CAPITALISM THE CREATOR

The Economic Foundations of
Modern Industrial Society

THE MACMILLAN COMPANY
NEW YORK · BOSTON · CHICAGO
DALLAS · ATLANTA · SAN FRANCISCO

MACMILLAN AND CO., LIMITED
LONDON · BOMBAY · CALCUTTA
MADRAS · MELBOURNE

THE MACMILLAN COMPANY
OF CANADA, LIMITED
TORONTO

Adam Smith

The portrait of Adam Smith, from which this reproduction has been made, was unknown until some forty years ago when the original oil painting was sold at auction in Edinburgh. It was for some ninety years in the possession of a family Muir in Kirkcaldy, where Adam Smith was born and spent the larger part of his life. Now in the possession of an eminent barrister of Edinburgh, John H. Romanes, W.S. A superb piece of work by an unknown hand. Regarded by Professor W. R. Scott and others who have examined it carefully as by far the finest and most characteristic portrait of Adam Smith in existence.

CAPITALISM
THE CREATOR,

The Economic Foundations of Modern Industrial Society

BY

CARL SNYDER

εἰ δὲ τοῦτ᾽ ἀγνοεῖς ὅτι πίστις ἀφορμὴ
τῶν πασῶν ἐστι μεγίστη πρὸς χρηματισμὸν,
πᾶν ἂν ἀγνοήσειας·

Demosthenes: For Phormio.
Loeb. I. 353.

With 44 Original Charts

NEW YORK
THE MACMILLAN COMPANY
1940

330.973
S67

NOV 7 1950

Macmillan 5.00

To the Prescient Mind of

ADAM SMITH

In his celebrated "Inquiry into the Nature and
Causes of the Wealth of Nations," 1776—not
the first to understand but perhaps the earliest
clearly to set forth the economic mechanism by
which the well-being and highest good of society is attained. In his lifetime his doctrines
found scant acclaim; still less in recent years.

CONTENTS

CONTENTS

THAT HE WHO RUNS MAY READ!

WITH A WORD ABOUT THE 44 CHARTS

The theses and conclusions in the present work rest upon the original research in quantitative economics which the writer has carried on in the last twenty years, summed up in several hundred original charts, of which a selection of 44 is herein presented. A hundred or more of these charts have been given in various papers in economic and statistical journals, of which a brief bibliography is later appended. It is hoped that in a volume to come, a further selection of the charts may be given.

To the mind of the writer it is the cumulative weight of these factual and statistical studies which provides such definite, quantitative proof as the theses contained in this volume may possess. It is the weakness of much economic writing that it does not attempt such factual foundations, but relies rather upon the plausibility of theoretical reasoning, more fitting to the domains of metaphysics than to a present day science.

The charts afford this advantage: they can be followed and studied without reference to the text, or the conclusions presented. They provide a rapid aperçu of the whole theme. On the other hand, by their complete detachment from the text, the reader who does not care for these newer methods of research need give them but the most cursory attention. He will find it all in the body of the text.

Finally: for the Rapid Reader. The main thesis is set forth in the introductory chapter: *By Way of a Preface*. And again, the entire argument is summed up in the eight brief chapters which stand at the close of the volume. There is no further "required reading."

For a "busy" Age! (As if it differs, in any serious degree, from hundreds of others, somewhere, in the last 5,000 years at the least, as the mounting evidence from the fascinating fields of archaeological discovery so vividly reveals.)

This volume is not intended as a systematic treatise. It is not written for economists, but for the larger public who take an intelligent interest in the affairs of this world, and the welfare of its peoples. There is perhaps undue reiteration of the main theses, in order that "he who runs may read," and comprehend.

LIST OF CHARTS AND DIAGRAMS

PREFACE

WHY—"CAPITALISM THE CREATOR"?

If we were to prophesy that in the year 1930 a population of fifty millions, better fed, clad, and lodged than the English of our time, will cover these islands, that Sussex and Huntingdonshire will be wealthier than the wealthiest parts of the West Riding of Yorkshire now are, that cultivation, rich as that of a flower-garden, will be carried up to the very tops of Ben Nevis and Helvellyn, that machines constructed on principles yet undiscovered will be in every house, that there will be no highways but railroads, no travelling but by steam, that our debt, vast as it seems to us, will appear to our great-grandchildren a trifling encumbrance, which might easily be paid off in a year or two, many people would think us insane.

We prophesy nothing; but this we say: If any person had told the Parliament which met in perplexity and terror after the crash in 1720 that in 1830 the wealth of England would surpass all their wildest dreams, that the annual revenue would equal the principal of that debt which they considered as an intolerable burden, that for one man of ten thousand pounds then living there would be five men of fifty thousand pounds, that London would be twice as large and twice as populous, and that nevertheless the rate of mortality would have diminished to one-half of what it then was, that the post-office would bring more into the exchequer than the excise and customs had brought in together under Charles the Second, that stage coaches would run from London to York in twenty-four hours, that men would be in the habit of sailing without wind, and would be beginning to ride without horses, our ancestors would have given as much credit to the prediction as they gave to Gulliver's Travels.

—T. B. MACAULAY: *Edinburgh Review;* 1830

WHY—"CAPITALISM THE CREATOR"?

(Apologia pro opera hac)

WHEN Adam Smith wrote his celebrated "Inquiry" into the Wealth of Nations, there were no measures of this Wealth, or of national income, or product, and scarce even of population. For one thing, even in prosperous England, already gaining the ascendency of the seas, there was then very little Wealth to measure. In Great Britain, now, perhaps a hundred times as much. And in the United States far more than that. 'Labor,' hand-labor, was the chief mode of production, the chief producer. Hence the very ancient doctrine to which even Adam Smith subscribed, that "Labor is the source of all wealth." There was then no successful steam engine in use—a few lumbering, clumsy steam pumps in the mines. The modern miracle of a real steam engine, almost the creator of the modern world, had already been invented by an obscure young man, in a small room in the same college in which Adam Smith had taught. Yet the latter thought so little of it that he refers to it casually as a 'fire engine.'

There were few factories, few good roads; needless to say, no 'rail' roads, no 'steam' ships; very little machinery of any kind. Only candle light to read by. Primitive days. 1776.

What a change!

I found recently a calculation as to the electric power now produced in the United States:—what it would mean in terms of 'human effort,' of '*labor*.' Present product now exceeds a hundred *billion* kw. hours per year. The mind can scarcely grasp the reality.

This, alone, it is reckoned, would be equal to the *human* power of half a billion men, working eight hours per day. This would mean ten times the entire present working population of the country, fifty times the number employed in all manufacturing, and about twenty-five hundred times the number now employed in electric power production. That is, if these employees "worked like horses." But they

3

do not; their "labor" is very light, mostly standing round and watching dials and dynamos, and polishing door-knobs. The 'work' is done by machines.

Who, and what, created this industry—so incredibly vast? Labor? In a sense, "labor" contributed almost nothing. It did not invent the dynamo, which produces all this electric power. That was the work of an untutored bookbinder's apprentice, who lives in fame as the greatest experimental genius of his age, and perhaps since Archimedes. Nor did 'labor' make any serious contribution to develop it. To perfect and make practical this epochal invention required the genius and skill of three generations and more, of thousands of trained engineers and physicists, a brilliant line extending from Faraday to Edison, Steinmetz, and Langmuir. Who paid for all this long travail of experimentation, and the salaries of all these technicians, involving the investment of tens of millions of dollars? Labor? No, it was Capital Savings; this, and this alone which has alike created this wondrous industry, and all our modern world of comfort, convenience, and luxury beside.

Such is the thesis of this volume. It is not offered as a 'theory,' but as an elemental reality. The findings here set forth are the fruit of some eighteen years of factual research and exploration, in a field still largely given over to emotional theorizing, and now sinking slowly into a quagmire of controversy and fantasy. The reader is warned that the findings, and the conclusions drawn, are by no means accepted by many teachers of present day economic doctrine.

The thesis here presented is simple, and unequivocal; in its general outline, not new. What is new, I would fain believe, is the proof; clear, statistical, and factual evidence. That thesis is that there is one way, and only one way, that any people, in all history, have ever risen from barbarism and poverty to affluence and culture; and that is by that concentrated and highly organized system of production and exchange which we call Capitalistic: one way, and one alone. Further, that it is solely by the accumulation (and concentration) of this Capital, and directly proportional to the *amount* of this accumulation, that the modern industrial nations have arisen: perhaps the sole way throughout the whole of eight or ten thousand years of economic history.

No principally agricultural or pastoral nation we know of has ever grown rich, powerful, and civilized. These are the fruits of

Wealth and Enterprise; and these, in turn, of organized industry and trade. As true today as in the most distant times of Babylonia and Sumeria, now known to us. Witness the astonishing rise in vigor and power of the Japanese Empire, under our own eyes.

Yet further: that all this represents the aggressive drive of the deepest and strongest of human motivations: the will to live, to gain, to discover, to conquer; and that whenever these begin to wane and weaken, and a nation is given over to visionaries, doctrinaires, and novices in "social experimentation," its decadence has begun.

Much of our knowledge of Capitalism in antiquity is new, the result of the fruitful excavations in Egypt and Asia Minor. Millions of clay tablets, telling the story of business and trade, that is, of Capitalism, of four thousand years ago. In this system, almost no material change, throughout the long stretch of recorded history. The commercial and industrial organization of ancient Babylon did not differ in any decisive way from our own—large business organizations, banks of deposit, insurance companies, holding companies, and, in general, a characteristic capitalistic organization of society.

If this was in full bloom thousands of years ago, there seems every reason to believe that it was even then an ancient institution, since we know that the further back we go, the slower is the pace of progress, or the rate of change; therefore that what has taken five hundred or a thousand years in modern times, may have taken five thousand or ten thousand years in very ancient days. Such at least may be inferred from the fascinating disclosures in recent years of archaeology, and what is now termed proto-history.

The immense quickening of pace which has come within the last few centuries, and most notably of all within the last hundred years or so, has obscured the long period of slow gestation and development that must have preceded our modern, historic time.

It seems clear that in modern days, and it may have been the same in ancient times, this accumulation of what we term wealth is largely the achievement of a relatively few individuals, gifted, for this special purpose, far beyond their fellows and their time. In all ages, great merchants and traders; great enterprisers. The most efficient agents for the accumulation of this essential base. Human, very human, envies, jealousy, and the like, obscure the fact of our debt to these especially capable types. We do not rebel at the idea of the exceptionally endowed poet or musician or painter. This we accept as a common-place. But the idea that the accumulators of great wealth belong in much the same category, and are vastly of more value to society, to civilization, and to the well-being of the people among whom they occur, seems to excite profound incredulity.

But if ever there was a living illustration, it is certainly our own United States: in the struggling Colonies, beginning in poverty and with scant equipment, growing slowly through two hundred years, then bursting forth as one of the marvels of economic achievement in all history. The story of England is not much different, or the Italy of the Renaissance, or scores of similar instances, as far back as the record extends.

What has especially distinguished our United States, aside from our freedom, our wealth of resources, and the vast new territory that lay open to development? Preeminently the use and the quick adoption of machinery and inventions. Identically the same basis for the wealth and commercial predominance of Great Britain. Much the same with modern Germany and other nations. What our plaintive 'modernists' bewail as the 'machine age' is precisely that which gives the greatest promise of the future, the opening of the gates of opportunity to the whole mass of the population. Without the creation of this Wealth, unimaginable.

And this wealth is not, as almost all the earlier economists assumed, the product of 'labor'; nine-tenths of it is directly the product of *machines;* these and these alone made possible the present day colossal aggregate of Capital. And in turn these machines were the product of brains and especial ability; quite literally a creation of genius, or of genii: inventors, contrivers, discoverers, enterprisers and accumulators—all conspiring in the economic wonder of today.

A wonder? Our present population could not survive without an amazing system of transportation, and a still greater achievement in goods and enjoyments produced. All these are but distantly the creation of "industry" or thrift, still less of "labor." They are the children rather of the minds who devised and found means for utilizing new processes, new instruments, by which the product of a day's work has (since the days of George Washington and Benjamin Franklin) been multiplied, on the average for the whole population, by at least ten. Were it not for these machines and processes, and the means of transportation, our present day fabulous accumulations would be inconceivable.

And what is the method, or mechanism, by which all this vast system of production and transportation has been created? Virtually, by placing this surplus, this capital accumulation, largely in the hands of a relatively few individuals, with rare gifts for the management and utilization of this surplus; all for the general good. The system that, for example, has in a single generation provided two-thirds or more of the people of the United States twenty-five millions of automobiles, and the general comfort and enjoyments which accompany this astounding achievement. All so unbelievable, in a way, that it is with difficulty that we truly understand the process by which this vast well-being has been attained.

The price—the reward to the rich and the exceptionally capable? A bagatelle. The actual 'consumption,' or expenditures of the three or four per cent of the population whom we class as "rich," is so slight as to be of no practical importance. All the rest of the income of this slender class is immediately turned back into industry, for the development of the country and for higher standards of living which an immensely larger part of the population now enjoys. Were the entire amount of the expenditures of this wealthy class secretly suppressed, we should scarcely know the difference. It would not increase the incomes or the enjoyments of the rest of the population by, at the most, more than something like five or six per cent. And the loss to the country of this exceptional talent and this genius for the organization and direction of industry would be indescribable, leading, as I see it, inevitably to a kind of inter-necine warfare of incompetents and brawlers.

In later years, the accumulation of this capital or surplus is largely the work of our great corporations, which now carry on perhaps 80 or 90 per cent of the industrial activity of the country. But even on the farms and in the smallest industries and individual trades and occupations, this influence of the mechanization of industry achieved through this surplus, is to be everywhere felt. Nowhere more so than on the farms. The fertility of the fields is no greater. But today the average worker on the farms can produce with machines from five to ten times as much with his individual effort as was possible in George Washington's day. Relatively the agricultural population has steadily declined for more than a hundred years, beginning with the invention of the steel plow, the harvesters, the reapers, and now the combines. Result: the release of a large part of the nation for its industrial and social development. Today the incomes of the farms are directly proportional to, and solely made possible by, the degree of their mechanization. All of it a part, and a vital part of this same "capitalistic" system. Much of this mechanizing done with borrowed capital.

Let us go further. Deep is the prejudice against avarice, and thirst for gain. And yet they are literally the most beneficent forces in modern society. Because the only possible way that this desire for gain and accumulation, and the "profit system" can be most effectively realized and advanced, is by the increase in the comforts and enjoyments of the whole population, or at least of by far the larger part. A submerged tenth, or perhaps more, of the incapable, the inefficient, the morons, and the derelicts, who have existed in every society since the beginning of time. Never smaller, never less, than now. Gradually to be eliminated, as they have been steadily eliminated through years of this spectacular industrial advance, through the improvement in the condition of the whole people, better feeding, and hopefully, in time, by a lowered birth rate. This is not a perfect world, and the dreamers who imagine that by fiat or edict or a "better system" it can easily be improved, ignore the inevitable and ever present differences in human ability. The distribution of this ability, as we now know, has probably not varied substantially in the five or ten thousand years under view: always a few very rich; in a former time the vast mass of the population ignorant and in wretched poverty. Both now rapidly disappearing in the more advanced nations, like our own. Famine, once widely prevalent, now almost unknown.

This system, or mode of industrial and social organization, has achieved in recent centuries results that must ever remain spectacular in the last degree, since nothing like it has ever before been known in history. This accumulation and utilization of capital, the 'division of labor' it provides, and the utilization of every kind of talent and unusual capability, has led to a volume and variety of production of goods, conveniences and satisfactions that almost defy enumeration. The last census takes record of some twenty thousand different 'trades,' or kinds of occupations, a large part of them unheard of a century ago, and a considerable part of them scarce a generation ago; such a diversification of industry and energy and enterprise as almost baffles the imagination; few to realize it in any detail, or in any comprehensive view. So extraordinary in its results, as compared with the hundreds of thousands of years of slow, creeping, plodding human effort.

And not an achievement of the human race as a whole, or any large part of it, but always and ever of a very few nations or peoples, and of the slenderest few among these: the 1 per cent, or one-tenth of 1 per cent, of the vast populations that have come and gone through all these countless millennia. These are the discoverers, the inventors, the contrivers, the enterprisers, the organizers, in a word, what we may call the 'genius' population. To these and these alone we owe *all*, for without them and their creations, their energy, their drive, their organizing power, our modern world simply would never have been, nor any civilization more than of the most primitive type. This 'genius type' has in our modern time, and especially within the last three or four centuries, found an opportunity for the play of talent and discovery lacking in the immensely larger part of the human epoch—possibly in but one-hundredth part of the time, let us say, since Peking man. Scant wonder that it has aroused, in many minds, intense feelings of antagonism, or distrust. Consider that some hundred years ago Sismondi, Rodbertus, and Marx were babbling of the vast "concentration" of Industry and Wealth and Ownership; an evil, a Menace! And precisely in this period, with the rise of the giant corporations and immense integrations of capital, never such an extraordinary diversification of industry, of effort, and of ownership. Consider that there are today ten or a dozen industries that produce possibly from one-third to one-half of the total present industrial output of the United States, that were scarcely heard of, forty or fifty years ago, none of them one hundred years back: electric power production, the oil industry, the motor industry, the newer chemical industry, rubber and rayon and radio, and scores of others. All practically creations of our own day.

And the ownership of these is divided up and distributed as it never was before; hundreds of thousands of shareholders, in literally hundreds of thousands of enterprises and corporations; with such an accumulation of wealth as even economic writers, and especially the socialistic dreamers of a century ago, could scarcely have conceived. Observe that in 1929 the income tax returns of the United States alone listed some forty thousand with incomes representing the equivalent of perhaps one million dollars of capital; and all this capital in the service of industry and in the service of the whole population of the United States; and the income directly from this, in dividends and in interest, aggregating but a slender part of our total National income, so slender a part that its equal distribution over the whole population would have made little material difference save to the utter dregs, the pauper and defective and criminal and incompetent substratum.

Yet more momentous, perhaps, the social side. When George Washington was inaugurated President of the new United States in New York in 1789, I believe the old slave market at the foot of Wall Street was still standing. Vividly recalling to mind that scarce one hundred and fifty years ago Slavery was prevalent over the larger part of the world, and only in England was there a strong sentiment for its abolition. That, in the premier capitalistic country of that time. Now hardly known anywhere, real slavery.

Even in England long after the Romans had come and gone, Slavery, white slavery, was still prevalent throughout the whole island. Impressively set forth in a famous passage in Taine:

Consider that so late as the Norman Conquest, in the eleventh century, the selling of men and women into slavery was a general custom in all parts of England. "You might have seen with sorrow long files of young people of both sexes and of the greatest beauty, bound with ropes and daily exposed for sale." So runs the word of a contemporary chronicler; and these were not captives of another race, not blacks nor prisoners of war, but "their nearest relatives and even their own children."

And this ancient institution had lasted not for thousands, but for tens of thousands of years. In all the higher civilizations of antiquity known to us it was an every day affair—in Babylonia, in Egypt, in Greece, in Rome, and for centuries thereafter over a good part of Europe; in Russia serfdom was not abolished until the last century. There are those who may suggest that Slavery was in reality a capitalistic institution. Perhaps in the earliest times. But it existed almost as strongly in the pastoral nations as in those in which capitalism was strong. But the point is that it was capitalism, and this alone, which *abolished* slavery. England being the first. It was when machinery began to come in that it was recognized that free labor was far more profitable than any slave system. In a word, the *machine* was the liberator. And the proof is evident in our own country. There Slavery existed where machinery was least, namely, in the South. Often said that the invention of the cotton gin really saved slavery, African slavery, in this country. But, to any considerable extent, only in the South. And, almost from the beginning of the Republic, evident that the South was losing ground. They were the wealthier of the colonies. At the time of the adoption of the Constitution, Virginia was not only the most populous State, but had the largest wealth. New York stood fourth or fifth.

From that time onward industry in the North grew at a far more rapid rate than in the South, so that by 1850 several Northern States were much richer than any Southern State. It was the boom in slaves, brought on by high prices for cotton in the 50's which, as Frederic Bancroft has pointed out, directly brought on the Civil War. The issue was almost inevitable from the beginning. At that time the North had more than two-thirds the wealth of the country, and three-fourths and more of its manufactures, a position which the original Northern States east of the Mississippi still hold. Slave labor could not compete with free labor. Slave industry could not compete with free industry. And all because of the machine. So I think it is clear that it was capitalism which destroyed this immemorial evil. It set free the workers to a degree never before realized. And that freedom has steadily spread over the whole world. These are factors that have been very little considered, but whose effect was unmistakable. In the 50's and 60's Karl Marx could talk about 'wage' slavery. But it was significant that he wrote and lived in the wealthiest and freest country then existing. Today these "wage slaves," of which he wrote so passionately, own millions of automobiles, at least in these United States, and have incomes, in normal times, far surpassing anything hitherto known.

So, as I see it, capitalism is destroying this 'wage slavery' just as irresistibly as it destroyed human slavery. And yet an incredible number of writers still cling to these Marxian idylls. A singular world.

This economic system here under review has brought not only freedom from absolute slavery, but likewise from the long hours of benumbing toil that was characteristic of the masses of the more civilized peoples up to hardly more than a century ago; giving time for recreational pleasures. It has provided likewise the means and the money for a vast system of public education of every kind, the introduction of common schools, the building and endowment of hundreds of colleges and universities all over the world, possessing today endowments running into the billions. An incredible out-pour of wealth and of capital to provide for a broader and more interesting life for the whole population.

Not always productive of unalloyed gain; often leading to and even breeding the strife and dissension which seem so strongly in-grained in the nature of man. For this we blame 'institutions,' in-stead of realizing that these fierce, combative and quarrelsome instincts have been characteristic of a large body of the human race from an immemorial time; in many ways the hallmark of the savage. And so remain to the present day.

Freedom from slavery, freedom from toil, freedom of opportu-nity and development. And yet more. This same capitalistic system has contributed marvelously to the advancement of science, dis-covery, invention, and technical development, so that today tech-nological science is sweeping all before it. For one thing it is destroying natural and national 'monopolies.' Of every sort and variety. We are no longer dependent upon a single country like Chile for our supply of nitrate, and the same is true of dozens of other chemicals. Soon we shall be independent of the rubber plan-tations, probably making synthetically a better and more durable rubber out of coal-tar and water. The great rubber plantations may conceivably some day go back to the jungle; estimated that even now an acre of plant for the manufacture of synthetic rubber-like plastic will produce 200 tons in *two hours* as compared with the 500 pounds of rubber that an acre of rubber trees will produce in *five years*.

Everywhere the same story, of a perfectly dumfounding ad-vance in knowledge and so in the average product per worker. All due to research and to machinery and to science, and to wise and beneficent management; and yet a part of the workers, who have contributed so little, would now claim the whole! The precipitate education of the masses has not been without its detriments and its dangers. It seems to have powerfully promoted discontent and 'class' feeling and envy, almost in proportion as it has brought com-fort and even a large measure of luxury. But at least we may per-haps look forward to a time, not distant, when the quarrelsome ape will not be fighting over patches of the earth, and the supposed ad-vantages of one section over another. If, as prophetic statistics sug-gest, the population will come to a standstill, the idea of 'crowding,' or the craving for 'expansion,' should gradually be ameliorated.

Yet further. With a larger understanding of this process, we may look forward to the prevention and practically the abolition of the periods of depression and unemployment, such as we have witnessed in an unparalleled degree within the last decennium. The product, as I think it is now clear, of ignorance and ineptitude. We shall have a real science of economics, instead of a bewildering jungle of conflicting theories and notions. It now seems definitely established that these periods of depression are almost wholly due to the over-expansion of bank credit, and the wild speculation which always ensues; and a wise banking policy will in the near future easily eliminate this. Not the part of over-optimism, but of sheer necessity. We *must* control these wide fluctuations of trade we called business 'cycles,' because it seems evident that an intelligent Government can scarcely continue in the face of such a debacle of industry as in these recent years.

Another orgy of so-called 'prosperity,' another wild outburst of speculation, aided and only possible through a huge expansion of bank credit, must inevitably bring us to the brink of another cataclysm. And the repetition of such a cataclysm would go far towards unsettling human reason and open the doors to another wave of 'social experimentation.' Perhaps even such a derogation of human freedom, of tyranny, as we see today in Russia and Germany.

The doctrines of economics, what used to be termed 'political economy,' were chiefly developed through the Industrial Revolution. But it has essentially lacked the guidance of adequate factual data, such as is available in the physical sciences. This in a considerable degree we now possess. And in another generation, we may hope economics will become a trustworthy guide to social policy.

It was inevitable, perhaps, that anything like a 'social science' should be the last to develop. Its bases are so largely statistical that it was only with the development of an enormous body of new knowledge that anything resembling a firmly grounded and truly scientific system could be established. It is coming; already the most fundamental elements of this knowledge are now available, as the pages to follow will endeavor to set forth.

THE MAINSPRINGS OF CIVILIZATION

When now I had for a long time reflected upon the uncertainty that pervaded all the mathematical results then existing as to the motions of the planets, it began to be repellent to me that the philosophers who would investigate with such extraordinary care the most insignificant details of the course of the heavenly bodies, should yet find no certain ground for the movement of the World Machine.
—COPERNICUS: *De Revolutionibus*

For Plato brings in the Egyptian priest, saying to Solon: "You Grecians are ever children, having no knowledge of antiquity, nor antiquity of knowledge."
—BACON: *Advancement of Learning*

Astronomy considered in its entirety is the finest monument of the human mind, the noblest essay of its intelligence. Seduced by the illusions of the senses and of self-pride, for a long time man considered himself as the centre of the movement of the stars; his vainglory has been punished by the terrors which its own ideas have inspired. At last the efforts of several centuries brushed aside the veil which concealed the system of the world. We discover ourselves upon a planet itself almost imperceptible in the vast extent of the solar system, which in its turn is only an insensible point in the immensity of space. The sublime results to which this discovery has led should suffice to console us for our extreme littleness, and the rank which it assigns to the earth. Let us treasure with solicitude, let us add to as we may, this store of higher knowledge, the most exquisite treasure of thinking beings.
—LAPLACE: *Exposition du Système du Monde*

CHAPTER I

THE MAINSPRINGS OF CIVILIZATION

1. *Animism and mechanism*

IT IS difficult for the human mind to believe that so varied and so complex a creation as our world could possibly be the result of a series of definite, relatively simple mechanisms. Least of all, that such mechanisms could be the sources and mainsprings of "civilization" in all its manifold aspects! [1]

Some forty thousand years ago when our rude forebears began to learn that roots or seeds thrust into ground would grow and produce food, there must have come recognition of the influence of the sun and the seasons. In Egypt, the annual rise of the Nile. They must have come to perceive the relation of cause and effect, between warmth, rainfall, flooding of fields, and product to spring therefrom; early to associate the position of the sun in the heavens and the seasons with times of planting and harvesting. But as they had few machines, tools, and devices of any kind, they could have had but slight concept of a mechanism. With the mythopoetic instinct of the race they peopled fields with elves and spirits, skies with gods and demons; to these, prayed and made offerings.

The concept of the solar system as a mechanism, with the sun its center and dominating force, came only after thousands of years of wonder and reflection and the attainment of a high stage of civilization. And then only to rare, percipient minds, like the famous Aristarchus, in the brilliant days of Alexandria.[2] From his observations and inductions slowly emerged the picture that we have today, a huge ball of earth whirling swiftly about another ball, a million times larger. But the full realization of the mechanical nature of the universe was dependent upon an invention, the telescope. After Galileo and the brilliant discoveries his new instrument made possible, incredible that this earth is the center of the universe, or the human race unique in creation.

In the three hundred years or more since this invention, the hu-

17

man vision has widened to the concept not of thousands, but of millions upon millions of suns like our own, many of them possibly carrying their cohort of planets, moons, asteroids, comets, and the like. More incredible still, the idea of binary suns, bodies of unbelievable magnitude revolving about each other and revealing that the relative simplicity of our solar system was not a characteristic of the universe of suns, but that there might be other, and to us, seemingly bizarre combinations. Today, the few interested in such matters have learned that these binary combinations of suns may conceivably be the rule rather than the exception. Dumfoundering in its implications, presenting us with a concept of creation immeasurably different from anything the imagination of a few generations ago could have compassed or even envisaged. All growing out of the invention of a single instrument of extraordinary simplicity, but requiring generations to develop and expand into the mighty telescopes that scan the skies today.

Despite the great popular interest in science, it is difficult even now for many to realize how significant a part of our daily habits, and even ways of thinking, are determined by this solar mechanism. We go to sleep when it is dark, get up when it is light, plant in Spring, harvest in Autumn, with scarcely a thought as to the determining factor. Dimly we may realize that all this planting, harvesting, and sale of product—what we call production and exchange of goods and services, of property and promises—are likewise founded upon this same mechanism, and that our whole economic life is broadly determined by the fundamental conditions imposed by the solar system.[3]

For centuries now the mechanistic principle that all physical phenomena represent the workings of a machine, has dominated the thinking and procedure in the "physical sciences"; though even here there is from time to time, a regular kind of animistic revolt against this rigid determinism. But usually short lived. In the biological sciences the influence of this mechanistic principle has been less evident. But it is steadily coming to be recognized that all life processes are simply a complicated form of chemism, that differ from any other kind of chemical reaction in no way, save in the mysterious association of certain combinations of the "organic" substances with feeling and consciousness. The idea that there is any impassable dividing line between the organic and the inorganic belongs to a generation that is gone.

A potent survival of the old animistic modes of thought still gives wide prevalence to the belief that the forces in our everyday life of getting and spending are 'human' forces; therefore, amenable to human control, and readily altered merely by an edict or the passage of a law. It is true enough that such human intervention, such laws and edicts, may for a brief time have a powerful effect. But almost wholly for evil. An ignorant workman may thrust a crowbar into a whirling electric generator, and if the crowbar is strong enough it may wreck a magnificent machine that may have cost millions of dollars and required the work of thousands of men. But it is clear enough, from the endless political experiments undertaken in many parts of the civilized world, that we are far from any understanding of the effects of such intervention in economic affairs, or of the serious consequences that may result. In other words, in many of the most important aspects of our lives, there is still slight consciousness of a mechanism at work.

The history of scientific progress is, in effect, a history of the gradual recognition and begrudging acceptance of the mechanistic concept. But in the so-called social sciences it cannot be said that the mechanistic concept has gained any great vogue. Particularly little in economic thought. There the mode of thinking has been largely of the syllogistic or deductive type. Certain rather obvious facts are marshaled in support of some sort of principle from which supposedly necessary consequences must flow. All presumably the result of institutions devised by men and subject to the control of new institutions to be devised by men.[4]

2. *The mechanical process: cause and effect*

Although the mechanism that controls the working of natural and social forces is invariably simple, the discovery of the mechanism is often difficult, requiring arduous research. The essence of a mechanism is the existence of an invariable cause from which follows an invariable effect. Cause and effect, the mechanical process. The discovery of the mechanism proceeds from the observation of effects and a search for causes. This is the foundation of scientific method.

When we inquire into any phenomenon—seek its cause—whether an earthquake or a growing plant or the perturbations of the moon (for, strangely enough, even the moon has perturbations)—we search for some factor that is invariably present. For example, we may have a garden with plants and flowers growing beautifully. Of a sudden they wither and die. Why? We note that there has been no rain; we supply water and the garden immediately revives. Evidently plants need water; and we do not find this strange because the fact has been noted from an immemorial time. On further seeking we find that plants need food, precisely like human beings and other animals. They need certain mineral salts—nitrates, phosphates, potash, and others; and when they lack these they die. Nothing strange about this now. But a hundred years ago when the great German chemist, Liebig, demonstrated the fact, many were incredulous.

Agriculture has been practiced by man for ten or twenty thousand years at least, and fertilizers such as manure have been in use for probably thousands of years. But no one sought to find precisely what in the manure or the humus made the soil more fertile. Some mysterious thing, like life itself. It was soon found, after Liebig's discoveries, that the manure or the humus was not needed at all, provided certain definite and well-known chemicals were supplied. Not even the soil was needful. The plants would grow in water, just as water lilies do. But under rigid conditions. Unless there was in the water or in the soil minute traces of certain other familiar minerals, like iron, there was no growth. There are apparently five or six of these minerals; the necessity of some of them —copper, boron, manganese, and magnesium—has been proved.

All this seems to be the identical process in virtually every field of modern knowledge. The same when we come to such things as the ups and downs of trade, what we call prosperity and depression, booms and panics. Even here we may gain no sure knowledge in any other fashion. We begin by seeking some one striking and always present feature—a cause—and then try to discover precisely how it works—its effect. When we examine this problem of so-called business 'cycles,' what seems the most conspicuous characteristic, the one feature common to every cycle?

At least one suggestive fact leaps out from the very form of the familiar phrase, the invariable linkage: booms and depressions. Are the two always associated? Is there never a depression without a boom? Apparently not. And again we may inquire, what is the most salient and invariable characteristic of booms? Here the answer is clear and definite. Never in history a boom without some

THE INDUSTRIAL U. S.
THE 14 NORTHEASTERN STATES (AREA 14%)

34 OTHER STATES   **THE 14 STATES**

POPULATION

| 51% | 49% |

MANUFACTURES

| 31% | 69% |

NATIONAL INCOME

| 40% | 60% |

I. THE INDUSTRIAL UNITED STATES

The United States have become the greatest manufacturing nation that ever existed, producing nearly one-half the total of manufactured goods of the civilized world. But this vast activity is largely confined to a small area in the northeastern part of the country, as depicted in the map above: 14 states with only 14 per cent of the land area have one-half the total population, producing seven-tenths of the manufactures, and have an estimated 60 per cent of the total national income. It is curious that this area attained to primacy in manufacturing in the earliest years of the new Republic, and has remained substantially unchanged ever since. Interesting to note, too, that much the same disparity was long true of the states of Europe, when Great Britain with its slender area was producing a large proportion of the manufactures of the whole continent. Now much the same thing is to be seen in the rise of Japan as a manufacturing area in Asia, despite its lack of 'great natural resources,' like coal, iron, copper and oil, or even of a large food supply. Energy and enterprise are perhaps the greatest economic assets of a nation.

kind of excited speculation—either in land, or in products like cotton or wheat, or commodities generally, or in great public undertakings like railways or power systems. In our own day most notably in stocks and company shares. So that, for one thing, we may definitely say: in the last sixty years, and to some extent in the last hundred years, there has never been a crisis, panic, or depression not directly preceded by a stock market boom. Here at least is one constant feature.

Is the stock market boom alone sufficient cause for panic, crisis, and depression? As yet, perhaps, no adequate proof. But at least one sure fact: the boom is an ineluctable antecedent of the depression. There have been scores of other factors adduced, mostly I believe imaginary, and the rest difficult to measure, or to prove. But here is no difficulty either of measurement or proof. And we may go much further and understand clearly the rationale. A great American, Simon Newcomb, one of our outstanding scientists and perhaps our most original writer on economics, laid the foundations of the explanation more than half a century ago. His central thesis was that the chief and sufficient cause of every depression was a diminution, as he termed it, of the societary circulation, or a curtailment of the current purchasing power.[6] The latter term does not imply any vapid and empty phrase like 'consumer buying' and all its endless cousins; but covers the whole wide range of buyers, including all the factories and mines, the railroads and public utilities, and myriad other industrial enterprises, just as much consumers as those who buy groceries or clothes or fineries, or go to the moving picture shows. Simon Newcomb did not fuss or fiddle over whether this or that product was to be listed as consumers' or producers' goods.

What did Simon Newcomb mean by a diminution of the societary circulation? He meant a reduction in all forms of circulating money,—even in his day very largely, and in our day 90 per cent or more of the total—bank credit. Which is saying simply that 90 per cent or more of all business transactions (retail trade included) is by means of checks. And why should this diminution be in itself the cause of a depression? The mechanism is simple. Between the general level of prices and the volume of bank credit, we now know there is always a definite balance, practically automatic; and whenever bank credit is created in excess or destroyed in sufficient amount, the price level rises or falls.[7] The reader is duly warned that this will be generally regarded, by many economists, as an overstatement or oversimplification; but the measurements and correlations presented in a later chapter, establish this relationship, I believe, beyond question.

Except during the World War and until 1933, the greatest creator and destroyer of bank credit has been stock market speculation. At the climax of the boom in 1929, for example, total loans on securities were around 14 or 15 billion dollars. In four years after, an equivalent volume of credit extinguished. Commercial loans also declined, of course, with the decline in prices; but the chief destroyer was the collapse of the stock market. Along with this diminution of the circulating medium went a reduction of tens of billions of dollars in the nominal value of stocks and bonds on various exchanges.

These two closely related forces combined to produce a series of related results: the destruction of confidence, a terrific drain upon the banks, an abrupt cessation of forward buying by business, and a consequent collapse of commodity prices, of land values, and of almost everything for which money is paid. The most unsettling factor, the precipitate decline in security values and in commodity prices. To all intents and purposes, the large majority of the banks of the country were by the early part of 1933 insolvent; on March 6 came the order for a general closing.[8] The first this country had known since the Civil War. What followed was inevitable: the heaviest decline in the volume of trade and manufacturing the country had experienced in at least a hundred years, and the greatest unemployment it had ever known.

Here, as I see it, we have in sharp relief forces and factors that create depression. But strangely not generally known, or sufficiently emphasized by writers on business cycles. For economics is pervaded by hundreds of fantastic theories offered as explanations of booms and depressions. And the confusion that characterizes these fine-spun theories has its origin in failure to realize that an understanding of the mechanism of business cycles—for that matter, the whole economic mechanism—requires the application of scientific method to economic problems.[9]

3. *Measurement and scientific method*

The infinite variety and range of measurements, computations, and experiments in the fields of physical and applied science today form a body of knowledge simply bewildering in its extent; in the feeling of certitude it builds up. Mostly in the latter respect that modern knowledge differs from that of the ancients. They guessed at what was the composition of bodies and had such answers as air, fire, and water. And this was the extent of the knowledge of the wisest of their wise men. Aristotle assuredly belongs among the greatest of philosophers; but his ideas upon such questions of chemistry and physics, if proposed today, would be thought simply childish and held in polite contempt. The idea that the air is composed of certain definite gases and that fire, rusting, and the like are processes of oxygenation, would have been to the ancients quite as incredible as some of the earlier achievements of modern science seemed in the days of Galileo and Descartes. Today grown almost commonplace.

But there are still relatively few who have any adequate idea of how truly marvelous the precision of this knowledge and these measurements has become. In many of the operations of a motor car factory today an accuracy of a thousandth of an inch is already long out of date; and devices are not lacking that afford an accuracy of a hundred-thousandth of an inch. Likewise devices that will measure ten-thousandths of a second. Others that will supply a vacuum within an electric light bulb or a radio tube amounting to but a millionth of an atmosphere. Nowhere guess work or an attempt to use a priori reasoning about such matters. This precision, this accuracy affords a degree of certitude in our knowledge that amounts nigh to a miracle.

All this new knowledge fits together in a remarkable manner, one kind of measurement or computation checking the accuracy of another. An example: thirty years ago an Austrian meteorologist brought forth a strange and almost unbelievable idea. His suggestion was that the continents float about on the surface of the earth much as a raft might be blown about on a pond. Promptly rejected by the authorities with the scorn that usually greets new ideas or discoveries. But Professor Wegener went on piling up his evidence until his idea took on a degree of plausibility. Actually it did explain some of the geological and geographical mysteries, such as

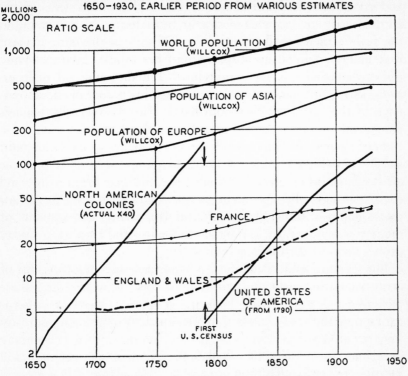

MOMENTUM OF WORLD POPULATION GROWTH
1650–1930. EARLIER PERIOD FROM VARIOUS ESTIMATES

MILLIONS

RATIO SCALE

WORLD POPULATION
(WILLCOX)

POPULATION OF ASIA
(WILLCOX)

POPULATION OF EUROPE
(WILLCOX)

NORTH AMERICAN
COLONIES
(ACTUAL X40)

FRANCE

ENGLAND & WALES

UNITED STATES
OF AMERICA
(FROM 1790)

FIRST
U. S. CENSUS

II. MOMENTUM OF WORLD POPULATION

It now seems an established fact that for some thousands of years, and until after the discovery of America, the world's population increased very slowly—perhaps for ten thousand years or more. Then suddenly an enormous expansion, as depicted in the chart above, showing that the estimate of the world's peoples has quadrupled in about 300 years. An extremely interesting fact that this rate of increase was shared about equally between Asia and Europe. But a much more rapid growth in Great Britain. Still more astonishing was the growth of the English colonies in America, which later became the United States; apparently a rather steady increase for well over 200 years, and up to the Civil War. Then a progressive slowing down of this increase, so that it is now estimated the United States may reach its maixmum population within the next 40 or 50 years. Perhaps not very much larger than now: around 180,000,000. A change involving some intricate social problems.

the existence of rich coal fields in Spitzbergen, within the Arctic circle. But proof was needed. Were the continents moving even now? Only actual measurement could provide the answer. And these measurements had to be of a then undreamt of accuracy at least to yield an answer within a lifetime. Fortunately, the radio can now be used for this necessarily delicate measurement. It may be some time still before decisive proof as to the Wegener theory of continental displacement is attained. But the scorn of the professors has faded. Although Wegener lost his life in an expedition to Greenland, his once fantastic theory may prove to be one of the great additions to our knowledge of the earth.

It has frequently been said that economics has made little solid advance in the last century or more. Many new theories have been put forward; few remain. Some even go so far as to hold that economics can never be more than an academic discussion of methods and principles of trade, finance, and exchange, and that its problems can not be resolved by the methods used in the exact or experimental sciences. And to a certain extent obviously true. But there are also innumerable economic phenomena susceptible to these methods; measurement and correlation. Take two or three questions where popular belief runs quite opposite to the available evidence as shown by numerous measurements extending over a long period of time.

1. Does the velocity of circulation, say, of money or of bank deposits, ordinarily affect the price level? The answer is that it does not. We can now measure both the velocity of demand deposits and variations in trade with considerable precision. The variations in velocity—that is, the rate of turnover of demand deposits—and the variations in the volume of trade, as measured in percentages of their norms, run remarkably close together. Thus, their effects tend to cancel each other. Their effect upon the price level is therefore slight. The only serious exceptions in the last fifty or sixty years were during 1928–29, when so large a part of bank checks, even outside New York, were simply drawn to and from brokers in the speculative purchase of stocks, and since 1933, when the large volume of government bonds sold to banks and the consequent increase in the quantity of bank deposits seems to have had a restraining effect on the velocity of demand deposits.[10]

2. Is there any evidence that the rate of increase in the total product, per capita in the United States, has been more rapid dur-

ing the last twenty-five years than during the preceding half century? There is no evidence of any material change in this respect. Measurements show that up to 1930 growth in per capita output over the past hundred years, measured in five- or ten-year periods, has been but slightly decrescent. Even the annual fluctuations in trade that come with booms and depressions do not materially affect the long term rate of growth.[11]

These are simply questions of fact that can be answered categorically once the relevant measurements have been made. And hundreds of such questions in the field of economic activity can be answered with the same assurance from measurements already made or from measurements that can readily be made. Not perhaps with the absolute certainty of astronomy; but it must be remembered that astronomical measurements date a long way back and have now been made literally by the millions. As a result, and almost solely as a result of these measurements and observations, we now speak of astronomical knowledge as the very paradigm of finality.

The question then arises, why, if these methods of measurement and correlation have been so marvelously successful and fruitful in the physical sciences, have they not been applied in the field of economics? The answer seems to be that digging out the material for all these measurements, from masses of statistical data not always readily available, is a deal of drudgery and requires very much patient labor and research. It is so much easier and so much pleasanter to collect a few scattered facts and from them spin fantasies that we call theories, forgetful how misleading, how full of pitfalls, this method must be.

4.   *Mechanism, measurement, and emotions*

In these pages there will be, perchance, wearisome repetition of a central thought, a dominating idea—that the prime retarding factor that delays and prevents the advancement of human knowledge, and of the race itself, is the ignorance born of the intense emotions inherent in our childish fantasies. We cling to these primitive fantasies, dreams, and comfort thoughts with an almost fanatical intensity. The history of human progress is mainly a record of the overcoming of these entrenched emotions. With a desperate effort mankind came to accept even such ideas as the shape and size of the earth, its place in space, and the origin and history of the human race. These discoveries and findings were, when made, a terrible blow to our feelings of importance, to our dignity. They seemed to threaten a kind of annihilation of all our hopes and dreams; and to a vast number of people, these feelings are still dominant and over-powering.

Although progress toward complete objectivity has been made in many important fields of knowledge there are still wide areas —in what used to be called moral philosophy—where the objectivity of scientific method is rejected. There is one aspect of the social sciences that is called normative, and that is devoted to the question of what ought to be.[12] This 'normative aspect' has affected every phase of the social sciences; even the descriptive and analytical phases of economics are full of the wishful thinking on what ought to be, rather than on the objective phenomena that are and must be. We refuse to believe that our economic world, no less than the physical world, is a mechanism, the central forces of which we may understand, but whose operations we can control only to a limited extent, and then only in accordance with the nature of its organization. We want to believe that we are masters of our fate, that we can shape our own destinies. But though we play a conscious part in this comedy, we cannot do with it what we will. In a very real sense, and despite appearances, the economic mechanism has made man what he is today, not man the mechanism. It was Spinoza who reminded us that a stone cast into the air and suddenly endowed with consciousness might readily believe it was moving of its own volition.

But this is the edge of the bogs of metaphysics. Subtly, slowly, these intense prejudices and antagonisms will fade, as they have from the minds of those influenced by the scientific spirit. Then we shall learn to understand the mechanisms, the forces, and the tropisms that determine human behavior and the character of human society. Already important strides have been taken on the way to a complete understanding of the economic structure. This progress has been made with the aid of the same implements of precision and certitude used in all science; that is to say, varied and accurate measurements and comparisons that establish definite correlations and associations.[13] But some day, surely, we shall have a true 'science' of economics.

ON THE RISE OF ECONOMICS AS A SCIENCE

The author takes a more hopeful view of the future development of economics than that commonly found in current discussion. He holds that nothing is needed to give the subject a recognized place among the sciences except to treat and develop it as a science. Of course this can be done only by men trained in the work of scientific research and at the same time conscious of the psychological basis on which economic doctrine must rest. To such investigators a most interesting and hopeful field of research is opened in the study of the laws growing out of the societary circulation. If the same amount and kind of research which have been applied to the development of the laws of electricity were applied to this subject, there is every reason to suppose that it would either settle many questions now in dispute, or would at least show how they were to be settled.

—SIMON NEWCOMB: *Principles of Political Economy*; 1884

A scientific study of economics . . . requires a certain acquaintance with the first principles of quantitative research. Most economists, however, have been brought up on other lines, and their equipment for quantitative thinking has often been defective. The result is that economic science has suffered at every stage of its growth from serious defects in quantitative thinking. The present state of the science offers clear evidence of this weakness.

—GUSTAV CASSEL: *On Quantitative Thinking in Economics*

The reason for the comparative neglect of American gold and silver by the economists and statesmen who attempted to explain the Price Revolution is not far to seek. Recognition of the fact that rising prices may stimulate industry and commerce is a distinctly recent achievement; but contemporary consumers grasped the significance of dear commodities, and producers understood the handicap to export industry imposed by high price levels relatively to those of other countries. Only with difficulty could mercantilists ascribe the advance of prices, which caused "evils" of such magnitude, to the accumulation of specie, the *summum bonum* in most of their eyes. At least in some instances it seems that the brevity of the discussions may have been due to a laudable desire to avoid expatiation upon the obvious; and, being pragmatists, the Spanish mercantilists devoted their attention to causes for which remedies compatible with their philosophy seemed attainable.

—EARL J. HAMILTON: *American Treasure and the Price Revolution in Spain, 1501–1650; 1934*

CHAPTER II

ON THE RISE OF ECONOMICS AS A SCIENCE

1. *The foundations for a quantitative economics*

THE reproach often leveled at economists is that so often they differ among themselves on many of the most fundamental questions.[1] A confusion of councils not peculiar to economics; perhaps characteristic of the early stages of all sciences. In the century that saw the beginnings of serious economic inquiry, there was a similar divergence of opinion in physics and chemistry. One most intriguing problem was the nature of heat, whether it was a substance, belonging to what were then termed the imponderables. A New Hampshire boy, who became Count Rumford, and was for a time acting ruler of Bavaria, observed that in boring cannon much heat was generated, just as did the early makers of fire from friction in the long ago. Of an inquiring mind, he undertook to measure the quantity, leading to what is now known as the mechanical equivalent of heat.

When Count Rumford was establishing these quantitative relations, the chemical theory in vogue was that heat was due to a substance named phlogiston, which entered into and departed from bodies hot or cold. Then a French chemist, Lavoisier, inquiring into the chemical nature of water, established that it was made up of two gases, and that in the combination of these gases heat was formed. Again in definite quantities. Therewith the phlogiston theory began to take wings and fly away. A characteristic of theories when measurement and experiment enter the field.

Economics still much in the phlogiston stage. As yet relatively little effort to provide economics with bases as solid as those which have proved so fruitful in experimental science and discovery. There are not lacking some eminent economists who seem to regard their 'discipline,' as it is so ominously termed, as a kind of theology or metaphysics in which definitive, quantitative proof is superfluous, or at best of slight utility.[2]

Some, among the proficient and understanding and those who are neither, hold to the belief that there is a radical difference between the social and physical sciences in that experimentation, so vital in the one, is practically impossible on any large scale in the other; therefore, that proof available in the field of economics can never be as convincing or as realistic as in physics or chemistry. I have already noted that the paradigm and queen of all the sciences is almost equally an 'observational' science, and that our vaunted astronomical certitude is in reality, to a large degree, simply a matter of inference. Yet there is hardly an intelligent person living who questions the foundations of astronomy or its principal conclusions. These latter, which were held unbelievable not four hundred years ago, are today taught to school children.

A step further. What is the actual difference between the kind of proof available in the field of economics and, say, of chemistry? Consider any of the paramount problems: business cycles, the influence of the rate of interest, the effect of changes in the quantity of money, the distribution of income. What is lacking in the economic proof? Simply endless and controlled experiment. If, for example, we ask for the proof that the air we breathe is composed almost wholly of nitrogen and oxygen in the proportion of four to one, the answer would be we can measure and weigh. But what proof that this is invariably true and has been for an almost indefinite time? Nothing more than constant repetition of the tests. The very first experiments of Priestley and Lavoisier were, for all purposes, convincing evidence. Since then, numberless repetitions of these experiments. From these we infer that the composition of the air remains unchanged; and we accept this conclusion as an indisputable fact.

Now, the observations obtainable in economic questions differ from these chiefly in number. We have, for example, adequate measures of only eight or ten business 'cycles,' and these differ in severity and in length, and to some extent in the underlying conditions that brought them about.[3] Probably no difficulty in understanding business cycles if we could have a hundred or more instances to study, and if they were sufficiently alike to be comparable. But those we have provide the basis for some reasonable degree of probability in the conclusions we draw, and provide the basis for some reasonable political and social action as well. If, for example, it is established, as I believe it is, that a commercial crisis is practically impossible without an excessive expansion of bank credit and then a sudden contraction of that credit, we have at least one definite fact upon which conclusions and policy may be based. In the same way I believe that we now have sufficient data, —that is, a sufficient number of repetitions under reasonably like conditions,—to decide between conflicting views on other economic questions.

Even experiments in economics of a certain type are not lacking; they never have been. Debasement of the currency has been a time-honored device of rulers and statesmen in all countries; probably since money came to be used. We know of a highly instructive experiment of this kind by Solon in Greece, about 600 B. C. And we know of similar experiments in many countries, in ancient, in medieval, and in modern times.[4] In fact, we have had numerous experiments in debasement during and since the World War; and on these experiments many able scholars have collected a mountain of observations. So too, numerous instances of a sudden increase in the quantity of the precious metals, and many observations of the effect on prices. We know that when the soldiers of Alexander returned with their immense booty after sacking the temples and treasuries of the East, there was an enormous rise in prices throughout all the Mediterranean trading world. And we have had a repetition of the same experiment in the conquests of Rome and Spain, and other countries. Always a revolution in prices. No doubt of the conclusion from these experiments.[5]

There have been likewise hundreds, if not thousands, of experiments in taxation and the levying of import and export duties. And so with a wide variety of other economic phenomena, particularly in money, banking, and prices. These experiments have provided a vast fund of valuable economic data, helpful in the development and support of economic theories and policies. Although deliberate and endless controlled experimentation, characteristic of the physical sciences, has not been possible, there have nevertheless been sufficient experiments and adequate observations for the foundations of a true science of economics.

2. *The useful art of economics*

A true science of economics would be invaluable in deciding the many difficult questions of policy with which governments are now and have always been confronted. Let us consider a few examples where a clear quantitative or factual knowledge might have profoundly affected not merely political and economic thought, but even great historical events. A striking instance was the relation of slavery to our civil polity. Now far enough away to be viewed with eyes unclouded by prejudice. In 1857 Hinton Rowan Helper of North Carolina published a remarkable volume, *The Impending Crisis*, in which he endeavored to show, through luminous comparisons gathered from the government census, that slavery was ruining the South, keeping its people poor, driving away capital and enterprise, and preventing the utilization of its rich natural resources; [6] while the industries of the North under free labor were expanding by leaps and bounds, those of the South were growing at a snail's pace. The book was a mine of factual information, unimpeachable logic, and colorful illustration. If ever there was a statistical demonstration of an economic truth, it was this. What was the fate of *The Impending Crisis?* Burned in the public square of the leading city of his native North Carolina; its publication prohibited by legislative enactments; and the man himself driven from the state as a traitor to the South. A vivid manifestation of economic ignorance and social prejudice.

As Helper revealed, the total number of slave holders or slave renters in the whole South did not exceed three or four hundred thousand; the bulk of the population had little capital, or was sunk in debt. Yet, swept by sectional prejudices and antagonisms, the legislatures voted for separation and war. Could the facts set forth in Helper's significant volume have been accessible and read and debated by every intelligent voter in the South, there might have been no war, and the 'irrepressible conflict' solved peaceably. In the minds of many the war set back the South, economically and industrially, a full generation.

Another example where a quantitative knowledge of the factors involved might have affected American political history: the United States did not adopt any real 'protective' tariffs until a half century or more after the beginnings of the Republic, that is, until the famous Walker Tariff Act of 1847. And at first customs duties were so moderate that they could not and did not have, a marked effect upon our international trade, or our industrial growth. Certainly not on industrial growth. High tariffs, really protective duties, were not enacted until the Civil War; and they did not become

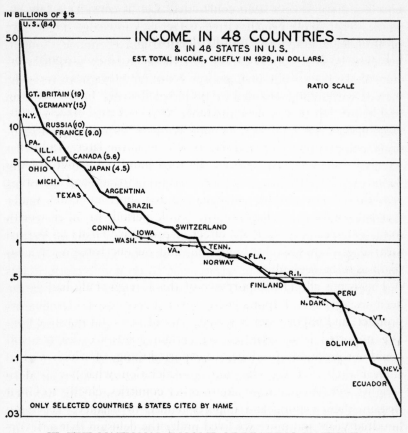

IN BILLIONS OF $'S

INCOME IN 48 COUNTRIES
& IN 48 STATES IN U.S.
EST. TOTAL INCOME, CHIEFLY IN 1929, IN DOLLARS.

RATIO SCALE

U.S. (84)
50

GT. BRITAIN (19)
GERMANY (15)
N.Y.
10   RUSSIA (10)
FRANCE (9.0)
PA.
ILL.
CALIF.   CANADA (5.6)
5   OHIO   JAPAN (4.5)
MICH.
TEXAS   ARGENTINA
BRAZIL
CONN.   SWITZERLAND
IOWA
WASH.
1   VA.   TENN.
NORWAY   FLA.
.5   R.I.
FINLAND
N.DAK.   PERU
VT.
BOLIVIA
.1   NEV.
ECUADOR

ONLY SELECTED COUNTRIES & STATES CITED BY NAME
.03

III. THE NATIONAL INCOME OF LEADING NATIONS

The League of Nations has published estimates from 48 of the principal countries as to their national income; and estimates of the incomes of various states of the Union have been made by the National Industrial Conference Board. A comparison of these two sets of estimates, given above, reveals the curious result that the differences shown between the nations closely resemble the disparities between the states. It will be seen that in 1929, when the world was at a top level of productivity and general depression had not yet set in, the income of the United States was apparently equal to that of the next six or seven richest countries combined. In turn, income in New York State was equal to that of the three or four next leading states. It is interesting that the wide disparity shown in the income tax returns of incomes of individuals (and of corporations) is almost exactly paralleled by the disparities between states and nations. In other words, here, as everywhere in all forms of income, talent, and ability, there is not the remotest approach to anything like 'equality,' and probably never can be. Inherent in human nature and in peoples and race.

a leading political issue until about a half century ago. What do we really know about the effects of these high tariffs on our international trade and on our industrial growth?

Elaborate data as to the value and character of our exports and imports are available from 1790. If we now plot these annual values from the beginning to the latest year what do we find? That the rate of growth of our foreign trade, while it varied widely from year to year, was over long periods comparatively steady; slightly higher, if anything, in the earlier time than in the later. And if we set these values against those of the total industrial growth of the nation, we find that the ratio between foreign trade and industrial growth did not sensibly change, but for short intervals, under special conditions, throughout the whole period. In other words, so far as we can discover, the effect of protective tariffs on our industrial growth was apparently nil, and on our foreign trade so slight as to be negligible.[7]

This is not all. The importance of this foreign trade has always been exaggerated. Exports were never a large part of our total product, and imports never a large part of our total consumption. We imported large quantities of certain goods we did not and could not profitably produce; we exported things of which we had a clear excess. If we take into consideration what we paid in freights, insurance and the like to other countries, chiefly to Great Britain, these exports and imports tended to balance. Yet for a hundred years and more we lived under the delusion that a 'favorable' balance of trade was an important factor in our industrial growth and development.

We have always been very largely a self-contained country, to a greater extent than any other leading industrial nation. Despite this, for almost eighty years the controversy over the tariff was a major political issue, the battle over 'protection' and free trade almost the dominating question in political struggles. These interminable controversies over the tariff were in large part simply over the difference between tweedle-dee and tweedle-dum. Yet the literature upon these subjects is stupendous, rising into thousands of volumes, and perhaps into millions of speeches. Hundreds of reputations were made on both sides in oratorical and literary battles over these inconsequential issues. Possibly it will be said that the political parties had to divide upon some kind of issues. Yet when the Democratic Party was in power, reductions in the tariffs amounted to little; a large part of the protective system remained. And all this pother from the lack of simple and easily accessible statistical proof.

And so with other instances of political controversy that could have been settled with more light and less heat by an unprejudiced examination of the facts, as revealed by statistical studies. Think of the endless war against 'monopolies!' There is no evidence that our industrial growth was ever deeply affected by them. The distribution of wealth and well-being remained practically unchanged throughout the whole period. They were never a 'menace' to our competitive system. But at frequent intervals, political leaders would call the country to a holy war against 'monopolies.' Entirely needless if we could weigh dispassionately the effect of monopolies as revealed by statistical studies. Similarly, the bitter struggle over utility rates and public ownership of utilities might be obviated if public policy could be guided by the evidence as to the efficiency of utility operation, and the relative economy of private and public management.

Yet another instance: the question of price changes. Do prices rise and fall simply because of changes in the relation between supply and demand? Undoubtedly these are important factors in a particular commodity. But at times all prices rise or fall very much together, not strictly in unison, but marching along, up and down, very much like a straggling army. What determines the *general* direction, the important rise or fall? Careful consideration of the variations in the total quantity of commodities sold or produced fails to disclose a satisfactory answer. There must be some other cause, long suspected to be the money factor. But verification of this view had to await two developments: first, accurate methods of measuring changes in prices as a whole; second, the precise formulation of the factors that must be measured in testing the relationship of money to prices. With the development of index numbers, and the statement of the 'equation of exchange' by Simon Newcomb in algebraic form, it became possible to test this hypothesis.

Something like a century and a half ago inquiring minds, observing this general tendency of prices to flock together, were led to an idea that has since developed into what is known as the 'general price level.' [8] The device was uncomplicated; it consisted in taking a variety of commodities and making an average of the percentage

changes in their prices; nothing difficult or recondite. But on theoretical grounds it was asserted that the idea of a general price level
was inherently absurd. So great an economist as Ricardo spent
much time and some scorn in the endeavor to prove that the whole
idea was preposterous; but offering only theoretical considerations
as proof.[9] But the idea grew steadily, despite the weight of this
great authority, and various tabulations were made. Comparison of
these, based upon a number of different commodities, often revealed a singular concordance. It seemed not to matter much
whether a few leading commodities were taken or an immense
variety. Today these price 'indexes,' as they are termed, exist in
large number for almost every commercial country; and comparisons for one country and another often reveal the same general
tendency and characteristics, especially where countries are on the
same monetary standard and more or less closely related through
trade.[10] Monthly, weekly, and even daily calculations of these indexes are now commonplace; published regularly in the newspapers. Ricardo's objections have been buried under the weight of
an enormous body of evidence that he was wrong. Index numbers
do measure price changes.

But the use of index numbers does not alone solve the question
of the cause of the rise and fall. With Newcomb's equation of societary circulation, better known as the equation of exchange, the
factors related to these price changes were lucidly formulated.[11]
Still a formidable difficulty, how to measure the magnitudes of the
factors. If, for example, the major determining element of price
changes is money, how shall its quantity be measured, especially in
recent times, when the chief medium of exchange in more highly
developed industrial countries is the bank deposit. The actual
amount of 'currency,' save as it influences or limits the quantity of
bank deposits, seems not to be a major factor. Currency, after all,
is only a kind of small change, or pocket money; and while the
quantity varies with the general price level, the relationship is by
no means precise.

And in the circulation of money, there is still another element,
the rate of turnover—the velocity of circulation. The money in
circulation—currency and deposits—is turned over a score and
more of times a year. When business is brisk, the velocity is high;
when dull times come, the velocity falls. And without reference
to the quantity of money in use. True, a marked increase in the

volume of money usually means a rise in its velocity. But this seems to be due to the fact that with a sizeable increase in money, there is a rise in prices and a consequent quickening of business and the volume of trade. At times there are exceptions, as in the past few years when bank deposits have increased heavily with a fall, and not a rise, in the rate of turnover. Is velocity then a wholly independent factor? And if so, what are the forces that determine its variations? A vast and at times acrimonious controversy.

It fell to the lot of the writer to measure anew the velocity of deposits. The calculation was quite simple, and disclosed nothing that was not fairly well known, namely, that velocity does vary, and at times independently of the quantity of money.[12] Then other measurements. There had been differences of opinion as to the extent of variations in trade. Could these variations likewise be closely measured? Not an easy problem, because trade in a country like the United States must grow. Several independent measurements were undertaken at about the same time, among others by the writer.[13] A comparison of these measurements in 1920 revealed fairly close agreement, some showing somewhat larger variations than others. We now have an idea of the rate of growth and of the variations in this rate. These measurements are satisfactory for all practical purposes, affording a good index of the variations of production and trade as a whole, variations so much exaggerated by many of the partial indexes that have been computed.

How do these variations in trade measured from their normal growth compare with the variations in monetary exchanges, that is, the velocity of bank deposits? The findings were that, in general, these variations were much alike; for long periods, almost identical.[14] The total of bank clearings, or preferably bank debits, even outside New York City, is at times considerably affected by violent speculation, especially upon the stock exchanges. But if these temporary aberrations are disregarded, it is certain that the ups and downs of deposit velocity correspond closely to the activity of trade. If variations in velocity and variations in the volume of trade, measured from its normal line of growth, are equal, then their influence cancels. The effective force in bringing about price changes then must be variations in the quantity of money compared with the normal rate of growth in production and trade. Another way of saying it is that if the amount of money and credit increases at the same rate as the growth of trade, the price level will necessarily be stable and unchanging. And, in fact, direct calculations have shown that this is so.[15]

Simon Newcomb never attempted a statistical verification of these relationships. But a young student at Cornell University, working for his doctorate, did essay these calculations twenty years later.[16] Professor Kemmerer's pioneer work was followed some years afterwards by that of Irving Fisher, with the same aim and using much the same methods.[17] But data for the necessary measurements were then lacking, and in particular gave no clue to the effect of a definite, slowly changing, long time rate of growth in the volume of trade. Fisher, and others who followed after, continued to treat the factor of velocity as generally an independent variable, and not as concomitant to the variations in the volume of trade, measured from its normal rate of growth.

Even when the interrelationship of the variations in velocity and the variations in trade were known, it was still necessary to devise a broader and more adequate index of prices.

The familiar indexes of commodity prices at wholesale, at first used in these studies, were unsatisfactory. What was needed: an index of all kinds of prices, of all things bought and sold, rather than the much narrower index of commodity prices.[18] For money is used not only in buying goods at wholesale, but in all transactions necessary to production and trade. Once a satisfactory general price level was devised, it could be seen how closely variations in prices followed variations in the quantity of money, when compared with the normal industrial growth. Other calculations, derived from bank clearings and trade, support the view that this general price level is an accurate device for measuring the effect of money on prices.[19]

Here is an important instance of the progress already made toward the development of a science of economics. Instead of the uncertainties, the confusion of unverified theories, the endless disputes, we have a trustworthy method of determining the relation of money to prices, a matter of enormous significance to the formulation of economic policy. This relationship was derived wholly from objective measurements, and from comparisons and correlations that these alone could provide. Consider the implications: Knowing the relationship of money to prices, and the predominant importance of bank credit, it becomes possible to control, or at least to limit, the wide fluctuations in business that we call booms

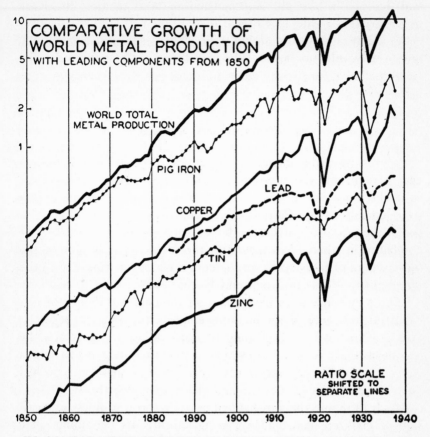

IV. COMPARATIVE GROWTH OF WORLD METAL PRODUCTION

Modern civilization is largely based upon the widening use of metals, as in railroads, steamships, electric power, equipment of mills, factories, and farms. The enormous increase in the wealth and income of the industrial nations of the world is chiefly due to growth in manufacturing and world-wide transportation, and this increase in turn implies a corresponding increase in metal production.

It will be seen that the total of metal mined and smelted has increased almost a hundred times within a space of 100 years—a truly astonishing fact! The large part of this increase is from the progress in iron and steel, with the progress in copper an important third. In the United States, steel production has grown to some fifty times that even of 1879. In the eighty years since the development of the Bessemer process, the total steel product has been far greater than in the previous six or eight thousand years since steel began to be made. And probably this was more or less true of the mining of copper, though copper has been in wide use for many thousands of years. And so also of tin. A similar increase is to be noted in the mining of coal.

and depressions. By use of the mechanism of credit control we might avoid the wild speculation of the boom that inevitably precedes depression. Little doubt that similar studies of economic questions would unquestionably lead to an understanding of the economic mechanism sufficient to guide us in avoiding serious errors of policy.

3. *Progress and prejudice*

Progress toward a science of economics, retarded by the indifference of some and the opposition of others, has not differed greatly from the history of all scientific advance. When a little more than two generations ago Pasteur, Koch, and their followers began to reveal the origin of infectious disease, and therewith the means of combating it, their ideas met with the usual opposition from the older school of physicians. In due course the latter passed from the stage and the ideas of Koch and Pasteur were hailed in triumph. Then the evidence as to inadequacy of the bacterial theory of disease, and still more of the methods employed to fight it, began to emerge. Now we are beginning to learn of the ultra-viruses, the organisms that are invisible even to the microscope, and to which many human ills are apparently due. The original concept had only to be enlarged, not radically changed or overthrown.

Much the same thing is happening today in the oldest occupation of civilized man, namely, in agriculture. Its beginnings date back at least ten thousand years, perhaps longer. But it was only a hundred years ago that Liebig and his followers began to introduce new methods of research. Liebig, like Pasteur, was a chemist and not a physiologist or agronomist. His ideas found little favor. Now in the last thirty years has come a new band of workers, following and extending the pathway blazed by Liebig, seeking to reduce agriculture, at least in its fundamentals, to an exact chemical science based on experiment and measurement. And they are meeting with the same antagonism and indifference from the old type of workers who have toiled so many years with such scant results.

Precisely the same attitude of indifference or active opposition towards the methods that may develop a real science of economics. The love of disputation and argumentation is deeply rooted in human nature, especially among teachers, preachers, and lawyers.

To them apparently any kind of mental gymnastics is so exciting, so seductive, that they seize upon it with joy. Hence the millions of sterile pages written on metaphysics, theology, and the law. And economics, as perhaps the most important of the current fields of metaphysics, has called forth a deluge of this futile, speculative writing. It is curious how wide a skepticism still prevails as to the value of exact measurement in this field. Some even go so far as to suggest that a 'science' of economics is impossible, from the very nature of the subject. They dwell upon the fact that we can scarcely submit banking or fiscal policies, and similar questions, to controlled experiment, under different combinations with a single variable, as do the workers in the physical sciences. And yet astronomy, the earliest of our sciences, cannot make use of controlled experiment, and must depend on the overwhelming number of its observations as a basis for certainty in its conclusions.

It must be obvious that the great difference in the relative progress of the physical sciences and of the social sciences is due to the difference in the methods they employ. And no one can inquire carefully into the striking difference in these methods without a surmise as to the source. And it is that the chemist and the physicist are trained to exact methods of investigation. They do not depend upon speculation, or content themselves with presenting ingenious hypotheses. Their method is one of constant check and verification. Every hypothesis, however plausible, every conclusion, however seductive, must meet the repeated test of precise measurement. Clearly until this method is applied to economic theory we cannot have any real science of economics. And in economics, this method can be utilized only by means of a wealth of observations and measurements, over long periods of time, exactly as in astronomy.[20]

There is hope for progress. For one reason and another, many nations are now building up a huge fund of statistical information concerning their economic activities. Beginning less than a century and a half ago with enumerations of the population, this use of counting was extended to every sort of human activity, especially on the economic side. As early as 1810, thanks largely to Alexander Hamilton's invaluable aide and one-time Assistant Secretary of the Treasury, Tench Coxe, this country had taken the first census of manufactures; long the sole undertaking of its kind.[21] Now nearly all nations are engaged in this and in hundreds of other enumerations, providing a vast fund of numerical data from which is rising a solid body of verifiable knowledge. And this development, though slow, is inevitable.

WHEN POWER CAME OF AGE

Long before the discovery of the New World, it was believed that new lands in the far West might be seen from the shores of the Canaries and the Azores. These illusive images were owing not to any extraordinary refraction of the rays of light, but produced by an eager longing for the distant and the unattained. The philosophy of the Greeks, the physical views of the Middle Ages, and even those of a more recent period have been eminently imbued with the charm springing from similar illusive phantoms of the imagination. At the limits of circumscribed knowledge, as from lofty island shore, the eye endeavours to penetrate to distant regions. The belief in the uncommon and the wonderful lends a definite outline to every manifestation of ideal creation; and the realm of fancy becomes thus involuntarily blended with the domain of reality.

—HUMBOLDT: *Cosmos*

The steam engine has increased indefinitely the mass of human comforts and enjoyments, and rendered cheap and accessible all over the world the materials of wealth and prosperity. It has armed the feeble hand of man with a power to which no limit can be assigned.

—LORD JEFFREY

It was remarkable to see the rapid increase that immediately took place in the cotton trade in England as soon as the new inventions were used. Thus, from a little over 1 million pounds weight of raw cotton imported into Great Britain, the import rose between 1771–75 to over 4 million, then was quadrupled to 18 million pounds weight in 1785, and no less than 56 million in the year 1800.

—H. DE B. GIBBINS: *Economic and Industrial Progress of the Century*

CHAPTER III

WHEN POWER CAME OF AGE

1. *The mechanism of progress*

THE one special purpose of this volume is to inculcate the doctrine that economics must be studied as a science, through measurement, as in other sciences, and through these to discover the mechanisms that govern economic phenomena. Further, to expound some of the factors which can be proven significant in our economic life, and to indicate how these may be profitably employed in promoting the general welfare.

Of the many significant economic mechanisms of which we already have statistical proof, none is of greater interest and importance to our well-being than the mechanism of progress. Every phase of economic policy, if it is to be directed toward the continued economic advance of our people, must be in step with this mechanism. And every policy of the government that prevents the working of this mechanism of progress must in the end affect the well-being of all members of the community, whether rich or poor, whether employer or employee.

We have in the United States a number of long-term economic series, especially those depicting industrial and economic growth through the last century and more, several from 1790 and 1800. Most strikingly these series reveal a steady rise in the annual value of the total output at a fairly constant rate over this whole period.[1] There have been occasional interruptions, due to business depression, but until the recent prolonged stagnation, these interruptions have had little effect on the long-term rate of growth. With recovery there has been, until the recent great depression, a resumption of growth, so that decennial series, at least, give no indication of any lasting effect of these business 'cycles' on our national progress. This growth has been fairly constant, although not always the same, in all the major fields of economic activity: in manufacturing, in transportation, in mining, in agriculture. And it should be added

47

that the evidence of this growth can be found not only in the series showing the value of output in terms of money, but also in 'deflated' series, and in series of the physical volume of output.

The explanation of this continued growth in production prior to 1930 is not to be found in the so-called 'efficiency' of the 'workers,' as so often assumed. Our workers have been healthier, better educated, and better trained. But it is questionable whether any increase in personal efficiency can entirely offset the steady diminution in the number of hours customarily worked. The reason for the growth in output over a century and more must be found in the improvements in the methods of production, the provision of new types of machinery, power, and in the increase in capital available per worker. The evidence for this is remarkably clear.

The increase in primary power employed in industry (measured in horse-power) has gone on at practically the same rate as the growth in physical product. The amount of goods produced per horse-power in industry has not materially changed in any decennium of the last century or more. Up to 1930 there has been a very slow secular decrease in output per unit of power. The prevailing idea of an outstanding gain in recent years is a delusion. Further, the annual value of the total manufactured product and the amount of capital actually employed through the last century and more (specifically since 1825 and presumably even earlier) have risen together, decade by decade, with only the slowest secular change; that is, invested capital has risen at a slightly higher rate than the value of the annual product. This indicates that on the average, for every dollar increase in the annual product of manufacture, disregarding price changes, there is required the investment of a dollar of new capital.

What is the source of this capital? Not the 'savings of the people,' for these provide little of the new capital required in industrial enterprises. The larger part comes directly from the companies and businesses themselves, in the funds set aside for surplus, and in over-allowance for depreciation and maintenance—the direct savings of industry itself; and, of course, from dividends and interest; and 90 per cent of net dividends paid to individuals by the 400,000 active corporations in the United States go to persons of incomes of $6,000 and over; 60 per cent to less than 100,000 persons.[2] The income tax returns reveal that income from interest payments is similarly concentrated in the higher income brackets.[3] Evident then that there is a distinct capital producing class; the people of high incomes, the larger owners of the leading industries; and that it is they who provide the capital for expansion.

There is practically no method of promoting economic progress other than through this provision of capital. The industrial advance of Russia under the Communist regime has been brought about solely by expropriation of the people, forced upon them by the distribution of relatively small incomes. Solely from this forced capital saving that they are able to produce new machinery and equipment at home, or to buy new machinery and equipment abroad.[4] The even more remarkable industrial advance in Japan, probably the most rapid advance of any country in recent times, has been based upon much the same mechanism. But here the method has been to maintain low wages, allowing high profits to the great industrialists, who have promptly used these profits to expand their capital equipment. Whether the method is that of Russia or Japan, where low workers' incomes have made possible rapid expansion, or whether the method is that of the United States, where hitherto a satisfactory rate of growth has been maintained with a fairly high level of workers' incomes, the mechanism has been essentially the same. All capital must come from savings. And under our system of free enterprise this capital has come largely from the savings of business enterprises and their owners.

The mode of distribution of income in most countries facilitates the accumulation of savings by successful business men. In almost all countries where an income tax law is in effect, the governments have published data as to how the incomes are distributed. When this information is analyzed it is found that the number of persons in each income class follows a regular gradation, expressible by a simple exponential equation.[5] From the rich to the poor there is a fairly even slope: That is, a very few—2 or 3 per cent of the population—have the highest incomes, a small number—12 or 14 per cent— have moderately large incomes, while the income of the bulk of the population ranges within narrow limits about the general average. The extraordinary thing about this pattern of income distribution is the degree of uniformity shown in different nations and at different times. In all countries for which we have adequate data, whether the United States, England, France, or Germany, this pattern of distribution of income is invariably found. Further, we find it in periods far apart, as for example in the United States as revealed by the tax returns of the short-lived income tax of 1864 to 1872, and again in all the years of the current income tax dating from 1913. And this distribution seems affected but little by prosperity or depression, as shown by the pattern of distribution in 1929 and in 1935.[6] This is the famous law on income distribution discovered by the eminent economist, Pareto. It seems of profound significance, for it shows clearly that inequality in income is a *normal* phenomenon; that the proportion of the people capable of gaining large incomes must always be small; and that the great source of saving for capital accumulation must of necessity be the incomes of the few people of wealth.[7]

It is sometimes argued that the cost of maintaining this mechanism of providing savings is unduly high. But the fact is that of the incomes that go to the very rich, a large part is directly reinvested in productive industry, where it works for the benefit of the whole population. The expenditure of the very rich for personal consumption is an inconsequential part of the national income. If all the personal expenditure of the rich were made available for distribution to the poor, it could add but little to their standard of living. And the savings of the rich cannot be used for ameliorating the condition of the poor without imperiling the capital supply. The prejudice that exists against the rich, and seems always to have existed against the rich, gives rise to recurring agitation for restricting their incomes. This is one of the great potential dangers to the continuation of the economic progress upon which is dependent the well-being both of the workers and of employers.

Here we have in brief the mechanism which governs our economic growth. If there is a failure of the capital supply there must be a halt in the growth of industrial production; stagnation and widespread unemployment. The manifest evidence of the last ten years confirms this view. In this decade, no net capital saving, no plant expansion, no increase in production or in well being; and we may add, no net profit in industry as a whole. Decisive negative evidence as convincing as the positive evidence of growth in the preceding hundred years. The lesson: we cannot destroy the capital supply—whether by taxation or by other ill-advised policies designed to redistribute the wealth to the farmer, to the laborer, or to the idle, without paying the piper.

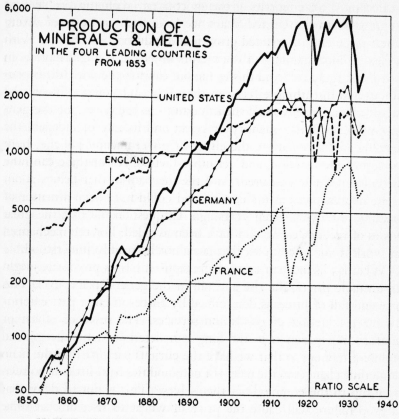

PRODUCTION OF
MINERALS & METALS
IN THE FOUR LEADING COUNTRIES
FROM 1853

UNITED STATES

ENGLAND

GERMANY

FRANCE

RATIO SCALE

V. THE CHIEF PRODUCER OF MINERALS AND METALS

For the last century and more, four nations have produced almost all the coal and iron which so largely have made possible our modern world. Through the nineteenth century England alone was providing most of this, almost more than all the rest. It was not until the middle of the last century that the United States came forward with a large product; now this nearly equals all the others, and if we were to include oil production as well, it would be far more than half, for oil is rapidly becoming everywhere the chief power producer, overtaking and exceeding coal. Since cheap power so largely influences industrial production, there seems little prospect that the primacy of the United States will be seriously challenged for many years, though Russia and Asia may become formidable factors.

2. *The mechanism of business cycles*

In almost all countries growing concern with the problem of depression. In the United States we have had ten years of severe unemployment, of arrested growth and industrial stagnation. With a clearer understanding of the factors involved, it might have been possible largely to avoid this economic catastrophe with all its profound and disturbing effects on the social and political life of the world. Here are involved such questions as the course of the general price level, the quantity of credit and its rate of increase, the influence of speculation, the effect of governmental policies, both of action and inaction, and yet other factors. All of these can now be estimated and measured. And the mechanism that brings about these depressions was understood and could have been a matter of common knowledge ten years ago. Unquestionable that the great losses of recent years could have been avoided. For the mechanism at work is not so complex that it cannot be readily understood.[8]

What is this mechanism of depression? It has its proximate origin in unstable prices, the rise and fall in the general price level. This rise and fall of prices is determined by forces in large part exterior to the production of goods and services. The price of wheat or cotton or pig iron is in the long run determined by the general value of money; so that we have the curious paradox that the main long time changes in the prices of commodities have little or no relationship to the commodities themselves.[9] This is not to deny that a crop failure will cause the price of wheat to rise; or that some prices may not rise or fall more or less than others. But the long run movement of prices is shaped primarily by this general factor of the value of money, which in turn is related to the quantity of money.

Now a commonplace that this 'quantity of money' consists very largely of bank deposits, and that changes in the price level are principally brought about by changes in bank credit. By far the larger part of the total business of the country is carried on by the use of bank checks. We now know from exhaustive studies, described in part above, that when the creation of bank credit proceeds more rapidly than the rate of growth in the nation's business prices rise. Not merely at wholesale, but every type of price including wages and security prices, and the prices of many other things not ordinarily included in the common concept. And when the creation of bank credit grows less rapidly than trade, and particularly when there is an actual diminution in the amount of bank credit, prices fall. Naturally this rise and fall in prices in turn brings about a quickening or retardation of business activity. Hence the significance of changing prices, and of expanding or contracting bank credit.

Now what brings about this more or less rapid expansion in bank credit, relative to the long period rate of growth in production and trade? Unquestionably speculation. In the last century this speculation was largely in land; [10] in recent times in securities, in urban real estate, and in commodities. But always we have found that the all important factor in a rapid expansion of bank credit is speculation. Once this speculation begins it feeds itself for a time. For the speculative demand for securities and real estate raises their prices, and with a rise in prices banks are willing to lend larger sums on these types of collateral. Thus the expansion of bank credit makes possible a general rise in prices. And this is the 'boom.' In turn, when it becomes difficult to get bank credit, except on onerous terms, or when the speculation has proceeded so far it becomes clear that there has been a general overvaluation of securities, real estate, and other types of property, the markets collapse. The sudden decline in the prices of speculative property results in a general calling in of loans by banks based on these types of collateral. With the decrease in the volume of bank credit, a general fall in prices. Business becomes unprofitable. This is the depression.

For all these stages of development in the process of boom and depression we have conclusive statistical evidence. Never do we find a depression without a preceding boom; and in general the greater the boom, the greater the depression. Nor can there be a boom of any magnitude unless it involves considerable speculation —in securities, real estate, or commodities. If bank credit were not made available the speculation could not proceed. And without speculation there would be no subsequent contraction of bank credit, and depression. The mechanism of boom and depression, thus stated in bare outline, is now definitely established. Is it too much to hope that, knowing what we do about business cycles, some attempt will be made to control the creation of bank credit, and avoid the costs of depression? Obviously, the avoidance of depression depends upon our understanding of credit control. Here, too, evidence of a definite mechanism that can be used to prevent the excessive creation and the rapid contraction.

3. *The factors of momentum and inertia*

Twenty years ago few could have anticipated the tangled skein of events that filled the ensuing years, events that so largely repeated the unsettlement, the disorganization, and the revolutionary tendencies that had followed the close of the Napoleonic Wars. True, in Russia there was a Communist State, the first attempt to carry out on a broad scale the revolutionary ideas of Marx and Engels. In Germany there was a new republic with a Socialist government in place of the Prussian monarchy and aristocracy. And there were mutterings of discontent in Italy and in other lands. But there was a brighter side too. The United States, rich and confident, was lending billions to crippled Europe, and resuming the sure and steady industrial growth of the preceding century. In the Far East Japan was pushing to the utmost the remarkable progress it had made prior to the World War, buying heavily the machinery and industrial equipment it required. At that time, who could have foreseen the unparalleled upheaval of recent years and the political anarchy? Is there anything we can learn from the history of these two decades?

The lesson, that can be verified from statistical studies already made, is that the world is governed by definite forces which shape the course of economic development and political events. These forces are rooted in human nature, and, as we are coming dimly to perceive, have subsisted with little change through thousands of years. Widening knowledge of the earlier development of the economic system has flooded with light an obscure and baffling subject, and has revealed the existence of certain forces, which cannot be materially altered in the present state of social development.

This central idea that we are governed by forces which we may for a time upset or disturb, but which we cannot completely control or modify, is derived from a familiar principle of physics: the concept of momentum and inertia.[11] Note, for example, the force of inertia, which tends to identify a product with the principal place of production. A striking instance is the famous city of Damascus, renowned for a cloth familiar to us today as damask. It likewise made marvelous swords before steel had come into common use. These were known as damascene. This remarkable city cultivated wonderful plums, still known to us as the 'damson' variety. In a similar way the island we call Cyprus became renowned for its copper and copper wares; the metal took its name from the island— in Greek, *Kypros*. So, too, the alloy of copper and tin we call bronze. Its name in Roman times was *aes Brundisium*, that, the metal of the city of Brundisium, which is our modern Brindisi.

In much the same way the famous Spanish city of Toledo gave its name to swords as well as to a kind of inlay-ware, just as China has given its name to products sent to foreign lands, so that to us 'china' may refer either to the country or to china ware. Similarly, japanning, the name we give to the process of varnishing. From Venice wonderful glass, and the window blinds used there. So also Sheffield steel and Sheffield plate. The word calico, applied to the cloth so largely produced in Calcutta. Endless other instances.

Now, the interesting thing about all this is that it served to accentuate a natural *monopoly* in these wares for the cities or countries from which they came. If a knife was, let us say, genuine 'Sheffield' or a plate was genuine 'china,' the buyer had little question of the quality of the product. Even when the art of reproduction had been learned by other communities and peoples, this preference for the original product still gave advantage in trade to the older sources of production. But this inertia could be overcome, as evidenced by the excellent reputation enjoyed by the 'china' of Dresden and the cutlery of Solingen.

Paradigm of the whole process of this momentum and inertia in economic life is the invention and development of the steam engine, with all its spectacular consequences. In its inception and establishment it went through all the usual pains of birth. Watt, even after he had worked out the principle and design, found his first products a failure for lack of skilled workmen to make a close-fitting piston. And there was the usual skepticism and hesitation among business men. Designed at first as a pumping engine for the coal mines of England; but the owners of the mines were slow to utilize this new kind of power. Finally the steam engine gained a foothold in industry through the genius of Watt, not only as an inventor but as a salesman. The first engines were sold on the installment plan, which we have somehow come to think of as a recent development, and which is actually as old as the hills. Familiar to Palestine in the days of Jesus, and doubtless far older.[12]

Once the steam engine had been perfected it was inevitably destined to the widest utility. Yet twenty years and more passed before it came to be applied to transportation on sea and on land. From these beginnings have come the huge fleets of steamships and the network of railroads that carry the commerce of the world on all the oceans and across all the continents. In industry, the use of steam power in the cotton mills and in the woolen factories gave rise to large scale production and the wide ramifications that followed. And the steam engine was a powerful impetus to scientific research, invention, and discovery. Not many years after the steam engine had been perfected eager minds like those of Faraday and Henry were at work upon the problem of utilizing the mystic force of electricity. And with the momentous discovery of electro-magnetic induction by Faraday, and with the invention of the dynamo and motor, the way was opened to the production and utilization of this new force of nature on an unparalleled scale. Extraordinary that the larger part of these revolutionary developments came from a single country, Great Britain.

Here, in truth, a perfect example of economic inertia and momentum. An epochal invention, the development of which is delayed for a time by the lack of technical skills capable of the precision required in the steam engine, and by the conservatism of business men. And when this inertia is overcome, the inevitable utilization of this new invention in every phase of economic life. This is the history of many of the important instruments and forces that have literally created and have dominated our modern industrial world, and that may determine the whole future development of mankind.

Even such a disturbing element as business 'cycles' cannot long overcome these forces of inertia and momentum. The world must have its supply of food; it must sow and reap and have its granaries to conserve the steady flow throughout the year, and from year to year when the forces of nature vary the yield of the fields. So, likewise, the world must be clothed; and it must spin and weave, and produce cotton, and wool, and flax. And it requires fuel to heat homes, and to provide light and power. The world must be taught, and served, and amused. The production, the transporta-

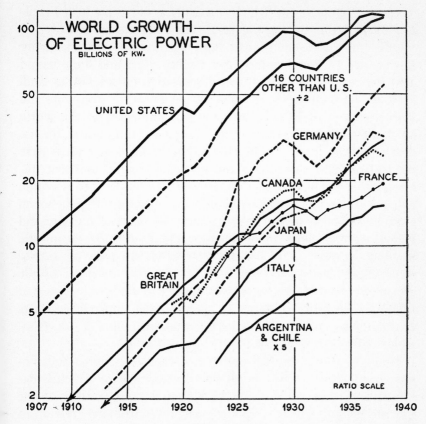

VI. THE ADVANCE IN THE USE OF ELECTRIC POWER

This country had a long lead in the wondrous development of electrical industry. It still holds this position, producing more electric power than the next six or eight countries combined. More than in almost any other industry, unless it be petroleum, electric power has come to be a kind of index of industrial progress; very roughly the advancement of a country may be measured by the amount of electric power it uses. In this regard the United States occupies much the same position as in industry in general. It is instructive that although the United States have vast water powers, more available than those of almost any other nation, electric power production from this source has steadily declined for a long period, in comparison with production by steam power. Save for relatively short distances, it is still cheaper to transport coal or oil than electricity, a simple fact that seems difficult for many minds to grasp. Only in rare instances are great water powers so situated as to be advantageous for use.

tion, and the distribution of these necessaries, comforts, and luxuries, together with the commercial and financial transactions they require, make up perhaps seven-eighths of the total economic activity of even so progressive a country as the United States. This economic activity varies normally from season to season, and from year to year. But the extent and importance of these natural fluctuations has been rather grotesquely exaggerated.[13] The experience of recent years has been far out of scale, and this difference is of profound significance.

The indexes by which the extent and exceptional character of the current depression (that is, since 1930) have been picturesquely brought to the public mind, tend to over-estimate the normal range and importance of these fluctuations.[14] If the tides of trade were really as violent as most of these graphic presentations of industrial activity would suggest, the business life of the country could hardly go on. In point of fact, the production of goods and services flows on, ordinarily, without wide fluctuation from low to high. The momentum of growth is tremendous and not easily overcome. Precisely this gives assurance of stability, and hope for security. When once we have learned the mechanism of the disturbing forces, and have instituted means for their control, these fluctuations might readily be reduced to an almost negligible minimum. We shall consider at length whether it is possible wholly to eliminate the wide variations in the expansion of credit and thus curb the speculation which makes possible the depression which inevitably follows.

More disturbing to our economic system and more difficult to control is the spirit of War, the love of fighting, that seems largely the prospect of plunder. It seems clear that these forces are inbred and to a high degree hereditary. There are peoples to whom war passions are more or less native and distinctive. This is certainly true among the animals, even down to the lowest orders. A colorful example is found in the world of ants; a noteworthy fact that ants are preyed upon by relatively few other animals, in this resembling the human race. And like the latter, their most dangerous enemies are of their own kind. Some of the most aggressive varieties present a singular analogy to the racial types which range through human history. Thus we read:

There are tropical ants which travel in great armies and are as savage as the ancient or may we now say, the present day Huns or Mongols;

they spend their lives mainly in destroying the nests of others and killing all insects in their way. These ants are blind, so that the size of an object in their path means nothing to them; tall trees are climbed and even human dwellings are invaded, in search of prey. When such an army enters a house, the owner must temporarily surrender.

In due course the countries in which these warlike and predatory ants are rife will wage a war of extermination. It is not impossible that in sheer self-defense the civilized and peaceful peoples of the earth may eventually be driven to the same procedure against the brigand and bandit nations. In every country we restrain and imprison the criminal classes and the violently insane. Civilization may be forced to take up arms against its enemies. But long before this, we must realize that the war spirit is largely engendered by economic disturbances and the feeling of economic insecurity. Not impossible that the psychology of the future will reveal that these feelings of insecurity and inferiority are strongly basic to the warlike impulse, and that the latter may be due to the fear or apprehension these feelings inspire. It seems clear that the life of the individual, and especially of the neurotic types, is often motivated by such feelings. There is reason to believe that they may take on a kind of mass mania, or produce what is often termed mass suggestion.

Be this as it may, it seems that these warlike and predatory impulses have been from an immemorial time an integral influence in shaping history. They too are a part of the momentum and inertia of human activity, and so deeply imbedded in some nations that their elimination will be slow. Curiously enough, it may be that the greatest hope lies just in what seems the greatest danger, namely, the advance in the technology of warfare. The writer was among the first to suggest that the coming of the airplane meant eventually the end of war. For a very obvious reason: whenever huge squadrons of airplanes, loaded with devastating explosives, gases, and inflammables, can bomb and butcher and burn peoples by the thousands, including kings, parliaments, generals, and munitions makers, the popularity of war will wane. When there is real danger in war, where hitherto it has been relatively slight, and when the cost of war becomes appalling, as it has not been hitherto, perhaps human society may eliminate the third and most formidable of the lethal scourges which have beset its history. War, like pestilence and

famine, will not yield to the moral improvement of man, but to
the advance of science and technology.

4. *Economics and mechanics*

Noted above that the stream of economic activity goes on ordinarily with little interruption. It is this economic inertia which
prevents the economic system from breaking down completely
under the impact of depression or war. Indeed, the impact of war
and depression has usually had little effect on the volume of production and trade, except perhaps during the depression of the last
decennium, or during the World War. And the disruptive forces
of war and depression have a characteristic mechanism of their
own, as can be seen from studies of the movement in prices, production, and income, during war and postwar periods.[15] Even
great technological changes, the major force for progress in our
economic life, are slow in their effects on the economic system. So
acute an observer as Adam Smith, who wrote the philosophy of the
industrial revolution into his *Wealth of Nations*, lived and died
blissfully unconscious of the stupendous consequences of the invention of his young friend and neighbor of early days, James
Watt.[16] When, however, the significance of these technological
changes becomes apparent to business men, they lead to salient
advances in economic activity. Here too, the uniformity of the
pattern of progress indicates that we have a mechanism at work.

Even the academic economists have come to recognize this in part.
When they speak of the equilibrium of supply and demand, the
relation of cost to price, they describe a mechanism at work.[17] But
they destroy their handiwork when they make this mechanism a
matter of deduction, rather than measurement and correlation.
And because this mechanism is not regarded as the result of natural
forces in the economic system, it is subjected to various methods
of control, designed to modify its effects. When these controls
result in failure, complex explanations are invented to show that
economics is after all a matter of human behavior, which is and
must remain beyond understanding. No attempt to study in detail
the mechanisms that pervade the economic system. No attempt to
discover, through scientific methods, why these mechanisms must
defeat the futile efforts of legislators and visionaries to change
them.

This difficulty in establishing the mechanistic nature of science is not unique to economics. It is equally true of all the social sciences. And in the past of course true of the physical and biological sciences. But little by little we are coming to accept the same forces as those which dominate the physical world, the idea of a definite order, of law and fixity, of mechanisms that control economic activity as they control the workings of the physical world. Our acceptance of these views must be slow, at first, because our economic attitudes are highly emotional, and because the mechanisms that control our economic life are more complex and less easily demonstrated than the mechanisms that control the physical world. But intelligent research must in the end be effective; it will provide the proofs; it will reveal the mechanisms at work in problems involving money and prices, prosperity and depression, wage rates and trade unions, profits and progress, and in the numerous other controversial questions which must be solved if we are to have stability, order, and progress in our economic life.

THE ANTIQUITY OF COMMERCE

Who hath taken this counsel against Tyre, the crowning city, whose merchants are princes, whose traffickers are the honourable of the earth?—ISAIAH

The History of *Commerce*, of the Invention of Arts, Rise of Manufactures, Progress of Trade, Change of its Seats, with the Reasons, Causes, &c., may also be made entertaining to Youth, and will be useful to all. And this, with the Accounts in other History of the prodigious Force and Effect of Engines and Machines used in War, will naturally introduce a Desire to be instructed in *Mechanicks*, and to be inform'd of the Principles of that Art by which weak Men perform such Wonders, Labour is sav'd, Manufactures expedited, &c. This will be the Time to show them Prints of antient and modern Machines, to explain them, to let them be copied, and to give Lectures in Mechanical Philosophy.
—BENJAMIN FRANKLIN: *Proposals Relating to the
Education of Youth in Pensilvania*

In the latter half of the 16th century, the joint-stock form of organization began its conquering career in England with the Russia Company and the Adventurers to Africa. The Bank of England (preceded by several continental institutions) adapted this form of banking and it spread slowly to other fields. But in 1776 Adam Smith argued that, in most lines of business, the joint-stock company was necessarily less efficient than the simpler organization in which one man or a few partners were giving strict attention to their personal interests. The enlarged capital needs of factories, however, the coming of railroads and the rapid growth in the volume of business, so altered the situation that within a century after the Wealth of Nations was published the joint-stock company in some of its proliferating variants became the dominating form of business organization outside of farming, retail trade, and the professions.
—WESLEY C. MITCHELL: *Business Cycles: The Problem and Its Setting*

CHAPTER IV

THE ANTIQUITY OF COMMERCE

1. *Historical perspective and economic understanding*

IN all human history no more singular phenomenon than the rise of great civilizations, not merely to affluence, but often to superb achievement, and their eventual decline, with only archaeological remains to bear evidence of their former glory. A perennial theme; still profoundly obscure. Involving natural as well as economic forces. First, it must be noted that hardly more than one-tenth of the earth's surface is fit for human habitation. Of the land, constituting one-fourth of the earth, half consists of tropical jungle, arctic wastes, rainless deserts, or mountainous areas with scant opportunity for human settlement. And of the rest, only one-half or two-thirds lies in the temperate isothermal belt of the Northern hemisphere that has always seemed the most favorable climate for human development. This isothermal belt is distinctly the zone of high civilization; it probably contains eighty per cent of the fertile arable land, and probably more than ninety per cent of the world's economic wealth.[1]

The present conclusions of archaeology are that this area has been inhabited by a human race not differing markedly from the present population for at least fifty or a hundred thousand years, and by more primitive men for perhaps half a million years. The invention of tools and the use of fire must have begun tens of thousand of years ago, at the least.[2] The larger part of this area has been known and traversed by commerce probably for many thousands of years. Trade routes are known that go back far into prehistoric time, and that stretch from the Baltic to the China Sea. Despite this, all the written history of this area is comprised in that of the last four or five thousand years. Within this historical period the forms of commerce and trade have changed but little, although undergoing tremendous development all over the world. This development, largely mechanical, is quite recent, and has come largely within the last two centuries.

Why was this development of economic life so long delayed, and why has it taken place chiefly in the narrow temperate belt of the northern hemisphere? Clearly it required the concurrence of modern science—physics, chemistry, geology, astronomy, and engineering. But always with stimulus of the vast natural wealth of this temperate belt. Within this limited area is included a large part of the coal, iron, copper, and oil resources, available for modern industry. From this area comes a sizeable part of the foodstuffs and fibers required to feed and clothe a progressive and growing population. It is especially the combination of these favorable natural conditions with powerful leaders that has given rise to the economic advance of the last two centuries. These resources and these men of genius have made it possible to concentrate within this limited area four-fifths of the urban population, four-fifths of the factory workers, and a corresponding proportion of the railway and shipping facilities.

When once the wealth and industry of a country have been developed in a given area where the natural resources abound and the spirit of enterprise is favorable, the element of inertia tends automatically to maintain economic concentration at that point.[3] And this will be true even when natural resources are no longer technically as favorable as they formerly were. Thus England's wealth of coal and iron gave rise to huge industries, which survived long after the local supply of coal and iron ore had dwindled. And in the United States, the steady movement of population to the West and the genesis of industry in the West seem not to have deeply affected the industrial supremacy of the older section. It is still true that half the population, and two-thirds or more of the wealth and income, and the same proportion of production of manufactured goods, are contained in fourteen of the smaller states lying east of the Mississippi and north of Mason and Dixon's line. When the industrial leadership of the older sections is lost, it must be not only through the discovery of superior resources elsewhere, but also through the weakening of the spirit of free enterprise.

This problem of the rise and fall of great civilizations is of profound importance. Why the rise and fall, not only of Rome, but of Memphis and Persepolis, of Athens and Alexandria? Why the rise and fall of the indigenous civilizations of the New World, that of the Incas and of the Mayas? On this interesting question many suggestions, but as yet no definite answer.

The investigations of Ellsworth Huntington on climatic changes are undoubtedly significant. The concentration of modern industrial development in the temperate regions of the northern hemisphere is evidence of the great influence of climate and temperature. Could the rise and fall of ancient civilizations have been related to climatic changes? Nothing more fascinating has come to our time than the evidence disclosed by archaeology and by other sciences, permitting the construction of a long time scale of temperatures. On this we have the work of Professor Douglass on tree rings, and the work of Antevs and others on the tiny varves, the alternating layers of clay and silt found along river banks.[4] Additional evidence has come from pollen grains, found buried in the peat bogs and preserved through thousands of years. This wealth of information has made it possible to construct a record of the climate and temperature of distant periods. There can be no doubt now that changes in climate and temperature have been a major factor in explaining the rise and fall of ancient civilizations.

More recently we have been learning the history of epidemics and plagues, which may have played such a fateful rôle in the history of empires.[5] Did Greece and Rome degenerate under the influence of malaria and perhaps other ravaging diseases? Another puzzle for the future. Similar forces, like destructive wars and famines, perhaps acting in a kind of conjuncture, may have sharply reinforced the effects of climatic change, though we have as yet no clinching evidence of this. But time, and the indefatigable labors of the archaeologists, may yet provide the answer. A decisive factor, the full influence of which has yet to be disclosed, may have been the varying degree of metallurgical development. It is evident that Rome could not have conquered the little portion of the world it knew without steel. And it is curious that the finest Roman swords and spears came from India, apparently the earliest home of steel making. Clearly it was steel plus gunpowder that made possible the swift conquest of America by the Spaniards.

We have yet another singular chapter in the history of human progress: The development of a native civilization in America, that just failed to reach the highest economic level, and that fell before the superior arms of the Conquistadors. The Incas of Peru had distinctly passed the Stone Age and understood the process and effects of metal alloys. They were fine workers in bronze and made other alloys with gold and copper. Their civilization was indigenous, and as our time periods go, quite ancient.[6] We have indubitable proof that agriculture in America was entirely of local origin, possibly as old or even older than that of the Old World. The independence of American agriculture is evident from the complete separation of the plants of the Old World and the new. For example: five of the leading cereals, wheat, barley, oats, rye, and sorghum, were unknown to the western hemisphere until the Spaniards came. And equally unknown to the Old World was maize (Indian corn), tobacco, potatoes, tomatoes, rubber, and a wide variety of medicinal plants such as those supplying cocaine and quinine. Even more convincing evidence of the separate development of the New World is found in the lack of horses, cattle, sheep, and many other animals.

The Incas had reached a fairly high stage of civilization. Their weaving of woolen yarns has never been surpassed. They were skilled potters, and real artists in metal working. They built remarkable roads and bridges. Suspension bridges spanned deep gorges, and roads a thousand miles long were spaced with huts at intervals of one and a half miles, where runners were housed who could carry a message from Cuzco to Bogatá, a thousand miles, in a week. The population of the New World was large. All told, the indigenous peoples might have numbered six or eight millions, possibly more.

Why did these people attain at such an early date so high a stage of culture and not reach the level of the Eurasian or Mediterranean peoples of the Old World? Perhaps we may have the answer in the absence of draft animals.[7] They had almost no beasts of burden, like horses or oxen or camels. For lack of these, agriculture and trade must have remained at a level below that attained in Europe and Asia. Far-reaching trade routes were impossible for the simple reason that there were scarcely any means of transport except human beings. Probably for this same reason they did not develop the wheel or the plow. A further handicap to the extension of trade was the absence of sea transportation.

All this, perhaps, explains why this talented people never found the treasures of North America, but left untouched the bounteous prairies and great forests, and all the wealth of coal and iron. They would probably have been unable to conquer the wandering tribes whom we later came to call Indians. The Incas and the Mayas were never conquering, adventuring, exploring peoples. Perhaps because of their vegetarian diet and the lack of abundant animal food

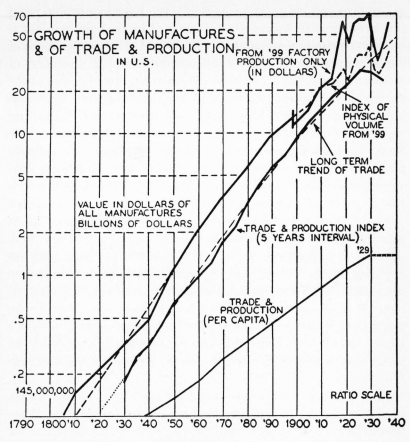

VII. GROWTH OF MANUFACTURES AND OF TRADE AND
PRODUCTION

The graph above is unique in two particulars: It records perhaps the most
remarkable industrial growth in the history of the world, and it is practically the
only such long time record that exists. The first census of manufacturers, anywhere,
was taken in the United States in 1810, and in later years long remained unknown.
The estimates for the period back to 1790 were made by Tench Cox, assistant to
Alexander Hamilton. The index of trade and production is by five-year intervals,
and is in physical units. Yet it will be seen that, up to the World War, it remained
closely parallel to the index of manufactures taken in dollar values. It reveals that
in every decennium from 1830 to 1930 the rate of growth remained almost
unchanged. Especially when taken on a per capita basis, as shown above; that is,
up to 1930. Then this magnificent progress stops for the first time in the history
of the country. Ten years of complete stagnation, no increase in wealth, production,
or plant, or in general well-being. A very significant fact, and prompting, it would
seem, a searching inquiry into the causes thereof.

Perhaps because of their inadequate weapons. But probably their ignorance of iron and coal was the decisive factor in their failure to advance further, since these resources, with the metallurgy and chemistry to which they gave rise, have been two powerful influences in the advance of civilization. And the absence of steel, and gunpowder, made it possible for them to be conquered by a comparatively small band of well armed Europeans.

Even after allowing for the tremendous importance of natural factors, for climate and temperature, for coal and iron and metallurgy, for means of transportation, and for military power, there must be other factors, such as economic and political organization, that have affected the rise and fall of nations. The economic factor has been stressed by many economists and historians, so that its significance is now generally known.

But the political factor in the rise and fall of nations, in economic policy, while given some consideration, has on the whole been neglected. Political pressure for improvement of the economic position of the masses must in the past, as it does today, have endangered to some extent the provision of an adequate supply of new capital necessary for technical and economic progress. On these questions, the economic and political aspects of progress, more will be said in succeeding chapters.[8]

2. The antiquity of commerce and trade

Discoveries, so recent even as the last ten years, have established beyond further question, the immense antiquity of the human race. In the caves of Chicoutien, near Peking, have been found the remains and especially the skulls of a considerable number of individuals imbedded in solid rock. It appears that this Peking man, as he is termed, lived at least half a million years ago and that he had fire and some rude tools. He was a cannibal, fond of human brains, and had implements to crack the skulls of his captives. These discoveries place a date for human beginnings much more distant than perhaps even the majority of anthropologists have been willing to believe. A race that had rude tools and could make fire, and that understood how to crack skulls in order to extract their contents must already have been old—as our human time reckoning goes, very old, possibly reaching back a million years at least.

So far as the still scanty evidence goes, the advancement from

Peking man to the recently discovered Palestine man of perhaps sixty thousand years ago, was almost incredibly slow, a very considerable development of brain capacity, but far less in what we term the arts of civilization. Even Palestine man still dwelt in caves. He is regarded by Sir Arthur Keith as probably the true predecessor of the present human species, homo sapiens. On the time reckoning here indicated, it took some four or five hundred thousand years to develop the skull cracking cannibals of the caves of Chicoutien into the men which in stature, and perhaps in intelligence, were not below that of many races of today.

This is the first striking fact that meets us in the history of our species: its immense antiquity and its unbelievably slow rate of progress from something not far above the higher apes.[9] This estimation of the time element and its correlative, the slow rate of human progress, is one of the fundamental generalizations in the slowly dawning science of man; but the rate of progress in, say, the last fifty thousand years, and especially in the last ten thousand years, has been notably accelerated. And that acceleration has been continuous, for we may now estimate that the progress of the last two or three thousand years has exceeded in importance that of the preceding twenty thousand years; and that in turn the preceding two hundred thousand years. We seem to have a distinct picture of an increscent rate of human progress. Profoundly as instructive as the background of our economic history.

With this record of the slow advance of man, it becomes clear that the highly developed institutions of our economic system cannot be of recent origin, but must have had their beginning far in the past. Contrary to a common belief, even among some historiographers, that modern forms of commerce and finance are perhaps only a few hundred years old. As we penetrate farther into the shadowy paths of prehistory, we see that the beginning of our economic institutions and forms dates back probably thousands of years. We know now that present procedures in banking and insurance, commercial law and customs, were in full flower in the golden days of Greece, and still earlier in Babylonia and along the Nile. The discovery of the code of Hammurabi, dating from 2100 B. C., establishes this beyond doubt. Long trade routes and sea voyages carried goods for exchange in the most distant lands.[10] There is legend that the continent of Africa was circumnavigated in the reign of Necho I, about 600 B. C. The account given by Herodotus and his naive arguments against the probability of the voyage seem actually to confirm the legend in an odd way. And we know that only a little later the famous Pythias had sailed far beyond the Pillars of Hercules and probably visited the lands of the Baltic. It is now certain that the tin mines and tin trade of Cornwall began long ago, perhaps antedating the glories of Greece. The Phoenicians were a vigorous race of traders and voyagers centuries before the able tyrant, Peisistratus, had laid the foundations of the future greatness of Athens.[11]

Even factory production must go back a long time. Interesting discoveries, confirming and extending this new knowledge, come year by year. A toy-making town on the banks of the Indus, Chanhu-Daru, was a forerunner of Nürnberg by at least four thousand years. Some of its creations have been found at distant points along the trade route on which it lay; and some of its attainments almost stagger belief; for example, an antique wristlet of tiny beads, found in a jewel box, the beads so fine that they could be strung forty to the inch. But strung only on hairs, since the aperture was so small that it is difficult to understand how these holes could have been accurately drilled without some kind of magnifying glass, which they possibly had. Chanhu-Daru was a purely neolithic town. The inhabitants seem to have had no metal tools. Sharppointed instruments were of flint and of obsidian, and in order to make these little beads, the tools must have been of extraordinary delicacy. Some of them, in fact, have been found. Here was a high degree of technical skill and technical achievement. From all this, and from much similar evidence, we gain a picture of the awe-inspiring antiquity of handicraft, or as we now say, manu-facture, which of course once meant making by hand.

The steadily mounting evidence in this field seems to have established one other highly instructive generalization: there has been little increase in our so-called human efficiency. The discoveries and investigations of a few marvelously gifted minds have immensely increased our equipment of instruments and machinery. But there has been no marked increase in the skill or dexterity of the individual worker. The wealth and affluence of modern nations is almost wholly the product of inventions, discoveries, contrivances and innovations, made by extraordinarily few individuals. The sole difference between the industry and productivity of our times and of a thousand or five thousand years ago is precisely in the use of these inventions and discoveries. The artisans of Chanhu-Daru must have had tools and implements of precision. But they had no steam engines or dynamos which have become the foundation stones of modern industry. Power! These, and the machines and devices they operate have come so swiftly we scarcely realize that before this last step in modern industry, there were skilled workers of rare capacity and intelligence, perhaps ten thousand years ago.

Now, if all this is true, if there were trade routes and sea voyages extending thousands of miles, and manufacturing and commerce, long before any written history; and if our modern economic institutions are a slow evolution from these, through thousands of years, what shall we say of the naiveté that would suppose that these institutions, and the whole organization of present day society, may be abruptly changed, as if by the wave of a hand. On a page of Plato there is an instructive sentence of the ancient Egyptian priest saying to Solon, poet, philosopher and reformer: "You Greeks are ever children, with no antiquity of knowledge and no knowledge of antiquity." [12] Twenty-five hundred years ago!

Even the spirit of economic reform is old. This Solon, it will be recalled, was the initiator of the famous Seisachtheia or 'shaking off of the burdens' (an earthquake!), the shaking off being, as usual, the repudiation of debts, canceling of mortgages, and devaluing of currency, lifting the weight of taxes no doubt 'from the many to the few,' precisely as in more recent days. Those who sometimes reflect upon the vanities of human endeavor may like to recall that this Seisachtheia was all over before Solon himself had passed from the scene. His successor was the astute Peisistratus, perhaps the greatest statesman of Grecian times. Pericles merely spent the wealth for which Peisistratus laid the foundations. It was the latter who began the coinage of the famous Athenian 'owls,' which became, for the next six hundred years, the prevailing currency of the Mediterranean, the pound sterling of that era.[13] And from history we know that a stable and widely accepted currency has been one of the principal aids to commercial adventure and wealth, precisely as it proved for Athens, the commercial leader of that portion of the world.

3. Cattle, chattels, and enterprise

Every schoolboy, as Macaulay used to say, is familiar with the fact that our word for capital possessions is just a translation from the Latin name for 'heads' of cattle, caput, and also that our word *chattels* had the same origin. Perhaps not so well-known that cattle were probably the earliest form of productive wealth, that they were long used as *money*, and that they stimulated to a large degree the development of commerce.

The domestication of cattle must have been one of the noteworthy steps toward civilization, and this process must have begun at an early stage in the history of man, far back in the period of the cave dwellers. The first domestic animal probably was the dog. Many breeds of dog are little removed from the wolf, jackal, fox, and other species, and there must have been weaker and less agile breeds that found it profitable to live in the vicinity of this strange prowling two-legged animal that was learning to get his food by killing other animals, by throwing rocks or hurling javelins and spears. And dogs must have been useful to man. They must have helped in the chase of wild boars and other beasts, and have had their reward with food. So it is that 'man's best friend' was perhaps his earliest, and therefore a potent factor in his mental and social development.

The goats and sheep came early into the domestic circle, the goat for its milk and the sheep for its warm wooly coat, and its meat. The cow, larger in size and harder to tame, must have come later; and the horse later still. It was harder to catch and to kill. But it is known that men very early learned to maneuver a herd of horses to the edge of a cliff and then drive them over. In the Rhone Valley and elsewhere there are findings of such strategic deposits of horses' bones, similar to the kitchen-middens of the seacoasts.

The interest of the process of domestication, of man as well as of animals, lies in its effect upon man himself. Sharpening his wits and increasing his intelligence. Cattle must have played a part in early economic development. They supplied the meat and dairy products that were an important part of the food supply; they provided leather, horn, and bone that were useful for clothing and tools; and they furnished the only means, other than human beings, of transport on land. Finally, they were truly capital, for they provided a form of investment from which a real income could be derived. Undoubtedly cattle were the first noteworthy form of 'conspicuous wealth.' Still an important part.

But sometimes far from bringing affluence, or well being. I have lately been reading what was to me an astonishing story to this

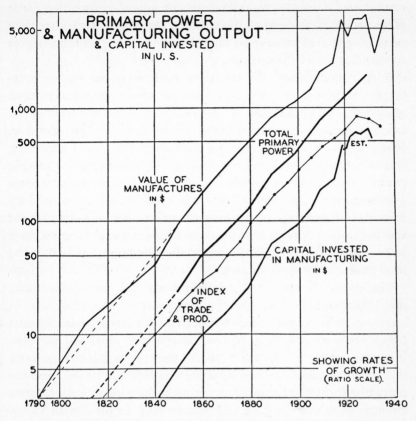

5,000

1,000

500

TOTAL
PRIMARY
POWER

EST.

VALUE OF
MANUFACTURES
IN $

100

50

CAPITAL INVESTED
IN MANUFACTURING
IN $

INDEX
OF
TRADE
& PROD.

10

5

SHOWING RATES
OF GROWTH
(RATIO SCALE).

1790 1800   1820   1840   1860   1880   1900   1920   1940

VIII. THE SOURCES OF OUR GREAT WEALTH AND INCOME

Another remarkable index is that above, of primary power employed to run machinery in industry, plotted with the value of manufactures and the index of trade and production shown in the preceding chart. It reveals that all three have grown almost at an identical rate, a little higher for primary power than for product. With this is shown the amount of capital investment in manufacturing, growing at a little higher rate than the others. Without this capital investment the really stupendous growth of product and of power would be impossible—the fundamental thesis of the present volume. It is noteworthy that with the great rise in prices in and since the World War, there has been a corresponding rise in the value of manufactures and the capital invested. That is, the capital investment must keep pace with the value of the product, a fact which some economic writers seem unable to understand. But this is really the whole secret of our national wealth, as is shown in the succeeding charts.

effect: that the poorest large population in the world has even now vastly greater possessions of this ancient form of capital than any other nation. According to the available data, India has today more cattle than the next five or six largest cattle-holding countries in the world: more than three times as many as our United States, more than four times as many as Russia, more than ten times as many as China. But this is only the beginning of the wonder. Indian consumption, both of milk and of beef, is the *lowest* of any large population. The singular thing is that this colossal holding of cattle, estimated at about 215 millions, is not for the purpose of supplying this huge population with meat and milk! The cattle are of low grade and produce little milk, very low in fat content. In some Hindu states the butchering of cattle is prohibited by law. Only foreigners, half-castes, and a few others eat beef in India. To the vast majority it is forbidden by their religious codes. The result: a large part of these people, especially the Hindus, are probably the most poorly nourished known.

The rest of the story is that India has not only this poorly nourished population, but has also the lowest per capita income of any large country. In good times the per capita income of the United States has been as high as $600 or $700 a year. That of India has been estimated as low as $25. Consider then the paradox: India with the largest possession of the most ancient form of wealth, and the particular form that has given us the name for capital, is the poorest country of which we have any trustworthy record. In India the development of capitalistic industry is still almost in its beginnings.

And this only a part of this unexampled situation. These vast holdings of cattle are precisely what is keeping India poor. The cattle eat up the fat of the land. They are literally ruining India and steadily reducing its area of fertile soil. The browsing cattle of India, like the cattle of our western plains, open the way to the terrible erosion from the tremendous rains. All told, the cost of maintaining this enormous cattle population has been estimated to be in excess of the cost of maintaining the government of India. "But few people in India count up profit and loss with respect to their cows; they do not keep them for profit. Many keep them for company, or for religious ceremonies, or to add social distinction. In reckoning the cost of India's village cattle it is necessary to ascribe a zero value to all food grazed, and to count the labor bestowed on herding, stabling, feeding and milking village cows as a labor of love." [14]

I know of no more acute differentiation between capital, or so-called 'wealth,' and the effective use of that capital under the typical modern capitalistic regime. The mere piling up of capital—whether cattle or machines—without directing the use of this capital in new and productive fields, is futile. Without enterprise capital remains sterile. For the same reason the presence or absence of abundant natural resources has not been a decisive factor in the well-being of a nation. England, for example, had few natural resources outside of her coal, and we might add her coasts; yet, until recently, England represented the highest stage of capitalism.[15] Russia, a nation of reputedly vast natural resources with an immense area, is still one of the poorest countries in the world. The United States has great resources. Nevertheless, half the population of the United States dwells in an area about the size of Germany; this area includes New England and the Middle Atlantic States. The vast stores of iron that have made the United States the leading steel producing country lie for the most part outside this area; and so does most of our coal. Yet this area does nearly two-thirds of the manufacturing of the country and has the highest per capita wealth and income of any section of the globe and naturally the highest provision of capital.

4. Trade, wealth, and civilization

In our modern world, with its enormous income and vast stores of wealth, it is difficult to realize the widespread poverty of ancient times, and that even now this acute poverty still survives over perhaps the greater part of the earth, as in Asia and Africa. Equally hard to realize how throughout tens of thousands of years the mass of humanity has lived close to the deadline of subsistence; alternating between famines and plagues.

Likewise difficult to realize that war and pillage have been an incessant characteristic of human society throughout an enormous span of time. There was so little to eat and so little to enjoy that there was almost perpetual strife over the possession of this little. The fertile lands of the ancient world were not of vast extent; most of them had to be carved out of the forests or built up by irrigation, or as in the natural overflow of the Nile. It was in these fertile areas that a settled society and the beginnings of wealth and civilization found root; and these valleys were the recurrent scene of savage warfare and slaughter. The apparent wealth of these areas, as reflected in their beautiful temples and in the legends that have come down to us of communities with enormous riches, has given a false impression, and has obscured the primal fact so essential to our economic understanding. It was the late Simon Patton who insisted so strongly that ours is the first age of a considerable surplus, the first enduring time of plenty.

Here and there in the cities, as in ancient Damascus, were the rude beginnings of manufacturing, the hand-crafts, the making of cloth, weapons, jewelry, toys and other goods. And with these the beginnings of trade by land and by sea. The latest discoveries, like that noted, of the toy town of Chanhu-Daru on the banks of the Indus, reveal how very ancient were these trade routes, how early the beginnings of industry; in full bloom definitely five or six thousand years ago, and quite possibly thousands of years before. Along these trade routes cities began to arise where they could make adequate fortification for protection against marauders of the deserts and the forests.

Noteworthy that trade, the manufacture and exchange of goods, has always been the chief source of wealth. Rarely or never have agricultural countries attained any high degree of wealth or civilization, for it is almost wholly from the wealth of a nation that the stimulus to art and culture is derived. In the rich valleys of the Nile and elsewhere, the possession of land could bring wealth to a very few,—the pharaohs and kings, and some of the nobility; but the amount of this wealth was small. And to this day we find in agriculture, all over the world, the work of small farms yielding but a meager subsistence to their owners.

The riches of Odysseus, king of the little island of Ithaca, are painstakingly enumerated in Homer, obviously as something of real note and achievement. And quite probably the barter of flocks was the beginning of any considerable trade. It may have been the herdsmen, the wanderers roaming in search of pasture, who were the first traders. And as owners of oxen, camels and horses, which provided the best means of transportation, they were in a favorable position to carry on. It was natural that these carriers and distributors should be a bold and adventurous type, not too distantly related to marauders and robbers. In the beginning, as with the Greeks and Phoenicians, there was a combination of the occupations of trader and pirate to a greater or lesser degree, creating a prejudice that has survived through all history. It is curious to note how the jealousy and suspicion of the merchant and the trader has persisted even to our own time, and how common is the belief that fraud and chicane are their inevitable characteristics.

In reality, the traders, with their wealth and energy and activity, were the first influential civilizers. It was the towns and cities, as the name 'city' implies, that gave rise to what we call civilization; and it was the traders, the merchants, and the carriers that made these aggregations possible. Now whether it was because of the boldness, the cunning or ability required, it is clear that the earliest capitalists, other than the primitive kings and priests, were the traders. They were the money makers and enterprisers. So from the earliest days we find banking, shipping, and mining, and all the complementary fields of industry and commerce, closely associated with the bolder spirits who were so engaged.

The wonder of it all is that once having made such a flourishing beginning this trade and industry should not have had the vast development of modern times. The ancient Babylonians, the Greeks, and later the Romans, apparently had banking facilities and considerable aggregations of capital.[16] They had a commerce that did not shrink before remarkably long voyages. There was a thriving commerce with India from the ports of the Red Sea; and some centuries before Alexander the Suez Canal had been cut through, for a long time remaining open to the passage of boats. The Ionians, the Phoenicians, and the Greeks were persistent colonizers, and had rich cities and plantations scattered all over the Mediterranean. They had mines in Spain; they voyaged to England for tin, and to the Baltic for amber.

Why seemingly an impassable limit? A difficult question and one that has engaged some of the keenest minds. A common explanation has been the prevalence of slave labor, and the peculiar disesteem in which commerce and business were held. Even the more civilized part of the world was dominated, as late as in Roman times, by warriors and plunderers. Julius Caesar a supreme example of this type. Other explanations include the insecurity of life and property, the burdensome taxes levied by the ruling classes, and the like. All no doubt contributory, but not decisive. There was another factor, a little difficult to understand in the light of the history of our own time. This was the prevalent lack of innovation and invention, a lack of highly motivated curiosity save in a few fields. Even the spirit of exploration and discovery did not change the ways of industry and trade. Life in Europe went on very much as before, until the coming of a new force; a force that, curiously enough, we now term power, so highly industrialized has our very language become. The advent of the Power Age.

What happened was a new implementing of industry, which gave a wondrous increase to the power of capital. It was large scale production, and large scale commerce and distribution, that opened wide the gates to capitalist enterprise, leading to industrial aggregates on a scale unknown before. And apparently it was just these increasing aggregations that themselves provided the capital supply for further extension and expansion of industry into new forms and new fields. This is the key to the whole economic development of the last two hundred years. Without this capital supply the expansion of industry that has been witnessed would have been quite impossible, save under state enterprise, and this form of economic organization has been neither successful nor enterprising. The paradox is that it was industry itself that from its high profits gained and supplied the capital that was needed.

It is clear that mere wealth could not of itself provide the incitement to progress that comes from industry and enterprise. This is evident from the history of Spain and Portugal. The discoveries and conquests of Cortez and Pizarro, and the later discoveries of gold in Brazil brought to these countries an astonishing flow of money; but this did not make either a great commercial nation. This unparalleled flood of precious metals spread, through the channels of commerce, into France, Holland, and England, and Germany; and it was in these countries that this inflow had its most fructifying effect. Almost identically the same thing, on a smaller scale, had happened in earlier times, when the Roman conquerors, and before them Alexander, had brought back vast stores of plunder. It is noteworthy that the distribution of these hoards of gold and silver in that distant day brought a tremendous rise in prices and periods of extravagant speculation and free spending, as Heichelheim and others have so interestingly set forth.[17]

In short, our present day industrial civilization is a plant that required for its development a combination of rare conditions. Iron had become an article of commerce, eagerly sought for a thousand or more years before the Christian era. Coal, it is true, was little known, but it was known, and it existed in a wide variety of countries. Why in the little island of England should the smelting of iron by coal be developed? And why there the invention of the steam engine, and so many other machines from which modern industry grew? Why did this insular people so swiftly develop commerce and finance on a world-wide scale? It may have been that their very isolation and freedom from attack was an important factor. The high stage of their seagoing commerce must have instilled a spirit of bold enterprise; and their profitable trade brought to them part of the wealth and capital required for the development of their industries and inventions.

And why then did their descendants in America carry on this powerful impulse to yet greater achievements? Why did not other nations and peoples catch up the flaming torch?

Here we touch upon one of the deepest problems of history, that of racial character. And to penetrate this we must go back.

CIVILIZATION AND CULTURE: GENESIS FROM GENIUS

The human mind enjoys today an enormous possession of ideas, heaped up, selected, sifted out by the centuries. The multitude of men have disappeared without contributing to this store a jot. Those who have had the fortune to add something, to leave something, should have their part in the glory and the recognition which is their due.

—JEAN SYLVAIN BAILLY: *Histoire de l'Astronomie Moderne*

Genius . . . which is the transcendent capacity of taking trouble first of all.

—THOMAS CARLYLE: *Life of Frederick the Great*

Chapter V

CIVILIZATION AND CULTURE: GENESIS FROM GENIUS

1. *The contribution of the masses*

THE evidence of the truly immense antiquity of the human race has come upon us so recently that we have only just begun to take stock of its significance. There are now discoveries of ancient fossil man in areas thousands of miles apart, dating back hundreds of thousands of years. Consider for a moment what this must imply in terms of mere numbers: the billions and billions of people that have been born, that lived, and died, through thousands of generations since the beginnings of man. A world population today of close to two billion, nearly half of whom live in the single continent of Asia. The mind is staggered before such a stupendous calculation. And the appalling part is that perhaps not one in a million of all these billions of human beings that have lived and died has left a lasting contribution to the advancement of the race.[1]

Nor is there evidence of any material change either now or in recent times. For example: the present population of Asia, numbering nearly a billion people, has contributed little to present day economic or scientific progress. Of their industries affecting the Western World, the most important, rubber, is a recent importation from Brazil. Whatever may have been true in a remote past, the important contributions from Asia within the last two or three thousand years have come from its extreme western fringe, Asia Minor. Of the three important inventions supposed to derive from China, the compass is probably a myth, for the Chinese were never a seafaring people; printing was never of real utility until the perfection of movable type in Europe; and gunpowder, of dubious value to civilization, was not developed far until it was imported into the Western World.

The early contributions of Babylonia and Persia to science, methods of reckoning, star observations, the alphabet, and much else, were of high value; but their influence on civilization was relatively slight until their adoption and improvement in Europe in the last three hundred years. For the rest, the human hordes that roamed the plains of Europe and Africa in these hundreds of thousands of years were equally destitute of any inventions or discoveries save of the most primitive types, such as wheels and levers, and rude instruments for tillage of the soil.

It may be said that all this is of slight importance in considering the problems of the present day. In truth, it is of profound significance. This essentially neolithic or primitive type of population constitutes a vast part of humanity now. We may estimate that to this kind of population would still belong perhaps three-fourths or four-fifths of the present human race, and even including our own country. In point of comforts and possessions—houses, motor cars, food, clothing, and amusements—the people of the United States have a far larger share than any other nation. And they have more schools, universities, books, newspapers, and radios—all the instruments of education—than any major power has ever had, past or present. Despite this huge expenditure on instruction for the common man, his contributions to progress in this country, as in other lands, have been slight.

Ninety years ago Henry Thomas Buckle created a deep stir by his insistence that there had been within historic times no moral improvement in mankind, that the whole process of its progress was intellectual.[2] Mere reflection, imagination, and philosophic reasoning, however, added little to human knowledge or to improvement in human conditions.

Even on the central themes of metaphysics we know little more than the untutored savage, save that we have a better idea of the infinities of time and space. So we may say that all the philosophers, from Aristotle and before to Kant and after, have added only a kind of edifying diversion of much the same nature as literature, music, and the arts, contributing to our entertainment, but supplying no new weapons for man's steady advance from ignorance to creative and God-like power.

If it is neither the common man nor the philosopher that has made possible the advance of the human race, who did, and how? The progress of man from chaos and darkness to order and light, from barbarism to civilization, has been almost solely the work of invention and discovery. The true creators, as much as man himself, are the tools and implements, the engines and machines that we use. We commonly think that these devices are human products, the results of human intelligence and human skill. In a sense they are, but only in a limited sense. It is rather genius and enterprise, combined with fortunate accidents, that have made most inventions and discoveries. They are not the work of the ordinary man or the reflective philosopher. In a broad sense, it is rather these inventions and discoveries which have civilized man.

2. *The civilizing process*

It is a commonplace that man is inferior to many of the animals in many ways—in size, in strength, in speed, or even in the basic senses. Many animals have a much stronger sense of smell, and others better vision or hearing. We know that many markedly surpass the human infant in its early life. Rats and mice, for example, will find their way out of a maze, or will find means of obtaining food placed out of easy reach, at a far earlier age than young children. Again, the behavior of homing pigeons and migratory birds requires a sense so acute that it is doubtful that man has developed any inborn capacities to such a high degree. So also with the equally astonishing behavior of ants and bees, spiders and wasps, in a far more primitive world; unbelievable had they not been carefully studied and trustworthily reported. Consider, too, the industry and the intelligence of the peaceful beaver, contributing more to the shaping of the present landscape than any other animal unless it is man. How absurd in the face of these amazing performances, to imagine that man has been more fully endowed with senses and capacities than his lowlier cousins.

The one outstanding capacity man seems to have had is a well developed brain, capable of much learning and remembering; this seems the decisive factor in human evolution. The greyhound and the cheetah are far fleeter; the tiger and the lion more ferocious; dogs, cats, and numerous other animals, have a more delicate sense of smell, that guides them to food and away from danger.[3] But none of these qualities seems as significant as the superiority of man's brain. This then is the clue to the process by which man rose to primacy among animals. It lay in the possession of a more integrative, capacious brain, an organ more capable of taking in, storing, modifying, and synthesizing the external stimuli we call experience.

Possessing such a brain man could make better use of his natural environment to shape it to his ends. For example, one of the more potent forces in human advancement has been fire. But it was not the work of man; it was a familiar phenomenon for millions of years before his evolution. The discovery of an artificial means of making fire was an accident, from the chipping of flints or the boring of wood and bone. The means of making fire were due to the possession of *tools*, of scrapers, borers, knives and drills; and these in turn were in the beginning all provided by nature. Man found rather than made his first crude tools. And even today many of the outstanding discoveries and inventions have been in part the result of chance. Many were found in the course of searching for something else.[4] Often we read that the idea flashed through the mind of the inventor, or that he awoke with the idea. In brief, all a product of the *unconscious*, which differs in man chiefly in the larger variety of his experiences and in their effect on his brain.

This inborn capacity thus to utilize experience, these accidentally discovered or unconsciously invented devices, are fundamentally the result of man's growing use of tools and processes that nature provided. We know, that man, in the course of evolution, acquired a larger brain than his cousins, the gorilla, the chimpanzee, and the orangutan.[6] This growth in the number and differentiation of the cells of his brain must have gone on for hundreds of thousands of years; but with no measurable improvement in the past fifty or sixty thousand years, if we may judge from the brain capacity of Palestine man. There would seem then no reason for anticipating, in any brief historic period in the future, any change in the constitution of the human brain or its qualities and faculties.

We have as yet not the slightest insight into the production of any kind of genius types. Animal and plant breeders are performing miracles in applying the science of heredity; but all the stimulating advance from the discoveries of Gregor Mendel and the geneticists has as yet given us no clue towards producing a breed of Newtons and Archimedes.

Possibly there is no distinct breed, because they appear so rarely and so sporadically, and seemingly without definite cause. They have often been likened to biological sports, and this analogy holds to this extent, that the genius type characteristically leaves few or no descendants. Whatever may be the forces that produce them, they do not thereafter breed true. An unusual number of them

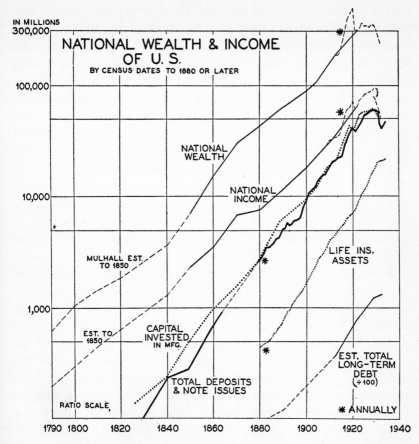

IN MILLIONS

NATIONAL WEALTH & INCOME
OF U. S.
BY CENSUS DATES TO 1880 OR LATER

300,000

100,000

NATIONAL
WEALTH

10,000

NATIONAL
INCOME

MULHALL EST.
TO 1850

LIFE INS.
ASSETS

1,000

EST. TO
1850

CAPITAL
INVESTED
IN MFG.

EST. TOTAL
LONG-TERM
DEBT
(÷100)

TOTAL DEPOSITS
& NOTE ISSUES

RATIO SCALE

✳ ANNUALLY

1790 1800   1820   1840   1860   1880   1900   1920   1940

IX. NATIONAL WEALTH AND INCOME OF THE UNITED STATES

We have official estimates of the increase of National Wealth, that is, taxable wealth, from 1850, and back of that some careful estimates by the English statistician Mulhall. Professor W. I. King has made similar estimates of National Income, from 1850; these have been here carried back to 1790 by comparisons with the increase of production and trade. With these are shown capital invested in manufacturing, and total deposits in banks, revealing how closely all of these factors are associated. It is precisely this increase in available capital and in bank deposits which has made possible the extraordinary growth of our national income and well-being. And when this capital supply is cut off, we have just such stagnation and social depression as in the ten years from 1930—leading to every conceivable economic vagary, and to a colossal loss in wealth, employment, and income. If we could but learn that here, at least, money (i.e., Capital) makes the mare go!

never marry. Whatever the biological explanation, we are certain of one thing: that the genius, whether an inventor, discoverer, or enterpriser, is a man of restless curiosity, trying always to get at the cause of things or to find new ways of doing them. Often his results are like those of Saul who found a crown while searching for his father's asses. The point is that the genius is in search of something, and that civilization is largely the result of his search. The genius is the hormone, the enzyme, the activator of human progress. There are few of him, and he provides the stimulus. We are only just beginning to realize the supreme importance of these genius types to society.

3.   The passionate amateurs: creators of civilization

A rare and fascinating breed are these passionate amateurs of innovation of all kinds. A prize example was our own Benjamin Franklin, a multifarious genius, certainly the greatest American. I have before me an amazing list of his accomplishments, compiled by the unbelievable Mr. Ripley. Franklin invented not only that famous stove, but the harmonica, the rocking chair, and the street lamp. He suggested the use of white duck clothing for tropical climates, and of plaster of Paris for fertilizer. He originated the political cartoon, the circulating library, daylight-saving time, and carrying newspapers by mail. He did not discover the Gulf Stream, as Mr. Ripley holds, but he probably was the first to measure it. He was also the first to chart the course of the northeast storms, and to establish the first street cleaning department and the first post office system in America. He had much to do with the founding of modern dentistry; was the author of an abbreviated English Prayer Book; and one of the early reformers of English spelling. He discovered that exhaled air is noxious, and originated a system of ventilation. And he was one of the greatest figures in American literature, politics, and economics. All this in addition to his really great discoveries in the field of electricity, which made him one of the founders of modern physics and one of the foremost men of science of his time.[7]

How much of this long citation is strictly accurate I cannot say; we may rely on Mr. Ripley. But it is certain that few men ever lived who, without any kind of formal training, save that given themselves, have turned their minds to such a wide variety of pursuits, and with such fruitful results. If we could have had one such genius in every century in the last ten thousand years since mankind reached some degree of civilization, we might not still be a world of armed warriors, ruled ofttimes by maniacs and assassins, and with much of our activities diverted to providing protection against the possible invasions of these Jenghiz Khans.

Be this as it may, these passionate inquirers and explorers are rare enough; yet the list would be long and go far back. We have few records of them in the earlier days. Archimedes was one, undoubtedly one of the most profound, a most extraordinary contriver, quite apart from his primacy in the field of mathematics. It is well known that he utilized the burning mirrors against enemy ships, and hurled at them Greek fire, the precursor of gunpowder. He invented the hydraulic screw, and doubtless much else. Archimedes attended school in Alexandria and in that sense was a university trained man. But in the field of mechanics, in which he was a pioneer, he was unquestionably an amateur.

There may have been many like him whose names are lost in antiquity. But as Draper so vividly portrays in his history, there was something in ancient times that seemed fatal to innovation.[8] Perhaps the social environment was not favorable. Babylon, Athens, Alexandria, and other metropolises had a relatively high civilization, —enormous wealth, wide commerce, good banking facilities, and a brilliant array of commercial law. But the passion for new contrivances was apparently rare. We know very little of the early history of mechanics and physical science; but we do know that much was lost and had to be reinvented and rediscovered in recent times.

In many instances, chance played a major rôle. Few events have been of greater significance in the history of the world than the discovery of America. And this, in many ways was an accident, the work of an amateur who apparently knew little of navigation, and who had no idea of discovering a new route to India, to say nothing of discovering 'a new world.' Probably one of the strangest combinations of luck, ignorance, and ambition of which history has any record. It seems likely that the letters from Toscanelli were a fabrication, that the grandiose ideas of opening up a new world were borrowed later from Cardinal d'Ailly, and that the whole adventure arose from a chance meeting with a shipwrecked sailor on the Island of Porto Santo. Whatever may be the facts, this turning point in world history was the work of a blunderer, apparently not a navigator, who could not even take an ordinary observation of his position at sea.[9]

A momentous scientific invention, the magnifying lens, seems also to have been due to chance. Whether the story of the observing apprentice is true or not, it is a fact that lenses had been known for centuries, if not for a thousand years and more (the Chinese claim an even earlier date), and that in all that time no one, so far as is known, ever stumbled on the principle of the telescope and the compound microscope. The man who made this epochal discovery was another passionate amateur, a professor of mathematics in a small university, who gave music lessons on the side to eke out his meagre salary. If it is true that the Chinese had spectacles long before our era, what a difference it would have made if there had been a Galileo among them in those early days. The proof needed for establishing the validity of the Copernican system, which Aristarchus had worked out seventeen hundred years before the Polish priest, could have been available long before. As it was, Galileo was the first to offer such decisive proof with his novel and fascinating device that thereafter the entire intelligent world was convinced.

Interesting to note the remarkable range of his talents. Galileo was a professor of mathematics, but it was as an amateur that he became the first of the renowned astronomical observers, and the founder of modern mechanics. He began his scientific quest, if we may believe the story, when as a boy he observed the swinging lamp and rediscovered the principle of the iso-chronism of the pendulum. Scarce any field of inquiry open to his day escaped his attention; his industry was prodigious. His complete works fill twenty and more large volumes, including some sixteen hundred letters on scientific subjects written chiefly to his friends. His reward: To die in little more than a hovel as the virtual prisoner of the Church.[10]

In vivid contrast, in the year of Galileo's disgrace and death, there was born in England a child destined to the highest honors while he lived and to be universally regarded as one of the foremost intellects of any age. It was because of his intense interest in machinery and such contrivances that Isaac Newton was sent to Cambridge; but it was his achievements in mathematics that brought him a chair in that university. His great discoveries were to marked degree intensely his own.

It is often said that achievements of genius are largely the product of a prevailing social stream. The tendencies or the environment in some ages are not conducive to innovation. But in a society that welcomes progress, inventions and discoveries abound. Almost as if the spirit of the time gives birth to these innovations, independently, as it were, of the inventors and discoverers themselves. Many notable instances where they have been made by several individuals independently, often in different countries, at almost the same time. Professor William F. Ogburn, a strong advocate of the theory of the social stream, has compiled a long list of such coincidences, covering a large part of the important inventions and discoveries of the last three hundred years.[11] And there are, of course, a considerable number of which the contrivers are unknown, indicating that probably the development was gradual and that many persons made contributions to the final form of the innovation. We may admit the influence of the social environment as a factor, as, for example, a vigorous spirit of enterprise, without overlooking the fundamental contributions of genius.

4. *Enterprise: Creator of wealth and well-being*

Few inquire just why the United States has become the richest nation that ever existed. Many think of it as 'natural' and inevitable. They speak of our great 'natural resources,' the energy of the people, the vast areas of free land, the more or less equal opportunities enjoyed in our democratic country. Unquestionably all these are of importance. But one factor, certainly, stands out beyond them all: the spirit of innovation, and the energy and acquisitiveness that go with it. The incentives were unusually high and the opportunities wide. There was a zest for achieving, and with this the everlasting lure of the *au-delà*, the just-beyond, that carried the tide of population steadily westward over vast plains and through unbroken forests. It is this that has made the United States so opulent. The same spirit of enterprise brought to England the industrial and commercial supremacy it enjoyed for some centuries. And while England and the United States forged ahead, neighboring nations like Spain and Mexico with equal opportunities and equal resources, remained relatively poor.

So, too, among men. Almost without exception the most successful and the richest men, in this and in other times began life as poor boys. It was no special privilege, no primacy of social position or family possessions that made men like George Washington, Stephen Girard, John Jacob Astor, and their like, the wealthiest of their day. Before he was twenty-one, George Washington, starting with nothing and earning his way as a young surveyor, was already a considerable landowner, and when he died he was probably our first 'millionaire.' Think of the spirit of the sixteen-year old Cornelius Vanderbilt, who borrowed one hundred dollars from his mother to buy a little sail boat as a ferry that he ran between Staten Island and New York, and lived to be the first man in the world to amass a fortune of a hundred million dollars. Notable that ninety per cent of the Vanderbilt fortune was gained in the last fifteen years of his life, after he had sold out his fleet of steam boats, built up through half a century, and began railroading with only the general experience of his career in water transportation to aid him.[12] It is this spirit that is characteristic of the United States, and that is synonymous with our reputation abroad.

This energy and enterprise has always been strong among the big business men of all countries and of all times. Pliny tells us that in his day it was the freedmen, manumitted slaves, who became the richest men of Rome. Many of the commercial lords of the Middle Ages and the Renaissance, men like Jakob Fugger and Jacques Coeur, rose to opulence from humble beginnings.[13] These types seem to possess a singular kind of drive that gives them an early lead on the road to fortune, and stimulated by their success, perhaps modest at the beginning, they carry on, gaining momentum as they go. When great wealth undermines the spirit of enterprise, in their successors, the fortunes decline, and often disappear.

Enterprise is the natural collaborator of inventive genius. What would James Watt have been but for the vision, the drive, and the wealth of Matthew Boulton, who advanced a very large sum for that day, of £40,000? Watt was poor, and his invention was not highly regarded. Adam Smith, for example, knew Watt at the University of Glasgow; but Adam Smith never mentions him, and in the whole of his great work Smith has only a few lines of

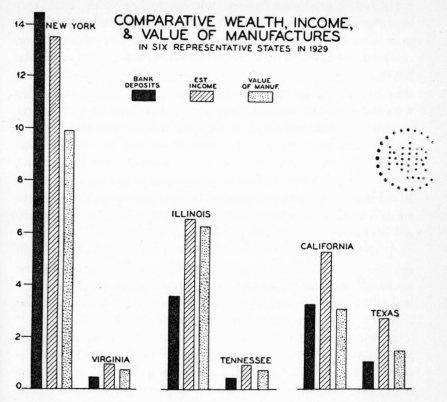

COMPARATIVE WEALTH, INCOME,
& VALUE OF MANUFACTURES
IN SIX REPRESENTATIVE STATES IN 1929

BANK DEPOSITS   EST INCOME   VALUE OF MANUF.

X. THE RELATIONS OF WEALTH, INCOME, AND MANUFACTURES

When the American Union was formed in 1789, Virginia was the richest and most prosperous state. New York stood about fifth. The relative income, value of manufactures, and bank deposits of the two states are shown for 1929. New York has no greater natural resources than Virginia, and no finer harbor. Indeed with its coal in its western section, Virginia was far superior. But the aggregate income of New York is now at least twelve times that of its former rival. So too, Illinois and Tennessee were settled about the same time, and now reveal a wide disparity. And so also California and Texas, although Texas has recently had an astonishing increase through its wealth from oil. The primary source of wealth and income is not in land, but in manufactures. The great manufacturing states are always the richest, have the highest wages, and have the highest standards of living.

obscure reference to a "fire engine," and that for the purpose of illustration.[14] Boulton had faith in Watt, but perhaps even his patience and his faith were severely tried. Ten years after Watt had produced a workable steam engine, it still could not be sold. Neither mine owners nor others would buy it. Even the bold and confident Boulton gave it up as a bad venture, and turned the direction over to Watt. The shy and cautious inventor made a real success of it, selling the engines on the installment plan with a guarantee of performance. Not the only instance of an inventive genius who possessed business ability. But it is clear that without the help of Boulton it would have been difficult to put the steam engine into use in the industries of England.[15] This is the great function of the enterpriser: he seeks innovations to utilize them. And although he often profits hugely from his use of new methods, all of society profits with him. The enterpriser is the pioneer in the land discovered by the inventor.

Now why do these adventurers engage so wholeheartedly in their work? For glory? No. Principally for gain; in part also because they are filled with the zest of achievement and domination that characterizes almost all these vigorous and talented types. The restless energy that made the Rembrandts and the Titians toil at their easels through long years, never satisfied, striving ever for perfection. The same with every kind of high ability. But, it is said, this is to forget the 'sordid' side of what we call 'money getting;' the 'vulgar' lust for wealth and power. And again, "why should the few have so much and the many so little?" The plaint of thousands of years, for the world of commerce and trade has never been different.

Many would have it that this tide of energy is now slowing down, that we have grown rich and languid, that enterprise no longer counts for what it did. Certainly a mistake; the evidence against it is overwhelming. Many men of our own generation have risen from small beginnings to tremendous wealth. In England Baron Nuffield has shown that even there men of initiative can still find opportunities for establishing huge businesses of their own; and in the United States Henry Ford has made the largest fortune in history, starting as a simple mechanic.

More important still, corporate enterprise has come to recognize the importance of research in science and technology. Two thousand corporations in this country, reporting to a committee of the National Academy of Science, are now, and have been for years, spending three-quarters of a million dollars a day on such research in the broadest sense. That is nearly a quarter of a billion dollars a year. Nothing like it in all the world's history. Those who despair of the future leave out of the picture the powerful momentum derived from inventions and discoveries since the beginning of the Industrial Revolution. Every invention or discovery tends to breed another, furnishes a stimulus to further inquiry. And this is precisely how science and technology have grown.

The momentum exists; the driving energy toward further achievement is here. There is no danger to progress from a disappearance of the spirit of enterprise. The danger is from its discouragement. Envy and jealousy of the rich and successful may take the familiar path of spoliation and pillage through artful forms of taxation. And the power to tax, we know, is the power to destroy. The vigor of enterprise has made America; it has created wealth for the masses; it has raised many large populations from the neolithic stage to civilization. Cripple this spirit and you stop this mighty advance.

5. Columbus, the compass, and enterprise

Men of adventure have lived in all countries at all times. But the earlier societies were not favorable to industrial progress. This was partly due to the contempt for business manifested by the philosophers of the time; and partly to the structure of society, largely founded on birth and status. But it was due to the difficulties of new enterprises in a world in which industry and commerce were not expanding, and in which the prospect of profits was so uncertain. Not until the commercial and price revolutions of the sixteenth and seventeenth centuries was the environment strongly encouraging to business undertakings. And these revolutions grew out of the discovery of America, made possible by the availability of the compass.

The navigators of the ancient world were adventurous almost beyond belief.[16] Even without the compass, they made voyages that stir the imagination. I have alluded to the circumnavigation of Africa by the Phoenicians in the reign of Necho I of Egypt. We have, as noted, authentic evidence that the Greek explorer, Pythias, had voyaged to the Baltic and had brought back a fascinating account of his travels. Herodotus describes a well established commerce with the Gold Coast of Africa, and the extraordinary methods of barter and exchange which must have required centuries for their development. Between the reported voyages of the Phoenicians around Africa, about 600 B. C., and the first rounding of the Cape of Good Hope in modern times by Vasco da Gama, more than 2,000 years elapsed. Why did Europe and Asia Minor ignore the sea route around Africa for so long?

Apparently the zest for adventure that was so strong among some of the ancient peoples was lost during the long blight of the Middle Ages. The wealth of Athens, and of Tyre and Alexandria was gained from trade. The agricultural poverty of Greece was the same then as it is today. A mountainous land with a few fertile valleys and a scant area of productive soil. The Phoenicians had no rich fertile lands. They were the most purely seafaring people known to history. Yet both the Greeks and the Phoenicians prospered famously. They were founders of colonies at Corinth and Carthage and elsewhere. They sent their wares to lands almost as distant as the New World. But though their ships travelled far, they were always within easy reach of land; and without a compass even these fearless sea-farers could not venture far into the open seas. Some later navigators did cross the Atlantic by accident or design—the Norsemen, the Basques, and perhaps the Irish—but made few settlements. For without the compass it was difficult to make long voyages with any confidence of arriving at the desired destination.

The history of the compass is lost in myth. There has recently been found a document that seems to record the first introduction of the compass in China, as about the 10th or 11th century. This credits the use of the northward pointing needle to the region around the Red Sea. In no wise improbable. For in the most distant day the Red Sea and the Indian Ocean were the scene of a thriving commerce. By what people the lodestone, known from very early times, was first put to its modern usage, we have as yet no record; but apparently it was not until the 8th to 10th centuries of our era. By the time of Columbus it was in common use. The long voyage across the Atlantic could scarcely have been undertaken in the fashion of Columbus without it. It does not matter whether Columbus sailed in search of 'a new world' or a new route to India. The voyage he made in all probability would have been undertaken by others within a few years if that fanatical soul had never been born.

The discovery of the New World truly opened a new page in human development. Beyond question the most dramatic event in all human history. It was not merely the finding of the new continents across the sea. Had they been countries like those already inhabited and known, their development and that of Europe might have been long delayed. It was the lure of gold and silver that unlocked the energies of our modern time. Nothing else could have stirred men to the unbelievable hardships of long marches across parched deserts and through virgin forests. It was the enormous stores of silver and some gold sent back that quickened the pace of industry and commerce in Europe, and led directly to the Industrial Revolution and our modern mechanical world.

The process by which this wondrous change was effected has been portrayed by Wiebe and others, and notably in the fascinating investigations of Earl Hamilton, whose volumes on the course of Spanish prices through the centuries just preceding and following the discovery of America are a monument of careful research.[17] From these we now have a full history of the amazing rise in prices that followed the opening of the mines of Mexico and Peru, and the import into Europe of immense quantities of silver, larger than any before known. Silver was and had been for thousands of years the chief medium of exchange; and the rise in prices that followed this vast inflow continued, as Professor Hamilton's studies reveal, virtually without interruption for the next century and a half. Its stimulating effect upon commerce and industry was unmistakable. It was the golden age of the enterpriser.

In our own time and in a preceding generation, we have seen a modern replica, on a modest scale, of this revolutionary event. The earlier of these two instances was the simultaneous discovery of gold in California and in Australia; the second, the curious combination of invention and new processes that made possible the workings of the Bloemfontein gold reefs of South Africa. Bringing to the world a greater store of gold than in all previous time.[18] But these modern inundations did not flow over a relatively arid soil; and so the rise of prices which each of these events occasioned was neither so lasting nor so profound. Reflect what it would mean in our own day if through five generations there had been an uninterrupted but very slow rise in the price level, instead of the spasmodic intervals of rise and fall we have known.

From the middle of the sixteenth to the end of the seventeenth century the price rise in Spain and in adjacent countries seems to have been very close to an average of one and a half per cent per annum. By 1568 this great rise in prices had already begun to focus the attention of statesmen and economists. Not without interest that in this year a French diplomat of singularly sagacious mind gave to this phenomenon a more lucid explanation than much or most of the writing on money and prices since. A minister of the king had been at pains to explain, first that the general rise in prices was not proven; second, with the usual perspicacity of statesmen, that this rise could not be due solely to the influx of the silver. Jean Bodin in his reply lucidly set forth that the great rise in prices was real, and had begun only after the inflow of the treasure, and therefore was due entirely to the new supplies of the precious metals.[19] It has remained for our own time, with the invention of price indexes, and accurate data on money and trade, to establish Bodin's thesis as impregnable.

Now as to the manner in which the price revolution brought industrial progress to the world. As the unbroken rise in prices continued generation after generation, it gave an enormous stimulus to every kind of commercial venture. The normal risks of trade were reduced almost to a minimum, providing a wonderful temptation to capital investment. The rewards were exceptionally large, and more than that quite general. In the days of Queen Elizabeth, when the chief risks to commerce were piracy and brigandage, the usual return on capital appears to have been about 17 per cent. When the rise in prices was in full swing the profits were even larger. The result: a steady increase in capital accumulation. And it was the profits accumulated by enterprisers that provided the means for the vast expansion of industry that followed the price revolution in England. Within hardly more than a century, the factory system began an astonishing growth, leading inevitably to an era of invention and mechanical improvement without parallel. Leading likewise, within a relatively brief time, as history goes, to the greatest rise in output ever recorded, bringing to the masses of the people a degree of comfort, health, and satisfaction not even experienced by the kings and lords of former times.

MALTHUSIAN MIRACLES

The age of miracles is forever here!
—THOMAS CARLYLE

The people must comprehend that they are themselves the cause of their own poverty.
—THOMAS ROBERT MALTHUS

In looking at crowded districts in modern times, it is a mistake to think that people are now less comfortable than they were formerly.

The dwellings of medieval laborers were hovels—the walls made of a few boards cemented with mud and leaves. Rushes and reeds or heather made the thatch for the roof. Inside the house there was a single room, or in some cases two rooms, not plastered and without floor, ceiling, chimney, fireplace or bed, and here the owner, his family and his animals, lived and died.

There was no sewage for the houses, no drainage, except surface drainage for the streets, no water supply beyond that provided by the town pump, and no knowledge of the simplest forms of sanitation. "Rye and oats furnished the bread and drink of the great body of the people in Europe." Cultivated herbage and roots were unknown in the agriculture of Britain before the end of the reign of Henry VIII.

"In the eleventh and twelfth centuries," William Farr said of England, "famine is recorded every fourteen years, on an average, and the people suffered twenty years of famine in two hundred years. In the thirteenth century the list exhibits the same proportion of famine: the addition of five years of high prices makes the proportion greater. Upon the whole, scarcities decreased during the three following centuries; but the average from 1201 to 1600 is the same, namely, seven famines and ten years of famine in a century."

Almost the entire population of a village were farmers, raising food by methods that were slow and wasteful.
—E. PARMALEE PRENTICE: *Hunger and History*

CHAPTER VI

MALTHUSIAN MIRACLES

1. *Politics, progress, and technology*

AN essential fact that stands out in all history is that the real sources of well-being are scientific and economic, not political and social.[1] In the long run it seems not to matter a great deal what form of government a people has, provided there is an opportunity for self-development and security for individual initiative.[2] Over a long period the general advance of nations seems to be much the same whether the countries are empires, kingdoms, republics, oligarchies, or tyrannies, provided always that the rulers are concerned with wealth rather than with war, with progress rather than with power. In our own time the superiority of democracy over dictatorship, as regards economic advancement, lies in its preference for the accumulation of capital rather than of cannon, in its encouragement of free enterprise rather than in a straitjacket economy.

There have been highly enlightened rulers and statesmen from the most ancient days: like Hammurabi in Babylonia, Solomon in Judea, Peisistratus and Pericles in Greece, Caesar and Augustus in Rome. The lapse of time lends a halo to their accomplishments; in any event, men of such distinction at the head of affairs were rare. But their achievements, we must note, were not related to economic progress, save with minor exceptions. In general, they were distinguished rather for military conquest, for enlightened rule, and for great public works. They could scarcely have understood the process by which the welfare of a people is most strongly promoted. They encouraged art, and even industry, but gave little aid to technical invention, the essential element for economic advance. King Solomon, Dionysius of Syracuse, and several of the Ptolemies in Alexandria were among the exceptions.

It is perhaps an impious thought; but contemplate what might have been the economic consequences if the millions of drachmas that were spent by Pericles on the Parthenon, and by others on the thousands of temples in Greece and other nations, and the expenditures for theatrical performances and the like, could have been devoted, even in part, to the advance of science and technology. Hero's prototype of the steam turbine might have become the real steam engine of Watt; the curious behavior of bits of paper when a stick of amber was rubbed briskly and brought near them might have led to the utilization of electricity, as it did two thousand years later. Political rulers in those days, as for the most part in our own, thought little of these things. The only technical achievements that seemed to arouse their interest and induce them to provide millions for experiment were devices for war and conquest. For these the nations have spent colossal sums, feeding the vanity of their kings, and their lust for grandeur. Even in our own enlightened country we have spent vastly more on foolish and needless armament, and billions more in bonuses, doles and relief, than the total expenditure upon scientific education and investigation in the entire history of the United States, if not the whole world.

Interesting to reflect that in this country, and in many others, it is the rich men, the capitalists, who have contributed the largest sums to universities and to institutes of technology. The Rockefellers, the Carnegies, the Mellons, the Armours, and many others, through their gifts have made possible the rapid development of varied institutions for higher education.[3] Only for the farming class, which has much political power, have any considerable sums been spent for research by governments. The results to date not conspicuous. The reapers of McCormick, the steel plows of Deere, the harvesters and mowers of other inventors, to say nothing of the railways and steamships, the tractor, the automobiles, the telephones, and the radios, have done more for the welfare of the farmers than all the efforts to 'aid agriculture' in two hundred years.

Fortunately, it has not been essential to await government initiative. The economic mechanism, through profits, savings and investment, has provided the means and the impulse towards the industrial advance of the last two centuries; the contribution of governments largely passive. They have encouraged enterprise to develop and expand new industries, and have provided security and order for society. Experience seems to indicate that this is the most effective rôle that government can play in the great drama. It is a functional rôle, not unimportant. But in these days of regulating, controlling, and 'planning,' it is well to recall that one of our ablest political philosophers, Thomas Jefferson, with rare insight, was a strong proponent of the doctrine that the best government is that which meddles least.[4]

2.   The steam engine and the power age

Recurrently, it would seem, a kind of cultural pessimism, dilettante despair, pervades the writings of the literary moralists.[5] At the end of the last century they wrote in sadness of the 'decline' of society, the exhaustion of effort, after the strenuous days of the nineteenth century. *Fin de siècle* was the cant phrase of the time. In the forty or fifty years that have since elapsed, probably never more intense activity. What the moralists and pessimists seem not to understand is the tremendous 'inertia and momentum' that has developed in our economic life—the direct result of the inventions and discoveries, the vast growth of capital for new industries, the spread of the spirit of industry and enterprise. What all this may mean to the world, to civilization, no man can yet measure. The rate of advance has been stepped up to a pace never before known. Today the productive power and the level of real income of a few nations has been increased five and ten times *per capita*. Most notably in highly industrialized countries like the United States, Great Britain, France, Germany; now spreading all over the world, even to Japan, to India, and to the distant islands of the Pacific. There is scarcely a land that has not felt this magic touch.

Undoubtedly the foremost single factor in this advance has been the invention of the steam engine and of other types of power that have grown out of it, directly or indirectly. This is not to say that other inventions and discoveries prior to the steam engine were of no significance. But none of these had the potency of Watt's device. Picture the rude beginnings of this epochal innovation. A prosperous iron industry had sprung up in Great Britain. But the ravage of the oak forests, to obtain charcoal, soon brought a serious difficulty. In England the further destruction of these forests was forbidden. Then necessity brought the 'coal-cooking' (coking) process, successfully developed by Abraham Darby and his son, which gave the iron industry a new and fabulous life.[6] But here again difficulties intervened. Soon, as the new coal mines had descended to sufficient depths, the water had to be pumped out, and this was expensive. The atmospheric engine used for pumping was converted by James Watt into modern steam power, the most effective instrument for developing the world's industries ever known. His contribution to human welfare may surpass that of any man who ever lived, for the amazing advance in scientific and technical investigation that followed was largely due to his achievement.

Fruitful now to reflect how slender were the beginnings. During Watt's lifetime few engines of more than twenty or thirty horsepower were built. These utilized steam pressures that now seem incredibly low. Watt himself believed that pressures higher than half a pound of steam were dangerous. Today gigantic steam turbines are built of more than one hundred and fifty thousand horsepower, utilizing steam pressures of twelve to fourteen hundred pounds, at a temperature of almost a thousand degrees Fahrenheit. Creating two hundred thousand kilowatts of electrical energy per hour. And with this an amazing reduction in the cost of power. In the early days of Watt's engines the consumption of coal per hour per horsepower was nearly ten pounds. Today these mighty turbines generate a thousand watt-hours of electricity on twelve ounces of coal—that is, nine ounces of coal per hour per horsepower—at a cost of not much more than one-tenth of a cent per kilowatt hour.[7] Such is the advance of little more than one hundred and fifty years.

The dramatic history of Watt's engines is known to every school boy: how a model of the old Newcomen pumping-engine was brought to him for repair; how he pondered the problem and hit upon the device of a separate condenser. From this simple but major improvement, a development without parallel. Yet the early engines of Watt were a failure, and even after his invention had become a technical success, it could not be sold. Such was the prejudice and inertia of the time. As I have related, it was Watt who became the salesman and successful director of the enterprise. Such a combination of business ability and inventive genius has seldom been seen. Throughout the ages he will be known as the father of the Power Age.

One invention quickly breeds another. This is the secret of all

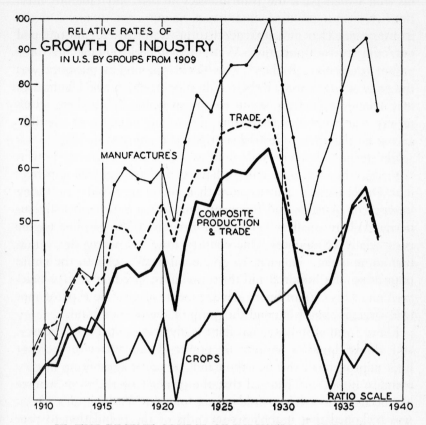

RELATIVE RATES OF
GROWTH OF INDUSTRY
IN U.S. BY GROUPS FROM 1909

TRADE

MANUFACTURES

COMPOSITE
PRODUCTION
& TRADE

CROPS

RATIO SCALE

1910   1915   1920   1925   1930   1935   1940

XI. THE RECENT COURSE OF INDUSTRIAL GROWTH

For a long period farming was the principal occupation of the settlers and their descendants in America. Even as late as Washington's day only about 5 per cent of the population lived in towns and villages. Today all this is sharply reversed and now less than one-fifth of the population is engaged in agriculture. And this tendency has been sharply increased in the last thirty years in which the growth of agriculture has almost ceased, while industrial production and especially manufactures have almost quadrupled; that is, up to 1929. Since then, as previously indicated, no further growth. More and more farms are becoming specialized in the production of poultry and eggs, dairy products and the like; and some of them are becoming veritable factories, organized just like a large industrial plant and equipped with expensive machinery. It is due to this fact that the incomes of thousands of farms in the United States now exceed $25,000 or more a year; yet agriculture as a whole is relatively a declining industry, as is set forth so vividly above.

industrial advance, and it is for this reason that never has invention risen to such a pitch of intensity as in our own time. With the steam engine came its application to other forms of industry, and especially to transportation. Watt himself took out patents for a steam locomotive. Richard Trevithick, George Stephenson, and the rest soon followed. Robert Fulton in America and Henry Bell in England applied the steam engine to boats. Before long steam power was employed in turning machines in factories, speedily giving England the industrial supremacy it enjoyed so long.

But steam no longer stands alone as the source of primary power. Already other forms of energy have gained tremendous impetus.[8] The Diesel engine, a little more than forty years old, is offering intense competition, and for many purposes it is economically superior. Where small power units are required, the gasoline engine is especially economical. One country now has nearly thirty million automobiles. Sufficient to give comfortable seats to the entire population of a hundred and thirty millions, speeding at fifty miles an hour. This extraordinary development, of a single type of motive force, is almost beyond the grasp of the human mind.

Every form of industry has felt the vivifying impetus of the new and almost limitless sources of power. Even agriculture. After little improvement through thousands of years, agriculture has become so highly mechanized that the product of the farm worker has been increased four-fold or six-fold. In Washington's day it was reckoned that it took six-sevenths of the population to produce a sufficient surplus of food for the one-seventh engaged in commerce and industry. Today this is reversed. One-seventh can now produce a surplus not only of food, but of other products of the soil required as raw materials for other industries.[9] A veritable revolution.

The wondrous growth of the United States has been almost wholly the product of this technical advance. With the tools that were available in Washington's time the workers of today could not, on the average, produce one-tenth of the present colossal output. And it is sufficiently clear, from the advance in our own day, that we are only at the beginning. The promise of the future is incalculable, and, I believe, can never be long arrested. For if one nation or people falters and lags behind, others will carry on. The industrial growth of England and the United States may be brought to a standstill through harmful and paralyzing legislation;

but, as ever, other nations will catch up the torch and carry it forward.

3. *Technology and Malthusianism*

Hard now to realize the pall that hung over the philosophic thinking of a hundred years or more ago. The spectre of 'Malthusianism,' the belief that future populations were doomed to misery, perhaps civilization with them. As a young vicar in a secluded parish, the Reverend Thomas Malthus had been profoundly stirred by estimates just then coming to be made, as to the long time rate of growth of the population in leading nations. Especially the very rapid increase in the newly founded republic of the United States. Of the latter, others had already taken notice, particularly Benjamin Franklin and Adam Smith.[10] The idea that seized the mind of the young vicar was that, unless restrained by the holocausts of war and the ravages of famine and disease, the population would tend steadily to increase at what he called a 'geometric' ratio, that is, a compound interest rate of growth, while the sustenance that could keep them alive was a simple function of the area. Therefore the only possible outcome was overpopulation, inadequate nourishment. The human race doomed to a Sisyphean treadmill. Even the wisest men of the time were deeply impressed by his thesis. Even John Stuart Mill. Malthusianism became the intellectual topic of the hour. A modest brochure expanded into a militant volume of which several editions were published. An example of the adventuring mind grown to a mild affectation of omniscience and certitude.[11]

Since the disturbing tract of Malthus, the man in the street has been familiar with the definite tendency of all kinds of animal life, the human race included, to outrun the food supply. The basic principle of 'the survival of the fittest.' Malthus himself would have been astonished enough if he had been told that less than one hundred and fifty years from the first publication of his essay, the United States would have a population of one hundred and thirty millions, and that the entire world, India, China, and Europe itself, would have a large if not equal increase. Malthus's bewilderment might have grown could he have known of the almost unimaginable antiquity of the human race. He was a clergyman and, despite his inquiring mind, probably accepted the familiar date in his day assigned to creation, 4004 B. C. Perhaps a hundred thousand years ago the human race had spread all over the earth, increasing its numbers but slowly; possibly little gain in many thousand years; then suddenly in the space of five or six generations an unparalleled rise, augmenting by three or four times in three or four generations.

The author of *An Essay on the Principle of Population* could not dream that the London of his day would be multiplied at least ten times in population in its whole area, and that there would be fifty cities or more in the world far more populous than the London he knew. Where, he would have asked, could the food supply for these immense numbers be grown? And if sufficient food could be produced, how would it be transported to these huge aggregations? All these modern miracles of production, of transportation, and the distribution of food we have come to accept as a kind of commonplace. Few realize how utterly impossible it all would have seemed, alike to Adam Smith and the Reverend Thomas Malthus of Seton Vicarage.

Part of the problem might have been envisaged: that is, the immense increase in the area under cultivation. This is the chief basis for the production of food for half of the world's population. Fertilizers and better methods of farming have added somewhat. The increase in agricultural output appears to have its major origin in the same force that has pervaded the textile industries, the metal industries, and all the rest. One thing and one alone: that is the discovery of new machinery, new processes, new sources of power.

This is what Malthus could not foresee: the marked increase in the productivity *per worker*, through the substitution of mechanical for manual labor. Malthus' statistics were perfectly sound; his fundamental thesis of an increase in population entirely correct. It has been realized in extreme degree. What he could not anticipate, what the wisest intellects of the time could not, was the import of mechanical invention.[12] When Malthus wrote there were few iron plows in the world. In most countries of the earth, the same clumsy, rattle-trap wooden affairs that had been in use for thousands of years. The iron plow in some ways marks a turning point in human history. Supplanted, half a century later, by the steel plow. Then came a series of remarkable contrivances, the mowing machine, the threshing machine, and the like. This was followed by the application of power to these machines. The result has been the conversion of the modern farm into an agricultural factory. And along with these, equally important inventions in the field of transportation, making farm products available to the most distant peoples, at astonishingly low cost.

A single example, to which I have referred elsewhere, is the reduction in the actual field time required to raise a bushel of wheat, from around sixty hours or more of human labor in 1830, to around two hours or less in 1930.[13] This reduction in the cost of a bushel of wheat is not due to any gain in the 'efficiency' of farm labor, but solely to the use of tractors, seeders, cultivators, mowing machines, and combines. In consequence farms have grown much larger, so that a farm of a thousand acres is less of a rarity today than one of two hundred acres a century ago. Along with this, there has also been notable improvement in farm chemistry and plant breeding. The result: in the more advanced countries, equipped with all this modern machinery and this new knowledge, as in the United States, we now have what is commonly called an agricultural 'surplus,' a development far from the wild dreams of the pessimists of the past; a true 'Malthusian miracle.'

A solution of the problem almost no one could have anticipated. The normal checks to population envisaged by Malthus were famine, plague, and war. With huge additions to the food supply, from all parts of the world, famine, except in the interiors of undeveloped countries like China, is now but little known. This same factor, adequate food, has also contributed to the decline in the death rate by the resistance to disease. Better nourishment in our time has been as important as improved sanitation, in minimizing the devastating effect of epidemics and plagues. The scourge of war remains. But as yet it is not a serious menace to the food supply of most large populations. Armies are larger and their armaments more effective, yet it may be doubted if the direct and indirect destruction of life in time of war is now as heavy as in earlier times. No modern war has wiped out population at the same rate as, for example, the Thirty-Years War. Is it too much to hope that a civilization that has made such progress will sometime succeed in abolishing this mass madness?

There are some who look upon the unprecedented gain in population as scarcely a blessing. It seems probable, however, that this increase, itself a result of the technical advance, has in turn been a strong stimulant thereto; a thesis set forth by Herbert Spencer.

Despite the apprehensions of the neo-Malthusians, there seems little to fear from mere increase. It is rather the character, the quality of this growing population to which Earnest Hooton has so sharply drawn attention, that presents the real problem.[14] It is the vast 'surge of the underworld' described by Ortega, the 'Vertikale Einbruch' so colorfully depicted by Walther Rathenau, the advent to power of the masses, aroused by ignorant and demagogic leaders, that threatens those characteristics of our society that we value so highly. This is the exigent problem which the increase has made acute. But it is well to remember that this 'surge of the underworld' has existed throughout historic times. There seems no more probability that it will gain wide supremacy now than in the days of Spartacus or Jack Cade.

4. Metallurgy and technical progress

Interesting to observe how much of technical advance has come from developments in metallurgy and chemistry. The first long step toward present day industrial civilization was taken by primitive men who discovered a way to smelt and temper what to them must have seemed a singular kind of rock. A far cry from King Solomon's industrial city of Ezion-Geber on the Red Sea to our Pittsburghs and Birminghams. While the Spenglers and their type can look forward only to a 'twilight of the gods,' the real gods—the chemists, metallurgists, and technicians—are creating the foundations for a future that may surpass the whole previous advance.

And this seems to be coming swiftly. A curious bit of archaeology, that as early as the seventh century the Japanese were employing the rare element molybdenum in the making of their beautiful swords, superb specimens of the metal worker's art. This rare material was known to the Romans, so it may be assumed that it had been known for centuries before their era. In any event, from the seventh century in Japan to the twentieth century in the western world seems a long sweep. In all these thirteen hundred years, no advance in the employment of one of the most extraordinary metals for the purposes of alloy.

We were beginning to discover the uses of molybdenum before the World War. Then the uncovering of a huge deposit in the state of Colorado, now estimated to contain perhaps nine-tenths of the known supply. The usual result: a precipitous decline in the

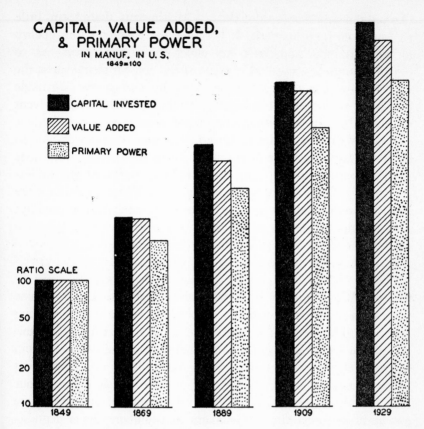

CAPITAL, VALUE ADDED,
& PRIMARY POWER
IN MANUF. IN U. S.
1849=100

CAPITAL INVESTED

VALUE ADDED

PRIMARY POWER

RATIO SCALE
100

50

20

10

1849   1869   1889   1909   1929

XII. THE INCREASE IN CAPITAL AND PRIMARY POWER USED

To many persons the ordinary charts, such as most of the preceding, are rather
difficult to follow. Chart VIII plotted the growth of capital in manufactures and
of primary power over a long period. Much the same thing is given in a different
form by 20-year periods in the chart above, which compares the amount of capital
invested, the 'value added' in manufacture (over the cost of raw materials), and
the number of horsepower used in primary power. The year 1849 is taken as 100;
and with this is shown the increase of each factor in successive 20-year periods.
A glance suffices to reveal how close is the association, very strongly suggesting,
perhaps even *proving* that increased product in manufacturing can only be attained
through the increased use of machinery, of which the amount of horsepower
employed is an excellent index. In turn, this increase in use of machinery and of
primary power is possible only through the increase in the capital employed. No
other conceivable way. It follows, therefore, that stoppage of the capital supply
(which is derived very largely from business profits) means: no further increase
in the industrial product. Therefore, no further gain in wages or in general well-
being. Precisely what has happened in this country in the ten years from 1929.

price, much like that in aluminium after the new electrolytic process had brought this other remarkable metal into wider use. Then in both an intensive search and discovery of new properties of alloys hitherto unsuspected. Today, thirty million motor cars owe to these much of their wondrous strength, endurance, and lightness. And with molybdenum and aluminium, a similar widening in the uses of nickel, chromium, tungsten, and others.

Until twenty or thirty years ago there were only three or four kinds of steel. Now the steel companies are making literally hundreds, most of them simply variations in the percentages of the components. Ordinary cast iron contains about 4 per cent carbon. Take this carbon out and put in 25 per cent nickel and the properties of iron are transformed. It becomes non-magnetic. Put in 46 per cent of nickel and the metal has the same heat expansion as glass and is used for lead-in wires for our electric light bulbs. Adding manganese renders steel so hard it cannot be machined and must be ground. Adding molybdenum makes it soft and workable. And so for almost a thousand varieties, suitable for nearly every conceivable use. The floor of a railway car made of thin alloy steel weighed less than the cork matting that covered it. To these alloys are to be added several thousand alloys of other metals, likewise of extraordinary utility. Probably four-fifths of them created since the Spanish American War. The automobile, the airplane, the stream-lined trains, the new cutting tools and machines, have all been made possible by astonishing new materials.

A parallel magic in the fields of chemistry. We think of the industry as rather new. Actually its American beginnings were in Boston fifteen years after the landing of the Mayflower, when John Winthrop, Jr. set up the first chemical laboratory in America in 1635.[15] In 1650 he organized the first American stock company, for the purpose of dealing in chemicals. The principal interests of this first company were salt and saltpeter, gunpowder, and such. This was soon followed by tanneries, fulling mills, glass works, and many other types of chemical enterprise. Surprising now to read of the many products known in early Colonial days. The chemical industry of the United States is a full three centuries old.

But the chief progress in metallurgy and in chemistry has come in our own generation. The promise it holds for the future is incalculable. If this advance continues for another generation we may by then have succeeded in solving some of the most troubling economic problems–even poverty. Unless, as Earnest Hooton suggests, we provide the moron with equipment for the conquest or destruction of civilization.

5. *Scientific imagination and technology*

We cannot see far into the future. Could discoverers and inventors see the ultimate forms of their work, they would scarce recognize the fruits of their labors. When our Hero of Alexandria, in the third century b. c., contrived a steam vessel to open and shut doors in the temple, and to rotate small vanes, he could not dream that this crude device would one day be transformed into a colossal turbine of a hundred and fifty thousand horsepower, producing a sufficient quantity of the mysterious power we call electricity to light a city.

Archimedes of Syracuse, working with his screws and levers, could hardly envisage the ponderous steam shovels of today, lifting fifty tons of rock at a scoop, as if it were a handful. Possibly he could, for he was given to fanciful dreams. Whose imagination could equal that of Archimedes when he said: δos μoι πov sτo και κινo τεν γεν ('give me whereon to stand and I will move the earth'). But even an Archimedes could scarcely have divined that from Galileo's measurement of the rate of fall of bodies, that is, the force of gravity, a method would be devised for weighing the sun, and many of the stars. Nor could even Galileo have guessed that when Newton observed the lovely band of colors of the solar spectrum, a method had been devised for one day discovering the chemical constitution of the sun and stars.

A century and more ago the eccentric English chemist, Lord Cavendish, discovered that the nitrogen and oxygen of the air might be united by the passage of an electric spark. Here was a possible source of supply for huge quantities of fertilizer needed for the fields, and for the ingredients of explosives. Thousands of experiments in an effort to extract this nitrogen in quantity. Slender results. Finally, some thirty years ago a distinguished Norwegian physicist, Birkeland, attempted to imitate, and thereby determine, the nature of the solar corona, the brilliant glow that surrounds the sun in an eclipse. He placed an electric arc in a powerful magnetic field, and produced a sheet of flame, creating an excellent imitation of the corona. But with unexpected by-effect. His apparatus generated a powerful gas that made it impossible to stay in the room. Rushing out, Birkeland sought his neighbor, the chemist Eyde, and excitedly dragged him into the laboratory. The chemist took a whiff of the air and exclaimed: "Nitric oxide; man, you have a fortune. You have solved the problem of a century." From this experiment the Birkeland-Eyde process of nitrogen fixation was born.

So almost without end. Not even among the most gifted has there ever been, or can there be, any very definite anticipation of the future. Yet 'the scientific use of the imagination,' of which Tyndall wrote so movingly, has been almost the basic element of all epochal discoveries.[16] These have not come, as a rule, from severely logical reasoning; rather the majority of which we have record seem more a spontaneous flash of insight and genius. A degree of genius is often required to foresee their practical uses. Which is why business men like Boulton have often been a dynamic force in making them useful to mankind.

CAPITALISM THE BENEFICENT

"Pecunia nervus rei publicae"
(Wealth, the sinew of the commonwealth)
—JEAN BODIN; 1568

The unassisted labour of a solitary individual, it is evident, is altogether unable to provide for him, such food, such cloaths and such lodging, as not only the luxury of the great, but as the natural appetites of the meanest peasant, are, in every civilized society, supposed to require. Observe in what manner a common day labourer in Britain or in Holland is accommodated with all these, and you will be sensible that his luxury is much superior to that of many an Indian prince, the absolute master of the lives and liberties of a thousand naked savages. The woolen coat which covers the day labourer, as coarse and rough as it may appear to be, could not be produced without the joint labour of a multitude of artists. The Shepherd, the Grazier, the Clipper, the Sorter of the Wool, the picker, the Comber, the Dyer, the Scribbler, the Spinner, the weaver, the fuller, the Dresser, must all join their different arts in order to make out this very homely production. Not to mention the merchants and carriers, who transport the materials from one of those artists to another, who often lives in a very distant country; how many other artists are employed in producing the tools even of the very meanest of these. I shall say nothing of so very complex a machine as the loom of the weaver or as the Mill of the Fuller; much less of the immense commerce and navigation, the Shipbuilding, the sail-making, the Rope-making, necessary to bring together the different drugs made use of by the Dyer, which often come from the remotest corners of the world; but consider only what a variety of labour is necessary to produce that very simple machine, the sheers of the Clipper. The miner, the builder of the furnace for smelting the ore, the burner of the Charcoal to be made use of in that operation, the feller of the timber of which that charcoal is made, the brickmaker, the bricklayer, the smelter, the mill wright, the forger, the smith, must all club their different industries in order to produce them. . . .
If we examine, I say, all those different conveniences and luxuries with which he is accommodated and consider what a variety of labour is employed about each of them, we shall be sensible that without the assistance and cooperation of many thousands, the very meanest person in civilized society could not be provided for, even in what we very falsely imagine, the easy and simple manner in which he is commonly accommodated. . . .
—ADAM SMITH. From the first draft of the *Wealth of Nations;* 1762

CHAPTER VII

CAPITALISM THE BENEFICENT

1. *The environment of capitalism*

DISCUSSION of the factors affecting economic progress has emphasized the significance of climate and 'natural' resources. It is evident that the temperate climate of North America is more conducive to energetic work than is the tropical and subtropical climate of South America. Nor can it be doubted that an important factor in industrial development is the abundance of such basic materials as coal and iron. Nations lacking one of these resources can build up large industries. But industrial development will be delayed and may never reach the highest level. It is partly because of supplies of coal and iron that Germany, and not Italy or France, became the leading industrial country of the continent.

Due emphasis has been given to the contribution of inventors and enterprisers, men of genius. But even great inventions may not be effective in advancing economic life, for these may be born out of time, when enterprisers are unable to make practical use of them, or when the economic environment is unfavorable. Consider, for example, the circumstances under which Hero (or Heron) of Alexandria produced his primitive steam engine. The congregation of peoples that came to dwell in Alexandria reached a level of civilization perhaps unsurpassed in its intellectual achievements.[1] They measured the circumference of the earth. The Copernican system was anticipated by Aristarchus of Alexandria, erudite mathematician and astronomer; to his theorems and demonstrations Copernicus added little. And yet even in this intellectual environment the discoveries of Hero bore no fruit. They seemed to remain sterile, and the development of the steam engine waited for another 1,900 years.

Why? It may be that a steam engine on a practical scale would not have been possible in lower Egypt, because there was no coal or iron. It may be that there was little need in the Egypt of that

119

time for inanimate power. It may be that there were no factory owners who could see a practical use of Hero's device. But all this is simply to say that the economic environment was unpropitious In Watt's time and country, a radical change. Plenty of coal and iron and materials required for fabricating the engine and supplying it with fuel; a distinct need for engines for pumping water in the coal mines. And there was a man of energy and enterprise, who saw the economic possibilities of the steam engine and was willing to provide the capital. Hero of Alexandria lived in Egypt, a land content forever to remain an agricultural country. James Watt lived in England, a land ready to take the lead in the industrial revolution. In short, Hero of Alexandria lived in pre-capitalist times; James Watt lived at the threshold of the great capitalist period.

2. *What capitalism is and what it does*

Definitions are dreary stuff. I propose, therefore, to show what capitalism is by considering what capitalism does.[2]

The Colorado River flowed a thousand miles and more through high-walled canyons to the sea, doing no useful work for man. An utter waste. At a strategic point a dam is flung across its course, creating a huge artificial lake that impounds something like a three years' flow of the river. An insurance fund for operations through a long spell of drought. This Boulder Dam is one of the mightiest creations of man. A part of the flow of the Colorado is pumped over a mountain chain to supply the city of Los Angeles and its environs, and to irrigate a wide area round about. A feat so far as I know never attempted before. The dam is used also to generate power, the electricity distributed to places several hundred miles away. Worthy of note that the river pumps its own water over the mountains, the power created by Boulder Dam is employed in part for this stupendous undertaking.

Yet other benefits from this engineering achievement. Three hundred miles or more below Boulder Dam is the wonderful Imperial Valley, the richest fruit-growing area that this earth has yet known. In itself an extraordinary creation, a product of irrigation. The Imperial Valley lies partly below sea level and has derived the water for its irrigation ditches from the Colorado River. Once a highly capricious stream; for this reason there have been in the past alternations of flood and drought. Boulder Dam will mean to Imperial Valley a steady and assured supply. It will impound the floods and feed them out as and when needed. Thus will the mighty powers of this mighty river be brought under the control of man.[3]

These are the things that every water power development does, whether the tremendous installations at Boulder Dam and Grand Coulee, or the numerous smaller undertakings throughout the country. And all this without depriving anyone of needful water. Some of the water is impounded temporarily; but the flow goes on just the same. The Colorado River will continue in the future as it has in the past million years. Impounding the excess flow will not consume the natural wealth of the area. On the contrary, the farmers and fruit growers of Imperial Valley will be benefited by the more certain and more even flow of water, and so too will the whole area this stupendous creation serves.

But this new and fruitful power is not to be had for nothing. It has required an enormous amount of human labor and materials, and means of transport. The machinery and supplies may all be made thousands of miles away; and this entails railway lines and motor roads across the desert. The steel for these huge constructions may be made in Pittsburgh, the iron ore may come from the Mesabi Range, the diamonds for drills from South Africa. All the workers who contribute, directly and indirectly, must be fed and housed and clothed and amused, for otherwise they cannot or will not work. What is it that makes this miracle of industry and engineering possible? What single force *creates* it all? The answer is the magical powers of capitalism, as strong in the economic world as gravitation in the physical.

What is this capitalism? It is the power of stored money. Into Boulder Dam and Grand Coulee have gone hundreds of millions of dollars. On the factories, mills, railways, steamships, and the machinery for all the industries of the United States has been expended hundreds of billions. Without this capital, in some form, the vast industries of the United States, as of the rest of the world, could not have come into being. In the construction of these factories and mills, and to open the mines and wells that yield the coal and oil, these billions had to be provided to sustain the workers employed. No other way in which this 'capital equipment' can be created. Whether a country has a free economy, as in the United

States, or a compulsory economy, as in Russia, the capital, the funds for building up productive industry, must be found.

The case of Boulder Dam. What produced this vast source of power? Not just the river, the stream that flows between the towering walls. Men of vision may see the potential power flowing by. But it is all as nothing if they have no capital to build the dam. For the use and profit of millions of people. Typical of the whole system. Popular imagination pictures capitalism as supporting a large population of idlers, wasters, and drones. In small part this is true. But the amount diverted from the total flow of income to provide for the luxurious consumption of the wastrels, is like the losses from the diversion of the Colorado River,—almost negligibly small. If the whole income so diverted were distributed, the income of the average person would not be increased by 3 per cent. And, in the long run, with loss to the multitude.

To revert to analogy: in order to carry the water of the Colorado to lower California, a part of the energy developed at Boulder Dam must be diverted to pump the water over the mountain chain. Identically the same with the System. The capital for our industrial enterprises comes from the few who divert part of their income from consumption to investment. Their function is just that of Boulder Dam: to impound the funds that create the capital equipment of the country. Which makes possible our colossal product and income.

Absolutely essential, if we are to have economic progress, that someone shall provide this capital: either the State or an economic class within it. But within the State, there is no class to insure the most effective use of these funds. Politicians and officials are rarely men of high business ability, and what is still more of import, they have no imperative interest in either efficiency or profit. In our society of free enterprise we have a mechanism marvelously effective, almost unbelievable in its simplicity, to attain all these ends.

Sometimes it is asked whether further economic progress is now necessary. It is said that we already produce sufficient 'goods' to provide for all reasonable needs; and that the problem of our day is to achieve a more equable distribution. A strabismic view. The product in our time is enormous compared with the past; but it is far from what is attainable in a near future. And much further gain is essential if we are to provide all the people with the material

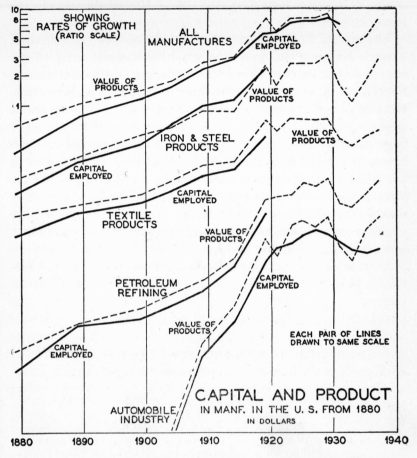

CAPITAL AND PRODUCT
IN MANF. IN THE U. S. FROM 1880
IN DOLLARS

XIII. THE RELATIONS OF CAPITAL TO PRODUCT IN DIFFERENT INDUSTRIES

In preceding charts the indispensable rôle of capital has been set forth for industry as a whole. The chart above shows how close is this association in each of the larger industries, when plotted together. Side by side, for each major type of manufacturing, is shown the varying rates of growth, compared with the aggregate for all manufactures. It is amazing to note how closely the increase in the value of the product in each is paralleled by the increase in the amount of capital employed, which of course varies with different industries. There seems no mistaking the fact that the amount of capital available is the limiting factor in the growth of every industry, and it is solely through the increase of the capital supply that a continuance of our industrial growth and social improvement is possible. Equally true, it would appear, for agriculture, as a later graph discloses.

means for comfort and culture. We cannot be content with present economic standards.

But further: The maintenance of *growth* is apparently an economic as well as a biological necessity.[4] Without it the joy of enterprise and achievement begins to fade; with it, the courage and self-reliance of a vigorous people. Some already fear we have come to the end of our wondrous advance. Grotesque! Even in severe depression, technology, invention, and scientific discovery have shown as remarkable progress as in any previous decennium. We have continued to devise new and better methods and machinery, despite the arrest of increase in our national income. And when we have finished with this decade of muddling, we may more than resume our normal rate of growth. But this only if we continue to provide the essential capital. If through present lack of understanding we dry up the source of capital, as we have, there can be no hope of achieving higher levels of economic well-being, or the social and economic security that is universally desired. Why?

3. *The wealth of this and other nations*

In a paper published some years ago I endeavored to offer detailed proof of the following propositions: [5]

1. The amazing wealth of the United States and of other rich industrial countries is due almost wholly to the astonishing growth of manufacturing, mining, transportation, and trade; very little to agriculture.

2. This tremendous industrial growth has required an adequate supply of new capital. Without this new capital supply, invention, discovery, and enterprise would have been ineffective.

3. This new capital is derived directly, and almost wholly, from the industries themselves, each industry providing its own capital through reinvestment. To this capital supply the so-called 'savings of the people' have contributed but a small share.

4. The average net realized gain per year, in the total reproductive capital employed in industry, seems to amount to not much more than 5 or 6 per cent of the national income.

5. This supply of new capital is derived almost wholly from the profits of industry. These profits, and therefore the supply of new capital, are largely due to the energy and initiative of a very few highly capable individuals with unusual talent for management and accumulation.

6. The larger the wealth and income of these few individuals, the greater the proportion of profits that is turned back into industry, for industrial expansion, and for the creation of new industries.

7. As the margin of net profit is small and precarious, whatever tends to limit profits or to reduce them is inimical to the continued growth of the country and opposed to the best interest of the whole population.

8. Finally, as the highest rate of savings is from the largest fortunes, it follows that until we can devise a more efficient system, the greater the concentration of income, the greater the capital supply, and therefore, the greater the gain in national well-being.

In support of these propositions I give a series of charts showing that in almost every line of industry for which adequate data are available, the rate of increase in product is strictly proportional to the rate of increase in capital, and that the more rapid the growth of this new capital the more rapid the growth of the industry.

Much of this argument runs strongly counterwise to the emotions, and therefore the beliefs, of a very large number of people, including many fervid writers upon this subject. It is instructive to observe how vague and fanciful are the ideas as to how and why the United States has become the richest country that has ever existed. Usually expressed in terms of the 'great natural resources,' the intelligence of our people, 'Yankee ingenuity,' and 'American enterprise.' These are all consequential factors. But of little avail without a steady increase of the means of utilizing these resources.

Many of the world's most important inventions cost in the beginning very little. But on their development enormous sums have been expended. The discovery of electro-magnetism by Faraday and his predecessors represented only a small sum, possibly amounting to a few thousand dollars. But it was thirty years after Faraday's discoveries, and complete demonstration of his theory, before a commercially successful dynamo. The work of many inventors, in several countries. All told, this meant the investment of hundreds of thousands of dollars, possibly several millions. And this was, in turn, only a small part of the capital necessary to extend this vast industry over the earth. The total capital in electrical enterprises in the United States alone now amounts to over twenty billions of dollars, with perhaps an equal sum for the rest of the world. Precisely the same in other fields.

With all this, huge losses. Inevitable. So the present capital investment can represent only a part of the total cost. How much more has been wasted in bad ventures, or in unworkable devices and inventions, can not be estimated. Unquestionably large. It follows that the large majority of thrifty people, with their relatively small savings, can not safely invest in venturesome enterprises, which most new industries are in the beginning. The one unfailing source of these funds has been the savings, direct or indirect, of the rich, or from profits retained for surplus.

The effect of this has been felt by everyone in every industry, whether wage-worker or business man. The gain from increased production has been shared, and shared in strict proportion, by all who have contributed either their labor or their capital. The incomes of our ancestors were astonishingly small. They had adequate food, shelter, and clothing, all largely homemade; but few comforts, and almost no luxuries. Transportation, save by water, was extremely difficult.[6] It took weeks to carry their slender surplus from the farms to the towns; and the products this surplus would buy were scant and dear. They worked long and hard, lived frugally, had scarcely more of material things than the populations of a thousand years before. Yet within the space of five or six generations, these straggling colonies were transformed into an industrial nation of incredible wealth, its population enjoying the highest standard of living in history. The fruit and flower of the capitalistic system.

The evidence that the wealth of the United States has been due to the beneficent effects of capitalism may be summarized as follows:

1. For every dollar of additional value added per annum in manufacturing, as far back at least as 1850, something more than an additional dollar of new capital has apparently been required. This ratio of capital to annual value of product has been rising slowly in the eighty years from 1850 to 1930, so that it now requires nearly twice as much capital to produce a given value of product.

2. The average money value of a physical unit of manufactures has changed little throughout this period, except in time of war, so that the ratio of capital to the physical product is approximately the same as for value added in manufacturing.

3. The ratio of capital invested to horsepower employed in manufacturing has risen in almost equal degree. It is evident, therefore, that there has been a steady increase in the average cost of a unit of machinery. That is, as the efficiency and output of machines have risen,

so also has the cost. It is for this reason that capital invested in manufacturing must rise somewhat more rapidly than the 'value added' in manufacturing.

4. The average wage per wage earner has risen steadily and proportionately, with the 'value added' and with the physical volume of manufactures. The ratio of wages to the total value of product has not materially changed in the last eighty years.

5. The entire increase in average wage per wage earner, or in real wages, has been due directly to one factor and to one alone: the growth in capital investment. This must be so, because wages are paid out of product, and the larger product per worker has been wholly due to the increased application of machinery.

6. The increase in mechanical equipment was possible only because of the increase in the supply of capital. Therefore, the well-being of the great body of workers has been improved solely through the provision of an adequate supply of capital for investment.

It should be added that for these propositions we have now statistical proof, largely set forth in the charts. Further, that this has always been the process of creating wealth, not only in the United States, but likewise in England, Germany, France, and in other industrial nations.

Nor is this method of increasing wealth confined to the older industrial countries of Western Europe and America. Strikingly illustrated in the case of Japan, in this generation. Fifty years ago the Japanese, highly gifted in other ways, were not noted as a mechanical or industrial people. Amazing to think that they had no coal, little iron, and that other resources were so largely lacking. They had no water power. They had to import virtually everything—their materials, methods, and machines. They were of quick intelligence, highly industrious, pertinacious. Their progress is one of the marvels of recent history. But it was not indigenous.

In the beginning the Japanese copied almost everything. They bought machinery, they borrowed ideas, they engaged foreign talent, and they utilized all these to the fullest. The start was difficult. They were patient and persevering. They were willing to make sacrifices. Their industrial development has been almost as ruthless as that of Russia in recent years. It has been directly the result of exploiting the mass of the Japanese people, and especially the farmers, for a definite purpose. By general report, the farming population of Japan is despairingly poor. And wages in industry have been kept down with an iron hand, so that the workers have enjoyed, as yet, relatively little of the fruits of this astonishing advance. Japan had to economize in order to achieve; without savings no amount of ambition or desire would have sufficed to realize their goal. What is the result? No country or people of which we have any record has risen so swiftly to power and position.

All this was the direct result of a definite process. The Japanese fully grasped the principle and the method of economic progress. They carried on with irresistible energy. To get machinery, to obtain the funds they had to scrimp and to save. Now the profits from their new industries provide the capital for further expansion. With this, Japan has become a nation of inventors and innovators, and shown in the highest degree the necessary qualities of enterprise. In consequence, it has already gained a formidable industrial position. This is what method may do. Reviewing all this, I wonder if other peoples will not follow their example, copy their methods, and adopt the same formula. With like results.

Apparently, this is much what Russia is doing now. It has followed the same formula, and almost the same method. Its rulers have ruthlessly starved the people, taken from them their wheat, in order to get valuta with which to buy German, English, and American machinery. No doubt they have made mistakes, and met many checks. Perchance they have attempted to drive their plans through too rapidly and somewhat beyond the capability of their people. Japan, at least in the beginning, took much longer, set a much slower pace. In Russia bloody purges come from political antagonisms. But it would be surprising if Russia does not carry through. If it succeeds, we may look for gigantic developments from that large and populous country. The essence of such achievement is that it is almost always fertile and stimulating. Just as England, the United States, and Germany have progressed from one epoch-making invention to another, probably so also will Russia and Japan.

4. Manufacture, commerce, and capitalism

As noted, nations grow rich and their peoples enjoy wide comforts only where the principal occupations are manufacturing and commerce.[7] This seems true not only among nations, but within a nation with geographic specialization, such as the United States. Quite astonishing to find that even now, after three hundred years, the industry and wealth of the United States are largely confined to a small area within the Northeast. Fourteen states with 14 per cent of the present continental area have nearly half of the population, three-fourths of all the manufacturing, and at least 60 per cent of the national income. This leaves for the other thirty-four states, with 86 per cent of the area, only one-half of the population, one-fourth of the manufacturing, and not more than 40 per cent of the national income. See map.

Almost all of these remaining thirty-four states are largely agricultural in character. Nor is this surprising. The larger part of the income of the country is derived from manufacturing, mining, and trade. The total net value of products on the farm, including meat, dairy, poultry, fruit, and truck products, does not exceed 10 or 12 per cent of the national dividend. There is no mistaking the import of these facts.

In a highly representative year, 1930, the seven leading manufacturing states, all of them in this Northeast area, produced something like 37 out of the 53 billion dollars of estimated manufactures, that is, 70 per cent of the total. Of the 25 billion dollars of income reported for income tax purposes, these seven states supplied 15 billions, that is 60 per cent. Contrast this with seven representative agricultural states. Their total manufactures amounted to only 2 billions of 53 billions—about 4 per cent.

Neither now nor throughout all history has farming been productive of any large amount of savings or capital. It does not lend itself notably to highly capitalized or mechanized organization. The present agricultural product would be impossible without machinery; but the amount of mechanization on farms so far is relatively small. In manufacturing the average capital investment per worker in the United States now amounts to something like $10,000, which is probably twice the average per worker for any other nation. But the value of all machinery on the farms of the United States amounts to less than $500 per farm, which means even less per farm worker.[8] The investment in machinery on the farm is a small part of the total value of the land and buildings and live stock. But this is the whole point. It is the machinery which creates the wealth.

The product per farm worker in the United States is higher than in any other country, due solely to the use of machinery, not to more fertile land, and not to the superiority of our agricultural methods. Yet the average nominal income of farm workers is the lowest of any large body of workers in the country. Probably not much more than half of the average wage in manufacturing.[9] As a result, a slowly dwindling farm population, that is now less than it was a quarter of a century ago. For the same reason: no such increase in the product per worker in agriculture as in manufacturing and kindred industries.

The difficulty, as already observed, is inherent, in agriculture; and so far as I can see there is no present way out, save by the continued lowering of the population engaged in agriculture and by raising the proportion engaged in other fields of industry. In this manner larger industrial markets may be made available to a smaller number of agricultural workers. To some extent it is possible to increase the size and efficiency of farms, and to increase the use of machinery on them. But by the nature of the industry, this alternative is limited, and it cannot obviate the need to shift more of our population into non-agricultural work. This last, it should be noted, is possible only if sufficient capital is available to expand our industries and to employ more workers. The old Greeks had a wise saying, that the gods themselves do not fight against necessity.

5.   The phantom of 'technological' unemployment

A century and a half ago there was in the important textile industry of Great Britain a violent commotion. In the weaving and spinning industries there were new machines by which one man could do the work of three, five, perhaps ten. And weavers and spinners were losing their jobs. Riots, smashing of the new machines, trouble. And endless economic writing, about the appearance of a new evil, what is now called 'technological' unemployment.[10] Regularly to be trotted out with every succeeding industrial depression as a stalking-horse, with regularly renewed discovery of its ominous character, threatening the 'foundations of society.' Now we have it with us again.

In the thirty years following the introduction of the spinning and weaving machines of Arkwright, Hargreaves, and others, the number of workers employed in the British textile industry was increased five-fold and more. And every important invention has had a similar effect, an increase in employment. The life of eco-

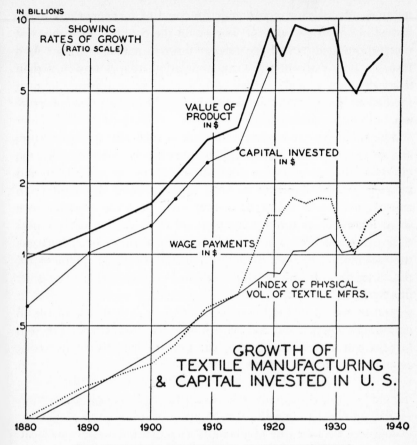

IN BILLIONS

SHOWING
RATES OF GROWTH
(RATIO SCALE)

VALUE OF
PRODUCT
IN $

CAPITAL INVESTED
IN $

WAGE PAYMENTS
IN $

INDEX OF PHYSICAL
VOL. OF TEXTILE MFRS.

GROWTH OF
TEXTILE MANUFACTURING
& CAPITAL INVESTED IN U. S.

XIV. GROWTH OF TEXTILE MANUFACTURING

We now extend the relations of capital, wages, and product a step farther, to note their effect not only upon general well-being but on the workers in individual industries. In each of the five succeeding charts is illustrated the intimate association which exists between the capital invested and the amounts paid in wages. The proportion of total income, that is, the total value of the product (or the "value added"), bears a nearly fixed relationship to the amount paid out in wages, this proportion changing only very slowly through the last 60 years or more. Whatever industry is investigated, the same relationship appears in each. In other words, it seems clear that only by increasing the capital investment is there provided new paths for employment and increase in wages. Never any greater folly than to suppose that wages may be arbitrarily raised through either political, social or union influences, without disturbance of the price level, lowered consumer demand, and a fall in employment. The Ford case in 1915 was a quite exceptional circumstance, and gave rise to a vast illusion. (In many instances shown, the amount of capital invested is not available since 1919, because of a strange omission by the Census Department.)

nomic conjectures and fantasies appears to be immortal. Always a flood of books to prove that, although the dire predictions in the past have invariably proved groundless and futile, *now*, at last, they are true. Governmental policies are usually based on this delusion.[11]

Obvious that there must be some way by which the expected, and 'inevitable' effects of new machinery, inventions, have been obviated, with no serious consequences, since the Industrial Revolution began. What is the process? It is the creation of new industries, the cheapening of products, and the expansion of the old. For this is clear: there must have been, with the cheapening of weaving and spinning a considerable increase in demand. The result, the expansion of what had been a minor industry into one of the major industries of the world. Where once there were thousands, there are now millions employed in the cotton industry alone. This in addition to the increase of employment in the machine making industries.

Scarce any one would contend that if the cost of an important or attractive article can be sharply reduced, the demand for such articles will not be much increased. This has happened repeatedly, as in the textile industry in the nineteenth century, and more recently in the automobile industry. Further, if expenditure, per individual on the goods reduced is less, there will be that much more available for expanding the consumption of other goods.[12] If there should still be a residue of unemployment, this is almost automatically absorbed by the introduction of new industries. Always there are hundreds or thousands of incipient inventions and discoveries by which, with the aid of sufficient capital, important new industries and new fields of employment may be developed.[13]

Witness the veritable outburst of invention and industrial discoveries in the last generation. Everyone is familiar with the list: the automobile, the radio, the telephone, the aeroplane, the gasoline engine, the Diesel engine, almost every phase of the electrical industry, and innumerable others. Every one of these has brought about more demand for labor, and especially for the highly skilled. Forty years ago the automobile was almost non-existent; today one of the leading industries in the country, employing, in all its ramifications, literally millions of men. Consider the number now employed in making, selling, repairing, and serving automobiles; the even larger number in providing gasoline, tires, roads. A total of more than 3,000,000 men. All these opportunities created within the lifetime of the majority of adults now living.

It is through these new industries that expansion is resumed, in every period following depression.[14] Obviously this process is not now coming to an end. Twenty times more money is being spent on technical investigations and in the development of new inventions and new processes than forty years ago. In the United States despite depression, the corporations of the country are spending nearly a quarter of a billion dollars a year on the highest type of technical and scientific research. And this is encouraged by fabulous rewards. An interesting example: Nearly fifty years ago, a shy student in Oberlin College heard his professor of chemistry say that a high reward awaited the man who could find an economical process for the extraction of aluminium from the bauxite clays. In a year or two, working in an improvised shop in his father's barn, the invention was made. Almost simultaneously the same discovery in France. When this boy, Charles Martin Hall, died nearly thirty years later, he had received a total of $23,000,000 in royalties. No end of such possibilities still exist.

It may be urged that in some industries an important invention may result in unemployment that is not relieved by new opportunities in other fields. But this is rare. The displacement of old skills by new processes is gradual. If an industry declines at about the same rate as its employees die or retire, there may be no unemployment at all. The industry merely fails to share in the industrial growth of the country. The displacement of horses and carriages by automobiles was not sudden. Ample time to reduce the number of persons employed in the older industry without depriving those already employed of their jobs. There is nothing cataclysmic, and little that is precipitate, in the rate of displacement of workers by new processes and inventions.

Not only common sense, but statistical evidence proves that wide-scale technological unemployment is imaginary. Throughout the last hundred and forty years, for which we now possess most definite knowledge, the number of workers employed has steadily increased relative to the population. Perhaps for the first half century after the founding of the new republic, the apparent increase may have been due largely to the conversion of industry from home to factory. All this had been largely completed by the end of the last century, so that the growth in industrial employment since then has been real. It was necessary that employment should thus increase more rapidly than population, for in the last hundred years or more the proportion of those over 21 has risen steadily from around 40 per cent in 1830 to around 60 per cent. With more to spend and more to consume.

The prevailing unemployment, about which there is so little understanding, has nothing to do with technical progress. Almost wholly the result of economic ignorance. In another generation, when these problems are more fully understood, our serious depressions will disappear.

SAVINGS: SINE QUA NON

By what a frugal man annually saves, he not only affords maintenance to an additional number of productive hands, for that or the ensuing year, but . . . he establishes as it were a perpetual fund for the maintenance of an equal number in all times to come. The perpetual allotment and destination of this fund, indeed, is not always guarded by an positive law, by an trust-right or deed or mortmain. It is always guarded, however, by a very powerful principle, the plain and evident interest of every individual to whom any share of it shall ever belong. No part of it can ever afterwards be employed to maintain any but productive hands, without an evident loss to the person who thus perverts it from its proper destination.

—ADAM SMITH: *The Wealth of Nations*

And with the growth of openings for the investment of capital there is a constant increase in that surplus of production over the necessaries of life, which gives the power to save. . . . Every increase in the arts of production, and in the capital accumulated to assist and support labour in future production, increased the surplus out of which more wealth could be accumulated. . . . Thus from step to step wealth and knowledge have grown, and with every step the power of saving wealth and extending knowledge has increased.

—ALFRED MARSHALL: *Principles of Economics*

A conspicuous trait of the dynamic age in which we live is to be seen in the rapid pace at which existing capital equipment is made obsolete by technical inventions and other innovations in the design and construction of consumption and capital goods. In 1934, the trade journal Power made a study of 454 "better-than-average" industrial power plants constituting nearly 10 per cent of industrial prime-mover capacity, and found 62 per cent of the equipment was over 10 years old, while 25 per cent was over 20 years. In 1935 the American Machinist made a study of the obsolescence of metal-working equipment, concluding that, because of the rapid improvement in machine design, metal working equipment was as a rule obsolete if not produced within the last 10 years. It took an inventory of the age of such machinery and found that 65 per cent of all the metal working equipment in the country was over 10 years old and presumably obsolete. The Interstate Commerce Commission records indicate that 61 per cent of the steam locomotives in the country were built over 20 years ago. These figures suggest the magnitude of capital obsolescence.

—WILLIAM F. OGBURN: *Technological Trends and National Policy*

CHAPTER VIII

SAVINGS: SINE QUA NON

1. *Parsimony and industry*

STRANGE are the fantasies that so largely dominate our minds, and perhaps the world. Until recent years, there were few to question the fundamental necessity of adequate savings for capital investment, the mainspring of economic progress. On this men of affairs and doctrinaires were at one. The leading English economists were emphatic in their insistence on the need for savings if the wealth of a country was to increase. True, some among the earlier Socialists saw in thrift a cause of unemployment; but until recently they stood almost alone.[1]

In this country, Benjamin Franklin, not always thought of as an original economist, yet deserving such designation, incessantly extolled the significance of saving to well-being.

> A penny saved is twopence clear;
> A pin a day 's a groat a year.[2]

Perhaps no work reflects more thoroughly the early American character, than *Poor Richard's Almanack*. A paean to the virtues of thrift.[3] One may wonder what he would have thought of a nation lost in dreams that the way to wealth is through prodigious spending.

The means by which nations are lifted from poverty to affluence were well expounded in the epochal work of Adam Smith. Difficult to improve his lucid presentation.

"Every increase or diminution of capital naturally tends to increase or diminish the real quantity of industry, the number of productive hands, and consequently the exchangeable value of the annual produce of the land and labour of the country, the real wealth and revenue of all its inhabitants.

"Whatever a person saves from his revenue he adds to his capital, and either employs it himself in maintaining an additional number of productive hands, or enables some other person to do so, by lending it to him for an interest, that is, for a share of the profits. As the capital of an individual can be increased only by what he saves from his annual revenue or his annual gains, so the capital of a society, which is the same with that of all the individuals who compose it, can be increased only in the same manner.

"Parsimony, by increasing the fund which is destined for the maintenance of productive hands, tends to increase the number of those hands whose labour adds to the value of the subject upon which it is bestowed. It tends therefore to increase the exchangeable value of the annual produce of the land and labour of the country. It puts into motion an additional quantity of industry, which gives an additional value to the annual produce." [4]

Adam Smith well understood the process of the wealth of nations; but he could not offer the proof. Only in the last twenty years have adequate data been available to reveal an almost dollar-for-dollar correspondence between the increase of capital and of the physical product. If common sense might lead to the same conclusion, it must be realized that it is not just upon common sense that this thesis rests. Fortunately, we now have statistical proof for every stage of the process. The basis for the principles set forth in this volume. [5]

2. The source of savings

The volume of savings in the United States available for all purposes—for consumers' investment such as housing, for public investment such as roads and schools, and for business investment such as factories and machinery—is estimated in ordinary times as approximately 15 per cent of the national income. [6] Probably a generous estimate. In 1929, even, possibly not more than 13 per cent; in some previous years perhaps more. Since 1930, on an average little or no savings. In 1929 the amount used for 'reproductive' capital—the net business investment except for inventories—was the largest in our history. And yet in that year, this was only slightly over four billion dollars, little more than 5 per cent of the national income. This in the peak year of our industrial history. A long way from the fantastic sums usually imagined by popular or emotional writers.

What is the source of these savings? They can come only from an excess of income over necessary expenditures. This excess is highest for those of high incomes. So the larger part of the savings must of necessity be so derived. There are always many who love to spend, and do. Particularly true of those with incomes ranging from $5,000 to $50,000. These perforce save little.

Receivers of the largest incomes are not as a rule extravagant spenders. Their active interest in business deprives them of the leisure for grand expenditures; and their early struggles have often so fixed their habits of thrift they are not strongly disposed to luxurious consumption. Their incomes are paid out of business profits, and in these profits, the insignia of success, they often take a profound pleasure. And this, and not 'ostentatious expenditure,' is their reward.

We have definite evidence that the wage earning class contributes no considerable part of our industrial, reproductive capital. Their savings are made largely for the purpose of future consumption, either in old age or by dependent widows and children. A part of these savings go to savings banks and insurance companies. The use of funds by such savings institutions is limited. Most of it is put into government bonds, and mortgages on homes and farms. Other savings of the wage class go directly into home-ownership, or through building and loan associations are made available for home-owners' loans.

For many it is difficult to believe that the savings of the great body of people in a nation so rich as the United States are in fact so small. They cannot accept such an estimate as that made by Clark Warburton, that something like 70 per cent of the population saves little or nothing.[7] But if the fifty millions gainfully employed in good times each saved as much as $100 a year, the total would only be five billion dollars—hardly half the estimated gross savings of the country in prosperous times. But if employees continued to do this year after year, they would soon bring about a material change in the distribution of income. Their ownership in industrial enterprises would be enormous.

Years ago I made a computation regarding the Pennsylvania Railroad: if from the beginning of the road, in 1829, every employee drawing a wage or salary had put aside five cents out of every dollar he received, and invested it in Pennsylvania Railroad stock, they would long ago have been the proprietors of the whole Pennsylvania system, and perhaps of other roads besides. Yet the truth is that employees generally are not large owners of stock in the enterprises in which they work.[8]

The further proof: From income tax returns we may ascertain the destination of almost every dollar that is paid out in dividends to income tax payers. There are only a million persons in the United States, even in prosperous times, with incomes over $5,000 a year, and only half a million with incomes over $10,000. But those with incomes of $5,000 and over receive something like 90 per cent of the total dividends distributed to individuals. The reported dividends in incomes under $5,000 a year amount to only about 10 per cent of this total. In other words, dividends are an unimportant part of the incomes of the latter class; while the higher incomes, especially those of $25,000 a year and over, are largely derived from dividends, and not from interest on bonds and mortgages, or income from other types of property.[9]

There are notable instances of a few large corporations with a large number of shareholders. One especially has expertly publicized the wide distribution of its ownership. Likewise, some utility companies, as in California, have made special drives to distribute their shares among their customers. Such instances are of interest, but they are rare, and do not affect the conclusion that corporate capital comes chiefly from large incomes. I have often wondered why the persons of moderate income do not invest more in some of our enterprises which have long, fine records of continued dividend payments and a justifiable reputation for good management. Their shares can be easily purchased at a very small commission. But small savings are more conveniently deposited in savings banks, or paid for life insurance or for the purchase of homes. If all these savings from modest incomes were put together, it would be a large sum. Yet it might still not equal, at a maximum, one-fourth or one-fifth of the total real invested capital in the United States.

I have been at pains to set all this out at length, to indicate that there is nothing surprising in the estimate that something like 70 per cent of the families in the United States save very little or nothing.[10] This conclusion is borne out by the finding, noted elsewhere, that only three or four out of every hundred who die leave enough property to make it worth probating. Nor does it follow that the small savings of this large proportion of families are due to an 'injustice.' Later the natural law governing the distribution of income will be considered. Meanwhile, it may be noted that those who do not save are nevertheless able to spend many

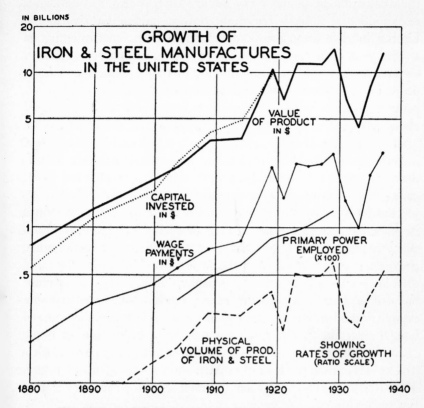

IN BILLIONS

GROWTH OF
IRON & STEEL MANUFACTURES
IN THE UNITED STATES

VALUE
OF PRODUCT
IN $

CAPITAL
INVESTED
IN $

WAGE
PAYMENTS
IN $

PRIMARY POWER
EMPLOYED
(X 100)

PHYSICAL
VOLUME OF PROD.
OF IRON & STEEL

SHOWING
RATES OF GROWTH
(RATIO SCALE)

20
10
5
1
.5

1880   1890   1900   1910   1920   1930   1940

XV. THE VAST GROWTH OF THE STEEL INDUSTRY

As everyone knows, with the birth of railroads and steamships, and with the ensuing rapid mechanization of industry, steel and iron have become the great basic products, and, one might add, basic to all prosperity as well. Interesting to note that throughout history war has had an especially stimulating effect, in endeavoring to provide better steel for guns and cannon. The Bessemer process was directly such an outgrowth. An industry often thought of as 'prince or pauper'; but in reality, of fairly steady growth (up to 1930). And here, as in every industry for which the data exist, we find the same relationship between the increase in wage payments and the increase of the capital employed. The astonishing fact about this relationship seems to be its fixity, that is, that for all practical purposes about the same amount of capital is required for a given increase in the product as 50 years ago. Quite contrary to many suppositions that the capital supply is no longer the paramount factor.

billions of dollars annually in owning and operating motor cars. They spend billions more on cosmetics, cigarettes, chewing gum, candies, soft drinks, hard liquors, movies and a wide variety of sports. In all a portentous sum, much in excess of the entire national income of a country as large and as prosperous as France. And as long as these consumption habits persist, there can be no hope for any considerable savings by the masses.

3. The destination of savings

What happens to our national savings and what effect do they have on the well-being of the people? Much more than half of the net savings are used for two purposes not directly related to the expansion of industry. In the decade of the 1920's about one-fourth of the total savings was used for residential construction, the funds for this purpose partly derived directly from savings of the home-owners; part borrowed from the savings of others, through building and loan associations, savings banks, and insurance companies.

In this same decade of the 1920's another fourth of total savings was used in constructing public works and for other government undertakings, the funds for this raised by the sale of bonds, purchased largely by the banks, insurance companies, and wealthy individuals. Some of this represented the accumulations of persons of moderate means; but probably much more the receivers of large incomes.

Thus the larger part of the total national savings was used for non-industrial, non-reproductive purposes. It is important, of course, to the health and comfort of the people to build habitable homes and schools and hospitals. But this type of investment in no way increases the capacity of industry to produce goods. It does not promote the expansion of industry, nor much increase the real income of the people. Much less than half, perhaps not over a third, of the savings in the decade of the 1920's was available for this important purpose.

The net annual savings for reproductive capital in this same period was probably not more than three to four billion dollars. Yet this relatively small amount made possible the economic progress of the country. The beneficiaries of this industrial gain, that is, the ultimate beneficiaries of these savings, were the whole body of the people, the workers no less than the managers and the owners. In fact, because taxes are largely derived from industrial incomes, the huge number of government employees were supported from the same source.

Consider now the further inference: If this entire fund requisite for continued economic progress were to be diverted to augment the incomes of the fifty million gainfully employed, it would amount to only sixty dollars per person per year, five dollars per person per month. With this additional income would the average working man do any more saving than now? And if he did, would these savings be available for this reproductive capital? The answer is easy. And the inevitable result would be industrial stagnation. New jobs available in industry would be steadily diminished, the general level of wages would no longer rise. And this great sacrifice for no better purpose than to enable wage earners to increase their expenditure by a dollar a week.

So: if higher wages come solely from increased production; if increased production comes solely from additional capital; and if this capital is derived almost wholly from profits, it must follow that the highest rate of profits will promote the greatest progress and increase of wages.

4. *There is no oversaving*

Already noted that, until recently, the chief proponents of the view that a community may save too much were among the brilliant group of Socialist writers of the nineteenth century. The leaders of this group—Sismondi, Rodbertus, Marx, and Hobson—developed the theory that business cycles are chiefly due to 'oversaving.' [11] The heart of the doctrine was that business depression was the result of insufficient consumption, and insufficient consumption was a necessary consequence of the saving of the rich! The extreme position was that taken by Rodbertus who declared that capitalists "must expend their income to the last penny in comforts and luxuries," for if they save, goods accumulate and "part of the workmen will have no work." [12] A view so fantastic that it is no longer held even by the ardent adherents of the doctrine.

The new dogma is rather that "savings limit consumption." [13] But how? Surely the workmen engaged upon the construction of a twenty million dollar steam turbine electric plant, or the like, must have food and comforts, along with their fellow workmen in consumption goods industries. The money they receive may have been immediately diverted from similar expenditures upon candy and cigarettes. But not, apparently, for long. Why? Because of that continuous "current-flow of monetary circulation" so admirably set forth by Simon Newcomb more than half a century ago. Unless savings are buried in the ground, or lie idle in the bank, thus reducing this monetary flow, they will join this continuous process the moment they are put to work. And it is prudence and foresight to put them to work in the safest and most profitable way. In all this there is inevitably a segregation of labor from one type of production or construction to another; but surely it is weird to imagine that under normal conditions this 'limits consumption' or reduces the national income.[14]

The softer pedal of the same idea is that there is more saving than can be profitably used in expanding business. This conclusion seems based on ignorance of the diverse opportunities always awaiting the use of capital, and the quantity of capital almost always needed for providing additional employment. One striking illustration: One of our large and progressive chemical companies states that over a period of six years they invested $22 million in a new process for the manufacture of dye-stuffs before a dollar of clear net profit was earned. A further investment of $21 million was made in this field during the next twelve years before sufficient profits were earned to pay back the accumulated losses.

Again, in this company's new process for the manufacture of synthetic ammonia and related products more than $27 millions were invested during a period of ten years, before the accumulated yearly operating results showed a dollar of net profits. The report adds: "Both of these newly developed industries are now distinct national assets, and these two new industries now provide employment for some 8,000 workers." It appears that to open these new fields of employment, this company invested nearly $9,000 of capital per worker. These two new industries represent high technological achievement, with high wages, and not 'unemployment.' The dyes and other chemicals they produce are far better, far cheaper, and more varied than those available before. This is a notable, but not an isolated instance of the varied opportunities that characterize our economic system.

In every generation there have been many to believe that this

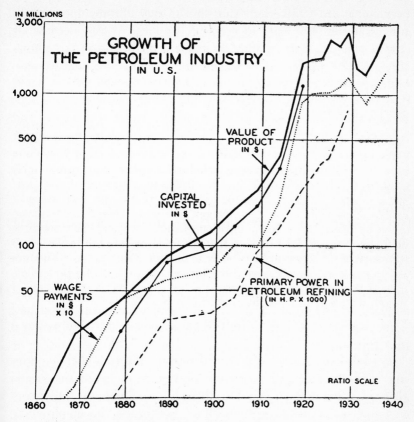

IN MILLIONS

GROWTH OF
THE PETROLEUM INDUSTRY
IN U. S.

3,000
1,000
500
100
50

VALUE OF
PRODUCT
IN $

CAPITAL
INVESTED
IN $

WAGE
PAYMENTS
IN $
X 10

PRIMARY POWER IN
PETROLEUM REFINING
(IN H. P. X 1000)

RATIO SCALE

1860 1870 1880 1890 1900 1910 1920 1930 1940

XVI. THE AMAZING GROWTH OF THE OIL INDUSTRY

The extraordinary advance in the use of petroleum is one of the spectacular features of the last 80 years or more. Now rapidly encroaching upon the use of coal, and promising perhaps to take rank as the most important single industry in our national economy. Likewise, likely to become a portentous factor in war. When its potentialities for vast conflagration become a reality. A whole nation might be devastated in a few days. There is a future of wondrous possibilities, for already new methods of oil drilling indicate that the supply is practically inexhaustible. It happens that we have data for this industry from 1860, as shown above, and here again it will be seen how close the relationship is between capital investment, product, wage payments, and the rest. Suppress the capital supply, that is, destroy or limit profits, and progress ceases. This is the lesson we must learn.

splendid prospect must soon come to an end, that 'the future does not offer the same opportunity as the past.' To these prophets of doom all is gray. But never to men of vision. Listen to a voice of fifty years ago:

"On whichever side we look we find that the progress and diffusion of knowledge are constantly leading to the adoption of new processes and new machinery which economize human effort on condition that some of the effort is spent a good while before the attainment of the ultimate ends to which it is directed.

"The rate of progress has sometimes been slow, and occasionally there has even been a great retrograde movement; but now we are moving on at a rapid pace that grows quicker every year; and we cannot guess where it will stop. On every side further openings are sure to offer themselves, all of which will tend to change the character of our social and industrial life, and to enable us to turn to account vast stores of capital in providing new gratifications and new ways of economizing effort by expending it in anticipation of distant wants. There seems to be no good reason for believing that we are anywhere near a stationary state in which there will be no new important wants to be satisfied; in which there will be no more room for profitably investing present effort in providing for the future, and in which the accumulation of wealth will cease to have any reward." [15]

This prophetic view of Alfred Marshall is as true today as when he wrote it.

Yet another variant of the same delusion is the view that 'oversaving' leads to excessive formation of capital in boom times, and that this capital is largely lost. Broadly speaking, the only way in which capital can really be 'lost' is through the employment of labor. Always in a period of expansion there is increased demand for construction materials, for machinery and equipment—all requiring a large number of workers. If this suppositious oversaving leads to reckless and unprofitable enterprise, the effect is not directly felt by the workers. And very little, as a rule, even by those who make the ventures. Naturally at times and in particular industries there will be unprofitable investment. Even so, there is often marked social benefit therefrom. It usually leads to the scrapping of antiquated equipment; and morale and management are kept at a high level. They are not wrong, I think, who hold that the losses from unprofitable investment do not deeply affect the national economy. We had an excellent example of this in the railroads. No end of these ventures proved unprofitable for a time, and that meant huge losses to the builders and investors. But eventually many of these bankrupt roads, as the industries of the country grew, became a distinct national asset. Almost every industry has similar experiences, particularly in the early stages of its development. In the meantime all these capital expenditures contribute to the increase of employment and the consequent consumption of goods.

The fundamental question is this: do these unprofitable investments in particular industries vitally affect the course of business; and do they produce depressions? We have clear evidence that unless this supposed 'over-investment' is accompanied by monetary inflation and consequent wild speculation, followed by the inevitable rise in interest rates and a severe contraction of credit, the effect is never serious, and readjustment not at all difficult. The crisis of 1929 was surely not due to 'over-investment.' And the ensuing depression might have been as short lived as the crisis of 1907 had there been no such tremendous monetary contraction. There seems little question that all these ideas and theories under view belong to a flimsy construct of the imagination.

THE PUBLIC UTILITY OF PROFITS

I hope that no teacher . . . will ever give any countenance to the pernicious belief that steady and honest service in satisfying the demand of the people for the necessaries and conveniences of life is something to be ashamed of because it is profitable. The modern workman and the modern trader can practise virtue as well as a Greek philosopher, a medieval begging friar, or a twentieth-century social reformer.

—EDWIN CANNAN: *Economica;* 1926

But it clearly does follow from the fact that the sole initiative in industry resides in the employing class, that it is exceedingly important that profits should be kept up to the point to encourage the largest production which can be maintained without repletion.

The margin of profit in ordinary business is so small that a reduction in profit . . . cannot fail to tell heavily upon the vitality of the commercial and industrial system.

—FRANCIS A. WALKER: *Money in Relation to Trade and Industry*

Chapter IX

THE PUBLIC UTILITY OF PROFITS

1. *Business organization and production*

It is not labor, as even Ricardo held and as Marx so fanatically believed, that is the 'source of all wealth.' Save in the most indirect way.[1] So long as everything was made by hand this dictum was largely true. But even from the earliest times other factors came into play; for example: organization, the division of labor. As soon as a gang or group could do a job in less time and with less labor than the same number separately, the factor of *organization* came to play a leading rôle. Growing in importance ever since.

Capacity for organization, the ability to get along with other men, the foresight to plan and manage is rare, and paid accordingly. Likewise it is noteworthy that these managers—business executives—are paid more or less in close relation with the size of the business.[2] It is easy to see why. The total of their salaries expressed as a percentage of the net earnings is not large—a matter of 2 or 3 per cent—but obviously the salaries paid on this basis by a corporation with a business of a billion dollars a year would be onerous to another of fifty or a hundred millions. For this reason, a large enterprise can command a higher grade of business talent and capacity than smaller enterprises.[3] This is not always true; boards of directors and owners of enterprises may make mistakes in judgment, quite like ordinary people. Thus much abler executives are occasionally found in smaller enterprises. But not as a rule.

Consider the inevitable effect if it were. If the majority of the competent men were at the head of the smaller companies, the latter would soon take the business away from the larger, and in time their positions would be reversed. This does happen from time to time. Older companies come to be affected with a kind of dry rot. The vigor and foresight that built them up disappear. And this gives the smaller enterprises their opportunity. Whole industries may be affected by a decline in the energy and ability of their managers. Up to ten or twenty years ago the steel industry in the United States and Great Britain was making little progress, measured either in the volume of output or in the quality. But steel makers in other countries like Germany were spending large sums on research and experimentation, and producing new kinds of steel, —high speed tool steel that will hold its cutting edge while it grows red hot; stainless steels, and others. Now we have almost a new industry. Perforce, of the fierce competition in different countries, something similar was going on here. Smaller, more enterprising companies were making sharp inroads on the larger. The latter were forced to adopt the same methods, and to find more capable executives to put these methods into effect. To get these men they had to pay higher salaries.

If 'labor were the creator of all wealth,' how absurd all this would be. And how needless. Who would pay salaries of fifty or a hundred thousand dollars to executives if there were a plentiful supply of capable managers at the wage rates of workingmen? No one. Clearly such salaries are paid because the contribution of these executives is worth their hire.[4] Even if the industries and the companies were owned by the workers themselves, they too, if they understood their business, would pay these same salaries and be glad to have the managers. Why? Simply because their labor, time and effort, competently directed, with better planning and management, would yield a larger return to the worker, than if they selected less able leaders at lower salaries.

The idea that high salaries and bonuses are a 'scandalous' part of an unjust economic system is, I believe, part of a wide misapprehension. The Soviet government in Russia began as a supposedly communistic state, that is, giving approximately an equal income to all. After ten years of effort to bring some order out of chaos, Russia turned a new leaf, and has begun to show the effect in its remarkable industrial growth. Where is the 'communistic state'? On the testimony of Max Eastman and of other competent, first-hand observers, Russia is sadly going the way of all capitalistic flesh: larger and larger salaries to the more competent, bonuses and other inducements to the workers.[5] And which workers? Those who produce more goods! In a word, this very interesting experiment in Russia, begun by theorists, revolutionaries, and dreamers, is taking on the methods and introducing the inequalities of reward to be found in a capitalistic society.[6] What they have today is a scheme of governmental enterprise, of 'state capitalism,' that in method and spirit, in its ruthless demand for product and in inducement to increase output, does not differ in any serious way from the most capably run capitalistic corporation in our highly capitalistic United States.

The system of large rewards to talent for organization and management is clearly not the artificial product of an 'artificial' system. Nor can it be abolished with the stroke of a pen. It lies deep in the most pervasive characteristics of human nature, that is, the natural and universal inequalities in talent and capacity. And exceptional talent must always be rewarded to call forth its best efforts. Else we have to believe that organizers do not contribute to production, and that they are not worth the small share of the total product that is paid them for their services.

What then becomes of the ancient fetish that 'labor is the creator of all wealth?' The simple fact is that the marked increase in production in the last hundred years is not due to an increase in the personal 'efficiency' of labor. The average number of hours of work has been reduced from twelve and fourteen per day a century ago to seven or eight per day in our time. The variety of skills, if not the quality of skill, required of the laborer today is actually much less than that of the artisan of a century ago. Much of the work in modern industry requires a greater degree of ability than was ever required before. This is particularly true of the makers and designers of machines. But the ordinary workingman, even one using delicate and expensive machinery, is seldom required to contribute more than a moderate amount of concentration and dexterity.

2.   *Surplus value and profits*

This doctrine that labor is the creator of all wealth was the foundation upon which Karl Marx built his celebrated theory of surplus value.[7] The value of a 'good,' he held, is determined by the quantity of socially necessary labor required for its production. In purchasing this labor, the business man does not pay the full value of the product; that is, wages are less than the value produced. The difference is the 'surplus value' which constitutes the income of the capitalist and the business man. Strange that this theory should have held the field so long; seductive even to writers not of socialistic or communistic leanings. The chief basis of attack on the taking of profits by business enterprise. Perfectly true that in calculating the price of a good the producer adds his profit to the wages he pays, and also the cost of his materials. This no sane writer would deny. The chief error seems to be that they imagine that these profits are enormous, and form a large part of the final cost to the consumer. The facts are the reverse.

A remarkable statement, issued not long ago, by what was for a long time the largest corporation on earth: After nearly forty years of its rather placid existence, we have forgotten the tremendous stir aroused by the formation of the United States Steel Corporation, the first 'billion dollar company' in existence. A storm of protest, and violent attacks in Congress and out; not to mention the derisive howls of joy from the followers of Marx, who saw therein the long awaited verification of his prophecy, of the steady concentration of wealth and industry into one vast tyranny. Came the ancient and sempiternal tirades against 'monopoly,' the deathless slogan of the demagogue from the beginning of organized industry.

Reflect then upon the consolidated statement for a ten year period, of 1928 to 1938, of this monster that had 'threatened the very foundations of society.' [8] This period was representative of the steel industry for the past forty years; it included three years of boom, three of extreme depression, and four of about average business. What do we find? In these ten years, the United States Steel Corporation received from its customers just under seven billion dollars. Where did all this money go? A total of three billions in wages and salaries, over 40 per cent; an unusually high percentage. But it is to be recalled that the United States Steel Corporation is a typical, 'vertical' combination, that it produces most of its own raw materials, and transports these in its own ships and railways. For this reason, wage payments were a much larger share of the product than in most manufacturing enterprises.

What of the remainder? 'Goods and services' purchased from others forms another two and one-half billions, more than one-third of the total receipts. Taxes, depreciation, and depletion (the corporation is the largest iron mining enterprise in the world) took nearly one billion more. Leaving a final net income 472 million. Slightly more than 6⅔ per cent of the total receipts, and less than 3 per cent of its capital assets. Actually the company paid out in

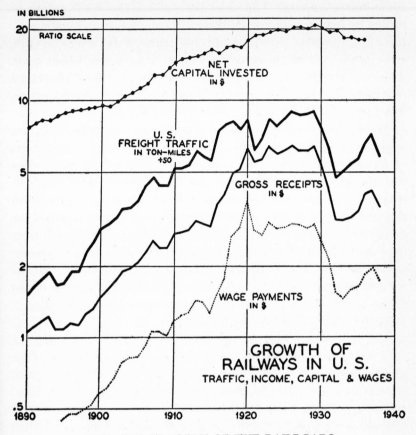

IN BILLIONS

20 — RATIO SCALE

NET
CAPITAL INVESTED
IN $

10

U. S.
FREIGHT TRAFFIC
IN TON-MILES
+50

5

GROSS RECEIPTS
IN $

2

WAGE PAYMENTS
IN $

1

GROWTH OF
RAILWAYS IN U. S.
TRAFFIC, INCOME, CAPITAL & WAGES

.5
1890   1900   1910   1920   1930   1940

XVII. THE TRAGEDY OF THE RAILROADS

For the first half of the last hundred years the expansion of the railroads over a continent was the most spectacular economic event in the history of any country. Beginning a little late, the railways of the United States soon so far surpassed those of any other country that up to recently our railway traffic, like our wealth and income, exceeded that of the next 6 or 8 largest countries combined. An extraordinary development. But when this remarkable growth is plotted over the full period, it will be seen that beginning some 30 years ago this wonderful growth began to abate. Chiefly, the deadly influence of governmental interference and domination. Result, most of our railway systems in the last 20 years have gone bankrupt and have had to be reorganized, with immense losses to their owners. They provided the cheapest transport of goods in the history of the world and performed a magnificent service; this was their reward. It will be seen how deeply the working man has been affected by this process of strangulation, the wage payments by the railroads having reached a peak in 1920, and steadily declining since. A tragic example of the effects of economic ignorance and insanity.

dividends a little more than this, drawing to the extent of 13 million on the surplus of previous years.

What a menace! One out of every sixteen dollars of receipts taken as profits and paid out to the owners of the corporation, who numbered a quarter of a million stockholders. The ancient story. If *all* profits had been wiped out, who save the stockholders would have known the difference? The public, the fifty millions gainfully employed? Or even the employees of this 'monstrous' monopoly?

The instance here considered is unusual, because practically from its inception the United States Steel Corporation has had no increase in its nominal capital. Almost all the huge outlay upon improvements and new construction, amounting to hundreds of millions of dollars, has been financed from the company's earnings. And this has represented no large present gain to the owners. Astonishing that in the last four years the average market value of the capital stock of the United States Steel Corporation was nearly that of 1902 in the first year of its existence. While the value of the product has risen steadily.

Further: Much ado over the high salaries paid by our large corporations, and many believe that these form a large proportion of the total of wages and salaries. These two items are not reported separately by the United States Steel Corporation, but several of our largest corporations published such details. The figures disclose that all payments in salaries of five thousand dollars and over, amount to only 3 or 4 per cent of the total of wages and salaries combined. And in the item of salaries is included the payment of many clerical workers, whose average salary is less than the average wage. Further, in these corporations the average wage of the worker was approximately the same as the average remuneration in both wages and salaries, including the salaries above five thousand dollars. The high salaries of corporate officers are as insignificant a part of this total, as dividends are of the total income of corporations. If all the high salaries were abolished, and the sum diverted to increase the pay envelopes of the workers, they would scarcely notice the difference.

3. *Profits are self-regulating*

Often we meet with the phrase 'outrageous' profits, or 'scandalous' monopoly, favorite themes of the reformatory mind. As far back as we possess any detailed history, there have been laws against usury, laws to limit prices (therefore profits), laws to curb monopolies, laws against combinations in 'restraint of trade.' Probably in every age and every country that has had written laws; that is, in the last four thousand years, and for aught we know thousands of years before.[9] Why this deep-rooted tendency? As if high profits were not only harmful, but also 'wrong'; a species of robbery. And so we find in governments of all ages and in our own United States, hundreds of enactments and proposals with this aim. Easy to see that profits can never long be unduly high; that they are naturally self-regulating, and can never for any length of time much exceed the going rate of interest.

Always we find the highest rates of nominal profits and of interest in the poorest countries, and especially in times when capital is scarce and the rewards of adventure large.[10] Even in England, as late as the seventeenth century, something like 17 per cent was the expected rate of return in maritime enterprise, just as now 7 per cent or less would be the expected net return. Further, that nominal profits are highest where wages and other incomes are lowest. A seeming paradox; but high profits are usually associated with high risks. In Great Britain in the seventeenth century the accumulated capital was relatively small, despite the high nominal profits. Great Britain was then not a rich country. As capital slowly accumulated and the risks of adventure declined, so also the rate of profit. Consequently, in the last half century or more, interest rates in Great Britain have been the lowest in the world. Given safety, stability, freedom from piracy and, it may be added, seizure of profits by unscrupulous governments, capital will accumulate rapidly, and the rate of interest and profit will fall.[11]

Very high profits, like high winnings in gambling, usually bring their own retribution. Men who grow suddenly rich are apt to lose their caution and engage in wild ventures, in which much of their capital is lost. But high profits are soon returned to labor, because the only way that capital can be profitably utilized, ultimately, is in the employment of labor. And if high profits are not dissipated in unprofitable ventures, the resulting increase in savings will bring about a fall in the interest rate. This process is accelerated whenever a particular industry, as the motor car or electric refrigerator, shows great promise; always a rush to engage in the new field.

Because of this self-limiting nature of profits, and because they are used to employ labor in expanding enterprise, it is difficult to understand the violent emotions aroused when a well-run business earns profits of 10 per cent rather than the usual 5.[12] And when these profits are earned by a huge business that dominates the industry, the popular resentment is easily aroused. As, for example, in the control of the aluminium industry by the late Mr. Mellon and his associates. Undoubtedly they made large profits, but not at the expense of the public. When these men took over the patents of an Ohio youngster this metal was selling for around $1.50 per pound. After thirty years of as near a monopoly as any industry of our day, the price of aluminium was around nine cents per pound. In their efforts to 'mulct' the consuming public these 'high binders' and 'thieves,' as they were freely called, reduced the price of the utensils made from aluminium by more than 90 per cent; meanwhile, as noted, paying the clever young man who invented the process a trifle of twenty-three million dollars in royalties.[13]

I do not know whether this is a typical monopoly, though I suspect that it is fairly representative. If we imagine that 'monopolies' are a means of gouging the public to make outrageous profits, why, in this instance and in almost every other, were prices steadily reduced? The obvious answer is to get more business, so as to make more aggregate profit. Why, for example, was it advantageous to Henry Ford, and to other makers of motor cars to reduce their prices to the lowest possible? Why did Ford make perhaps ten times the aggregate profits of all the companies manufacturing high-priced cars? Because he turned back to the public the greater part of the benefit of the increased efficiency resulting from his large scale production. For a time Henry Ford had almost as absolute a monopoly in the motor industry as the Mellons had in aluminium. Although his net realized profits were near to a billion dollars in thirty years, and that from an initial capital of $29,000, the public gained as much and more from the fine cars he sold at an astonishingly low price. And it should be added that Ford paid the highest wages in the automobile industry.

Perhaps it will be said that a distinction should be made between

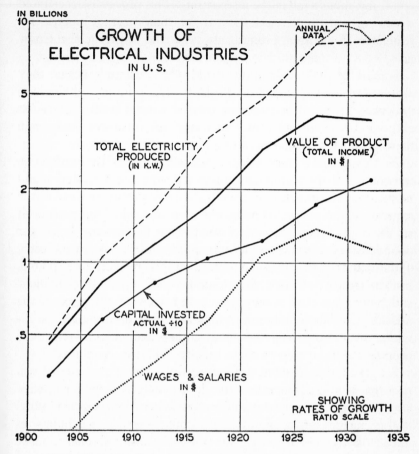

IN BILLIONS

GROWTH OF
ELECTRICAL INDUSTRIES
IN U. S.

ANNUAL DATA

TOTAL ELECTRICITY
PRODUCED
(IN K.W.)

VALUE OF PRODUCT
(TOTAL INCOME)
IN $

CAPITAL INVESTED
ACTUAL ÷10
IN $

WAGES & SALARIES
IN $

SHOWING
RATES OF GROWTH
RATIO SCALE

XVIII. THE PRODIGIOUS GROWTH OF ELECTRIC POWER

The spectacular advance in the use of electricity was one of the miracles of the nineteenth century, but it is in our own time that electricity has entered so intimately into our daily lives, and likewise into almost every kind of industry. The production of electric power, as shown in a preceding chart, has grown at an amazing rate. But under what influence? A glance at the chart shows the invariable answer—increase of product through increase in the capital invested. No other possible way. And this capital supply is derived very largely from the profits in the industry itself. Relatively little outside capital. This capital is invested in giant power stations and endless transmission lines, which cannot be built out of air. Yet forty-odd governmental commissions are now engaged in an effort to curtail the profits of this industry in order that further improvement and further reduction in the cost of electricity may not take place. It is a singular spectacle, especially in the light of the tragedy depicted in the preceding chart.

'good' and 'bad' trusts. The distinction seems idle. From the point of view of general benefits, there are no 'bad' trusts. Consider the Standard Oil Company, for many years the target of the trust-busters, and of none too savory fame. Mr. Rockefeller made a great fortune, selling oil all over the world. He acquired a virtual monopoly. But he did this by making better and cheaper oil than his competitors. True that his competition was ruthless; but the public was and is the ultimate beneficiary, not only in lower prices and better product, but in other ways.

To be sure the profits of Mr. Rockefeller and Mr. Ford were unusual. But to what were these profits devoted? To vain or ostentatious expenditures by Mr. Ford or Mr. Rockefeller? Scarcely 2 per cent for personal expenditures of any kind. The monopoly profits, carefully and wisely invested, went to the increase of the hundred billions or more of active capital employed in the industry of the country, to increase the product per worker, to raise the general standard of living. In addition, much of Mr. Rockefeller's profits were devoted to educational and scientific purposes; three quarters of a billion dollars, to lasting benefit to all mankind.

It has been duly noted that the inventions and technical improvements in the equipment used in industry require a continually increasing investment per worker. In manufacturing, this investment has risen steadily, from a few hundred dollars per worker a hundred years ago, to approximately ten thousand dollars per worker. No one imagines that an employer would buy new machinery if it did not pay. But it is only by providing this additional or improved equipment that the product per worker can be increased to any extent. A current advertisement depicts an extraordinary new machine for rolling steel in a Cleveland steel works. This will turn out a sheet of steel eight feet wide at the rate of twenty-five *miles* an hour. One hundred years ago there was no rolling machine. This mechanism is the result of a long course of inventions and improvements, made by many talented and highly skilled individuals. But unless adequate funds are available for building such equipment, there could be no means of using it.

The same in every line of industry. Take, for example, a modern Leviathan, the 'Queen Mary' or the 'Normandie.' The men who man them, and the laborers who worked on their construction, possess no higher efficiency than those of fifty or one hundred years ago. If the cost of transportation on such ships is lower, and the quality of transportation higher, it is due entirely to the huge investment, rising to sixty or seventy million dollars for a single vessel. Without such investment, modern ocean transport would be impossible.

Or consider a modern printing press, turning out hundreds of thousands of printed papers per hour, at a speed almost terrifying to watch. Almost inconceivable that a substance like paper can be whirled through monstrous rollers with such rapidity and not be torn to shreds. These printing presses are again the product not of the worker but of inventive talent. Compare their output with that of an ancient hand press such as may be found in the museums. It is the *investment* in these machines that makes it possible to sell a modern newspaper of forty or fifty pages for two or three cents.

The use of such equipment, whether in steel, in transportation, or in publishing, is possible only if sufficient capital is available for its purchase. Why should additional capital at times be so difficult to obtain in so rich a country as the United States? Simply because new capital for industry is derived almost wholly from profits, and these profits, despite popular impression, are often low, and limited. If savings were large, capital would be far cheaper. In point of fact, the average rate of interest over a long period has not materially changed in the last half century. But at times sharply dear.[14] If capital savings were greater, more up-to-date machinery would be employed. But profits in industry are restricted by intense competition. The constant aim of every manufacturer is to produce at a lower cost than his competitior in order to sell a larger quantity of goods.

So also the rate of improvement in machinery, the cost of developing and installing new inventions, the discovery of new processes, impose a sharp limitation upon the rate of investment. Industry as a whole cannot advance much faster than this rate of improvement. The whole process, therefore, is interlinked in such complete fashion that we have here, in a real sense, a nearly automatic mechanism. The very nature of competition restricts business profits; this limits savings; and the rate of savings and technical achievement limits the fund for reproductive capital. This reproductive capital then determines real income and rate of growth in production.

Another aspect of profits as a factor in industrial progress. Unless business enterprises can make profits they have no inducement to invest in new equipment.[15] There are always industries that can make use of new equipment, but often their profits are so small they do not have sufficient credit to borrow the necessary funds on acceptable terms. The railroads have been a notable example. A large proportion of their locomotives are said to be twenty years out-of-date. The new equipment would result in lowered operating costs. There is an instance where a company replaced fifty outworn locomotives with seven of the modern type. Such new equipment could be used effectively by nearly all the railways. But their profits are so small and uncertain, they cannot secure the needed capital. We here have a typical instance of the necessity of adequate profits to induce enterprises to invest, and lenders to provide the funds at a satisfactory rate of interest.

Further, unless profits are sufficiently high to make ownership of stocks and bonds both desirable and secure, the cost of new capital will be so high that business enterprises will be unable to issue new securities. Finally, with inadequate profits the principal of savings for use in industry will be depleted. Because profits stimulate production and assure economic progress, it may be doubted whether any policy that has in view the limitation of profits, whether for the purpose of diminishing prices or for increasing wages, can be justified. We may go further and say that the one and only certain method of increasing real wages for all working men is to maintain this adequate level of profits.

THE SOLE BASIS FOR HIGH WAGES

The wages of a working man are ultimately coincident with what he produces, after the deduction of rent, taxes, and the interest of capital.

—W. S. Jevons: *Theory of Political Economy*

The richer the world is in capital, the richer the worker is in productive power. Into this region of thought we may not now go; but what we may properly note is that at every point in the period of growing wealth, labor will find its natural rate of pay fixed by the law that we have now before us. Fifty years hence wages will be higher than they are to-day; but they will be fixed by the final productivity of labor in that later and more fruitful industrial state.

—J. B. Clark: *The Distribution of Wealth; 1891*

FUNDAMENTALS

1. All material welfare depends upon high productivity.

2. Our present industrial system in the United States is the most efficient that the world has ever known.

3. A ten-year normal increase in per capita production under our present system represents a greater gain for the worker than any that is possible as the result of any conceivable redistribution of profits.

4. This normal increase in production can only go forward with ample investments in new productive equipment and with the assurance of a living wage for such investments.

—M. C. Rorty: *Problems in Current Economics*

CHAPTER X

THE SOLE BASIS FOR HIGH WAGES

1. *Why the high wages characteristic of the United States?*

ADAM SMITH ended his 7-year task of writing his "Wealth of Nations" in the year the American colonies declared their Independence. Towards the end of his work, he paid a visit to London and there met the celebrated Dr. Franklin, 'greatest American.' Adam Smith formed therewith a firm friendship, which probably accounts for his accurate knowledge of economic conditions in the Colonies, better known to Franklin, perhaps, than any other American then living. And in the first chapter of this celebrated work is to be found this interesting survey of wages in the Colonies:

"It is not the actual greatness of national weath, but its *continual increase*, which occasions *a rise in the wages* of labour. It is not, accordingly, in the richest countries, but in the most thriving, or in those which are growing rich the fastest, that the wages of labour are highest. England is certainly, in the present times, a much richer country than any part of North America. The wages of labour, however, are much higher in North America than in any part of England. In the province of New York, common labourers earn (1773) three shillings and sixpence currency, equal to two shillings sterling, a day; ship carpenters, ten shillings and sixpence currency, with a pint of rum worth sixpence sterling, equal in all to six shillings and sixpence sterling; house carpenters and bricklayers, eight shillings currency, equal to four shillings and sixpence sterling; journeymen tailors, five shillings currency, equal to about two shillings and tenpence sterling. These prices are all above the London price; and wages are said to be as high in the other colonies as in New York. The price of provisions is everywhere in North America much lower than in England. A dearth has never been known there. In the worst seasons, they have always had a sufficiency for themselves, though less for exportation. If the money price of labour, therefore, be higher than it is anywhere in the mother country, its real price, the real command of the necessaries and conveniences of life which it conveys to the labourer, must be higher in a still greater proportion.

"The liberal reward of labour as it is the necessary effect so it is the natural symptom of increasing national wealth. . . .

"But though North America is not yet so rich as England, it is much more thriving, and advancing with much greater rapidity to the further acquisition of riches."

To the 'liberal reward of labour' two factors especially contributed. One was the abundance of free and fairly fertile land; the other was 3,000 miles of perilous ocean and slow travel.

The land in general was to be had almost for the taking. And so these hardy settlers swarmed up the rivers, the only available means then of transportation for themselves or for their produce. They were for the most part a rugged and daring type who were not afraid of hard work. Also not inclined to work for others when there was such wide opportunity to carve out a home for themselves.

The obvious result was that he who wished to employ labor had to pay what was for the time counted as high wages. Labor was in demand. This fact was likewise a stimulant to large families which were characteristic of this early period; families of 8, 10 or more, were not uncommon. And in general they throve. The death rate was high, but the hardy survived. As a result the colonies grew rapidly from the beginning, the population doubling about once in 20 or 25 years, two or three times the rate of increase for example in Great Britain. Vigorous boys, and girls as well, were an immense help at harvest time and in other ways. Immigration was small; it was not until many years later when the United States had become a nation of many millions, new methods of transportation had been found, that the foreign element was of much importance. Even nearly up to our Civil War, the population of the country was highly indigenous.

There was a corresponding demand for cloth and household goods. Not always was it homespun or homemade. There was a strong protective barrier for home production. With the long sea voyage, the importation of goods from England was difficult. On the other hand, so was the export of American products, explaining why the international trade of America has always been relatively small. This was naturally a high incentive to home industries; and here was yet another element of the large demand for labor.

In general, with a corresponding effect upon wages. Good wages, in their turn, afforded a rising demand for produce and for such 'manu-factures,' for machinery of any kind was scant. This in turn gave early a strong incentive for labor saving inventions. As these multiplied the product was increased, the profits were good, and wages accordingly steadily rose. From a very early time the consumptive demand was relatively high.

Easy to see that all this meant a corresponding demand for capital, and a high rate of interest. When small amounts could command ten or twelve per cent there was a forceful impetus to saving, far greater than when this rate had fallen to five or six per cent. So we find our leading philosophers early preaching the high rewards of thrift; and the terse and vivid writings of 'Poor Richard's Almanack' were eagerly read, and had a very definite effect.

So we find early in America high rates of interest, a high rate of saving, and high rates of wages all going hand in hand. In a way each stimulated the other. And very soon, likewise, the invention and use of machinery, with a corresponding increase in the product per worker.

These were the factors that promoted the rapid growth of the colonies, and then of the new nation, and not its imaginary 'great natural resources.' And not large immigration, for that was small as compared with the growth of the population. Equally there was little influx of foreign capital, some, but not much. It was not merely an indigenous population, but a highly indigenous industry that laid the foundation for the future greatness of the United States.

There was an abundant supply of wood for fuel and other uses. Therefore the use of coal and the expansion of the coal mines was in the beginning dilatory. So too, in large part, the iron mines. For the most part the iron industry was dependent upon the bogs and scattered small deposits. It was late before the enormous wealth of the country in coal and iron began to be disclosed, and utilized. With a plentiful supply of excellent timber, the colonies were early ship builders and ships were needed as the only practical form of transportation. Roads were very few. Travel was mainly by horseback and the local movement of goods was relatively slight. But the river and coast-wise trade, and later ocean transport, was vigorously extended. And so with other industries.

The invention of the cotton gin by a Connecticut Yankee gave a powerful stimulus to the production of this comparatively new fiber; but it is extraordinary that almost from the beginning the evolution of the cotton spinning industry was in the North, not in the South. A more driving and energetic people. The early profits of the plantations first from tobacco and later from cotton, brought affluence to the large land holders of the South, but the type and spirit of capitalism prevalent in that land did not readily lend itself to the rapid development of manufacturing and trade. And it is always from these latter that wealth and capital rapidly accumulate. The result was that even with a smaller population in the earlier periods, the growth of industry was far more prominent in the Northern states. In colonial days and up to the time of the first census, Virginia was the most populous and the richest of the colonies. But the industrial development of the next 50 years wrought deep and revolutionary change; far more to the North than to the South. And so we find the first banks, the earliest signs of rising industry, were developed, rather than in the South, in thrifty New England and in New York and in Pennsylvania.

High wages are never characteristic of a typically agricultural population; these arrive where industry can be more concentrated, production intensified, and commerce and trade more markedly developed.

2. *Capital and wages*

There is a widespread belief, not only among workers, but also among many others, that the average rate of wages is somehow the result of 'custom,' or 'bargaining power,' or similar factors: always with a nod to the 'cost of living,' and the like. Therefore, that a higher level of wages could be brought about by laws, through setting a higher customary standard, or by trade unions, through increasing the 'bargaining power' of labor![1]

The thesis presented in this volume is that the average wage in any country at any time is, to borrow a Pavlovian phrase, a strictly conditioned reflex; that neither the capitalist nor the employer, the wage earner or the labor union, sentiment or law, has anything to do with fixing this wage; that it is determined by definite measurable factors: the average product per worker, which in turn is rigorously determined by the amount of capital employed in industry, the degree of mechanization of production, and the number of hours worked.[2]

Neither law, nor custom, nor 'bargaining power' can affect money wages; with an artificial level of money wages, prices will also be higher, and the 'cost of living,' and the average real wage

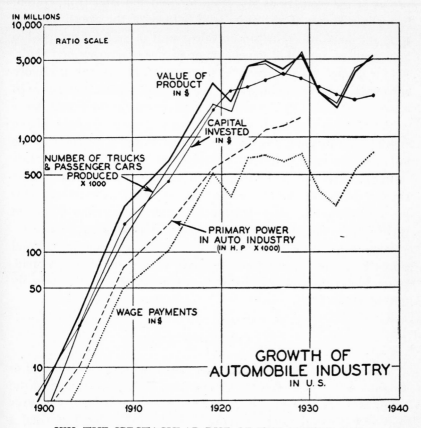

IN MILLIONS
10,000

RATIO SCALE

5,000

VALUE OF
PRODUCT
IN $

CAPITAL
INVESTED
IN $

1,000

NUMBER OF TRUCKS
& PASSENGER CARS
PRODUCED
X 1000

500

PRIMARY POWER
IN AUTO INDUSTRY
(IN H. P X 1000)

100

50

WAGE PAYMENTS
IN $

GROWTH OF
AUTOMOBILE INDUSTRY
IN U. S.

10

1900   1910   1920   1930   1940

XIX. THE SPECTACULAR RISE OF THE MOTOR CAR

If in 1900 anyone had predicted that in the next forty years a new form of transportation would repeat the prodigious growth of the railways from 1840 to 1890, he would probably have been regarded as a dreamer. It is quite amazing to find that in both these two instances the rate of increase was nearly identical. Yet in 1900 the railways of the United States were the finest and the most extensive in the world, and in addition thereto there had been a great growth of electric trolley systems and the like. Today the trolley systems are largely grass-grown, and the total capital invested in motor cars—in their manufacture and upkeep—is probably greater than the total in railways. A quite incredible feat. A precise example of the capitalistic method working without restraint. No herds of governmental officials standing about to fix prices or limit profits. And those profits in the motor car industry were huge, beyond that of any other industry almost in this period. Result, a nearly perfect picture of an industry creating itself; it had very little outside capital until later years; its capital was derived almost wholly from profits.

for the same volume of employment will thus remain the same. Further, an arbitrary increase in money wages may have an adverse effect on employment, and thus diminish the real income of the working class.[3]

If the prevalent illusions regarding wages had any factual basis, if the average wage were even in slight degree a matter of law, volition or custom, we should not find the high correlation that exists between the wages paid and the determining factors: the amount of capital employed in industry and the degree of technical development. This correlation is proof that these factors determine the average wage so closely that, given certain details as to the wealth and income per capita of a country, and the amount of machinery employed in industry, one could easily estimate the average wages paid. And this would probably hold for any country, at any stage of its industrial development.[4]

This thesis seems borne out by the industrial history of the American colonies, as well as by later days. In early times, anything in the way of manufactured goods or articles were relatively dear, because most of them were made in England. Not many skilled artisans came from the mother country to the wilds of America. Transport was extremely slow—six weeks was a fast voyage—and charges were correspondingly high. All these factors conspired to develop an economy in which high wages and high prices were the rule.

The inevitable result: the price of capital—the interest rate—was high. This meant that where capital found employment in America, its rewards were large. And with high profits in business, accumulation not difficult. Yet another factor: the frugality and industry of the people. There were few luxuries and fewer frivolities on which the people of that time could spend much, and habits of thrift were taught and practiced. Capital was thus accumulated, and when new methods of production were introduced, America was in a position to adopt the new devices. There was the will, the incentive, the capital, and the spirit of enterprise.

The beginnings were small. Already in late colonial days a considerable industry had developed, notably the making of iron.[6] But the needful capital of American industry was predominantly of domestic origin. An error to believe England was a large investor in America in the early nineteenth century. But opportunities here for business venture, under the prevailing conditions of a scarcity of goods, high prices, high profits, and high wages, soon had the expected effect. And it is to this, rather than to our fabled 'natural resources,' that the prodigious industrial development which followed was due.[7] A fortunate combination of economic conditions which more or less continued until the new spirit of emotional humanitarianism.

Now very remarkable to find that when statistics were first gathered on these matters, about a century ago, the United States already ranked high in the amount of capital investment per worker. The indissoluble combination of high profits and rapid capital accumulation were in evidence; likewise the steady increase in wages. Today this capital investment per worker the highest in the world.

This association of capital investment and average wages is too strongly in evidence to imagine it merely fortuitous. A direct relation of cause and effect. Almost conclusive proof afforded by the fact that even in the present century this high rate of industrial development and increase in wages continued nearly without a break. The same rate of increase in the product per worker that had prevailed in the preceding century continued in the new—until 1930.[8] Then, for the first time in our industrial history, this magical era came to a prolonged standstill.

This close relation between capital and the rate of wages seems to hold for all countries for which we possess the requisite data. But not always true of different industries in the same country. There is, nevertheless, a strong tendency for those with large capital investment per worker to pay higher wages than industries with less. In steel, motor cars, chemicals, meat packing, and in other highly capitalized industries, wages will be higher than in agriculture, for example, and in other industries with comparatively little capital. The reason is manifest.

3. *High wages and prosperity*

We now have ample statistical evidence to establish the following propositions:

1. Taken broadly, real wages are determined by the product per worker, and are a fairly fixed share of the value of the product. Unless, then, the product can be increased, the level of real wages cannot.

2. The product per worker is determined in the long run by the capital investment per worker, which makes possible the use of new machinery, new processes, and new methods of production.

3. The rate of growth of capital investment and of aggregate product has been approximately the same in this country for a century or more, indicating that an increase in product is dependent on the provision of additional capital.

4. The rate of growth of total wages and of total product has been nearly the same, so that over long periods the share of the product going to labor has remained nearly constant.

If these propositions are true, it follows that the rate of wages paid by employers is fixed automatically, and to all intents cannot be materially altered by any arbitrary action of either the employer or the employed. To many it will seem a paradox that neither the hard-fisted nor the philanthropic employer, neither the militant laborer nor the meek, has any material influence upon the average real wage paid and received.[9] Or that strikes and lockouts are rarely of the slightest avail. Almost always an enormous loss. They may at times correct inequalities between different industries; but they can never affect the real wage for the country as a whole.

Suppose, for example, that Henry Ford, when he first introduced the five dollars a day minimum in his factory, had found that his costs had risen so as to wipe out all profit. How long could he have continued in business? Only so long as he could borrow money; and if this had continued he would inevitably have been ruined.

If the tale is true, Henry Ford had little to do with this unique adventure, save to give the idea his approval. It originated, it is said, in a conference, and was adopted for quite another reason than the familiar one. Just at that time the motor car business was having a tremendous boom. Orders were piling up that could not be filled. Impossible at the time to expand the plant quickly. Some one hit upon the idea that to boost the wage rate sharply would draw the best workmen from the other motor car factories, and increase the output. This it did, according to the account, by something like 20 per cent. And 20 per cent was about the average rate of increase in Ford's wages. In this instance, the higher wages paid for themselves in increased 'efficiency' and in increased product per worker.

In the long run, this is the sole way in which there can be any increase in wages in the country as a whole. It is easy to say that higher wages raise 'buying power' and therefore increase consumption. But this is as absurd as to think one can lift one's self by his boot straps. If wages were increased all around, this would raise all costs of production, and so the price of everything that workingmen buy; there would be no increase in real wages. Prosperity and high wages cannot come by decree or by Major Douglas schemes and the like, as the countless fiat-money enthusiasts imagine. Nor can we agree with the vociferous group who insist on the necessity of high wages 'to avoid depression.' The foundation is the ineradicable belief that profits are a large part of the income produced by industry; and that the owners of industry, the rich 3 per cent, or the 'Sixty Families,' absorb much that might otherwise go to the 'workers.' From this they conclude that the workers do not receive enough in wages to purchase the goods they produce; hence periodical crises resulting from the poverty of the masses.[10]

If the net realized profits of industry, taken over a period including good years and bad, do not amount to much more than 5 per cent of the total national income, how could complete extinction of profits, by adding them to wages, increase the incomes of the wage earners by more than 8 or 10 per cent? With all the fateful consequences.

All this seems scarcely to need reiteration. Nevertheless, it is amazing to find that many believe that by some kind of hocus-pocus higher wages could be paid and consumption thereby increased. They forget that every business man is endeavoring to make profits, and to make all he can; that if he can increase his sales he will pay the highest wages required to get the necessary labor. Equally true that the employer will try to pay the lowest possible wage; and nevertheless will have to pay the highest wage possible at any given time, for no other reason than to increase his output and profits to the utmost. So, if the whole process of wages and employment is thus immutably fixed, it is not surprising to find that throughout the period for which we have trustworthy information, the proportion of industrial income paid out as wages has shown little change, and that very slowly.

The national income is simply the money value of the national product. The product per worker in the United States, as shown at decennial intervals during the last century, has increased at approximately 2 per cent per annum. Over this same period, wages have tended to increase at a rate slightly below this, about 1½ per annum. The explanation of this difference seems to be as follows.

The amount of capital invested in industry, for example in manufacturing, has tended to increase a little faster than the physical product. If wages had risen at just the same rate as the product per worker, it would follow that the rate of profit in industry would have decreased steadily. Actually, it seems to have been in the last century remarkably constant. And this was possible because wages have risen slightly less than output.

It seems clear, then, that the fixing of wages is a determinate process, not subject to the will either of the employers or the employed. It is possible, of course, to raise or lower the differences in wages between industries. But a rise in one industry must be at the expense of workers in other industries, who will pay higher prices for the goods they consume. Further, a general rise in wages, at the expense of profits, would soon reduce the volume of employment and thus diminish the total income of wage earners. Therefore illusory to believe that such a general rise is possible without destroying the mechanism of economic progress. Nor is it possible to change even relative wages without setting up disturbances in the economic system.[11] Differences in wages are usually the result of differences in ability, skill, training and education. In all ages, and in all countries for which we have any records, we find approximately the same differences in wages among the various occupations. The wage 'scale' has remained curiously fixed; and this undoubtedly is because the distribution of complex abilities has remained unchanged. We must conclude from this that the automatic determination of wages by competition alone can result in a stable wage system, insuring workers a share in economic progress while maintaining the necessary expansion in the capital supply.

4.   The rôle of labor unions

If this conclusion is well grounded, it may then be asked: what utility can labor unions have? Their influence upon the average rate of wages is for the most part nil. What workers in one industry may force from their employers is paid for by all other workers in the increased price of these particular products. But the effect of labor unions upon industry may be disastrous. Even before the war England and Germany seem to have reached a point approaching industrial stagnation; that is to say, the increase in the product per worker in these countries in the last quarter of a century has been

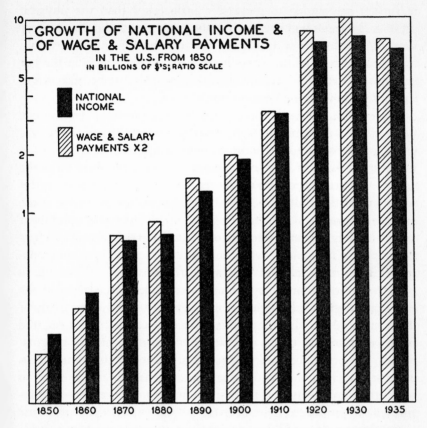

GROWTH OF NATIONAL INCOME &
OF WAGE & SALARY PAYMENTS
IN THE U.S. FROM 1850
IN BILLIONS OF $'S; RATIO SCALE

NATIONAL
INCOME

WAGE & SALARY
PAYMENTS X2

1850 1860 1870 1880 1890 1900 1910 1920 1930 1935

XX. NATIONAL INCOME AND WAGE AND SALARY PAYMENTS

Through the eighty years in which trustworthy information is available, it will be seen how close the relation of national income, that is, the well-being of all the population, to wage and salary payments of workers; practically unchanged. Another example of what I have termed the automatic relationships of industry: they are not the result of any individual will or of arbitrary interference by labor unions, but, as noted, inherent in the business structure. And this includes of course the share of capital in industry, as well as wages and the cost of materials. Something that, so far as can be determined, no human agency could materially alter. But the proportion going to capital is so small that if all profits were to be abolished and these amounts were applied to wages and salaries, the increase in the latter would be slight. But at what a cost, alike to the nation and to the workers, for it is solely from profits that the capital for expanding industry, and for employment, comes.

extremely small. This has been obscured by the economic upheavals of the war, and the almost invariable monetary inflations it brought about. But the cause goes beyond these factors, and this is becoming more and more evident. It is these two countries that were the most highly unionized. In this same period, the product per worker in the United States, and the average rate of wages, have risen notably, just as they did in England and in Germany in an earlier time.

The control of industry by labor unions seems to have as its major effect a deadening influence upon enterprise and innovation, and it is to these factors that an increase in product is surely due.[12] The restless drive of business men for greater achievement cannot thrive in an atmosphere of repression. In general, almost from the beginning of the Industrial Revolution, the instinct of the worker has been opposed to innovations; and time after time they have fought bitterly the introduction of labor saving machinery. They see only that machinery replaces workers. Hence their inveterate opposition to new methods and new processes.

Of course the more enlightened labor leaders understand quite well that progressively higher wages depend upon a continued increase in product. But they are powerless because, like the politicians, they are the leaders of a huge number of uninformed minds, with strong prejudices and almost ineradicable beliefs. Hence, just as with politicians, they could not gain power if they were frankly to tell their followers that the union can do no more than correct differentials in wages, and keep in check unintelligent and unscrupulous employers. They are in the power of the crowd spirit; they must follow this crowd spirit. For this reason, labor unions are seldom a constructive factor in economic progress.

When the demands for higher wages are not met, there is usually an attempt to coerce employers through strikes. Apart from the fact that strikes are often accompanied by violence and destruction of valuable property, the interruption of employment must diminish the general wage fund. For during the strike wage earners lose the earnings they would ordinarily have, employers lose the profits on the production they would ordinarily undertake.[13] All this must increase the difficulty of maintaining the capital supply, and not only endangers the future rise in wage rates, but may actually necessitate a reduction. Thus, the principal weapon used by labor to secure its demands must retard the economic factor so essential to their own interests.

It would seem, therefore, that the attempt to raise wages through action of labor unions, particularly when accompanied by strikes, can only work harm. Capital is notoriously timid, and wisely so, for the returns are small and the risks great. Hundreds of millions of capital are lost annually through bad investment, poor management, or the invention of new devices and the discovery of new processes that render equipment obsolete. Unless business men can expect fair profits, they will not undertake new ventures upon which higher wages are so dependent. If unusual profits are realized, a further expansion of industry, increased production per worker and higher wages. When Ferdinand Lassalle made his famous pronouncement of an 'Iron Law' of wages, he spoke wisely, although not well.[14] There is an Iron Law; and it is precisely such a process as I have endeavored to portray. It is not a question of volition, of good will, or of the power of labor. And every effort to interfere with this mechanism has hindered rather than helped.

Nor does it appear that all this would be essentially different under another economic system. We may have state capitalism or private capitalism; but in any event we must have capital and savings. The whole question at issue is which is the superior system. In Russia state capitalism is now being tried on an unparalleled scale. The complete regimentation required under such a system is tyrannical, and it is doubtful whether economic efficiency is possible under tyranny. It has been tried often enough. Freedom, even the limited amount that is possible in modern society, is precious and indispensable, and this includes the opportunity for individual initiative that we call free enterprise. It may be that for a time, under the spell of a kind of religious enthusiasm, the workers will submit to the tyranny of such a regimented economy. But such enthusiasm is not conducive to economic efficiency.

Further, it may be doubted whether a system of state capitalism will bring forward the high types of ability for management characteristic of free enterprise. Political ability and business ability are at wide variance. Under state capitalism, positions depend on political skill; under private capitalism, leadership depends on business ability. Political skill is manifested in winning votes, gaining popular applause, developing and controlling political machines. Business ability is shown by adroit organization of production, by economy in production, by an understanding of market conditions. It seems impossible to entrust industrial leadership to men chosen for politi-

cal rather than business ability without impairing economic efficiency. For this reason, and many others, private capitalism is
superior to state capitalism in the production of goods, and therefore in the promotion of the general well-being.

5. *Protection and wages*

There has been a considerable amount of nonsense written on
both sides of the question whether protection or free trade is more
conducive to a high level of wages. Of course, by putting a heavy
tariff upon a product, for example sugar, a country like the United
States may enable the domestic producers of sugar to pay higher
wages. But this means that these are paid by all the workers and
consumers in the higher price. The sugar duty is, in effect, a compulsory bonus for sugar production, paid by the consumers, en-
abling the industry to pay wages high enough to obtain an adequate labor supply.

For some industries such a bonus may be defended upon long-
term grounds: that it protects an infant industry capable in ma-
turity of producing goods at less than foreign cost. In the United
States this has generally required the development of new machinery and better processes than those used in other countries.
The difficulty with protection is that the artificial stimulation of
industry tends to produce a wage scale so high that the industries
must claim the continuing need of protective tariffs, even when
they cannot be justified on other grounds.

It is evident, however, that there is here no great evil, such as
was so vehemently maintained for a long time by the advocates of
free trade. The proof is that in the United States, where the doctrine of 'protection' has been carried to apogean lengths, many industries once in need of such protection are now able to compete
in world markets. Witness the steady growth of our exports to
other lands of all kinds of machinery. The stimulus to invention
that the introduction of a new industry always generates account
in part for the superiority of American machinery. For most protected industries could not have survived without adopting new
methods and new processes. And the example of innovation in
these industries has been infectious, tending effectively to stimulate
enterprise in every field.

Quite possible that, eventually, the increased mechanization and the lowered costs might have come without 'protection'; but clearly at a slower rate. These protective tariffs have not been the only factor, by any means. I have pointed out that wages were high in the colonies long before we were a nation, owing to the opportunities presented by immense tracts of free and fertile land. Further, that these wages continued to advance a long time before protective tariffs were introduced. From the beginning the United States were among the foremost countries in adopting mechanization. Protective tariffs were merely an adjunct and an aid to what would undoubtedly have taken place sooner or later without them. But the cost of hastening the process through protection was not high, and it seemed well worth incurring.

It must be emphasized that protection, as any other factor in economic progress, can only be significant as it stimulates increased production, increased capital investment, and increased saving. On the whole, protection has had this effect. It stimulated new industries, and diverted this country from undue specialization in agriculture. It helped in converting the country from low income products to high income goods. The higher incomes made possible greater accumulation, and the new industries provided a profitable field for investing the increased savings. This resulted in a further increase in total product, incomes, saving, and investment: the usual process. Finally, the larger profits that unquestionably were made in the protected industries, provided an important source of the very type of savings seeking use in industrial expansion.

In view of these various ways in which protection stimulated the growth of the capital supply, and ultimately production, it cannot be doubted that protective tariffs have been a factor, although scarcely a major factor, in the steady rise in the average rate of wages for American labor.

ALL AS OLD AS DIOCLETIAN

—Rabbi Akiba was wont to say: Everything is given on pledge, and a net is spread for all the living: the shop is open, and the dealer gives credit, and the ledger lies open, and the hand writes, and whosoever wishes to borrow may come and borrow; but the collectors go round continually every day, and exact payment from man whether he wills or not; and they have whereon they can rely in their demand; and the judgment is a judgment of truth; and everything is prepared for the feast.

—From the *Talmud; circa* 30 A.D.

"The natural effort of every individual to better his own condition, when suffered to exert itself with freedom and security, is so powerful a principle that it is, alone, and without any assistance, not only capable of carrying on the society to vealth and prosperity, but of surmounting a hundred impertinent obstructions with which the folly of human laws too often encumbers its operations."

—Adam Smith: *The Wealth of Nations*

Under the compulsory arbitration which socialism would necessitate . . . the regulators, pursuing their personal interests . . . would not be met by the combined resistance of all workers; and their power, unchecked as now by refusals to work save on prescribed terms, would grow and ramify and consolidate until it became irresistible. . . . When from regulation of the workers by the bureaucracy we turn to the bureaucracy itself, and ask how it is to be regulated, there is no satisfactory answer. . . . Under such conditions there must arise a new aristocracy, for the support of which the masses would toil; and which, being consolidated, would wield a power far beyond that of any past aristocracy.

—Herbert Spencer; 1853

CHAPTER XI

ALL AS OLD AS DIOCLETIAN

1. *Interruption of economic progress*

ALTHOUGH growth and progress are a distinctive characteristic of our modern economic society, they do not proceed without interruptions. At least, that has been the experience of the last 150 years. A curious halt or a retardation of economic life, which we call depression.[1] In a sense this depression, when it is merely a decline in the secular rate of growth, is perhaps inevitable. Because growth depends on new inventions, new processes, and other innovations, it must in short periods be somewhat uneven. And if such irregularity is to be termed a business 'cycle,' then perhaps such cycles are an intrinsic part of a progressive economic system.

But if the only type of depression were of this sort—a brief interruption of growth—there would be no reason to be disturbed. The depressions of 1924 and 1927 were of this nature. They involved little more than a slight halt in the rate of growth, with the previous rate of expansion soon resumed. In fact, only the more sensitive indicators of business conditions show these depressions, and such indicators obviously exaggerate the magnitude of the change.

But there are times when the volume of production and trade not only fails to grow at the usual rate, but seriously declines. Such depressions are much less frequent, and even here their magnitudes are scarcely as great as most business indexes show.

This brief statement of the nature of the rise and fall in business activity differs widely from the commonly held view. The very term 'business cycle' usually brings to mind a force operating in the economic system possessing a strong element of regularity, and perhaps inevitability. Something resembling solar and lunar cycles, and cycles of temperature and rainfall.[2] In brief, movements that result from the play of strong natural forces. In the writer's belief, a mistaken view. The term business cycles, although long used—it was common in the last century—gained its wide vogue largely from the admirable work of Wesley C. Mitchell and his associates.[3] As used by him, the term was without objection. It described simply a recurring 'round of events,' as recovery, prosperity, recession, and depression. But used by others as a kind of natural economic process, with a meaning all its own. Full of problems of infinite complexity. Dear to many hearts.

It is characteristic of our minds that they are strongly disinclined to clear-cut conclusions, especially simple ones. Perhaps because we prefer mystery and obscurity, and feel a sense of disillusionment when a simple answer is found. So in most scientific questions. For thousands of years men must have reflected upon the marvelous variety of plants and animals that populate the earth. Why so many? And such incredible variety? Was it simply for the amusement, or to display the ingenuity, of a great Artificer? Yet when Darwin and his followers proposed a very simple and rational explanation of this spectacular variety, there was an almost universal outcry of indignation. Much the same in the field of medicine when Pasteur offered his demonstrations and proofs of the germ origins of disease. So in an earlier day at the revelations of the immensity of geological time. Almost invariably incredulity, if not a strongly emotionalized resistance.

Much the same attitude prevalent toward cycles of depression. They are held to be 'inherent' in the economic system, regular in their recurrence, bewildering in their complexity, and not susceptible of control. And usually this belief is regarded as a justification for doing nothing towards control. If this is the reality, then we must resign ourselves to an irregular and unpredictable recurrence of these serious calamities. If these forces are not controlled, they may, as in the last ten years throughout the world, check human progress, if they do not wreck civilization and bring a return to barbarism. It is the writer's view that the large part of the unrest, the anarchic conditions, the ruthless invasions, and the barbaric butcheries now at flood tide, are fundamentally due to economic ignorance and to primitive economic superstitions.

In our own country, if we had clearly understood that such wild and extreme speculation as that from 1925 to 1929 would bring the disaster we have experienced, would we have hesitated then to exercise reasonable means of control? Hardly any even of the wisest of our statesmen and financiers could foresee such a prostration of industry, to say nothing of the fateful social upheaval, with its strange train of muddled thinking and muddled action.[4] Precisely this ignorance that made these events possible, with their profound repercussions all over the world. But there is no need to take such a passive attitude toward these disturbances because the means are at hand to minimize and even avoid them.

2. *Mild and deep depressions*

For some years it has been evident that our better known business indexes exaggerate the fluctuations in business activity that they are designed to measure.[5] They are based on more sensitive series that distort and magnify the variations in the normal growth of industry and trade. The 'pig iron type,' as I have termed them. The reality is that the bulk of our vast business activity, production, distribution, and trade, goes on in fairly regular fashion, affected very little by the forces that show such violent changes in many business barometers. With this in mind, I constructed a comprehensive index of the volume of production and trade in which production, distribution, and retail trade are given the larger weight, and in which the significance of financial activity is minimized.[6] This index has usually shown much less fluctuation than most other indexes, and affords a close measure of our normal industrial growth. With this we may estimate the deficit of the last ten years.[7]

The cost of the prevailing depression, that has now proceeded for a decade, is so fabulously great that it is difficult to believe. If we define the cost as the real loss through inadequate production, using the 1929 level as a basis for calculation, the accumulated deficiency in production through 1939 was approximately two and a half times the production of 1929. If we estimate the national income for 1929 at $80 billion, a conservative estimate that does not include capital gains, the loss through deficient production in terms of 1929 dollars is nearly $200 billion. But the industry of the country has normally grown in this generation at the rate of slightly less than 4 per cent per annum. Even if we allow a rate of growth of only 3 per cent, it would mean that in 1939 we should be producing goods and services at a level 40 per cent above that of 1929. In terms of 1929 dollars, the national income for 1939 normally would exceed $110 billion. And in each year prior to 1939 we should have been adding steadily to our income, so that after a decade of depression the accumulated deficit of actual production from the normally growing level of production is approximately four times the real income of 1929, or fully $320 billion in terms of 1929 dollars.

Not only has the country lost the income it could have produced in this decade of deep depression, but the effect on its productive capital will never be made good. If we reckon, as seems probable, the normal net realized savings for reproductive industry, that is, for new industrial capital, at the conservative average of $4 billion in '29, then in this decade we should have added to the really active and productive capital of the nation $30 to $40 billion. To gain some idea of what this means, note that this 30 to 40 billion would probably exceed the net realized savings for reproductive capital in the United States for the whole 19th century. It would have meant the addition of at least one-third to the active industrial capital of the nation as it stood in 1929. In reality, in this period there was apparently no net realized gain in active capital, no increase in the nation's productive plant, no increase in the power to produce goods and services. This is a fair statement of what the depression cost this country in one decade. The price of economic ignorance and mistaken judgment.[8]

But it will be asked, if this colossal loss was really due to economic ignorance and to mistaken judgments and policies, how could it have been avoided? Did not both administrations in power during these years do everything they knew to end the depression and to bring about recovery? According to their lights. But the primal effort seemed to be to save the gold standard, rather than to stop the disastrous shrinkage in bank credit. Sending the price level down at the most precipitous rate in forty years. Thereafter a variety of bizarre activities, vast government expenditures, priming the pump, and the like. All fundamentally futile, for they had destroyed *credit*, confidence. Extremely interesting that in many languages the word "credit" has a double significance: The first sense of trust, faith. The second of loaning money—granting credit; as trade credit, and bank credit. Much the same in French: The word "creance" means not only *trust* and *belief*, but also a *debt* and *owing money*. The same in German. The Germanic word *Glaubiger* has two meanings; a *believer*, and a *creditor*.

In the last decennium, in the United States, such an undermining of this faith, trust, confidence, scarcely known in a hundred years. And a corresponding destruction of real credit, bank credit,

DIVISION OF INCOME IN ALL MANUF.
IN U. S. BY CENSUS YEARS FROM 1849

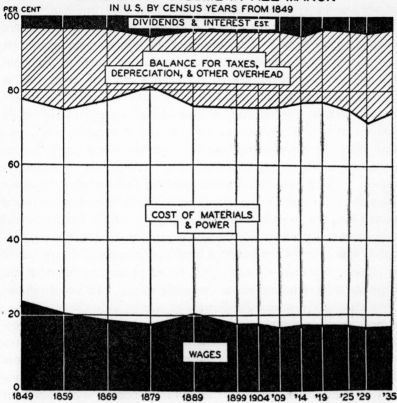

XXI. THE SHARE OF THE WORKERS IN INDUSTRY

We now have had a careful governmental census of our largest single industry—manufactures—giving great detail as to wage payments, profits, and the like, from 1850. Study well the tableau; note how slightly the relationships have changed through all this long period. The share of dividends and interest payments, amazingly small, remains practically the same; the amounts paid in taxes and other overhead, and the cost of materials and power, have increased a little; and as a result the share of wages has had a slight decline. Suggesting strongly that all these relationships are inherent in the nature of business organization and could not well be materially changed. If all profits were abolished, it would mean very little gain to the workers, and a very great loss; for no business can survive without profits, just as no business can continue successfully without paying the highest wages which it can possibly afford. Otherwise, it will lose its best workingmen, and its product will suffer.

of unexampled magnitude. In two years, 1930–32, we had a reduction of more than $15 billion of bank credit, one-third of this 'life-blood' of commerce and trade. More than one-half of the banks of the country were unable to continue normal operations, many actually failing. The whole credit structure collapsed.[9] It was not only impossible to secure loans, but even to maintain loans that had been considered perfectly sound. In panic, and in what they felt to be self-protection, the banks were forced to call loans or to refuse credit even to their best customers. Hundreds of business enterprises, some of them extremely important, went to the wall. The physical volume of production and trade fell in greater proportion than in any previous depression in our history.

If in 1930 or 1931 it had been proposed deliberately to destroy one-third the nation's currency, with which the retail business of the country is mainly carried on, there would have been an overwhelming protest. Yet we deliberately permitted the destruction of one-third of our essential bank credit, essential to the actual production of goods, without a great deal of protest, and without any adequate understanding of its inevitable effect. The proof: in the Autumn of 1931, when the depression was steadily deepening and extending all over the world, the discount rate of the Federal Reserve banks was *raised*—raised instead of lowered—in order to 'protect' our gold. We had billions of gold, a huge excess, far more than we had any need for, and yet in panic we increased the pressure, forcing the banks to further contract credit. With the result that the depression in this country was far deeper than elsewhere. Great Britain wise in long experience, promptly suspended gold payments. Other countries followed.[10] But not the United States, the richest of all. Hence the prolonged disturbance.

When this essential step was taken, the recovery was prompt. If the government had done no more, we might readily have soon returned to the 1929 level of production and trade, and continued our previous growth. But the zeal for mistaken 'reform' was too strong. The good that was accomplished by an effective monetary policy was largely offset by drastic agricultural restriction; by regulation of industrial production, of prices, wages, hours, and labor relations; by unnecessary restriction of the securities markets; by punitive taxation, that discouraged investment; by large wasteful expenditure in 'priming the pump.' And along with these a torrent of irresponsible denunciation of business and business men.

At a time when the confidence of the country was still very low.
Result: the industries of the country at ebb tide, and eight or ten
million out of work for ten long years. Why?

3. Theories, fantasies, and prejudices

A characteristic by-product of all depressions is a deluge of economic 'literature.' Thousands of pamphlets, papers and books, each
purporting to give the one true cause of all our ills, and invariably
providing the infallible remedy, a 'panacea.' It was ever thus. The
first annual report of the Commissioner of Labor, in 1886, concerned with industrial depressions, was written by an able economist,
Carroll D. Wright. He reports that three Congressional committees took testimony on the causes of the depression of 1873–78,
and in this testimony one hundred and eighty causes of depression
were suggested. They fell into the following classes: [11]

Administration poli-
    cies
Agitators
Business enterprise
Capital (nine causes)
Cigar factories
Confidence
Consumption
Corporations
Corruption in govern-
    ment
Credit
Crises
Currency (27 causes)
Debts (two causes)
Demand
Depression
Destitution
Education (eight
    causes)
Electricity
Employment
Extravagance (three
    causes)
Fashions
Food
Franchises
Girls
Immigration
Imports
Income tax
Indebtedness
Indolence
Indulgences
Intemperance
Interest rates
Invention
Knowledge
Labor (21 causes)
Laws (eight causes)
Legislation (four
    causes)
Machinery (two
    causes)
Miscalculation
Mismanagement
Monopoly (six causes)
National debt
Necessaries of life
Non-producers
Panic
Passes on railroads
Produce exchange
Production (two
    causes)
Products
Profits
Railroads (eight
    causes)
Reaction
Revenue
Sanitary conditions
Speculative era
Speculation
Steam power
Stimulation
Stocks
Systems (12 causes)
Tariffs (six causes)
Taxation (nine
    causes)
Telegraph rates
Tobacco
Values
War (two causes)
Work

It is reassuring to find that all our familiar friends, 'over-production,' underconsumption, monopolies, labor-saving machinery, maldistribution, undue accumulation of wealth, et alia, sine finis, are all included in the 180 'causes' presented to the Congressional committees investigating the depression of 1873.

All these time-worn theories of depression alive and kicking today. But not more numerous than others concerning wealth, well-being, and prosperity. A perennial example that high wages 'create' prosperity, and, therefore, that in depression wages must not be reduced! If the quantitative relationships set forth in these pages are valid, there is no such thing as an absolutely high or low level of wages. The fundamental fact is that ordinarily the wages paid to labor are the highest that industry can afford to pay. There are times, as illustrated in our current period, when with a violent fall in prices and the resistance of labor unions to wage changes, wages may be relatively too high for industry to carry on. As Simon Newcomb long ago pointed out, this is one of the main forces that prolong depression: the difficulty of readjusting wages to the prevailing price level. In the end this adjustment must be made. There is no escape. The return of prosperity usually comes when wages have been so adjusted.

If there is no serious fall in the general price level of commodities and of other values, no such lowering of wages is necessary, because the depression will be brief. All illustrated in the great boom, crisis, and short depression that preceded and followed the panic of 1907. Normally the fall in the price level determines the duration of depressions, and as this is purely a function of the monetary or credit supply, it follows that if this credit supply is properly maintained, no such fall in prices or in wages is necessary.[12] Nor will it take place. These are among the elementary findings of quantitative economics.

Rising money wages can, in the long run, signify only one of two things: first, a decrease in the value of money, that is rising prices with a decline in the purchasing power of the dollar; or an increase in the average product per worker, prices not rising. Questions of fact and not of theory. It follows that an attempt to increase wages beyond the levels established by prices and production cannot insure prosperity. On the contrary, inevitably the end of prosperity, for the simple reason that no industry can continue to pay more than the fixed proportion of its income in wages,

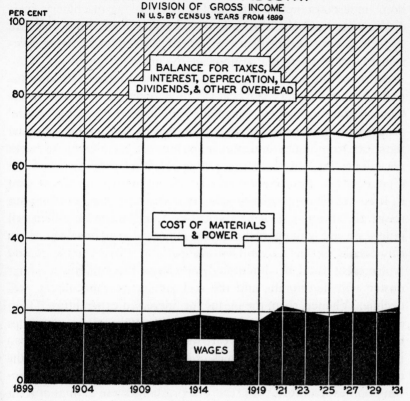

MEN'S CLOTHING INDUSTRY
DIVISION OF GROSS INCOME
IN U.S. BY CENSUS YEARS FROM 1899

PER CENT

BALANCE FOR TAXES, INTEREST, DEPRECIATION, DIVIDENDS,& OTHER OVERHEAD

COST OF MATERIALS & POWER

WAGES

100

80

60

40

20

0

1899   1904   1909   1914   1919 '21 '23 '25 '27 '29 '31

XXII. THE SHARE OF THE "WORKERS" IN THE CLOTHING INDUSTRY

In the preceding chart it has been shown how narrowly the percentage of wages to the income in manufacturing as a whole has fluctuated in the last eighty years. It is interesting to find how this fixity of relationship has been maintained even in a turbulent industry in which the labor unions have been extremely influential—the clothing industry. It will be seen in each of the three categories shown—wages, cost of materials, overhead and profits—how little the percentages have changed in the last forty years; repeating again the old, old story, which apparently work-ingmen cannot believe, that the labor unions have no material influence upon the wages paid, any more than have the proprietors or the managers of the industry. Wages in the long-run are fixed automatically and cannot be materially changed by any artifice or interference, or law. If employers paid higher than the nature of the industry could tolerate, they would go bankrupt; if they paid less than the highest wages, they would gain only the poorest workingmen, while the more capable workers would go to more successful enterprises, and their profits would vanish. One difficulty of a large part of economic writing is that it does not employ simple bookkeeping.

which is determined by the nature of the productive process in the industry itself.[13]

Whence, then, the almost universal delusion of the 1920's that 'high wages' insured prosperity? Largely the result of another delusion, that of stimulating consumption by 'increased spending.' Measurement of the factors affecting economic progress has revealed that not more than 15 per cent of the national income is withheld from expenditure on consumption; very little real 'saving.' About 10 per cent goes to investment in residential and public construction, 'creating homes' and similar purposes. Only about 5 per cent net goes to increase the reproductive capital of industry. And this 5 per cent is expended for construction purposes of some sort, that is, it is spent for machinery and labor and materials, creating the means for an increase of product. This fund cannot be diminished unless we are willing to have our industrial progress stop, as in the decade of this Great Depression. Nor can the renewal and replacement fund be diminished; otherwise the equipment of industry will deteriorate, and the real income of the country will decline. Whence, then, the means for 'increased expenditure'?

Ordinarily (not in recent years!) the expenditure for consumption goods goes on year by year, with little fluctuation other than in the normal increase. In times of depression the savings and the expenditure for investment fall sharply, far more than the consumption expenditure.[14] In severe depressions these savings and investments may fall to zero. Times of depression no longer mean any heavy increase in savings deposits or in commercial deposits, or in hoarded money. Income is reduced and expenditure is reduced therewith, but usually with a further decrease in savings. How fantastic, then, to assume that spending can be increased merely by a will to do so. Obviously to increase spending it is necessary to increase employment and income. And that requires an increase in investment, particularly in reproductive capital, which is seldom available in depression. It is absurd to think that business men will be induced to invest by raising wages and increasing costs and increasing the difficulty of making the very moderate profits necessary to finance industry.

In spite of nostrums and delusions a rational and statistical explanation of all these troublous disturbances does exist, and with it a simple means for their elimination.

Two difficulties must be faced. The first is the profound ignorance of the mechanism of depression, so that instead of the relatively simple means of control, the usual procedure is resort to abortive efforts at 'priming the pump' or arbitrary control of prices and production of various sorts, all as old as Diocletian and without exception invariable failures. The second difficulty is that well-intentioned business men may misunderstand the measures needful for control—they regard any attempt at mitigating the insanity of booms as interference with free enterprise. But effective means of avoiding depressions involve neither regulation of individual initiative or of individual enterprise. It means little more than regulating the increase or decrease of bank credit. Such regulation will only remotely touch the decisions of individual business men with reference to their particular problems of production, employment, and prices. It is not, therefore, a modification or limitation of the basic principle of free enterprise upon which our economic structure is based.

First as to the fundamental problem.

THE MECHANISM OF BUSINESS CYCLES

The causes of alternating periods of inflation and depression of commercial activity . . . are intimately connected with . . . changes in the purchasing power of money. For when prices are likely to rise, people rush to borrow money and buy goods, and thus help prices to rise; business is inflated, and is managed recklessly and wastefully. . . . When afterwards credit is shaken and prices begin to fall, everyone wants to get rid of commodities and get hold of money which is rapidly rising in value; this makes prices fall all the faster, and the further fall makes credit shrink even more, and thus for a long time prices fall because prices have fallen."

—ALFRED MARSHALL: *Principles of Economics*

Analyzing business cycles means neither more nor less than analyzing the economic process of the capitalist era. Most of us discover this truth which at once reveals the nature of the task and also its formidable dimensions. Cycles are not, like tonsils, separable things that might be treated by themselves, but are, like the beat of the heart, of the essence of the organism that displays them.

—JOSEPH A. SCHUMPETER: *Business Cycles*

CHAPTER XII

THE MECHANISM OF BUSINESS CYCLES

1. *The natural history of depressions*

SOME six hundred years ago there died a gentle and accomplished Franciscan friar, equally well known to the princely courts and theological schools of his day, deriving his name from the little village in Surrey where he was born: William of Occam, or Ockam as it is now spelled.[1] Those were the good old days when philosophers were concerned with the soul and the hereafter, very much as modern philosophers now prattle about the fate of capitalism and the future of economic planning. Theological disputation was then the vogue, much as economic controversy now. Apparently the gentle William grew weary of these endless disputes and empty logomachies; and so invented a philosophical tool which came in later days to be known as Occam's Razor. This rule set forth the idea, as he quaintly termed it, that "entities," meaning 'explanations,' shall not be needlessly multiplied; sometimes called the Law of Parsimony, which means very simply that we shall not go on inventing possibilities or fantasies when we have already an adequate explanation. Perhaps the counsel of perfection.

But think of what the application of such a rule might do to the endless theories that depressions are caused by 'over-production,' or 'over-population,' or 'over-saving,' or over-building, or over-something-else. And if not over, then under-something: 'under-consumption,' under-investment, under-supply of money or capital.[2] And for each and all of these endless theories, we have of course a corresponding multiplicity of remedial measures. What an accumulation of nonsense might be cut away by a ruthless use of Occam's Razor!

Let us consider further the process that brings about this slump in production, employment and prices, that we call a depression. Universal agreement that the most characteristic feature of these 'cycles' lies in their alternating periods of boom and recession. The booms preceding major depressions invariably terminated by a crisis; in the century gone by, some six of these of major proportions: 1837, '57, '73, '93, 1907, and 1929.[3] In the earlier part of the past century it was land speculation; more recently the stock market, and city real estate. All these concomitant with the great eras of canal building, railroad building, gigantic corporate mergers and the like. What are the noteworthy features common to all? At least six: [4]

1. Every crisis preceded by a period of high prosperity. Production increasing, but as a rule only at slightly more than the normal rate of growth. Great activity, particularly of a speculative kind, that gives the illusion of more prosperity than actually exists. Business men highly optimistic. A general belief that we have passed the days of depressions, and entered upon a 'new era' of unending prosperity.

2. Every such period characterized by easy money and easy credit. This means always an excessive increase in the quantity of bank credit, accompanied always by rising prices. Especially real estate and the stock markets. Often likewise in commodities, almost always in metals.

3. The rise in prices in the real estate or stock markets, or in commodities, is always accompanied by an outbreak of wild speculation. This is facilitated by the ease of borrowing money at low interest rates, though once under way, it may continue for a time after rates have risen considerably, often heavily.

4. When speculation has continued for some time and interest rates rise, there is evidence of a shortage of credit, and soon fear of the consequences. Bank credit becomes especially difficult to obtain. At this stage, a check to the rise in prices.

5. When prices stop rising, while interest rates increase, there soon follows a selling movement, with a sharp fall in prices, particularly of stocks, but also, to a lesser extent, later of real estate; interest rates continue high. Banks call in loans. The volume of bank credit is sharply curtailed. The general price level begins to fall. Numerous bank and business failures.

6. The collapse of speculation and the fall in prices leads to a sharp check to business, and this to a decline in production and employment. Gloom and depression are the rule, and this continues for a more or less extended period until bank credit is no longer curtailed, interest rates decline, and prices more stable.

Much debt has been liquidated, depending on the severity of the recession; there is readjustment in wage rates. Only when these final conditions exist—the resumption of lending by banks, the halt in the price decline, low interest rates, and proper wage rates— will business again expand.

Is all this invariable? Is it possible to have depression without each of these features? Apparently not. Every serious depression has been preceded by such a period of boom and wild speculation. Every period of speculation accompanied by an unusual credit expansion. This alone makes possible the continuance of the rise to higher and higher levels. The credit expansion is the inescapable and invariable cause of a general rise in prices. When the limit of credit expansion is reached, as it must be in time, speculation for the continued rise can go no further. Prices of securities fall first. With the decline in share values, banks must call in loans, for the collateral is no longer adequate to support them. Once this credit contraction is under way, prices in general must begin to fall, and business becomes unprofitable.

The major factor, the dominant factor, leading to depression is therefore invariably the expansion of bank credit, which alone makes possible the speculative boom; and the ensuing contraction of bank credit that brings the collapse of speculative activity.[5]

2.   *The Great Depression of 1929–'40–?*

If, then, these depressions are to be avoided, the absolute essential is intelligent control of the expansion of this bank credit, princi- pally in order to prevent the contraction. The method of control is well-enough known; but at the crucial point, just what no one wants; business men especially. The reason is that rarely are periods of very active trade regarded as 'booms.' Some clever man once said that prosperity is always just ahead or just behind us; never with us. And so with 'booms.' Almost every business man and most economic writers declared in 1929 there were no heavy stocks of goods; some of our most distinguished prophets were quite certain that no serious depression was in sight. In the light of later developments we call these men mistaken. And yet I am not cer- tain they did not correctly state the facts. What proof have we now that so late as the Spring of 1929 there were threatening accumulations of stocks of finished goods, or raw materials and the like? Department store stocks in 1929 were actually less, on an average, than in 1928. Stocks of manufactured goods in 1929 were less than 2 per cent above the level of 1928. It is true that stocks of raw materials rose sharply in 1929, but this was after the decline in trade had begun.[6]

Nor was there any clear evidence of over-expansion. The rate of industrial growth in the eight years prior to 1929 was not unheard of in this country. Taken as a whole, it was only about the average rate of growth over the preceding forty years; less than the average rate in the last half of the 19th century.[7] We have now a wide variety of careful measures, sufficiently inclusive to show the facts. The economists and business men who confidently declared there was no 'overproduction' were, I think, in the right. Yet their deductions and predictions were disastrously wrong. There was over-expansion in bank credit, generating the wildest boom in stocks in this century.

As noted, at the peak in 1929, total loans on securities were between 14 and 15 billion dollars. The funds lent by banks to finance the purchase of securities became part of the 'money supply' of the country. When the stock market crashed, as always the banks began calling loans. In two years a huge amount of bank credit extinguished. These closely related forces—the collapse of the stock market and the reduction in bank credit—combined to bring the usual train of results: the destruction of confidence, a heavy drain on banks and their reserves, an abrupt cessation of all forward buying by business, collapse in commodity prices, land values, and almost everything for which money is paid. What followed was inevitable: the heaviest decline in volume of trade and manufacturing the country had experienced in at least a hundred years; and the greatest unemployment it had ever known.[8] The majority of the banks of the country were in a dangerous, if not actually insolvent, position by the early part of 1933. On March 5th came the order for a general closing, the first this country had witnessed since the Civil War.[9]

Here we had in sharp relief for the first time in a generation the forces that create deep depression. In many ways the crisis of 1907 bore a striking resemblance, in its antecedents, to that of 1929.[10] Prior to 1907 there had been the same vigorous growth of trade and wealth, a prolonged rise in commodity prices, and still more in land values, and the same tremendous outburst of security spec-

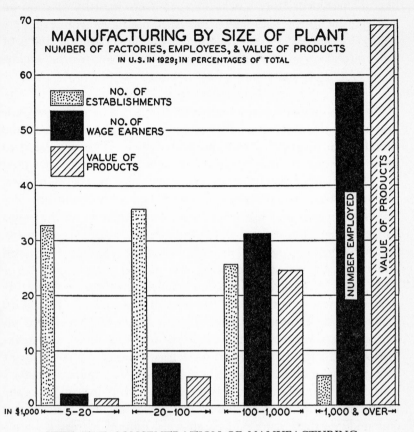

MANUFACTURING BY SIZE OF PLANT
NUMBER OF FACTORIES, EMPLOYEES, & VALUE OF PRODUCTS
IN U.S. IN 1929; IN PERCENTAGES OF TOTAL

NO. OF ESTABLISHMENTS

NO. OF WAGE EARNERS

VALUE OF PRODUCTS

IN $1,000   5-20   20-100   100-1,000   1,000 & OVER

XXIII. THE CONCENTRATION OF MANUFACTURING

In manufacturing, the smaller establishments greatly outnumber the larger, but their product is in inverse proportion to their number. The plants having a product valued at $1,000,000 or more per year turn out more goods than all the rest combined; likewise they employ more workers than all the others, though their number is less than 10 per cent of the total. This includes every kind of manufacturing, and shows the same tendency: that the highest efficiency is attained by the largest enterprises, resulting in the lowest costs. So they are able to pay the highest wages and to obtain the most capable workingmen; each factor strongly influencing the other. This 'concentration of industry,' far from being a 'menace' or an evil, as many fanciful writers believe, is a salient example of the principle of 'the greatest good to the greatest number'—the greatest good to the workers, for they receive the highest wages; and the greatest good to the vast consuming public, who obtain the necessities, the comforts, and the luxuries of life at the lowest possible cost. If it had not been for this concentration, it seems unlikely that the United States would today be the foremost manufacturing country in the world.

ulation. Security prices, too, had risen to an unprecedented height, and along with this, as always, a parallel expansion in bank credit. There followed the same precipitate fall in security values, the same unsettlement of confidence, and a very sharp contraction of commerce and trade. But it was all over within ten or twelve months.

Why the extraordinary contrast with 1929? The difference was that after 1907 there was no great contraction of bank credit, and therefore no heavy fall in commodity prices. The panic led to a temporary suspension of specie payments, and the use of Clearing House Certificates. But no sharp shrinkage of the circulating medium. Business had money enough. And after the fright was over the deposits that had been withdrawn began to return to the banks. Business confidence was soon restored, normal conditions began to prevail, and within a year business recovery was well under way. In 1929, what a different sequence! First of all a heavy drain of gold, with its consequent depletion of the reserves. Instead of a vigorous effort on the part of the Federal Reserve to counteract these influences by heavy purchases of government securities, there was hesitation and delay: fear of a renewal of speculation, and another great rise in security prices.

In reality, such a sharp rise would have done more to restore confidence than perhaps any other single factor. Instead, the prevailing policy resulted in lower and lower security prices, and commodity prices; bank and commercial failures increased alarmingly. The avalanche had started. The economic morale of the country went to pieces. No doubt all this was accentuated by events abroad. But a bold course would have disregarded these. There was still an abundance of gold, ample foundations for a liberal credit policy. We were an enormously rich country. Industry and trade were intrinsically sound. There were 'maladjustments,' no doubt, but no greater proportionately than in others of preceding periods.

It is, of course, always easy long after such events to mount the judicial throne and scatter censure with a lavish hand. The fault here was one of lack of knowledge and understanding, not confined to official bodies. In the present state of economic doctrine it would not have been easy to choose a more fortunate course. Difficult under any circumstances to get commissions and boards that will follow a fearless policy. Especially in dark depression with confusion of counsel. The rare combination of insight and courage that was required is scarce at any time. It was a lamentable misfortune that the one man who seemed to have acquired these qualities in unique degree died in the Autumn of 1928. From years of close association, not unmarked by differences of view, I had come to regard Benjamin Strong, the first Governor of the Federal Reserve Bank of New York, as perhaps the most prescient financier this country had produced since Alexander Hamilton.[11] Nor have the passing years changed this view. I still hold the belief that could this man have had twelve months more of vigorous health, we might have ended the depression in 1930, and with this the long drawn out world crisis that so profoundly affected the ensuing political developments. Not without interest that within a year of this Great Britain seemed to have found its feet and rose steadily in industrial activity, while our United States continued the downward course until the Spring of 1933.

3. *World factors in depression*

In the preceding has been sketched the effects of wild speculation and the perversion of our monetary system to the uses of speculators. Our failure inevitably brought about critical economic and financial conditions abroad. And the economic collapse in other countries in turn increased the difficulty of bringing about recovery in the United States.

After the World War we became heavy lenders abroad, which undoubtedly went far toward bringing about the astonishing recovery attained by some nations. With characteristic enthusiasm, we lent billions of dollars to European countries. So rapid was the recovery, largely the effect of our lending, and so plentiful the funds in the European money markets, that almost inevitably a great speculative movement developed, notably in Germany following its era of inflation. Wisely or not, there was a heavy flow of short term funds to the German money markets. And always it is these short term funds, moving from market to market, that create most of the trouble. When the crisis came, there was a heavy withdrawal of funds and a terrific contraction of credit to German industry as well as to the stock markets. The result was a drastic collapse; it could not have been otherwise.

When the Wall Street crash of 1929 brought our orgy of speculation to an end, it was inevitable that this should temporarily at least stop foreign lending. But in 1930, we were still lending abroad on a large scale. The foreign securities issued in that year exceeded those of 1929, although considerably less than those of the five years from 1924 to 1928. As liquidation and credit contraction in this country continued, it necessitated the withdrawal of short term funds from abroad, from London as well as from Berlin and other centers. It meant a general cessation of lending, because in a similar way it curtailed the lending power of other countries, such as Great Britain. It was almost two full years before the effect of our monetary policy was severely felt in Germany. There the crisis did not come until the Summer of 1931. Unquestionably the major factor in their crisis was the continued contraction of bank credit in the United States and the consequent deepening depression in our industries.

The crash in Germany and the temporary closing of the German banks brought with it the same economic paralysis that we experienced in the United States in 1930.[12] From Germany, the severe depression spread to all the smaller countries of Central Europe, many of whom were dependent upon German trade for their prosperity. And thus the depression became worldwide. Its beginning certainly in the United States. Its European center was as clearly Germany and her immediate dependencies. And we have proof that it was a financial, banking, and monetary phenomenon, and not a crisis of trade or industry, not the result of overproduction and the like. This is apparent from the highly instructive course of events in two other powerful industrial countries: Russia and Japan.

The revolutionary character of the Russian government largely cut off Russia from the financial and commercial current of the rest of the world. It was in singular degree a highly autonomous land. The ironical fact is that because of its communism, it was prevented from borrowing large sums abroad, and, therefore, saved from the profound depression that affected almost every other nation except Japan.

The case of Japan is even more convincing proof that the depression did not have its origin in industrial and commercial factors. Japan had made heavy purchases of machinery abroad; and with this machinery it had developed the largest industrial enterprises on the vast continent of Asia. Not content with this, it had gone boldly into the world markets, competing actively not only in the Far East and in South America, but even in the United States. To take one instance: despite an adverse tariff, it flooded this country with cheap electric bulbs and compelled our manufacturers to improve their methods and cut their prices to meet this competition. In a world almost universally affected, Japan felt virtually no depression. It continued its astonishing rate of industrial growth, which exceeded that of any other nation, possibly excepting Russia, in the last quarter of a century. Alone among the great commercial nations, Japan persisted in its prosperity. In that country there was little contraction of credit. On the contrary, banks continued to make loans to industry throughout the world depression.

In view of all this, it would seem merely senseless babble to suggest that the world depression was due simply to disturbances in industry and trade. It was most active and severe in the United States and Germany, the two large countries that suffered the heaviest decline in their banking resources. No such depression in the countries in which this disastrous credit contraction did not take place. Great Britain as a financial center and as the foremost country in international trade, felt these disturbances severely. But its recovery was prompt. While the United States continued for two more years in ever deepening gloom, and even then had only spasmodic recovery, Great Britain has been as prosperous as at any time during the last quarter of a century. A striking contrast.[13]

One central fact seems to stand out in bold relief: no nation can any longer suffer these excessive expansions and ensuing contractions of bank credit; economic and social stability depend chiefly upon monetary stability. An undue expansion of bank credit brings about not only a general rise in prices, but most harmful of all, promotes speculation in securities; and the effect is to force a further expansion of borrowing; then the usual crisis. Obviously we can no longer permit such debauchery of the share markets in this reckless fashion. Just as a broken rail or an open switch may mean a terrible railway disaster, so does precisely the same sort of thing bring disaster to the whole commercial world. What is yet more important, society as well.

This is the fundamental fact we must understand if our present day civilization is to survive. We have learned the definite effect, the widespread suffering, that cholera, plague, and yellow fever entail. The nations have spent millions in research to prevent them.

But the epidemics of the economic and financial world, more harmful than any plagues, continue unrestrained, or are treated with a variety of nostrums reminiscent of our treatment of disease in the Dark Ages. Just as research and control have banished these deadly epidemics, so only through research and control can we hope to abolish the disturbances that afflict our industrial and economic life.

4. *The depression of 1937*

The depression that began with the crisis of 1929 continued with growing severity until the Spring of 1933. Then, with the suspension of the gold standard, production bounded upward in a great and sudden surge. No man can say with certainty that under favorable conditions this upswing in business might have continued without serious interruption until our industries had been restored to their normal level and normal rate of growth. Perhaps under any circumstances, recovery would have halted before full employment was again attained. Actually, the recovery after 1933 and until 1937 was of the spasmodic type, frequently interrupted and after a short time resumed. If we may judge from the protests of business leaders, these interruptions in recovery were due to the radical measures inaugurated in an attempt by legislation to correct evils, real or imaginary. One thing is certain: these innovations had a harmful effect upon business confidence. Just as a plant can flourish only with adequate light, warmth, and moisture, so business can thrive only in an atmosphere of confidence. Destroy this confidence and continued economic progress is impossible. More than two thousand years ago Demosthenes, in his defence of Phormion, gave utterance to his famous phrase: *"Pistis megale aphorme"* – credit, confidence, is the great spur to business. If in the turmoil of political conflict, this fundamental truth is forgotten, we must suffer.

In the Autumn of 1937 the business world and many of the business prognosticators received a rude jolt. The moderate degree of prosperity that had been attained after more than four years of intermittent advance was suddenly lost.[14] The stock market fell precipitately, as did production and employment. Very unexpectedly, we were faced with a new depression, and a bad one. What was the trouble? In the earlier part of the year, we had the so-called

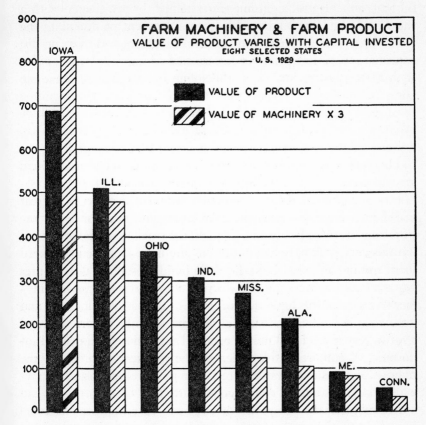

FARM MACHINERY & FARM PRODUCT
VALUE OF PRODUCT VARIES WITH CAPITAL INVESTED
EIGHT SELECTED STATES
—— U. S. 1929 ——

■ VALUE OF PRODUCT

▨ VALUE OF MACHINERY X 3

XXIV. THE CAPITALISTIC SYSTEM ON THE FARM

Most people would probably say that the production of the farms largely depend upon the industry and the hard work of the farmers. But the chart above reveals the reality. The value of the product, that is, the farm income, depends almost wholly, nowadays, on the amount of machinery employed. This varies from state to state in a most striking way. Iowa is the richest farm state in per capita income, and its investment in farm machinery is, likewise, the largest—larger, even, than that in the great state of Illinois and eight or ten times as much as that in a sizable majority of other farm states. See how closely the product varies with the *amount* of this investment. It has been estimated that an Iowa farmer, for example, can produce ten or twelve times as much per worker employed as would be possible without this investment in machinery. In Canada there is a thousand-acre wheat farm which normally employs only five or six workers, even in the harvest season. Almost everything is done by machinery.

war-boom, in steel, copper and allied industries. Orders were flowing in from every side. Tremendous military expenditures all over
the world. And the billions that our government was handing out
for doles, work projects, and similar adventures were having the
expected effect. Prosperity at last seemed in sight. Labor troubles,
with their sit-down strikes, so threatening in the Spring, were apparently abating. The prospects for an European conflagration
seemed on the decline. The United States had an immense backlog
of eight years' inadequate renewal of plants and properties, to say
nothing of the halt in the normal growth. For once, at least, the
soothsayers who assured the country that business was sound,
seemed right. Then suddenly the picture changed.

Few of the usual stigmata of depression seemed present. No vast
increase in bank borrowings, as in 1928 and 1929, save by the
government; there had been a boom in the stock markets, of course,
but this very strikingly had not meant any huge increase in brokers'
loans and in bank credit. No boom in building such as usually pre-
sages a business recession. Production was heavy in certain lines,
but it was not the high tide of 1928. The business indexes that
gave such an indication were clearly misleading, distorted by an
overweight of steel and motor cars and their closely associated industries. A comprehensive index of the physical volume of production and trade shows definitely that the level of business activity in 1937 was nearly 15 per cent below that of 1929.

In brief, that the prosperity of 1937 was very mild, far removed
from a boom. Nevertheless, at the first suggestions of government
retrenchment, curtailment of relief expenditure and similar outlays,
there was a sudden clouding of the skies. No mistaking the source
of the trouble: the unstable base of government spending. The
moment this was removed, the structure collapsed. And the collapse was rapid precisely because business had no confidence in the
soundness of the edifice. The only sound basis for prosperity is the
investment of reproductive capital, in search of a profit. Any other
stimulus to business activity can provide only an uncertain foundation that must collapse when it is withdrawn.

One may well ask: why did government expenditure not result
in an expansion of investment and provide a sound foundation for
prosperity? [15] This is a very rich country, still full of energy and
enterprise. There was no slowing down of the urge to progress.
It is noteworthy that in the midst of the longest and worst depres-

sion this country had ever known, business was spending tremendous sums on research and investigation, to find new fields for investment. There was a marked advance in industrial technique and efficiency.

Under favorable circumstances these new developments would lead to active and prosperous business. Labor disturbances had begun to abate by the Autumn of 1937, and while they contributed somewhat to the termination of the mild prosperity of that year, they were not, perhaps, the major factor. More important was the sharp and undesirable rise in wages. Fantastic to think that at a time of tremendous unemployment, when wage rates were already excessive, labor could ask and receive wages as high as, and in some industries higher than, in the boom year of 1929, when the volume of production and trade was much above the 1937 level.

The main responsibility, however, lay in governmental policies. The huge deficit led to a fear that future taxes and costs of production would be higher, so that investment undertaken then might become unprofitable because of the necessity of future increases in taxation. Along with this there was widespread fear of 'inflation,' based on the possibility that the debt might grow so large and so burdensome that a heavy rise in prices would be needed to diminish its real magnitude. With all this, incessant denunciation of 'business' and of business practices. It was unavoidable that business men and investors should lose confidence in the outlook.

Worth noting, too, that after all the evils arising from the contraction of bank credit following the crisis of 1929, the Federal Reserve authorities again initiated a contraction of bank credit in the midst of the inadequate prosperity of 1937. By raising the reserve requirements to the maximum allowed under the present law, that is, double the basic reserve requirements, the Federal Reserve authorities compelled banks throughout the country to withdraw funds from New York. These withdrawals, together with the higher reserves required, wiped out the excess reserves of the New York banks. To replenish their reserves they sold government bonds. The result: a decline in bond prices, and a rise in bond yields. The market for new securities became unfavorable, and funds were not forthcoming to finance new investment.[16] It cannot be said that this raising of the reserve requirements was the major factor in the depression of 1937; but it did have an unfavorable effect, and it indicates how far we still are from understanding the proper use of our monetary system.

5. Debt, depression, and discontent

Yet further: Always after a violent fall in prices, there looms on the horizon the spectre of 'long-term debt.' It never fails. And always with its appearance comes a variety of theories concerning the rôle of this debt in depressions. I make bold to say it is never a *cause*, although it may be a potent factor later. And therein, I think, lies whatever menace it may contain.

The mechanism of this is extremely simple. A severe fall in prices never comes save after a long and usually violent rise. This was as true after the Civil War as after the World War. Immediately after the World War, there was a rather sharp fall, but not serious. The danger comes from the prolonged fall in prices that usually begins years after hostilities are ended. Now rising prices are always a period of high optimism, widespread speculation, and increase in debt. At such times, lenders share the prevailing optimism and lend freely, bankers as well as others. When the decline in prices comes the debts incurred in this period become burdensome. Then comes the talk of the 'depression brought on by debt'; the usual commotion, and serious discontent among debtors, particularly farmers And political upheavals.

This is not to say that long term debt is not a powerful factor in the continuance of depressions. Obviously a factor. All this was vividly set forth by Simon Newcomb, and others, more than half a century ago. Newcomb, especially. It was his early belief that depressions arise solely from the contraction of what he called the 'societary circulation,' that is, chiefly bank credit, and the consequent fall in prices. He held that if wages and all other costs could be reduced in a corresponding degree with the price decline, there would be only a temporary disturbance; no serious depression. But his 'all other costs' included, of course, long term debt; this likewise must be scaled in the same degree.[17] But this process would be (and is) profoundly perturbing, involving bankruptcies, receiverships, and their long train of evil.

But this is not what the 'debt theorists' have in mind. They believe rather that it is the creation of the debt itself that brings about

he depression.[18] We now have adequate evidence to show that in
a broad way the creation and the increase of long term debt is a
fairly definite function of the increase in production and trade and
in the general price level. The increase of debt, other than for construction and speculation, represents very largely the borrowings
of younger men, taking over the farm or the business of previous
owners. A careful inquiry as to farm debt has established this
clearly. With rising prices and general prosperity the average
farmer realizes his long standing dream of selling out at high tide.
And in an atmosphere of general confidence and good profits this
is easy.

There would be no danger in all this, if there were no later fall
in prices. There is no evidence, it would seem, that the mere increase in debt has any particular influence upon the price level, or
the state of trade. The fall in prices is a monetary phenomenon,
resulting from the inability of the banks to maintain the volume of
credit required to finance production and trade at ever rising
prices. Without depression there would be no difficulty in meeting the charges on the existing debt. Even with mild depression, the
debt would not be unmanageable, except to the relatively few business men who borrowed for speculative purposes, or for unprofitable enterprises. But in disastrous recessions even well managed
enterprises may have difficulty in meeting debt charges. When
their financial structure is undermined, they have difficulty in obtaining funds for financing current production, to say nothing of
the increase of capital. In this way the burden of debt may intensify and prolong a major depression. But this is far from saying
that it is the cause.

The long term debt is a necessary and normal part of the development of industry.[19] In short periods, say during boom and
depression, its dimensions do not rise or fall appreciably. Ordinarily
the debt grows rather steadily, along with the normal increase in
the amount of capital invested in industry, and with the volume of
production from which the funds are derived to meet the debt
charges. The ratio of long term debt to the total volume of trade
has generally remained extraordinarily stable. It is all a part of the
mechanism of economic progress, not to be changed for imagina-
tive plans for promoting stability. When we have once learned the
lesson of preventing depression by avoiding speculation and the

excessive creation of bank credit, and by avoiding the subsequen contraction of credit and the fall in prices when the speculativ boom has burst, there can be no danger in our customary financin; of capital development through the issue of bonds, mortgages, o other evidences of debt.

HEART OF THE PROBLEM: CREDIT CONTROL

For all future time the period through which we are now living will come to form one of the most important chapters in monetary history, and it will likewise offer the richest materials on which to draw for studying the question of the effects of a misguided monetary policy.

—GUSTAV CASSEL: *Money and Foreign Exchange After 1914*

The decline in the purchasing power of gold has disclosed a weakness in the gold standard. The stability in the value of gold depends on the accumulated stocks being used in proportion to the annual supply. But just because the stocks are large the quantity in use as currency is large. The demand for gold as currency, by withdrawing this large quantity from other uses, tends to keep the value of gold up. But if a great part of the demand is destroyed by the adoption of paper money in place of gold, the supplies set free are great in proportion to the world's industrial demand, and have to be absorbed as currency, in the area in which gold continues to be used for that purpose. The more restricted this area, the more marked will be the effect on the value of gold. At the present time gold prices have fully doubled, or in other words, the value of gold in relation to commodities has been halved.

—R. G. HAWTREY: *Monetary Reconstruction*

The positive credit guide here proposed is the normal rate of growth of production. Central banks should aim at so regulating the reserves of the banking system that the outstanding credit built upon those reserves will expand at the same rate as the long-term growth of production. There is enough credit when the curves of credit growth and production growth parallel each other. More than this is too much; less than this is too little.

—LIONEL D. EDIE: *The Banks and Prosperity*

CHAPTER XIII

HEART OF THE PROBLEM: CREDIT CONTROL

1. *Monetary control and business confidence*

THE view expressed in this volume that, au fond, depressions are chiefly the result of speculative bank borrowings, seems to many extreme; too simple.[1] It seems hard to understand that the credit created by speculative activity is the same as all other credit; it enters the channels of business and trade throughout the nation. The creation of billions of dollars of bank credit in New York and other cities through the borrowing of the speculators is not limited in its effect to the markets or to the areas about New York. This bank credit is an addition to the 'circulating medium' of the whole country. It makes practically no difference, ultimately, who makes the loans or what they are first used for. Once created, they mingle with the general flow of credit, and may be used by a sheep ranch in Idaho, a sugar plantation in Louisiana, or a woolen mill in Maine. And they may be and are used many times.

In turn, when the loan on which the bank deposit was based is extinguished, that is, when the loan is paid, the reverse process takes place. There is then a corresponding contraction of the circulating medium. And if the contraction is sufficiently large, as after 1929, a severe depression of industry and trade becomes inevitable.

In this view, then, the problem of controlling depression is simply one of controlling the expansion and, likewise, the contraction of bank credit. It is essential that speculation should be held in check in order to prevent an excess of credit. This has not been clearly understood, and in the past the banking authorities have failed in their efforts because they have come too late, as in 1929. But unquestionably they have the power to control credit; and if this power were expertly used, they could limit bank loans to the amount needed to finance the normal growth in production and trade.[2] There can be now no doubt that the Federal Reserve authorities have this power. But there is another side to credit control. If, for any reason, depression has come, it is equally essential that the banking authorities do whatever they can to prevent the contraction of bank credit, and so encourage business recovery. And the Federal Reserve authorities have likewise the means to aid, by the heavy purchase of government bonds, and so maintain excess reserves.

But unless business men are willing to borrow, there can be little recovery. And business men will borrow only when they have confidence in the future. This necessary relation of credit to confidence is the heart of any sound program for recovery.[3] Few men will borrow money and incur debt for the joy of it; just as they will not invest in new machinery or in new enterprise unless they have faith that the enterprise will be a success or that the new machinery will be profitable.

True they may borrow money in dire distress to protect themselves if possible from failure. But here the question of confidence steps in from the bank's side. No banker will deliberately lend money unless he has a reasonable degree of assurance that the borrower can or will be able to pay. He may in times of grave difficulty lend bravely to protect his clients. Yet even here his actions must be guided by his confidence in his client, for he is lending other people's money, not his own. And he has a great responsibility to those who have shown faith in his bank, and in his business judgment as well as his honesty. Confidence is a delicate plant that grows slowly and as easily wilts. It must be cultivated with care, for it bears a precious fruit. And clearly a nation, no less than an individual, must be certain that *its* actions inspire trust in the business community. Otherwise neither can prosper. It is recorded that when John D. Rockefeller was a boy of ten or eleven, he had saved from his scant earnings of thirty-five cents for a ten-hour day, the sum of fifty dollars. Then he heard that a nearby farmer would pay 7 per cent interest. The boy lent the money. At the end of the year, when the loan was paid with interest of $3.50, Mr. Rockefeller said that he counted up that this interest was equal to ten days hard work, and determined thereafter that he would make money work for him. But it was not from lending that Rockefeller acquired his amazing fortune. At nineteen he went into business with another young man. The firm was successful and bore an excellent reputation, but they lacked capital. Mr.

Rockefeller went to an elderly gentleman with whom he had business dealings and asked for a loan of $2,000, hoping to get half of
it. He was astonished to find that the old gentleman lent him the
entire sum. This confidence that others had in him enabled Rockefeller to prosper greatly, and to found the Standard Oil Company
when he was only thirty.[4]

Are not nations in the same position as individuals, with respect
to the necessity of inspiring confidence? When Alexander Hamilton at thirty-three became the first Secretary of the Treasury of
the United States, one of his earliest acts was to valorize the bonds
which had been issued. A terrible uproar and scandalous charges
followed. The bonds had been selling at a discount of 70 to 80
per cent. Many were held by foreign investors in England and
Holland. In spite of the opposition, Washington stood behind his
young financial genius. It proved a wise step. Confidence was
quickly established in the new government, and it was soon possible for business enterprises to borrow abroad. At home, too, the
confidence of creditors in the honesty and stability of domestic
obligations was immeasurably improved. Thus the young industries of the country were nourished and built up to their present
high state of development.[5]

For many reasons, the faith of business men in the destiny of
American business is now at a lower level than at any time perhaps
since the founding of the republic. It is imperative that confidence
be restored. Agitation for ill-considered reforms that invariably
accompany depression has always an upsetting effect, and so too
the many hastily instituted changes in our economic and financial
structure. This drift away from our traditional economic principles
has gone far, and has lead to huge governmental deficits that have
undermined the faith of business men in the soundness of our public finance. There can be no reasonable doubt that wise economic
and fiscal policies would quickly restore that confidence essential
to sustained recovery.

2. *The nature of credit control*

In larger view, there is, of course, a danger that business men will
confuse credit control with the general tendency to increase regulation of business. Not unjustified. But a policy of credit management, designed especially to limit speculative forces upsetting nor-

mal growth and prosperity, is far from this. It does not attempt to 'regulate business,' but only to insure sound financial *and* speculative conditions; for speculation itself is not an evil, save in its extremes. Unquestionably a powerful stimulant to capital accumulation. Nor does credit regulation involve the establishment of any powerful and offensive bureaucracy. Wise control is no complicated or mysterious process. In summary as follows:

1. The production of the national income and national comfort requires a *definite* sum of money and commercial credit.[6] The 'money' is mainly in the form of bank deposits; the credit in the various forms in which sellers extend credit to their customers. The total amount of commercial credit that can be so extended is closely related to the amount of bank deposits; and these in turn are fixed by the forces that determine the supply of *money*. With a given money supply, goods and services will have a certain average level of prices. The variations of this general price level result solely from the ratio between the amount of bank deposits and the total volume of trade. Long disputed; now definitely established. Illustrated in the chart on the relations of Trade, Credit, and the General Level of Prices.

2. Bank deposits are chiefly created by loans of the commercial banks to their customers; but also in part by purchase by the banks of government bonds and other securities. In the long run the amount of these loans and investments, and therefore of bank deposits, is almost automatically determined by the amount of bank reserves. The upper limit of loans and investments is practically fixed by the law governing required reserves; the lower limit by the desire of the banks to obtain sufficient income to at least meet expenses. The principal income of banks is from their loans and investments.

3. There is a widespread belief that the interest rate is a powerful factor in determining the demand for bank loans, and that it thus exercises a great influence upon trade and enterprise. As a matter of fact, the average rates of interest paid by business men vary within rather narrow limits, and are not ordinarily a decisive factor in determining whether business men should borrow or banks lend.[7] But there are upper limits at which these rates become very important. Few business enterprises can afford to borrow money at more than 6 or 7, at most 8 per cent, depending on the part of the country in which they operate. Whenever the rate of

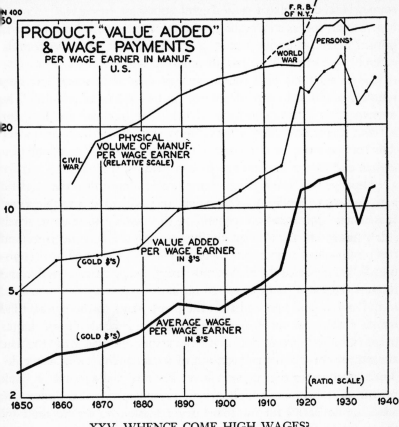

PRODUCT, "VALUE ADDED"
& WAGE PAYMENTS
PER WAGE EARNER IN MANUF.
U. S.

F. R. B.
OF N.Y.

WORLD
WAR

PERSONS'

20

PHYSICAL
VOLUME OF MANUF.
PER WAGE EARNER
(RELATIVE SCALE)

CIVIL
WAR

10

VALUE ADDED
PER WAGE EARNER
IN $'S

(GOLD $'S)

5

AVERAGE WAGE
PER WAGE EARNER
IN $'S

(GOLD $'S)

(RATIO SCALE)

2

1850   1860   1870   1880   1890   1900   1910   1920   1930   1940

XXV. WHENCE COME HIGH WAGES?

A vast number of people believe that the fixing of wages is a more or less arbitrary act of the employers, or the companies; and even employers, in part, share this delusion. Neither the employee nor the employer nor the workers' unions can materially affect the wages paid. They are fixed chiefly by one definite factor, that is, by the value added to the product. The higher this value added per worker, the higher the wage; and, to all intents, this is the end of it. Competent employers will always pay the highest possible wage in order to get the best workmen. But, at the same time, he will always pay the least possible wage in order to keep the cost of his products as low as possible so that he may undersell his rivals. The amount he can pay and does pay is fixed by the nature of his business and by its mode of organization.

interest is forced up above these limits, business borrowing largely ceases. For two reasons: business men can see no profit from borrowing, and the rise of the interest rate to these critical points is everywhere recognized as a danger signal.

4. What forces these interest rates up to and beyond these critical points, if business men, as a rule, cannot afford to borrow at such high rates? It is, for all practical purposes, the borrowing of the speculators. They alone can pay these high rates. The men who expect to make a profit of 20, 50, or 100 per cent by holding securities for a few months care little how high the interest rate is.[8] But the wisest of the speculators pay close attention to the rate because they have learned that it means a check to prosperity, and an end to any boom, in stocks, or land, or the like.

5. Speculative borrowings thus largely determine the interest rate, and so, to a considerable extent, the *volume* of bank deposits. It is when bank loans are expanding to finance speculation, when stock prices are rising, that business is brisk. Everyone comes to feel optimistic at such a time, because we are a ticker-minded country. Few seem to realize that this rising stock market will force interest rates to a point at which business enterprises cannot afford to pay. So up and up. And then the panic, the familiar 'crisis.' One would think that the bankers, especially the heads of the larger banks, with long experience and large responsibilities, would realize the dangers of this over-expansion of bank credit. They never do. Time after time, the 'conservative' bankers make loans on such securities at prevailing high prices, presumably because they are adequate collateral for the loans made. Certainly, we cannot look to the banks for restraint at times when speculation goes mad.[9]

6. The Federal Reserve System was created in 1913 largely for just this purpose. But the Reserve officials cannot be much wiser or more foresighted than the bankers from whom they are usually chosen, although the Federal Reserve Banks and many of the larger commercial banks have had some wise and prudent men. What then is the answer? If the principal factor is the *volume* of bank credit, and changes in this volume are chiefly due to speculation, then the key is simply to limit speculation. This is feasible only by controlling the volume of bank credit, maintaining its increase at a fixed and pre-determined rate per annum; this rate determined by the normal rate of growth of industry and trade, which in our generation we now know has been about 4 per cent

per annum.[10] If we had used this simple rule from 1920 to 1929, we should have had no undue expansion of credit, no wild speculation, no crash; for the simplest of reasons. If the credit supply is thus sharply limited, the speculator will bid up the interest rates to a point at which business cannot afford to borrow. Therefore, a temporary check to business activity and the end of speculation for the rise.

We cannot, in an immense country like the United States, expect to have perfect control, or an absolutely stable price level, or freedom from mild variations in business undertakings. But all these are of no consequence. On the contrary, they are of the highest utility in promoting efficiency and good management, more investment, and greater productivity. In summary, they are really stimulants to industrial progress. But with no undue expansion of bank credit, we shall have no marked variation in the general price level, and therefore in values of every kind; no heavy fall in wages, as in times of prolonged depression, but a steady increase with the progress of technology and the growth of capital investment. And with the end of these deep and prolonged depressions we could avoid the social upheavals that invariably accompany economic disturbance. In brief, we would have not only stability, but also sanity, progress, and peace.—Too dull?—Perhaps!

3. *The rediscount rate and reserves*

The effect of interest rates in limiting the demand for bank credit has long been known, and since 1866 has been almost officially regarded by the Bank of England as the chief instrument for control. A high rate of interest in comparison with prospective profits, will ordinarily decrease the demand for credit. For this reason, when excessive borrowing gave evidence of the development of unsound conditions, the Bank could easily halt the expansion by raising its rates. Nothing novel in this view; it was stated in similar terms far back by Ricardo, in his *Principles*. "The applications to the bank for money, then, depend on the comparison between the rate of profits that may be made by the employment of it and the rate at which they are willing to lend it. If they charge less than the market rate of interest, there is no amount of money which they might not lend; if they charge more than that rate none but spendthrifts and prodigals would be found to borrow." [11] Though Ricardo was speaking of the Bank of England, the same principle applies to all. In the past it has often been denied that the interest rate is so significant in controlling credit; but it is now of general concord that *high* interest rates do limit the demand.

England was the first country to develop an acute concern over credit control, since it was there that modern industrialism began, and there that the present great banking companies were born. It was in England, too, that industrial 'crises,' particularly severe crises, first appeared. In fact, the theory of control was largely formulated from observation of the behavior of British banks and British business during the credit 'cycles,' as they were called, of the nineteenth century. By the middle of the century it was generally accepted. The process and theory of this method was fully set forth by Walter Bagehot, celebrated editor of the London *Economist*, in the remarkable volume called "Lombard Street," published in the Spring of 1873. There Bagehot set forth the doctrine that it was the business of a central bank like the Bank of England to lend freely in a crisis, and up to the very limit of its resources, *but at a high rate*.[12] A high rate in a central market like London had for one immediate effect the drawing in of large funds from the continent, so that the normal freezing of deposits in a crisis was avoided, and the path opened for a speedy return to normal conditions.

As a result, Great Britain has had no serious money panic since the acceptance of this view, though it should be added, that it was for a time strongly resisted by the officials of the Bank. The United States, on the other hand, has done badly. It has had four or five major financial crises, and several minor ones.[13] It was largely to end these banking crises that our Reserve System came into being. But it is obvious that the full lesson has yet to be learned. Perhaps in fear of assuming the responsibility, the officials of the Federal Reserve System have steadfastly denied their ability to control credit and the behavior of prices.[14] And yet, unless the Reserve officials recognize their powers and realize the necessity of fully using them, we can scarcely hope to avoid such crises and their appalling effect upon industry, employment, and the morale of our people.

This unwillingness is the more remarkable because the Federal Reserve Act places in the hands of the Reserve Banks and the

Board of Governors greater powers than have been enjoyed by the Bank of England, even in very recent years. For not only may the Federal Reserve determine the conditions and terms under which member banks may rediscount or borrow from the Reserve Banks, but it may directly determine the reserves required against deposits of member banks. In addition to this, the Federal Reserve Banks may expand or contract credit by buying and selling government securities and fix the terms under which they will purchase acceptances.[15] What further powers can they possibly need to regulate effectively the volume of bank credit?

The actual mechanism of control is simple. By law, the banks in the Federal Reserve System, comprising a very large part of the total banking strength of the country, are required to keep with the Reserve Banks a certain percentage of their deposits. Prior to 1934, these reserves were on an average 10 per cent of the demand deposits. Now, when the required reserves were definitely known, as in former times, the commercial banks commonly extended their loans to the limit. When no acceptable loans were available, they purchased government securities and some few others, so as to maintain the largest possible proportion of earning assets. Whenever there was need, the banks could, and still can, take some of their assets to the Reserve Banks and rediscount them, or use them as collateral for a loan. This is what normally happens when pressure for funds is high and reserves are at approximately the legal limit. It follows that at such times the banks are exceptionally sensitive to the pressure of these rediscount rates. Originally it was supposed that this would be an adequate means for credit control.

But in creating the Reserve System, a secondary means of control was added. This provided that the Reserve Banks might invest their assets in government securities, and some few others, which supplied a wonderful lever for smooth operation, alike for acceleration and deceleration. For in times of pressure, when it was felt necessary to check the expanding credit, the Reserve Banks could sell securities to the market, thus withdrawing funds, and thereby reduce the reserves of the member banks. And in the same way, when the money market needed easing and encouragement, they could go into the open market and buy securities. The effect of this was to increase the reserves of the member banks. This latter method did not come into use until the Reserve Banks themselves were in need of 'earning assets,' and employed this means to increase their revenues. The effect was so unmistakable that the method has been repeatedly employed to ease the markets and encourage lending by putting the banks in funds.[16]

The Federal Reserve Banks are thus provided with two powerful means of maintaining control. The first is the rediscount rate, the second the purchase and sale of government securities. The procedure is much that of a locomotive engineer. The latter can put on or take off steam as he desires, and in this way increase his speed. Or he may use his brakes, applying or releasing them. When applying his brakes he will first shut off steam. And when he wishes speed he will simply release the brakes and open the throttle. The analogy may be applied to the practices of the Federal Reserve Banks. The rediscount rate is a brake that can be employed to halt undue expansion; the purchase or sale of securities can be used in either way, to check or to expand. Skillfully employed, these two agencies are adequate for any normal emergencies.

But under the new law, yet a third agency has been added: that of varying reserve requirements of the member banks. Originally these requirements were fixed by law and could be changed only by act of Congress. Under the new law, they may be raised or lowered at the discretion of the Board of Governors of the System. It is a method that can be highly effective, if properly administered. It was employed in 1937 when the reserve requirements were doubled. A drastic step, and in the judgment of competent critics much too effective. It may have contributed towards the marked decline in industry and in the security markets. Experience is often a poignant teacher. The action of the Board in raising reserve requirements, it was thought, would be taken as a warning, checking the rising tide of speculation without injury to the nation's business. Apparently an erroneous view. It was a peculiar situation. There was widespread demand for action by the reserve system to prevent inflation. But it is always difficult, as this instance revealed, to operate credit control in an effective manner when confidence has been impaired by enormous losses and threatened by huge governmental deficits. The situation was abnormal and not likely to recur when more usual and, it may be hoped, more natural business and financial conditions prevail.

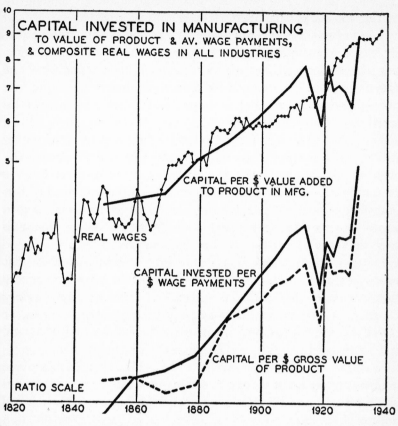

CAPITAL INVESTED IN MANUFACTURING
TO VALUE OF PRODUCT & AV. WAGE PAYMENTS,
& COMPOSITE REAL WAGES IN ALL INDUSTRIES

CAPITAL PER $ VALUE ADDED
TO PRODUCT IN MFG.

REAL WAGES

CAPITAL INVESTED PER
$ WAGE PAYMENTS

CAPITAL PER $ GROSS VALUE
OF PRODUCT

RATIO SCALE

1820   1840   1860   1880   1900   1920   1940

XXVI. CAPITAL INVESTED, VALUE ADDED, AND WAGE PAYMENTS

In order to bring out more clearly the very close relationship shown in the preceding chart, I have here made closer comparison of these three factors, showing, first, that real wages are a direct function of the invested capital, as the amount of capital invested is to this value added. Second, how closely the capital invested per dollar of wage payments corresponds to the capital per dollar of the value of the produce, which is very much the same thing as the preceding. If all employers could learn and if all workers could understand the force which really determines the amount and rate of wages paid, we would have few labor troubles, and quite possibly would have less interference from labor unions. It seems paradoxical, to the workingman, that the greater the profits earned, the more his wages will rise. The typical viewpoint is the reverse: high profits mean 'mulcting the workers.' A prize example of economic infantilism!

4. *Credit control in the 1920's*

There has been a widespread inclination to deny that credit control can always be effective; a viewpoint frequently expressed by Federal Reserve officials. As evidence of this, it is said that in the period before the great crisis of 1929 credit control was tried and failed. I should like to consider how the monetary policy of the 1920's was developed, and to what extent it succeeded in its objectives.

Following the close of the World War there was, it will be recalled, general apprehension as to the effect in this and other countries of restoring an immense number of men—in America some four millions—to their previous occupations. Grave doubts whether it could be done at all. And during the war there had been, as during all wars, a rapid and extended rise in prices; and there was almost universal expectation that, as after our Civil War, there would be a heavy fall in prices. Many economists took this view, and one of the ablest went so far as to publish an elaborate tract describing how we might deal with this situation: *Factors of Safety When Prices Drop.*[17] For a time it looked as if such a fall were in process. Then an abrupt turn, and a wild rise, in commodity prices, at a swifter rate than at any time during the war.

This rise through 1920 was so violent that even business men were apprehensive of its effect. There was a strong call for repressive measures. Finally, after a long wait, the Federal Reserve Board approved the policy Governor Benjamin Strong had so urgently presented and allowed the Federal Reserve Bank of New York to raise its discount rate to 6 per cent. Even this did not bring an immediate check, and so in May the New York rate was again raised, this time to 7 per cent. Probably a needless step; the 6 per cent rate would, as later experience suggested, have been sufficient. At any rate, there was an abrupt fall in the stock market, and then in commodity prices, bringing on the depression of 1921. Just as every violent fall in prices will do.

During this depression an unusual situation developed. The Reserve Banks during and after the war had rapidly increased the manifold services they had been called upon to perform, particularly as government fiscal agents. A corresponding increase in operating expenses. Towards the end of 1921 several Reserve Banks found themselves facing a deficit, and while some had surpluses, others had not. So to acquire some earning assets, they began considerable purchases of government securities. Within six months the fall in prices had stopped, business began to recover and confidence returned. A rather magical result which did not escape the attention of careful observers, and most notably of Governor Strong.[18]

Then through 1922 and into 1923 there was a sharp rise in several types of price and a corresponding expansion of bank credit, with a renewed outbreak of speculation. Because of this the Reserve Banks again intervened by raising discount rates. Again a sharp check to the rise in prices, and likewise to trade. So, in 1924, not as a means of meeting expenses but as a deliberate policy, Governor Strong proposed that the Federal Reserve Banks again lower their rates and buy heavily of government securities. The foresight of a statesman. The recession in business was soon over and normal conditions restored.

A little later an episode that has been gravely misunderstood. It has served, under the skillful handling of some who were opposed to Governor Strong's policies, and perhaps jealous of the domination of the Reserve Bank of New York, to cloud the fine reputation he had built up. In the spring of 1927 the Bank of England was apprehensive that England's return to the gold standard might have been premature, and with his long experience and foresight Governor Norman proposed to Governor Strong that the two banks cooperate towards tiding over the possible stringency that might develop at the peak of London demands in the autumn. This was done. In the summer of 1927 the Federal Reserve renewed its purchases of government securities and lowered its rate, with precisely this intent and only this intent, to relieve the pressure on London during the peak of its seasonal needs.

This action aroused in some minds very active dissent. Stock speculation had been rife through 1925, and again in 1927; credit had been expanding, and some were fearful of the outcome. The action of the Reserve Banks naturally stimulated the stock markets anew and Governor Strong was warned that he might face a difficult situation. He did not need the warning. His long experience had taught him to expect precisely such a result. And he did not fear it. It was his belief, and the writer was able to bring forward evidence to support this, that the discount rate could check any stock market boom that might break out. By no means widely understood, Governor Strong's plan anticipated proper repressive measures as soon as the autumnal demands upon the Bank of England had been met. But this part of the program was long delayed, and in February, 1928, Governor Strong was stricken with a fatal illness; in October he died. It was not until August that, in response to his constant urgings, the New York rate had been raised to 5 per cent. Wholly inadequate. The market boom went on, gathering momentum for another year. Not until August, 1929, was the rate finally raised to the decisive 6 per cent. Within six weeks the backbone of the craziest speculation the country had seen for a generation or more was broken.

The general lesson of the 1920's is unmistakable. The discount rate in New York and elsewhere does have a powerful effect. Whenever this rate is high enough, a boom is checked. But this policy must be pursued courageously; otherwise useless. The boom goes on to its fatal issue. The policy of raising rates must of course include the sale of government securities, to deprive the banks of funds that are being used to finance speculation. That such a policy can be effective was shown in 1920, in '23, in '26, and belatedly in '29. If Governor Strong's plan of restricting reserve credit had been followed, from early in 1928, the later phase of wild speculation could easily have been avoided.

But credit control can encourage recovery as well as restrict a boom. The effect of Reserve policy in 1921, in '24, and in '27 was unquestionably favorable. After the long delay in '29, the vacillating and timid policy that followed could not be effective.[19]

A profound misfortune that such a brilliant beginning should come to such an end. In credit control we have a powerful mechanism that might be used to maintain a degree of economic stability such as this country has hitherto never enjoyed. With the continuance of destructive depression, and the failure of a variety of monetary experiments, we have deep skepticism instead. Abortive efforts at arbitrary control of prices and production, all as old as Diocletian, and always a failure from time immemorial.

Unless we learn to control credit, we face, I think, the danger of endless extension of arbitrary regulation of business. That is why it is so important to realize the implications of the period under view. For every period of highly optimistic prosperity is bound to produce speculative activity, and therefore undue credit expansion. And this invariably means crisis and depression. This is the Shorter Catechism of economics:

Never a depression without a preceding boom. Never a boom and high prosperity without an outbreak of speculation. Never such an outbreak that has not ended in a financial crisis. Check the speculation in time, and we shall have no serious depressions. But if a depression does appear, we have abundant means of counteracting its influence and bringing about a restoration of normal prosperity. No mystery in this, as in time we shall learn.

PARETO'S LAW OF UNIVERSAL INEQUALITY

The population of the earth is distributed with great unevenness over its land surface. Well over a half (57 per cent) of the total land area of the earth is occupied by only four and a half per cent of the total population of the world. And about 81 per cent of the earth's total land area contains only 18¼ per cent of the world's population. Only a little over 5 per cent of the land area of the earth (densities of 200 and above) contains 52.5 per cent of its population.

—RAYMOND PEARL: *The Natural History of Population;* 1939

Those possessed of the qualities for leadership must not only be given a free field; they must also be stimulated to the full exercise of their gifts. Inequality of some sort appears to be indispensable as a stimulus.

—F. W. TAUSSIG: *Principles of Economics*

CHAPTER XIV

PARETO'S LAW OF UNIVERSAL INEQUALITY

1. The prevalence of natural inequalities

THROUGHOUT the whole range of nature, inequality, disparity, wide differences are the rule.[1] Little equality of any kind anywhere on earth. Even among the planets and the stars. The suns themselves, which we now know to be numbered by the billions, vary unbelievably in size, in density, in temperature, in every characteristic. There are dwarf suns as there are dwarf peas. The dwarf suns have such an amazing density, their force of gravity is so great, that a pint measure of their substance would 'weigh' a ton. One of the most colossal of the suns, at least in bulk, Epsilon Aurigae, has a density so thin that we might sail right through it—it would take considerable time at the present speed of the earth—and never know it.

So in all animal, and even plant life. Some so minute as to defy even the finest microscopes, some towering like the giant sequoias. Some may live only in water, as the plankton and whales; others may live in the desert and exist almost without water. And these forms of life may vary from the ultra-microscopic microbes or viruses to the lordly elephant and the monstrous grampus. Nothing equal anywhere, not in size, nor strength, nor in intelligence. The continents themselves differ in area, in population, in natural resources. The largest of the continents, Asia, is more than four times the size of Europe. The population of Asia is over twice that of Europe, three times that of North America and Africa combined. The soil, the coal, the iron, the forests, every diversity of resources is most unequally distributed.[2]

Not only in the endowments of nature, but in the achievements of man, countries differ just as widely. Perhaps two-thirds of the population of the earth cannot read or write, have few tools, almost no machines, live at a level incomparably below our own. The United States alone possess more machinery and utilize more mechanical power, for example, than all the rest of the world together; and yet it has scarce 6 per cent of the world's population. Perforce of this amazing development of machinery and of mechanical power we have greater wealth and income than any other five countries combined. And our *per capita* wealth and income, our economic standards, are far above those of other countries.

Why this tremendous inequality? Why should wealth and physical resources and the capacity to produce be distributed among the nations and the peoples so differently? And why *used* so differently? The resources of the United States in coal and iron are possibly no greater than those of India and China. Today these two nations together have perhaps six or seven times the population. Yet their combined production is far less than that of the United States. And it must be added that these two Asiatic countries have an old civilization with a remarkable record of early achievement. A full two thousand years ago India was producing the finest steel in the world; and the ancient accomplishments of the Chinese are proverbial. Why, then, the extraordinary difference in the tempo of development between the oldest and the newest of the great countries?

Precisely the same in all the ways and walks of life. Within the United States itself we find the same extraordinary differences among the states—in size, in population, and in wealth and income. In area the states range from the empire of Texas, 266 thousand square miles, to the little county of Rhode Island, 1248. In population the states range from more than 13 millions in New York to only a hundred thousand in Nevada. And differences of the same sort are to be found in every phase of economic life. The same wide differences in total production, in agricultural production, in industrial production; in total income and in per capita income; in capital invested in industry and in machinery used in agriculture; in wealth and in taxes. For all practical purposes, there is hardly any field of endeavor in which equality can be found even among the states of our own country. Or any others.

These differences in peoples and in countries are not new. They are at least as old as the culture and civilization of man as shown by archaeological records. Thus, all through history we find races with a talent for navigation, trading, and adventure. Far back in the dim mists there was a people in southern Arabia in the land of Magan, known to the Babylonians and to the Egyptians, who had

all these characteristics and seemed the predecessors of the Phoenicians. They were ship builders, explorers, and miners, and they
distributed their products to the surrounding nations. And then as
their successors, there was the race that founded Tyre and Sidon
and Carthage, a peculiar people who never had large land possessions, only narrow strips along the shores. But the Phoenicians had
large cities and a widespread commerce, and they sailed long distances. There is some evidence that they were regular voyagers
from the Mediterranean down the west coast of Africa. They went
in search of gold and ivory, and it is known to this day as the Gold
Coast, though there has been little gold found there in the last
thousand years and more. And so formidable was the strength of
the Phoenicians and their settlements that, as we know, Carthage
contended with Rome for supremacy in the Mediterranean. Every
school boy knows the story of Hannibal at the gates of Rome.

And then the Greeks, or as probably one should say the Hel-
lenes, a northern race with beginnings in Crete and Asia Minor,
and then in Greece proper. A people whose origin is still a mystery,
possibly the product of the great Doric and kindred invasions. For
centuries they were rivals of the Phoenicians; and they spread their
power far over the Mediterranean, occupying something of the
position in the commercial world as the British in our own time.
They were first of all navigators, traders, free booters and pirates;
but destined to become the light of that ancient day. They did not
invent the alphabet, or banking, or coinage, or sailing ships; but
one by one they took up all these things and carried them forward
to become the foremost merchants and bankers of that period. For
600 years the Athenian Owls, as they were known, silver coins and
some gold, were the international currency of the Mediterranean
region and even far beyond. Perhaps these people did not have true
bills of exchange, any more than did the Babylonian bankers; but
they did have a system of drafts by which travellers could carry
purchasing power in safety to the most distant lands. It is noteworthy that so large a number of their most famous men boasted
of their wide travels, among them Democritus, Herodotus, and
Thales.

And as they became rich and founded distant cities like Syracuse
and ancient Massilia, the present day Marseilles, they took up letters
and the arts, and especially sculpture and architecture. Some of their
creations, like the Parthenon, and the sculpture of Phidias, have

never been surpassed. They adventured profoundly in literature; had their poets and dramatists and grammarians, whose creations remain after two thousand years among the finest products of the human mind. And likewise in the fields of science and philosophy. Their final flowering, in the city founded by Alexander, marks the apogee of Mediterranean civilization. And all of it growing out of a people that first distinguished itself in trade.

Centuries later came the Italian commercial cities, Venice and Genoa and others, that maintained a wide trade with the Orient, carrying the wares of Western Europe to the East and returning with the special products of these lands. It was in these cities that modern banking arose. These were the first to adopt the Arabic notation and the new business arithmetic with its cipher, or zero position. There also the beginnings of modern bookkeeping.[3] And with their economic progress, came the Renaissance in the cultural life of the world. Later still the Portuguese and then the Dutch, once the leading commercial nations of Europe, and still holding large possessions in Africa and the Far East. After them the English, an insular people on a small island, growing up, as it were, from semi-barbarism, who apparently gained but little from three hundred years of Roman occupation, but changed profoundly with the coming of the Saxons and the Danes. Destined to become the most far-flung trading nation that the world has ever known, and a land of great wealth, invention, science, and philosophy.

Consider that the chief contributions to modern civilization have always been made by one or two nations, standing out as the leaders of their time. Then as now, the bulk of the peoples of the world were plodding along in their accustomed ways, gradually adopting the innovations of their leaders. Obviously a tremendous difference in the capacity of a people to add to the progress of mankind. Why did the Chinese, for example, never rise to leadership? They had the magnetic needle very early, but they were not daring navigators. They had gunpowder probably before any other nation, but they were not mighty warriors. Never in the vanguard. With not a tithe of their numbers, why did the English rise to a kind of world dominion? For a hundred years and more England was the primal land of colonization, commerce, and invention. The English perfected the steam engine, and new processes for making steel. They devised all of the important textile machinery, and they discovered the means of manufacturing electricity. Countless other contributions

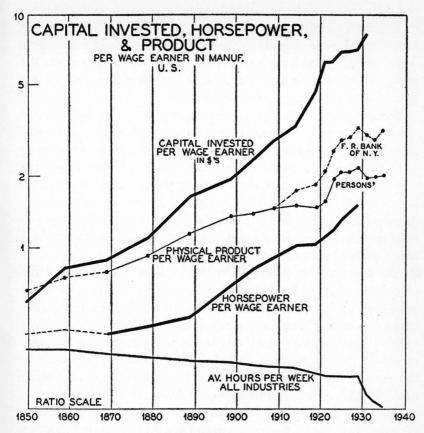

CAPITAL INVESTED, HORSEPOWER, & PRODUCT
PER WAGE EARNER IN MANUF.
U. S.

CAPITAL INVESTED PER WAGE EARNER
IN $'S

F. R. BANK OF N. Y.

PERSONS'

PHYSICAL PRODUCT PER WAGE EARNER

HORSEPOWER PER WAGE EARNER

AV. HOURS PER WEEK ALL INDUSTRIES

RATIO SCALE

XXVII. THE CAPITAL INVESTMENT AND THE WAGE OF THE WORKER

As indicated in the preceding chart, the wage is dependent upon the value added; and now we see that this value added per worker is a function not of the energy or ability of the worker but solely the amount of capital invested; that is to say, the amount of machinery employed in the product. This in turn means the amount of horsepower per wage-earner. This, and this alone, has made it possible for the average manufacturer in the United States to turn out nearly twice as much in goods per worker as that in any other country. He has twice the machinery, which means twice the capital invested. It is this that makes possible the steady lowering in the number of hours worked, in the face of a steady rise in wage payments. The product of a century of invention and progress, after perhaps five or ten thousand years of little change—and vast poverty.

to modern civilization. And England still remains the creator of the most extensive empire the earth has ever known.

It would seem that genius is as narrowly distributed among the peoples and races, as it is rare and confined to a slender number in the countries that have risen highest and produced most. It is an enigma, but nevertheless a fact, which we must accept as a part of the scheme of creation. And so perhaps it will always remain. The scepter of the British Empire may pass, and in turn the United States may lose the industrial supremacy of the world. Leadership will be handed over to other nations, with new talents and surpassing vigor perhaps it will arise in the lands of the East. We cannot see far into the future; but this much we know: the qualities of genius or talent will remain unequally distributed by nations or races, and among the peoples of these. The bulk of the earth's population may still remain the hewers of wood and the drawers of water. We cannot equalize human ability.

But it is not only in invention and in the arts and in other high accomplishments that we find this inequality. It covers the whole range of human faculties in the individual. Few indeed of more than one talent. The most familiar fact of everyday experience Who does not recall in his childhood the youngster who was so adept at shooting marbles that other boys would not play with him except with heavy odds? So in every kind of sport and occupation I suppose there are, at a modest estimate, three million youngsters now working their heads off trying to pitch a curved ball like Dizzy Dean or Carl Hubbell. In my youth I spent hours upon hours at it I can hardly recall anything at which I ever worked harder; a total failure. With all this practice by millions of boys, but few rise to be pitching stars.

And the same in every variety of technical skill. The extraordinary dexterity of Dr. Alexis Carrel in tying knots with two fingers and in working with needle and thread, were the foundation of his amazing accomplishments in surgery. Skill of the same high order is required to become a marvelous golf or tennis player, or an extraordinary billiard player, or a chess master. It is worth noting that unusual accomplishment in these fields is often shown by young men—chess prodigies capable of competing with the masters Some competence in sports may be gained with practice, by many persons; to the genius complete mastery comes with comparative ease. The same throughout all the professions. But very few lawyers doctors, or clergymen rise to fame or fortune among the hundreds of thousands of competitors. But even a successful clergyman can make a fortune. The late Dr. DeWitt Talmage, a noted preacher of the last generation, was a remarkable money maker, equally successful as a popular writer or a platform orator.[4] He died with a considerable accumulation.

Little need to pile up instances of the wide variances in ability and accomplishment in all the fields of human endeavor. Obvious that these exist everywhere, and are common to all the world. The only question is whether these differences may be measured and compared; and whether there is any wide general conformity to which we might give the name of a "law." Highly important to know whether these differences we see all about us are at haphazard, not to say pure chance, or whether they reveal similarities and regularities capable of measurement, analysis, and explanation. Very little available data. A fertile field for investigation. But there is one in which the data are abundant, comprehensive, and of profound social import. That is the distribution of Income. Available in many countries. Not only are the data on this distribution most complete, but the acquisition of income is everywhere an important part of the social activity of persons in all occupations. So these differences of income have aroused the interest of many able economists, and even occasional statesmen: primarily to determine the facts, though in many instances with a thought of methods or policies designed to minimize glaring inequalities, or destroy them.

2. Pareto's Law of Income Distribution

But throughout all history we find record of exceptionally rich men, rich, of course, relative to the wealth or possessions of their time. Homer, if it was Homer who wrote "The Odyssey," reports a peasant as saying that Odysseus, 'King' of Ithaca, "was twenty times as rich as any man known;" and he gives a tabulation of his flocks of cattle, sheep, horse, and the like. The first 'Tyrant' of Athens and perhaps the greatest statesman of Greece, was Peisistratus, who made a fortune in the silver mines of Laureion, and raised a private army with which he seized the reins of power. In the golden days of Pericles the wealth of the leading bankers like Pasion and Phormion was traditional. These bankers were once freedmen, as were most all the bankers and many of the rich men of antiquity. Fruits of the lofty disdain of 'trade.' In Roman days Pliny tells of the enormous fortunes of Caesar, Pompey, and Crassus (the "plunderbund"), and adds, "their fortunes, however, were small compared with the huge accumulations of some of the rich freedmen of our own time."

The same in later days. Wherever we find a highly developed society, with thriving trade and broadening activities, we find individuals of conspicuous wealth. The period of the Renaissance was 'rich,' not only in art, but in a commercial sense. And in this period bold financiers and merchants arose in many of the European countries. The Medici in Florence, rising from humble circumstances, acquired immense wealth, became patrons of the arts, and founded a dynasty. The Fuggers amassed an even larger fortune. Starting as weavers, and turning to commerce and banking, in the course of a century and a half they became the richest family in Europe. In France, Jacques Coeur followed the same pattern. The son of a merchant, he rose to opulence through his numerous activities in shipping, commerce, and banking. These three great financial families of this period came principally from the 'lower' ranks.

Our day presents the same picture; the rich men are richer and more numerous simply because the modern world is more populous and more productive. Among the English fortunes were those of the banking families, the Rothschilds and the Barings, but the largest were made in industry. One ironmaster of the early industrial period started 'at the bottom,' and died in a castle leaving a million and a half pounds. Another accumulation of this period, amounting to five million pounds, had its source in the manufacture of carpets by machinery. The notable German fortunes of the Krupps, the Siemens, and the Rathenaus, had their origin in the iron, steel, and electrical industries. The great fortunes of the aristocracy, those of the Duke of Westminster and Prince Henckel von Donnersmarck, were generally the result of large ownership of urban land. But many noble families augmented their wealth by close association with banking and industrial houses.

The paragon of all, our own United States, long known as the 'land of millionaires.' From the birth of the nation. Beginning with George Washington; probably our first real millionaire. Another who began poor, but by the time he was nineteen had already earned enough to possess fifteen hundred acres of land. Washington's fortune came entirely from land; and although land has contributed to some large American fortunes, the much more usual source in this country has been industry, transportation, and trade. John Jacob Astor, after three years as a furrier's apprentice in London, reached these shores in proud possession of one new suit of clothes, twenty-five dollars, and five flutes. The growth of the fur trade of the Pacific Northwest brought him vast holdings. The elder Vanderbilt began his business life on his sixteenth birthday when he borrowed one hundred dollars from his thrifty mother to operate a ferry. He left a fortune of a hundred millions. Andrew Carnegie came to this country in the steerage, began as a telegrapher, became a steel magnate, and accumulated nearly half a billion. Rockefeller had a year's schooling in a commercial college, and like Carnegie began his career in a job paying about four dollars a week. His unparalleled benefactions totalled at least 800 millions. When Henry Ford formed his company he had no capital to invest; only his invention and his business ability. Today perhaps the one living billionaire.

It is not only in making money, but in accumulating it, saving it, that these wide differences exist. Mr. Rockefeller, for example, was said to have remarked about his brother that William was a much smarter man than he, and made much more money: but somehow he did not hold on to it. The two faculties, we definitely know, are often sharply differentiated. William Rockefeller started in the oil business with his brother, at nearly the same age. He was a tremendous plunger in the stock markets, and was supposed to have had at times a very large fortune. But when he died a few years ago, his estate equalled only about one-tenth what his brother had then given away. Here seemed almost complete equality of opportunity and, more than that, a certain inevitability of making a large fortune through association with his brother's exceptional business talent. Another younger brother also went into the oil business, but never made any such success, although he did become a millionaire.

Are these rich men throughout all history merely accidents, of good fortune? A childish belief. When he began, Ford knew nothing of gasoline engines; Rockefeller knew nothing about oil refining; Carnegie knew nothing about steel making; Vanderbilt did not go into railroading until he was 68 years old, and 90 of the 100 millions he died with were gained in the fifteen remaining years of his life. The almost invariable record that the richest men have started as poor boys, as a rule devoid of any special opportunity, seems to suggest that here is a special form of talent as distinct, as real, and probably as vital to civilization and to progress as the genius of a Titian, a Shakespeare, a Newton, a Faraday, or any of the supreme figures of the ages. Everywhere, in every way, and in every age, the genius has been a rarity—one in millions.

From all of which arises a problem of profound interest: does the distribution of this talent and ability, especially as shown by income, follow any definite law? This was the question considered nearly half a century ago by a rarely endowed young engineer, born in Paris of Italian parentage, gifted far beyond the common lot, and destined to become one of the original thinkers of his time: Vilfredo Pareto.[5] His outstanding discovery as to the distribution of incomes is known as Pareto's Law, and the graphic figure that depicts this distribution is generally known as the Pareto Curve. In simplest terms, the law states that the larger incomes are received by comparatively few people, the number with large incomes more numerous, and as the incomes decrease, the number receiving these lower incomes steadily increases in a very smooth curve. If we represent graphically by logarithms the various levels of income and the number of persons in receipt of each level of income, the 'curve' so drawn will be a straight line.[6] This does not strictly hold at the extremities, the highest and the lowest incomes.[7]

Pareto's 'Law,' it should be emphasized, is entirely empirical, a finding of fact.[8] Pareto did not attempt to offer an explanation. He was content to test the validity of his conclusion on the distribution of income through all periods and all places for which data were available. And his test showed conclusively that this distribution followed the same pattern, with slight variations in all cases. Not only was this true for contemporary distributions in several European countries and provinces; but it was equally true for Augsburg and Basel in various years of the fifteenth century. Invariably, the curve of distribution follows the general pattern described by Pareto's Law.

A curious instance cited by Pareto revealed that this same distribution obtained in Peru, in the time of the Spanish domination at the end of the eighteenth century. A terrible plague put a severe strain on the funds of the church and the government. To acquire the needed money, a kind of amulet or 'bulla,' said to have come down from the crusades, was sold to the people as protection against the plague. "Every inhabitant, Spanish, Creole or mixed, was forced to buy, at a price fixed by the government, a bulla which he believed

sential for his safety . . . The price of the bulla varied according
the rank of the people." The historian Robertson gave the num-
er of persons in each class who bought these amulets. When Pareto
otted the distribution of the buyer by rank, in this case equivalent
income class, he found that it approximated the usual curve of
stribution.[9]

The profound results of Pareto's investigations have been sub-
antiated by later tests. Dr. A. L. Bowley on several occasions has
own that the distribution of income in Great Britain, so far as it
revealed by income tax returns, follows Pareto's Law.[10] Lord
amp independently made a similar verification. In fact, he reported
at one could estimate the number of income recipients in the lower
vels, if data on the number for the higher levels were available.[11]
hus, Pareto's law has proven a useful tool for economists, statis-
cians, and Treasury officials, concerned with these problems.

In turn, a study of the distribution of income in the United States
es far to substantiate the finds of investigators in other countries.
Ve have now in this country several series showing the distribution
various times. The returns for the years of the Civil War income
x, 1864 to 1872, and the income tax returns since 1913, show a
rong conformity to income distribution pattern of Pareto's Law.[12]
addition to these income tax returns, various other estimates of
come distribution, such as those of W. I. King, von Szeliski, Rufus
ucker and the National Resources Committee, show the same gen-
al distribution, and suggest that this has not changed materially
the industrial advances since the Civil War, or by the inroads of
e great depression.

Pareto's findings were received, as many great discoveries, with
epticism and resentment, as if it were a new kind of "iron law" in
conomics, which indeed it really was. To many the idea of such
xity in the distribution of wealth is repellent. An attitude not
ncommon toward economic realities. Throughout the whole de-
elopment of science this idea of fixity or "law" seems to arouse an
stinctive antagonism; and it is noteworthy that almost all the dis-
ussions of the validity of the evidence for Pareto's Law have been
oncerned with the social desirability of the conclusions that may
e drawn from it.

Pareto's results were published in 1896, and have had more than
he usual amount of attack. The slope of the Pareto curve, it is said,
not constant. But Pareto himself was aware that it varied to some

extent at different times and in various places. But part of this m.
be due simply to the unreliability of the data. More particular
critics have endeavored to show that the straight line of the Pare
curve is not, in fact, perfectly straight; that there are perceptib
deflections. In particular, Frederick R. Macaulay has devoted mu
time and ability to prove that the supposed regularity of the curve
factitious and deceptive, and that the aberrations are in reality
larger import than Pareto supposed. In the use of logarithms, the
variations are minimized if not hidden. This is likewise the view
Professor Shirras from a searching examination of the income t
returns of India.[13]

To my mind, all this is to ignore the broad implications of the da
which seem unquestionable and clear. It is not highly important th
Pareto's Curve should provide mathematical precision for estimati
the number of persons at every level of income. The very nature
the material, its heterogeneity and the inherent difficulty of assuri
accuracy in collecting it preclude such an assumption. The fact th
sufficient conformity to Pareto's Law is found by leading statisticia
in England and in the United States to warrant the use of this fo
mula in making estimates of the numbers of persons receiving incon
at various levels, shows that the distribution is not haphazard, a
that there are fundamental forces behind it.[14]

Possible to say even more. Not only is the distribution of incon
among the people of a country in accordance with a definite la
but the same or similar differences in income may be seen in eve
field of economic activity. Even the distribution of incomes in ag
culture follows much the same pattern as the distribution of incom
in industry. The same in governmental salaries, in the learned pr
fessions, and even in so equalitarian a field as teaching.

3. *The distribution of income of various types*

So accustomed are we to the idea that ours is a democratic for
of government, that we do not readily think of governmental salari
as fundamentally similar in their distributions to incomes deriv
from private employment and production. None the less a defin
fact. For example, few think of the President as receiving a very hi
salary, comparable to the highest paid to the managers of successf
corporations. But the total amount, with all perquisites and allo
ances, is not far from $400,000 per year. To this must be added tl

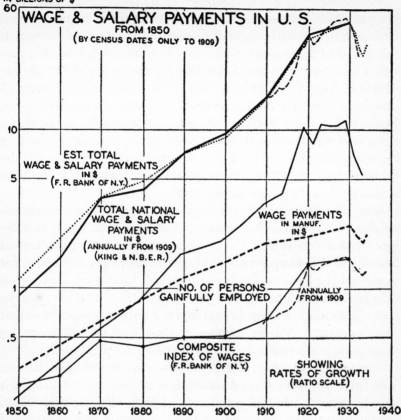

WAGE & SALARY PAYMENTS IN U. S.
FROM 1850
(BY CENSUS DATES ONLY TO 1909)

EST. TOTAL
WAGE & SALARY PAYMENTS
IN $
(F. R. BANK OF N.Y.)

TOTAL NATIONAL
WAGE & SALARY
PAYMENTS
IN $
(ANNUALLY FROM 1909)
(KING & N.B.E.R.)

WAGE PAYMENTS
IN MANUF.
IN $

NO. OF PERSONS
GAINFULLY EMPLOYED

ANNUALLY
FROM 1909

COMPOSITE
INDEX OF WAGES
(F.R.BANK OF N.Y.)

SHOWING
RATES OF GROWTH
(RATIO SCALE)

XXVIII. A HIGH TEST OF THE ACCURACY OF WAGE AND INCOME DATA

Above is a remarkable demonstration of the substantial accuracy of the statistical data now available. Here are census reports as to the number of persons 'gainfully employed,' and below this is a composite index of 'wages paid.' Now, if these data were accurate, multiplying the index of wages by the number employed would give the total of wage and salary payments, such as is shown in the upper dotted line. By the side of this is given the estimates of actual wage and salary payments in the United States for the period under view—the earlier estimates being those of Professor W. I. King. The correlation between these two upper lines was unexpected, and could not have been possible over such a long period save for the substantial accuracy of the different indexes employed. Notice how closely, in turn, the total of 'wage payments in manufacturing' corresponds to the increase in total national wage payments.

exemption from state income taxes that all federal employees enjoy.

Yet further: if all official salaries in the country are graded by income classes, we should find that the comparable Pareto curve is more heavily skewed than that of most other income distributions in the United States of which we have any definite record. The reason is that there are some large official salaries—the President, the Mayor of New York, the Governor of New York and governors of other states; then the moderate number of intermediate salaries from $5,000 to $15,000, and a tremendous number of employees at salaries equal to or less than that of skilled labor. In the latter class would be included the school teachers, clerks, the police and firemen, the postal employees, all of whom generally receive rather less than skilled workers in private employment.

Much the same distribution of governmental incomes appears to be true of the next richest country, Great Britain. But it is noteworthy that the skew of the curve is *less* than that of the United States! There is a larger number of salaries above $25,000 a year, for in general the higher officials of the British Empire are better paid than in the United States, with the natural effect that the governmental personnel of Great Britain has been distinctly superior to that of this country. A large number of these well paid positions are permanent, while relatively few in this country are. In fact, we have no equivalent of the Administrative Class of the British Civil Service. The latter seems the natural result of an empire organization, as it may be termed, which requires men of high administrative talent, who must be attracted by adequate remuneration and an extended tenure of office. Worth noting that the oral examination for the Administrative Class of the British Civil Service is of the same informal type that a modern industrialist might use in selecting an executive for a great concern.[15]

But it is not only in governmental salaries that we find rather wide inequalities in distribution of income; even in agriculture the inequalities are of much the same order. The Department of Agriculture in Washington has recently completed two valuable studies of the distribution of farm income. Two computations have been made: one of total farm income; the other of income from products sold from the farm (the cash income). We have plotted these curves of the distribution with similar distribution curves of total National Income and income from other occupations, and have found that these various curves do not differ widely.[16]

Important to note the striking facts shown by these curves of total farm income and cash income. Of the total farm produce sold, one-half is derived from 11 per cent of the number of farms. This estimate has been widely noted but seemingly without recognition of its significance. It goes without saying that this distribution of income on farms is not strictly a measure of business ability, since some farms are large, some more fertile, and some have more machinery than others. And cash income is not the same as net income. In larger farms with more employees, much borrowed capital and more machinery much less of cash income remains as net. But in agriculture, as an industry, we have large scale production and small scale, profitable production and unprofitable. By and large, the incomes therein must be related to differing degrees of farming and business ability in either field.

Another interesting result of this census is that an astonishing number of farmers are very well-to-do. According to this calculation, there are at least 25,000 farms in the country with cash production of $20,000 per year or more. Since from this we may project the higher brackets with some degree of accuracy, following the Pareto Law, we may be sure that there are a considerable number of farms with incomes of $50,000 and $100,000 per year, and even more. In other words, this inquiry on farm income reveals that among the farm population, precisely as among the urban population, there are very rich and very successful men. And that in the distribution of opportunity, ability, and achievement, farming does not differ fundamentally from industry, trade, or finance.

As in every other kind of industry, there are sharp and natural limitations to the rewards from agricultural enterprise. No one, for example, would imagine it possible to become a billionaire out of manufacturing velocipedes. One might be a very efficient grower of peanuts or pecans, watermelons or citrus fruits, and with diligent application one might build up a handsome fortune. But nothing like in the aggregate what similar ability might yield in, say, the oil business, or in the manufacture of motor cars.

Of all this there is an exceedingly instructive example, the famous Dalrymple farm of a generation ago, in North Dakota, at one time reckoned as one of the largest, if not the largest, farm in the world. Mr. Dalrymple, its owner, had inherited a considerable fortune. In addition, he was highly respected for his energy and business ability. Several times offered positions in corporations at salaries much above his profits on his farm. Mr. Dalrymple's own conclusion, after years of experience, was that wheat farming is not a very profitable occupation, and that if he had sold his lands and invested his money, to earn 4 per cent, he could have accepted one of the positions offered him, and had a far larger income. The farm was eventually broken up and sold. The conclusion, then, must be that while relatively high incomes may be gained from successful farming, these incomes are as rare as from successful enterprise in any other line. The distribution of ability, then, is everywhere much the same.

4.   *The distribution of corporate profits*

The largest inequality of all is found in the distribution of corporate income. The obvious reason is the wide differences in the size of corporations, and in the ability with which they are managed. Almost from the beginning it would appear that superior management led to the development of large enterprises and large companies. From the most ancient time. The famous Marashu Sons Company in ancient Babylonia was one of the earliest of these companies. But similar organizations seem to have been prevalent in every period of history. During the rebirth of business enterprise and industry in Europe that followed the Renaissance, similar large aggregations of capital were developed, as illustrated by the Medici, and the Fuggers. All born of the broad expansion of commerce in that period.

With the invention of the steam engine and the incoming of the Industrial Revolution, large enterprises have grown apace. And this growth regularly trotted out as an increasing menace. A favorite bugbear of economic 'reformers.' The ancient and faded cry of "monopoly," still raised from time to time as justification for more governmental meddling and control of business. The same intense jealousy towards large enterprises that has subsisted through hundreds, if not thousands, of years. And yet in spite of this fierce antagonism, successful enterprises have steadily grown in size; each generation attaining larger and larger units. Many still recall the huge outcry over the formation of our first "billion dollar corporation." The sole reason for this steady advance of large-scale operation must be that it is economically more efficient. It produces and sells better goods for less money. Aided by the standardization of brands and the growing confidence of the public in their wares.

But why should larger business organizations be more efficient? Because of increasing specialization of talent, and the combination of these different types of ability. When it is possible to have an aggregation of specialists with fine team work, the inevitable result is more effective management with production at lower cost. And the proof is that the larger and more successful enterprises have grown steadily with industry and commerce itself. Probably our leading corporations today are not much larger, relatively, than, for example, the undertakings of Thomas Hancock in the Massachusetts Bay Colony two hundred years ago. But hundreds and thousands of times as large in an absolute sense.

Probably the native ability of business men is no higher today than five hundred, or perchance five thousand years ago. Very doubtful whether the Fords and Rockefellers of our time were any more capable, shrewd, and farseeing than the Medici or the Sons of Marashu. But they are creating larger enterprises, turning out much larger product with much greater economy. Not only because they have the advantage of machine and power production; but also because they command more varieties of talent, may now utilize them more effectively than was possible in earlier days.

These differences in size and in the quality of managerial talent account largely for the tremendous inequality in the profits earned by corporations. Consider the following: of more than half a million corporations in the United States making income tax returns in the peak year of 1929, only 270,000 reported any net income. Of these 270,000 corporations reporting net income, half of 1 per cent earned 60 per cent of the net income of all corporations; and fewer than 2 per cent of the 270,000 earned 75 per cent of the total net. We have here quite the most unequal distribution of income of any type for which we have data in this country.[17]

These data are for all corporations. In trade, profits were distributed with slightly less inequality, in manufacturing and in mining with about the same inequality, in transportation and in public utility industries more. Thus, among these latter less than 1 per cent of the number earned 90 per cent of the total net. A striking inequality, but understandable when we consider that railroads and electrical utilities can operate economically only on a very large scale.

Endless fret and pother whether a few men or a few corporations may come to dominate all industry. And the records of corporate profits are cited as evidence of this tendency. In reality this is quite inconceivable, simply because of the steady diversification of industry and the constant stream of new processes, inventions, and discoveries. An outstanding instance is the United States Steel Corporation. No nearer now to absolute domination in steel or to a 'monopoly' than at its inception forty years ago. The smaller steel companies have shown more vigor and enterprise, more business intelligence, than the combination formed in 1900. The remarkable progress of recent years in this industry has been largely due to the initiative of the smaller companies. Indicating perchance that there is in any given period a size at which efficiency is at a maximum. We can rely upon the steady advance of industrial methods to forestall any threat to independence that may arise from the larger producing units.

Equally absurd to suppose that these huge organizations, even those called "monopolies," can seriously 'prey' upon the public. For the obvious reason that each and all of them is especially interested in producing and in selling at the lowest profitable price. In no other way can they maintain their primacy. Undue profits invite more vigorous competition, and incite the cupidity of other enterprisers, so that no large 'monopoly' has ever remained such for any great length of time. Success in any field is the surest stimulus to competition. In the long run the only way that any producer can command a wide market is by making better or cheaper goods, from both of which the public must benefit. It is only when large organization contributes to further efficiency by utilizing the best talent in every branch of the business that they can compete with the smaller organizations. The fact that corporate profits are so concentrated, so unequally distributed, is the best proof that large organizations do succeed in combining the most effective, specialized ability. With profit to the whole of society.

THE DISTRIBUTION OF HUMAN ABILITIES

There never was in the world two opinions alike, no more than two hairs or two grains; the most universal quality is diversity.

—MICHEL DE MONTAIGNE: *Of the Resemblance of*
Children to Their Fathers

Differences in income and wealth are after all the necessary results of physical and mental differences. Sometimes these differences in income are greater, sometimes less, finding a counterpoise in some institutions, enhanced by others, largely in consequence of the expanded borders of society within which personal superiority can manifest itself. The connection between personal differences and differences in income is not always the same. But as these differences persist, we can say they are normal, so that differences in income represent differences in capacity, superior or inferior work resulting from these differences in capacity, and the value that society gives to such differences in work.

—GUSTAV SCHMOLLER: *Jahrbuch für Gesetzgebung,*
Verwaltung und Volkswirtschaft; 1895

CHAPTER XV

THE DISTRIBUTION OF HUMAN ABILITIES

1. *Inequality and probability*

THE prevalence of inequality and disparity throughout the whole range of nature is patent enough. But in no field save in business, as evinced by income and wealth, has this inequality been regarded as undesirable. Great success in the arts and sciences is hailed as a contribution to cultural and technical progress. But the success of the business man, the large income he gains and the wealth he accumulates, is widely held a social bane; chiefly because it involves economic inequality. Such an attitude overlooks the fundamental fact that the successful business man not only contributes to his own advancement, but to that of the entire country.

Beyond that, it is part of a universal scheme. This inequality in income follows a general pattern, which has persisted over an immense period of time, and in practically every progressive society. Important to reflect that all this must be due to natural forces, and that if this be true, it must be difficult, if not impossible, to eliminate this inequality without destroying the mechanism which promotes welfare.

The distribution of many simple characteristics of human capacity follows what is known as the normal probability curve.[1] Fully verified by experience. The wide range over which this normal distribution is found indicates that this law may be applied to practically all types of inequality. This pattern of distribution is found not only for physical characteristics, such as height, weight, and head size, but also for mental characteristics, such as memory, speed, and accuracy. Just as typewriting tests will show a comparatively large number of persons with moderate speed; smaller numbers faster or slower than this mode. It is probable that if we could devise satisfactory tests for measuring such characteristics as judgment and perseverance, we should find that the distribution of these characteristics is of much the same type.

253

2. *Complex abilities and fundamental faculties*

But when differences of *attainment* are considered, they do not follow this pattern of the normal probability curve. In some instances, perhaps. But in many instances, the curve is sharply skewed. That is, the number of persons superior to the mode tends to be much smaller than the number in the inferior groups. The aptitude of college students in learning, as evidenced by grades, seems on the whole to follow the normal pattern. But in some fields, particularly the physical sciences, the proportion of failures is more than the normal expectation. And the more difficult the field of endeavor, the more varied the qualities required, the greater the skew. Thus, in business, in which achievement may be measured by income, the distribution shows a marked skewness. And if we had similar measures of attainment in the arts, we should find that the pattern of distribution of success strongly resembles the distribution of income. A matter of common knowledge that the number of persons with exceptional artistic ability is far less than the number with average talents.

The explanation is perhaps obvious. Achievement of a high sort is always a combination of several fundamental faculties. For example, even fast running is a complex of abilities. But it does not require as many fundamentals for outstanding success, as say, hurdling or broad jumping. An exceptional hurdler must have not only the speed of a sprinter, but he must be a good jumper. So, too, a broad jumper must be a fast runner in order to get the momentum that produces a long jump, and in addition get a forward kick into it. It is because hurdlers and broad jumpers require these extra faculties that the differences between them tend to be somewhat greater than the differences between sprinters.

Much the same can be seen in other types of sport. The requirements for safe hitting and for home run hitting in league baseball are much the same, except that home run hitters must be able to hit for longer distances. For this reason the differences between safe hitters will not be so great as those between home run hitters. And this is borne out by the batting records for the major leagues. Hitting ability follows a curve much like the normal probability curve. But the distribution of home run hitting is sharply skewed. There is an instance of a very capable ball player in a major league who has not hit a home run in more than 1,200 games. This does not prevent him from hitting safely.

If one could measure the fundamental faculties necessary for success in any type of undertaking, it would then be possible to predict the pattern of distribution. Unfortunately, not many studies of this type. We do have some. For forty years, Professor Carl Seashore of the State University of Iowa, has been working with intelligence and perseverance on the fundamental capacities required in musical achievement.[2] His measures of the fundamentals endeavor to segregate the different factors involved in singing or in playing music; and he has devised means of measuring individual capacity in each of these special traits. With stimulating and significant results.

Professor Seashore found that there are four especial faculties which may be directly measured and compared. Each of these has long been known, and their physical nature studied. Ever since the days of Helmholtz, well over half a century ago. The great work of the German physicist on the physiology of tone production laid the foundation for a new science. Professor Seashore has provided measures which permit a numerical gradation in these four essentials.

First, the sense of pitch. Some persons have so acute a sense that a single note sung or played can be identified by them at its precise position on the musical scale. Known as absolute pitch. A rare talent. But everyone has this sense in some degree, save a few who are actually tone deaf. If we did not have this faculty we could not enjoy music.

Second, the sense for time and rhythm. Almost everyone has it, even those that cannot play or sing. Its significance in music is seen, for example, in modern jazz, which is almost all rhythm. Some would say that modern fads or fashions in music have little "music," meaning little of the elements other than rhythm.

Third, of tonal intensity, the loudness or softness of a given note. Only the deaf entirely lack this faculty, but a fine sense for this is an important factor, for example, in piano playing. Often referred to as fine musical feeling. Nevertheless, rather surprising in its simplicity; many non-musical persons have it in a high degree.

Last of the four is the sense of tone 'color,' or as the physicists call it, timbre. Basically an acute hearing for the upper partials or reverberations of every musical note that is struck. It is these upper partials and their blending which give 'color' to the different instruments; some very striking, as the English 'horn,' the French horn and other unusual instruments of the orchestra. They give a wide diversity to the different types, as witness the violin and the xylophone. It is largely this sense of tone color which gives an acute enjoyment of orchestral playing. Likewise, it is the basis for the differences in the character or color of different voices, as the flutelike quality of a Melba as contrasted with the rich warmth of a Flagstad or a Lili Lehmann.

In addition to these four Professor Seashore would add a sense of sonance and consonance, the blending of one tone with others, as in the recognition of a musical chord. Not so easily measurable. But Professor Seashore does not suggest that these are all the musical faculties, or that high ability, even near perfection, in these determines whether one may be a great singer, violinist, or pianist. Far from it. Even with all these a person without quick reaction time, or agile fingers, could never become an outstanding performer. But it is certain that without a fine sense of pitch, for example, one could never become a famous violinist though he might become a piano virtuoso. Without a keen sense of time and rhythm no one could be master of the exquisite *nuance* or the *tempo rubato* that gives the delicate finish and charm to the finest musical performances. The point is that without these basic faculties the highest achievement in music is inconceivable. And at least these four can be measured.

As to the larger import of these findings. None of these qualities is related, or paired naturally with any other. They are independent attributes; that is to say, in Mendelian parlance, they are "unit characters." Just as distinct as height, weight, skin, and color. They are not merely psychic in the ordinary usage of that term. They are physical faculties, and if the physical basis is absent, the faculties are also. Simply the lack of the necessary physical apparatus may make a person tone deaf.

Note that these faculties are not linked in any statistical way. There is not the remotest expectation from a fine sense of pitch that one has a keen feeling for rhythm. Qualities just as different as skill in drawing and mathematical ingenuity. Further, these faculties are innate, that is, inborn. No kind of training will supply the lack. Practice may enormously improve some of them, as the dexterity of the violinist or the pianist. But with club fingers this is impossible. And the proof that it is impossible to supply the deficiency is that with the expenditure of millions of dollars in training children we still cannot considerably increase the number who attain high rank. This, it seems to me, is Professor Seashore's outstanding contribution. His tests, it may be noted, have been recorded for the phonograph, and may be obtained in the shops.

But the importance of this remarkable work lies far outside the limited field of music, or esthetics. It is so far as I know the first successful foray into the broad field of physical measurement of the faculties basic to any particular type of ability. I am not forgetting the fine pioneering work of the other leaders: Thorndike, Yerkes, Terman, Spearman, and others who have made contributions in this field. But here is a study of a novel kind. The implication is that talent, of every type, and especially of the higher grades, is native, and cannot be acquired by training, or education, that this training is often a waste of time and money and effort.

The social significance of these tests goes deeper. The Seashore tests indicate that *all* the various talents and capacities are distributed in more or less the same fashion. All this, of course, remains to be finally demonstrated by numerous experiments, analyzing the fundamentals in types of talent. But, as noted, thousands of measurements have shown that a wide variety of physical characteristics are distributed according to the curve, that is, with very few in the top-most rank. If much the same distribution is found for every fundamental faculty, and if each faculty is essentially a unit character, combining these discrete faculties in a high degree, very high talent of any kind must be rare. That is, on the law of probability anything approaching what we call genius will be just as we find it everywhere: possessed by very few. Further, if these discrete capacities have a re-inforcing effect, the difference between high talent and mere talent will be immense.

All of which readily suggests that the attempts, through all the ages, towards a redistribution of wealth are as futile as a legislative enactment, that the population shall consist of a stipulated number of Paganinis, Edisons, or chess wizards like Paul Morphy. But futile as such an attempt would be, it might be extremely harmful. Such endeavors must discourage enterprise, diminish the wealth and income of the successful business men who utilize their savings for the accumulation of capital, and prevent the improvement in general well-being through the introduction of new machinery, new equipment, and new processes.

3. *The faculties required for business success*

Most great fortunes have sprung from highly individual under
takings. Mr. Rockefeller *created* the Standard Oil Company, M
Carnegie his steel company, Mr. Vanderbilt the New York Centra
Railroad. Almost every special industry that we have has been i
large part such a creation of some strong, commanding busine:
genius. Take the very largest, in point of capital investment th
greatest in the world, the American Telephone and Telegraph Con
pany. Very largely due to the late Theodore Vail, a man of excep
tional energy and capacity, who apparently did not care much abou
accumulating an immense fortune. His joy was in the building up o
a vast enterprise. Much the same may be said of the General Electri
Company, largely the achievement of Mr. Coffin.

While the accumulation of wealth is incident to business succes:
it does not follow that all business men seek only to make money
Many of them regard the building up of a large enterprise as o
more consequence. The two more or less go together. With succes
profits will be large, and the business man may become rich; an
with these profits it will be possible to expand yet further. Many o
the qualities found in a successful business man are exactly thos
which characterize success in all fields of endeavor—whether tha
of artist, scientist, or soldier; as vision, initiative, and fathomle:
courage. Take the case of General Grant, perhaps our greatest mili
tary figure, at least so ranked by leading military authorities.

When the war broke out Grant was "down and out," virtuall
cashiered from the army because of drunkenness, an utter failure i
business, clerking at thirty dollars a month for his two brothers in
little store in Galena, Illinois. When recruiting began he had not
friend. He went down to Springfield. One day came an opportunity
There was a regiment of hoodlums from Chicago whom nobod
could control. Grant was small of stature, but in an hour after h
had taken command he had faced down the chief bully and di:
turber of the regiment, and in two weeks' time had the best drille
company in the regiment. He was sent off to war, and soon turne
up in front of the Confederate forts at Donaldson on the river. I
vain he sought permission to attack; the vacillating Halleck mad
no reply. Grant then sent a telegram: "If I have no peremptory orde
to the contrary I shall cross the river at midnight." He crossed, an
in forty-eight hours he was a national hero, the first general who ha

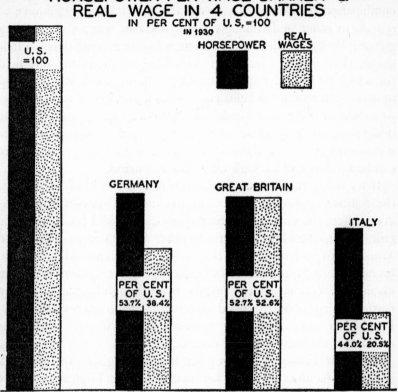

HORSEPOWER PER WAGE EARNER &
REAL WAGE IN 4 COUNTRIES
IN PER CENT OF U.S.=100
IN 1930

HORSEPOWER   REAL WAGES

U.S.
=100

GERMANY   GREAT BRITAIN

ITALY

PER CENT
OF U.S.
53.7% 38.4%

PER CENT
OF U.S.
52.7% 52.6%

PER CENT
OF U.S.
44.0% 20.5%

XXIX. WHY WAGES IN AMERICA ARE SO HIGH

Preceding charts have shown how closely the total product in manufacturing
corresponds to the amount of mechanical power employed. In the chart above, the
horsepower in use and 'real wages' in the United States are for comparison taken
as 100: and those in the other countries, as percentages of this. It will be seen, for
example, how nearly the power employed and real wages in Great Britain and in
the United States correspond. But in Germany and in Italy the wages paid, per
horsepower employed, are considerably less. The data for this chart were compiled
by the International Labor Office at Geneva in 1931, and were as impartial as
could be made. Even with some allowance for error, the broad fact stands out
clearly enough, which these pages have endeavored to enforce: it is machinery and
power which create high wages, and not labor unions or benevolent employers.

won a signal victory for the North. In another eighteen months he was in command of the Western Army.

The war gave Grant opportunity for the exercise of his especial combination of talents. Not always the ones that are conducive to success in other undertakings. Though Grant was an outstanding general, he was a failure as President, a failure as a politician, a failure in Wall Street, a failure in everything except in this one field for which he had the requisite qualities. Among those who find joy in detraction and in the belittlement of others, there was disposition to believe that because Grant was a failure in everything else he undertook, it must have been chance that gave him his fame. Chance it undoubtedly was, and that the accident of a major war. But there can be no doubt of his high talent for command.

If we study the lives of the famous in every field of attainment, the genius in music, in science, in invention, in statesmanship, it is everywhere the same: the special qualities required for the specific task. Often, like Grant, failures in other undertakings: Fulton and Morse, born inventors, were both mediocre painters. Mark Twain, literary genius, was a failure in business ventures. Edison, marvel in his field, was an indifferent business man; though he accumulated a fortune. Wagner nearly ended his career in prison as a revolutionary. Possible to add innumerable instances in which great talent was manifested exclusively in one direction.

Professor Taussig, who has given much thought to the question, adds other faculties necessary for success in trade. High among these he places judgment. "The successful business man must be able to foresee possibilities, to estimate with sagacity the outcome in the future. Especially is this necessary in new venture; and it is in new ventures that the qualities of generalship are most called for and the largest profits are reaped . . . Not infrequently those who are supposed to have the requisite judgment do not possess it. Personality tells, but may be deceptive—a vigorous presence, incisive speech kindling enthusiasm. Time and again an individual with such a personality secures a hold and a following, and is enabled to embark on large ventures. Yet finally he comes to grief because in the end he proves not to have the saving quality of judgment." [3]

Courage to venture is equally important. Executive ability, knowing how to handle men, is another. This faculty manifests itself especially in the selection of able subordinates. Highly desirable, too, that he have some understanding of the technics of industry; a though here, an able executive, cognizant of the importance of technological advance may make good his own deficiency by the selection of assistants who are familiar with the new methods and the new equipment.

From all of which, this, at least, is evident: that, as Professor Taussig avers, "in the business career, as compared with most others, inborn capacity counts more, training and environment less. Environment and ease of start seem to be of consequence in what we may call the middle range of the occupations—the businesses of moderate scale—requiring a substantial capital and yielding respectable middle-class income, but calling for no unusual degree of judgment or administrative ability . . . But in the upper range of the business world, in the large enterprises which dominate more and more the industry of modern times, native ability tells." Where the fundamental faculties are lacking, no amount of training can make good the deficiency and produce a real captain of industry.

The absolute level of success, however, obviously depends not only on these conditions, but also on economic environment. That is to say, no matter how able a man may be, he cannot accumulate a very large fortune in a poverty stricken community. Our rich men are far wealthier today than a century ago because the wealth and productive capacity of the country is far larger. Quite improbable that the money makers of our time have more native ability than in former times. Mr. Rockefeller would unquestionably have accumulated a fortune regardless of the specific economic environment in which he lived. He had already made a very large fortune in the oil business, when oil was still used principally for lighting; the development of cheap motor cars created a fabulous demand for gasoline: Mr. Rockefeller became a billionaire. Even as an ordinary merchant, he would have been a rich man; as the head of the Standard Oil combination, he would have been a millionaire; but he could not have become a billionaire without the development of the cheap motor car.

From this we may draw an interesting speculation. If the creation of large fortunes depends on qualities which, being inborn are not likely to change much from one generation to another, we should expect to find that there has been a steady progression in the estimated amounts of the fortunes of our richest men, from George Washington down to the present day. Difficult to estimate closely some of these earlier fortunes; but it would appear that there is a fairly definite relation between the size of these fortunes and the size of the National Income. In other words, George Washington and Stephen Girard possibly amassed as large fortunes for their times as John D. Rockefeller or Henry Ford. This is, of course, difficult to confirm. But if we compare the more trustworthy estimates of the fortunes of John Jacob Astor, who died in 1848, and Commodore Vanderbilt, who died in 1877, with those of the present time, this relationship seems not improbable.

Yet great fortunes require other faculties than those necessary for business success. Not infrequently we find men with a strong money-making faculty who seem unable to save any considerable part of their gains. A quite human characteristic. About eighty or ninety out of every hundred persons gainfully employed either save nothing, or the most modest amounts; and the proof is that around 97 per cent of persons dying do not leave property enough to make a probated will necessary.[5] Amazing when the high level of income that normally prevails in the United States is taken into account. The larger part of the workers receive wages equal in purchasing power to six or eight times that of a century ago. But they save little, or nothing. The attraction of wares, stimulated by clever advertising, seems too great to be resisted. Even people with incomes in the higher levels, from $5,000 to $15,000, contribute but a small part of the savings of the country. To them, too, the lure of social prestige, through a high level of expenditure is likewise strong. Only the highest incomes contribute largely, especially the capital for reproductive enterprise. It is not just because only the highest incomes can contribute heavily; but that the tradition of thrift seems especially strong among those who attain the highest economic success. Their absorption in business seems to outweigh the joys of spending.

Still enough of Veblen's 'ostentatious expenditure' to stir intensely the normal feelings of envy and resentment toward great riches. Jesus could offer the rich man but a slight chance of getting to heaven. But why no such jealousy when the wealth is gained from artistic achievement? We admire, may even envy, the exquisite genius of a Paderewski or a Toscanini. These may receive high reward for their talent and even accumulate wealth; but they do not inspire such enmity. Raphael, for example, was for his time perhaps the wealthiest painter we have known. Yet no one regards such reward in artistic capacity as a 'danger to the social system;' congresses or parliaments do not pass laws in a fantastic effort to 'dimin-

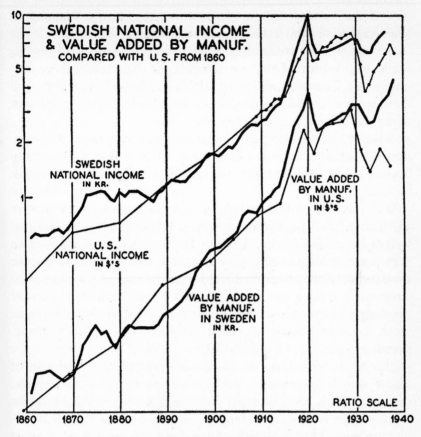

XXX. THE REMARKABLE PARALLEL OF SWEDEN
AND THE UNITED STATES

Sweden is a small country, with less than one twentieth the population of the United States. But it is the only other country with long time measures of its income from 1860. Interesting to compare the growth of this income with that of the United States, as in the chart above. How singularly they have grown to-gether, percentage-wise. Still more interesting to note that, precisely as in the United States, this increase in income has been due very largely to the increase in manufacturing, and that the rate of this growth has, through the last 80 years, been almost identical with that of this country, and has been faster during this period than any of the larger countries of Europe. Sweden's highly intelligent countrymen have very carefully nurtured the system by which they have grown to wealth and comfort. Having gained this, they have not striven to crush it, as seems to have been the case in the United States.

ish inequality' in artistic ability. Discontent and resentment toward success seems almost entirely confined to those whose fortunes have been gained in trade. Relic of an ancient snobbery.

Artistic genius is everywhere regarded as contributing to the cultural development of the community, providing new sources of satisfaction. But, to a high degree, the business man does very much the same. It is he who contributes most to the economic development of the community, providing higher incomes and better living standards for all. Nevertheless, a large number of people do feel that in the distribution of income and in the accumulation of wealth there is some kind of extreme unfairness, which ought to be 'corrected by law.'

Why this difference in attitude? The obvious answer is that money and income are a most intimate part of all our lives, and represent well-nigh universal desire. Almost everybody has an active part in our economic life, but few, very few, in artistic fields. This is why envy can never be so personal and so general toward the successful artist as it is toward the business man. Psychologically, the roots of this antipathy to great wealth, especially the feeling about *gold*, go much deeper, down to the earliest experiences of childhood, as the Freudian psychology has disclosed.

Beyond all this, there is a widespread belief that exceptional wealth usually represents some kind of chicanery or "unfair advantage." There are many who believe that most anybody could make money who would 'stoop' to the 'ignominious' methods of business men. That some riches have derived from dishonest practices is no doubt true. But the fortunes of nearly all men of great wealth have come from successful production and distribution. Creating 'goods.'

Then there is the doctrine that all profits have their origin in the 'exploitation' of labor. This is the well-known socialist view: that labor is 'expropriated' when capitalists retain the 'surplus value' as profits. Tersely put by the revolutionary Proudhon, when he said, "Property is theft." [6]

Finally, there is the well-nigh universal belief that a large part of large incomes is inherited; and so we have a widespread feeling that inheritances should be heavily taxed. This belief seems clearly at variance with the ascertainable facts. First, that most very rich men were born poor. I have compiled a list of twenty-five of the largest fortunes in American history, and in this list there is a single instance of great wealth built upon an inheritance. That was the late Andrew W. Mellon. (Perhaps also William H. Vanderbilt.) Pierpont Morgan had at one time a large estate, but did not die with any such possessions as Mr. Mellon. Practically all the rest had in their youth felt "the stimulating sting of poverty." Indeed, of these the list is so long, the instances so many, in almost every country and every age, that I have wondered whether this was not a strongly predisposing factor towards sizeable accumulations. Obviously the rich young man, born to affluence, rarely knowing what it is to work for a living, and having everything that money can buy, does not as a rule value money very highly. Nor is he usually inclined to work hard and scrimp and save to make more. Perhaps too we have here the explanation why no vast fortunes continue to grow as in the vigor of their creators. Among the forty thousand "millionaires" of 1929 estimated from the income returns, there was probably not one in 25, if one in 30, whose wealth was derived from inheritance.

It would seem that the only basis on which redistribution could be justified would be on the theory that it is not the absolute levels of income, but differences that are important to welfare and happiness. But this would imply that lower levels of income more equally distributed are more conducive to general well-being than higher incomes less equally distributed.[7] It would suggest that equal poverty is to be preferred to unequal wealth! And such a view was actually set forth by the famous socialist, Ferdinand Lassalle, contemporary of Karl Marx, that it would be better to have the working classes live on a *lower standard*, provided there was less difference between them and the 'upper' classes! "Every human suffering and every human privation, as well as every human satisfaction, and consequently the situation of each part of humanity," said Lassalle, "can be measured only in comparison with the situation in which are found other men of the same time." The French economist, Leroy-Beaulieu observes that according to Lassalle "it is not the absolute situation of the laboring population that matters; it is the relative situation. That the workers should be well fed, well housed, well furnished, well clothed, that they have leisure, that they enjoy the security of tomorrow and the rest of old age, all this is of no importance . . . if other men have a table more refined, palaces more ample, personal property more agreeable."[8]

An astonishing notion, Narcissism to the nth! A doctrine not likely to gain vogue among the working men of America. Who would exchange the high living standard that generally prevails in the United States, for poverty stricken equality? [9] If this is the strongest case for redistribution, we can depend on the common sense of our people to reject it, especially when they realize that such efforts must result in a lower output and in generally lower incomes.

MAN CANNOT LIVE BY BREAD ALONE

The presence of a body of well-instructed men, who have not to labour for their daily bread, is important to a degree which cannot be overestimated; as all high intellectual work is carried on by them, and on such work material progress of all kinds mainly depends, not to mention other and higher advantages.

—CHARLES DARWIN

The world has never had a good definition of the word liberty, and the American people, just now, are much in need of one.

—ABRAHAM LINCOLN

CHAPTER XVI

MAN CANNOT LIVE BY BREAD ALONE

1. *Inequality of income and economic progress*

INEQUALITY of income, it is agreed, is universal. Further, that the degree of inequality seems not to have been very different in this country 70 years ago from what it is today. And the same in England.[1] A recent analysis of the degree of inequality based on a most elaborate study undertaken under government supervision, that made by the National Resources Committee of the distribution of income in 1935–1936, may therefore be regarded as fairly typical for all periods. This compilation showed that in 1935–1936 the total national income of 60 billion dollars was distributed among nearly 40 million families and individuals living alone. Less than 10 per cent of the entire income went to those having incomes of $15,000 or more. Slightly less than 10 per cent went to the moderately rich with incomes from $5,000 to $15,000. The great middle group, constituting nearly 17 million families and single individuals, had incomes ranging from $1,000 to $2,500. This middle group formed a little less than one half of the income receivers and their share in the total income also a little less than one half.[2] In short, their average income was near the average for the country as a whole. No redistribution of income could affect this broad group. Redistribution would then seriously affect only the group we have called the 'rich,' to whom 10 per cent of the total income is distributed, and the 'submerged' one-fifth earning $600 a year or less.

The group receiving incomes of $15,000 a year or more consists mainly of those who show in high degree a combination of those faculties requisite to business success; while the group with incomes of $600 or less obviously consists of those who have failed to contribute efficient work in the various occupations. Taking from the rich to give to this submerged one-fifth would be to penalize the successful to endow the failures. The sociological and biological implications of such a policy are apparent. Much may be said in favor of relieving distress among the unfortunate and deserving poor; it would be disastrous by governmental action to reward the incompetent and the shiftless. A reward for incompetence must encourage the growth of incompetence; and in known periods it has.

What, now, becomes of the 10 per cent of the total national income distributed to the rich and the additional 10 per cent distributed to the moderately rich? A considerable part unquestionably goes to consumption, particularly for those with incomes from below $15,000 a year. But much of it is saved to form the capital necessary for the expansion of established industry and the development of new. The portion so devoted amounts scarcely to 5 per cent of the national income. Yet it is this saving, this addition to the capital supply, which alone makes possible economic growth. Without it we cannot have an increase in production, or in real income. Retard the flow of savings and progress must slow down.

If the incomes of the rich are diminished, their consumption may decrease slightly; but the far more serious effect will be the decrease of their savings. Without these savings, the capital necessary to implement new processes, new inventions, new techniques of production will be inadequate; production and income cannot continue to rise. In the end everyone, and especially the great middle group of workers, farmers, and business men, would all feel the effect.

2.   *The share of labor*

Astonishing that the share of the total income going to wages has been constant as far back as we have adequate record. A computation by W. I. King shows that this has been true since 1850; and other studies indicate much the same.[4] The explanation is not difficult. The comprehensive data that we have on production and capital investment provide the answer. The amount paid in wages has steadily paralleled the output. The volume of production in turn has risen only slightly less than the capital invested.

These relations are practically constant, and determined by natural conditions that cannot be changed. As to the share going to capital over long periods, good times and bad, it is so small that it only about equals the going rate of interest.[5] Some successful business men earn much more, otherwise there could be no great fortunes. On the other hand, some enterprises earn nothing, and some even lose their capital. When an average is struck, the net return is almost unbelievably small. If in the last century the whole of it had gone to 'labor,' it would not have increased wages by 10 per cent. In recent years, the increase would have been near zero.

Apparently not one person in a thousand is aware of this narrow margin of profit, or that it depends almost wholly on the efficiency of management. Subtract this, and the enterprise is a failure, as about 90 per cent of all such undertakings actually are.

Can the distribution of income, determined by economic forces, be altered by law? The evidence, it seems to me, indicates that it never has. Enormously rich men have existed throughout all known history. Their fortunes, tremendous for their time, were accumulated under the most diverse forms of government, and under the most diverse economic conditions. One thing and only one thing seems to have been common to all of them. That is, possession of the faculties required for business success. A fact never more in evidence than in and since the World War.

No period of our history has been marked by more extreme changes than this last quarter century. War and inflation, great prosperity, and overwhelming depression. And throughout, the distribution of income tax returns has varied little.[6] In the last six years, with all the equalitarian legislation designed to diminish inequality, difficult to discern any definite trend in the slopes of the curves.

This is the more significant because of the enormous difference in the actual amounts of the total income reported from year to year for income tax purposes. Probably the most violent decline in our history. After 1837 there was a heavy fall in the production of non-agricultural goods, perhaps equal to that of 1929 to 1932. But in 1837 more than three quarters of the population was still on the farms, while in 1929 less than one quarter. The conclusion seems obvious. Neither legislative enactment nor economic conditions can alter human capacity.

These results for the United States seem to find confirmation from the investigations of Lord Stamp and Professor Bowley as to the distribution of income in Great Britain. These eminent authorities have given much attention to the question, and their conclusion was that so far as any available data could reveal, there had been no marked variation.[7]

Apparent substantiation of the Pareto thesis. In a century marked by profound economic change, in which England became the leading industrial and commercial country of the world; by wide monetary changes, with the demonetization of silver in nearly all countries, paper money inflation in almost every country; by a world war involving most major powers; by heavy government taxation and colossal borrowing; by social legislation of every variety. And throughout a century the division of income in England remained much the same.

Here are the two most highly developed industrial nations, and two which have the most complete information on their income and its distribution. Both yield substantially the same evidence.

3. *Attempts at redistribution and economic progress*

Though legislation designed to redistribute wealth must be ineffectual, it is certain to have repercussions of major import. Always the attempt at redistribution through government intervention has required enormous taxation of large incomes, and the expenditure of these revenues mainly for the benefit of the lowest income group, the 'submerged.'

If out of the profits of successful business the government takes a large part in the form of taxation, the return to business men must fall below even the prevailing rate of interest. The reward for success is no longer commensurate with the risks that are inevitably a part of all business. Thus, if the investment of a million dollars may yield a profit of $100,000, under effective management, a tax of 60 per cent on such incomes will reduce the net yield to $40,000, or 4 per cent. Such a return is not compensatory when even a modest allowance is made for risk. The business man with capital to invest will prefer to buy tax exempt securities when available; and if they are not, he may decide to keep his funds idle. This unescapable. And when business men will no longer take the risk because the return has become inadequate, unemployment must result. As it has.

Identically the same with wage legislation. If a minimum wage is set for a particular occupation, in which labor has been paid much less, the higher rate of wages can not be made effective. Employers are always compelled, by competition, to pay all that they can afford. If legislation now prescribes a higher rate, business must diminish the amount of employment.[8] Such an attempt to increase wages through legislation may actually result in a decrease in the total amount of wages paid out. Further, these higher wages will be only partially borne by the employers, but will be passed on in the

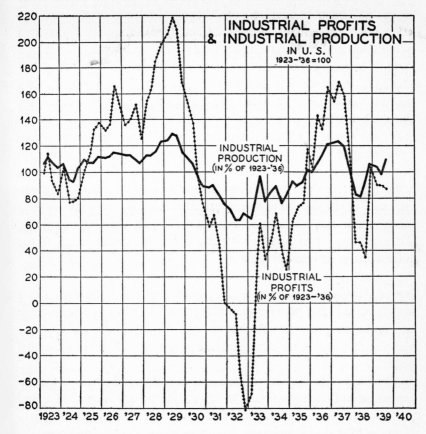

XXXI. INDUSTRIAL PROFITS AND INDUSTRIAL PRODUCTION

Many believe that the great corporations and their owners, because of their wealth and power, do not suffer as seriously in times of depression as the "workers," that is, their employees. Interesting to find clear evidence that the corporations and employers have far greater losses from depressions than the workers. In the chart above, the correspondence between the volume of the product and the profits realized in a wide variety of industries, making perhaps three-fourths or more of the total industrial profit, is vividly illustrated. That this correspondence is surprisingly exact is set forth in the following chart. Actually for every variation in the product, the fall in profits is three or four times as great, while wages, as a rule, change but little—unless the depression is very long.

form of higher prices. While minimum wage legislation may for a time give higher wages to a lesser number employed, these higher wages will be at the expense of other workers and consumers; and every industry will be likewise affected, and the total volume of production and employment lowered.

How much of the unemployment of this decade of the 1930's is due to the attempt to maintain excessive wage rates, it is impossible to say. Not to be overlooked that from the very beginning of the depression, strong pressure was put on employers by the government not to cut wages. Perhaps the first major depression in which no drastic revision of wage rates was undertaken. Not until 1932 were wages reduced to any noticeable extent; and by 1935 rates were higher than in 1929, despite the tremendous unemployment. Actually in the decade of the severe depression of the 1930's hourly wage rates in factories rose more than in the very prosperous 1920's.[ ] To consider, when reasons are sought for the continuance of the huge volume of unemployment.

Again, the little saved by the mass of the people is not, and should not be, invested in the promotion of new or untried industries. These savings should not be so invested because the risks of capital loss in new industries, new processes, new inventions, is high. Only people with large incomes and accumulated wealth can afford to take such risks.

The bulk of the savings of the people goes into homes, public investment and such purposes, in which the return is moderate and risks almost entirely absent. The funds for the expansion of reproductive capital, in new and growing industries, come from the savings of the rich, particularly those with incomes of more than $15,000 a year. As noted, the savings they provide for reproductive capital probably does not exceed five or six per cent of the national income.[10] The late Colonel Rorty was inclined to believe that it was considerably less—possibly not much over 4 per cent. However small as this contribution is to the capital supply, without it progress would be impossible, for there would be no way of implementing the new processes, the new inventions, in the new and growing industries.

Needless to repeat that these new industries which widen employment, stimulate other industries, increase competition, force other improvements, and most important of all, are the main instruments in raising wages. When they are successful, these new enterprises often make high profits and therefore can afford to pay much higher wages than in declining or stagnant industries. Therefore the capital so invested has a spermatic and stimulating effect which is lacking in the capital invested in homes, good roads, and similar comforts. With the present organization of society, this fund for new industries, and expansion and renovation of the old, can come from only one source: from the rich, who have more than they can spend and who can afford to risk millions, in the aggregate, in new undertakings.

It follows that the confiscation of profits, or a large part of them, and the scattering of these funds to the lower income groups, must extinguish the capital supply hitherto available for reproductive enterprise. Progress is impossible; we should virtually reach the Stationary State envisaged by John Stuart Mill.[11] Indeed this seems just what we have done in the last decade. In this period we have had colossal and unexampled government expenditure, derived from unprecedented taxes and governmental borrowing; profits have been almost extinguished. For a number of years the industries of the country, on balance, have had no clear profit.[12]

The discouragement of industry and enterprise has been expensive. Hitherto, the country has always recovered depression losses and resumed normal growth in a relatively short time—almost never more than three years. In this period the average number of unemployed, over and above the average number in the preceding decade, was not less than five or six millions, and was probably much more. The beneficiaries of the policies of the past few years could not have been the workers as a whole. These have paid heavily for the destruction of confidence and the halt in progress.

I should be far from suggesting this tremendous national loss was due wholly to the effort to reform society. The depression had its origin, at least, in quite other forces—the same forces of boom and speculation that have caused all other depressions. And depression continued for some time before the reformatory legislation. But this legislation did help to prolong the period. The revival that began with the new administration never reached the level of 1929, still less of the secular trend.

This six years' experiment has proved one thing: government may tax and borrow and spend, but it cannot change the general pattern of income distribution. Beyond the direct beneficiaries of government doles, the inequality will persist. Further, the discouragement of enterprise must result in sending millions who might have been self-supporting workers into this group of relief recipients. If we are determined to adopt a policy of governmental intervention to diminish inequality, we must accept a stationary state.

4. *Inequality and happiness*

To many, I am aware, the principles here set forth will seem austere and forbidding doctrine. Some are overwhelmed by the thought that the distribution of ability, whether in the arts or in the sciences, whether in work or in play, is determined by inborn qualities that bring about wide differences in achievement. But I do not regard these natural differences, whether in business or in other fields, as 'condemning' large numbers of people to 'poverty and mediocrity.' So far from that I find in this very pattern of distribution of income and achievement the hope for the highest levels of material well-being and personal happiness.

Given this pattern of distribution, it follows that a rise in the total income must affect favorably every group in the community.[1] Economic progress does not result in exclusive benefits to any one class. If men already rich grow richer, it is also true that those with lesser incomes likewise gain. There can be no monopoly of the fruit of economic advance; we all go forward together. Here, it seems to me, is a doctrine of high optimism. Poverty will be banished from the earth. For a century and a half we took giant strides in that direction. We can reach the goal of a whole nation of well-paid workers only if we can maintain the economic progress characteristic of our country until recent years. I find in the constancy of the pattern of distribution proof that the interests of every group in the community are fundamentally the same. No class can, or does, benefit by the expropriation of others.

Insofar as the general level of well-being depends upon an adequate supply of material things we can be certain that with favorable economic conditions, both well-being and individual happiness will be greater in the future than in the past. If the capital necessary for the effective use of new inventions and new processes is provided little reason to doubt that the total income of the country, and in every field of work, will increase.

But man cannot live by bread alone. Among other things, he requires a sense of achievement to attain happiness. Successful business men and many workers acquire this through their daily tasks. But others need distinction in other fields for the full development of their personalities. Does the distribution of ability offer the prospect of a moderate degree of achievement for nearly every person in some field of endeavor for which his natural capacity fits him? I think it does.

Suppose that it is true that for every genius there are, say, twenty or fifty men of high talent, a thousand of marked ability, and ten thousand above their fellows in capability, in ingenuity, or in strength. There is an infinite variety in human talent, and infinite ways in which to display it. There is almost no one who cannot excel in some fashion, to some extent, to do at least one thing better than his immediate fellows.

The famous Professor Huxley of an earlier day, whom I think of as one of the clearest of English philosophers, once said that life was like a game of cards in which we are dealt hands of varying value and left to play the game as best we can. And that seems to me a very graphic statement of the implications in Pareto's law. It does not tell us just how we may gain distinction, wealth, or happiness. But it does tell us to search for something wherein we have a special aptitude, and to seek achievement in that field. Extraordinary what a vast variety of things there are to do in this world. Not all of them will bring fame or admiration. But they will provide much personal satisfaction.

Far from declining, the pace of human progress seems, if anything, to be accelerating. And almost everyone can do some new or useful, some one unusual or interesting thing. And opportunity? Never was anything like it. Consider only the possibilities for research: the fact that the two thousand leading corporations that now report regularly each year to the National Academy of Sciences their expenditures for scientific research now pay out, all told, nearly $250 millions a year. All this opens wide the gates to thousands of gifted young men. An opportunity for scientific achievement with expenses paid!

And this is only a part of the picture. We cannot all be scientists, discoverers, or inventors. But there are hundreds of other opportunities to excel, as entertainers, actors, singers, pianists, artists, theologians, philosophers, poets, politicians, ball players. Opportunities unlimited. Great dexterity or strength or skill have always their meed of fame, their admirers and competitors: the Dizzy Deans, the Willie Hoppes, the Donald Budges, the Jack Dempseys. And though the fame and admiration is seldom great, the "village Hampdens" and "mute inglorious Miltons" have yet their audiences.

But this is not the whole story. We must recognize that many of the notably successful have not been very happy. Reflect upon the deep-seated and pervasive pessimism of Shakespeare or Carlyle and of many others like them. Certainly in the field of politics or what is called 'statesmanship,' the career of Bismarck represented as high attainment as any of his century; but all this left him only with an embittered sense of futility. Largely a question of temperament. There is a joy in simply understanding, and learning. "I am one," wrote the ancient Confucius, "who in the pursuit of knowledge forgot his sorrows, and did not feel that old age was coming on." Perhaps an ideal existence.

5. *The means to achievement and happiness*

But if the individual may not always attain, possibly a higher type of education, or training, may do much. If music ability, or the capacity to organize a successful business, or to be a star athlete, or to accumulate a fortune—if all this is determined by inborn characteristics, then why should not the aim of education be towards the discovery in the individual of some particular aptitude or ability? For in this direction, as I see it, lies the hope of happiness, and the joy of achieving.

For this purpose away then with routine, with regimentation, with trying to fit round minds into square holes. The everlasting source of mortification and chagrin, and the sense of failure and futility. It has sometimes seemed to me that present education is, in large part, a mild asylum of dullness. Of what earthly good to teach tens of millions of children identically the same things, by rote? What is the gain? That hundreds of millions will learn to read tabloid newspapers and 'adventure' magazines, with the slaughter of vast forests to provide pulp for all this mush and slush.

We spend vastly more per capita on education than any other large nation. With what apparent aim? To establish a monstrous system of unconscious regimentation and uniformity. We have now in Germany, a sufficiently horrible example of an unabashed effort to force such a scheme of uniformitarianism to the limit. To create in Germany seventy or eighty million animated sausages, identically

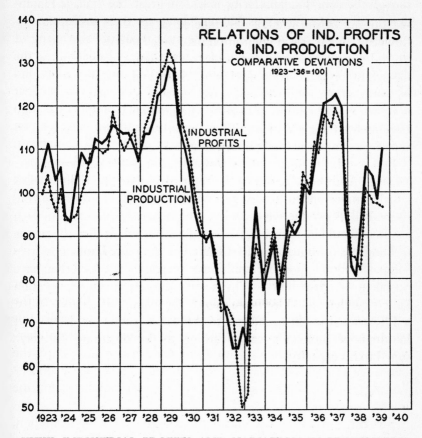

XXXII. INDUSTRIAL PROFITS AND VARIATION IN PRODUCTION

In the preceding chart, the percentage variations between industrial profits and production revealed that the drop in profits in depressions is usually three or four times that of the fall in the physical volume. In the chart above, the extreme of the fluctuations in the profits is made equal to the variation in the volume of production, thereby revealing the exact relationship which really exists between the two. This chart shows that the amount of profits realized by industries as a whole can be predicted from the volume of the product, so that no one has more interest in maintaining economic stability than the industrialist and enterpriser. Yet it is quite certain that no one has a larger ignorance of the reasons for these variations in product, and thereby in profits. The cause of these fluctuations is portrayed in the next two charts.

alike! What incredible waste: sausages for men! It will fail, and it memory go echoing through the halls of history with homeric laugh ter. But not before wars of unparalleled savagery, in which the fin flower of an European civilization may be engulfed.

And always a danger that under subtle guise, something of th like might happen even in the United States and in Britain and othe nations that may still boast of some measure of human freedom. I our present day education neglects the individual and seeks merel to regiment the child in a uniform pattern of culture, where is ou superiority over the totalitarian countries?

In a word, the purpose of a real education is *"la carriere aux le talents."* And the selection of the right person for the right work i equally important to society as a whole, the sole means of utilizing to the full its productive capacity. The material benefits from sucl a system would be immense, but not more important than the rescu of hundreds of thousands of frustrated, disappointed, unhappy live —impaled upon impossible ambitions of careers, for which they hav no talent or adaptability. Why should the selection of a vocatior be left to chance? Why not a *search* for talent and ability? Wha a difference it might mean—not to thousands—the favored few—bu hundreds of thousands, each learning to do something distinctl suited to his capacity.

SEISACHTHEIA THROUGH THE AGES

There is no grievance that is a fit object of redress by mob law.

—ABRAHAM LINCOLN

Nothing is more odious than the majority, for it consists of a few powerful leaders, a certain number of accommodating scoundrels and submissive weaklings, and a mass of men who trudge after them without thinking, or knowing their own minds.

—JOHANN WOLFGANG VON GOETHE

CHAPTER XVII

SEISACHTHEIA THROUGH THE AGES

1. *Humanitarianism and state action*

WHEN nations grow rich and powerful, they become conscious of the inequalities in society. Poverty becomes a sort of moral issue, and equalitarianism a distant ideal. And when political power comes into the hands of the socially minded, attempts are made towards revolutionary change. Legislation is enacted for the purpose. Usually with slender result. So difficult to overcome the natural differences of capacity, talent, foresight, and energy. Economic stratification remains. Even in Russia, in the most far-reaching attempt to establish a socialistic society yet made, there still exists a wide inequality. Mr. Max Eastman, an ardent socialist, writes bitterly of "The End of Socialism in Russia." The facts adduced by Eastman, and others, as to the disparity of wages and salaries seem to confirm his view. He endeavors to show that this disparity between the workers and superintendents and managers is rather greater in Russia than in ultra-capitalistic America.[1]

Why is it that attempts to diminish inequality by state action have invariably failed? Simply, I think, because inequality is a universal law of nature. The differences in income are a reflection of differences in economic worth. So long as human nature remains as it is (little prospect of rapid change) this economic inequality seems inevitable. No law, no edict can change the fundamentals of human capacity, which remain the same under socialism as under other isms. A hint of this is in the following dispatch from the Moscow correspondent of *The New York Times* (Feb. 5, 1939): "Soviet industrial leaders are finding that people work here from the same motives that they work in the capitalistic system. Some work for pride of accomplishment, or for the benefit of their fellow men. Some work to get the highest possible financial reward. Some work because if they do not they will starve." [2]

Yet from an immemorial time moralists and reformers have

283

wrestled with the problem. In ancient Greek and Hebrew history there is evidence of this same attitude toward the rich, the capitalist the successful business man, that we find in later days. The reforms of Solon grew out of the same feeling. Plutarch tells us that the disparity of fortune between the rich and the poor was then at it height. And Solon's reforms consisted largely in relieving the poor of their debts, shifting the economic burden from the impecunious to the rich.[3] So it seems to have been all through history.

It is possible that this thirst for equality is not wholly the reflection of the noblest motives. In some instances, it is clear that it is often a rationalized jealousy and antagonism. Soon as business enterprise become organized and there is a segregation of classes into workers owners and managers, antagonism must rise. Acutely in evidence in the time of Jesus. Dr. Erich Fromm, in a fascinating little volume has vividly set forth the extremes of social and economic status in Palestine during and before the Roman occupancy: great poverty among the masses and wealth and possessions among the upper strata.[4]

So we find very early attempts toward communistic societies even in ancient Palestine. One of these was the religious sect of the Essenes, from which Jesus was supposed to have come: based not only on communism but also on asceticism. The attitude of Jesus toward the rich and the poor seems clearly portrayed in manifold passages in the New Testament.[5] We have no means of knowing how authentic are these because a considerable part of the New Testament contains interpolations by the later followers and disciples of Jesus, during the two or three centuries in which the oral tradition alone existed, before being set down in Greek. Interesting that the teachings of Jesus were not first recorded in ancient Hebrew, or the common speech of the Jews of that time, Aramaic. The translation into Aramaic appears to have been of a much later date. The beginnings of the Christian tradition were among the Greek-speaking peoples, perhaps because Greek was then the prevalent language of the eastern Mediterranean, just as it later became the common language of the whole Mediterranean area.

Whatever may have been the teachings of Jesus himself, it is certain that early Christianity aimed toward a distinctly communistic form of society, and it seems scarcely probable that this would have been true had this not represented beliefs and the actual teachings of the Master. Such episodes as are recorded of Jesus driving the money changers from the Temple fit well with the earliest Christian tradition; this, at least, could scarcely be mere fiction.[6] The incident is the more instructive since we know that the temples were the original banks, accepting savings and making loans. And the 'money changers' in Jerusalem had a quite legitimate and useful function. The faithful who came to Jerusalem were drawn from widely different parts of the country, and brought with them their own money, which had to be converted into the currency of that city that they might defray their expenses.

Important to note that a large part of the Christian antagonism at that time to wealth and property arose from the fact that the early capitalist system was built upon slavery, always widely prevalent in primitive societies. The philosopher Nietzsche depicted early Christianity as essentially a 'slave religion,' and it was clearly in its essence a revolt against this form of capitalism, just as in many times in subsequent history. But the people who in modern times devoted their efforts to the abolition of slavery, although deeply religious, were generally men of wealth and enterprise. I have noted that the abolitionist movement in England and America coincided with the beginning of modern industrialism, and largely grew therefrom.

Early Christianity drew no distinction in its opposition to great riches; other ancient societies conceived a difference between wealth derived from agriculture and from commercial and financial enterprise. As in our own times! In the golden days of Pericles, business and 'money-getting' were looked upon as something in which a man of culture could scarcely indulge. The occupation of the aristocrat was statecraft or lordly acres.[7] A great portion of the active managers of business in ancient times were slaves, or freedmen who had shown extraordinary business ability. They were among the richest men of Athens, and later in Rome.

This early antagonism to wealth and enterprise throws light on our current problems. In the period when the Industrial Revolution was bringing to England wealth and well-being far beyond the dreams of an earlier generation, the political life of the country was dominated by strife between the landed interest and 'trade.' Now with the growing influence of the 'people,' the 'working' classes, political parties in all the great industrial countries are concerned with capturing the support of 'labor.' And so we have endless legislation, guaranteeing a minimum wage, limiting hours, providing unemployment benefits, old age retirement funds, and a host of other benefits under the flaming banner of 'social security.' In addition, to providing work on government projects and home relief for those unable to work. For agriculture, a smaller but nearly as important political group as labor, a wide variety of aids and benefits. In fact, most every economic group has been offered the most generous encouragement—from public funds. Save one.

If we may judge from experience, such legislation will be as effective in abolishing inequality as in the past. The forces governing remuneration, and trade in general, seem beyond effective control through legislative enactments. In that sense the new legislation is futile, but not without danger. For every attempt to establish economic equalitarianism seems to impose a heavy burden on the country in the form of increased government costs, a destruction of enterprise and achievement, and a diminution in the capital supply. Fatal!

2. *The futility of equalitarianism*

We know the power of words in prejudicing the views and acts of men, the learned as well as the unlearned. There may be some who are immune to the *argumentum ad populum;* obviously not many. The most recent experience has shown how easily people are affected by an appeal for an 'American' standard of living, for a 'living wage,' for 'social' security, for 'sharing' the wealth, for old age pensions, and for other alluring proposals, always in high sounding terms implying the 'justice' and equality that motivates them.

But we know how basic, how unchanging, are the impulses and motivations of all human activity, economic and non-economic: the love of war and fighting, of acquisition, accumulation, and wealth, of ostentation and display; the vanity of rulers in monstrous monuments erected in the hope that they may thus survive to the most distant eras. Likewise the lust for power and conquest, the ceaseless struggles of classes and of peoples. Of ruthlessness, murder, of the seizure of lands belonging to other nations, of which we recently have had shocking examples. All these are so old and so deeply rooted they may not be radically changed by any fiat or decree.

Difficult to see how economic equality can be imposed in an economic world motivated by a desire for wealth and power, and in which differences in capacity and energy are so wide. Among a few favored peoples, industrial development has been almost miraculous,

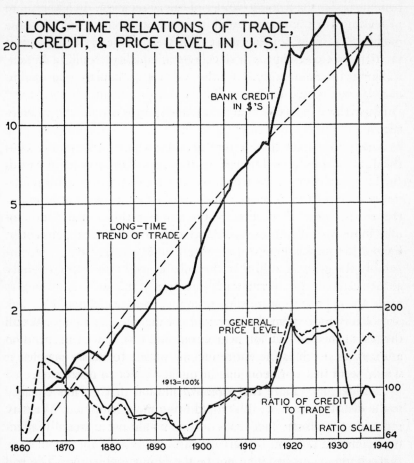

LONG-TIME RELATIONS OF TRADE, CREDIT, & PRICE LEVEL IN U. S.

BANK CREDIT IN $'S

LONG-TIME TREND OF TRADE

GENERAL PRICE LEVEL

1913=100%

RATIO OF CREDIT TO TRADE

RATIO SCALE

XXXIII. WHAT FIXES THE PRICE LEVEL AND THE WAGE LEVEL?

Exhaustive study has made it possible to measure closely the rate of industrial growth in the United States, through the last 80 or 100 years, and with this, the fluctuations from its normal line. Up to 1930 an astonishing continuity of growth, shown above as the "Long Time Trend of Trade." With this, the actual amount of bank deposits in the United States. What is the relationship between the two? Divide one by the other, and you have what is called the Trade-Credit ratio. Observe, now, the fourth line, a broad index of the "General Price Level," that is, the average of all kinds of prices. Observe how close is the correspondence of these two lines up to 1930, showing that, under normal conditions, the price level is determined almost entirely by the volume of bank credit. This, in turn, largely determines the wage level.

and with it has come a degree of comfort, education, recreation, and well-being for the masses unknown to any previous time. With a wondrous promise for the future. The fruit of the system. Nor is it clear that a closer approach to economic equality would be beneficial in the broadest sense. A healthy, vigorous, stimulating inequality may be one of the most impelling spurs to human advancement.[8] And it is this advancement alone that gives high, inspiriting value to life.

Noteworthy that these efforts towards equalitarianism are confined almost wholly to diminishing the personal differences in wealth and income within our own country. But the differences in economic status are far greater between this and other countries. For example, that the people of the United States own two-thirds of the automobiles in the world; yet they comprise only a little over 6 per cent of the world's population. Motor cars are an expensive luxury, incomparably the greatest in history. It probably costs the average family at least $300 a year to run an automobile, if adequate allowance is made for depreciation, repairs, insurance, and accidents. This sum is probably more than the average *total* income, per family, for all the rest of the 1900 million peoples on the earth. If we can spend on a luxury as much as the entire income of less fortunate peoples, it would seem that our economic inequality is not so distressing.

Consider once more the perennial illusion that greater equality in the distribution of wealth would bring more happiness. We may put aside the prosaic fact that equality would not materially affect the economic position of perhaps three-fourths of the population. But economic equality may not be the ultimate objective. The real purpose is the abolition of all 'class distinctions,' complete sameness of economic status. This, it is held, is the one sure road to happiness because it would mean 'the rule of justice.' But this injustice is not confined to the ability to make money or to hold property. It concerns every variety of human talent. Is it not equally unjust that a few should have superlative gifts, while the rest of the world is so deficient and dull? These talented few will be courted and admired far above their fellow men. Must they too be reduced to a level with ordinary people? Equalitarians will say that all this is absurd; that they mean to give the widest opportunity to every kind of talent. Precisely this that has led to large income and great wealth.

The idea of human equality in any save the most limited scope is one of the world's supreme illusions. We would loathe it, and find in it only infinite boredom. Every intelligent person believes in equality before the law, unmodified by accidents of birth, of race, or creed. The vast majority of intelligent people would heartily support any feasible project that would bring a reasonable amount of comfort and, let us hope, contentment to every human being. But does this comfort and contentment arise solely from the amount of this world's goods that we possess? An extraordinary number of people of marked ability already care little for wealth, so common are sufficient incomes. Faraday was one of the happiest of men, even though much of his life was spent in two not very commodious rooms at the Royal Institution in London.[9]

The idea of equality is a will-o'-the-wisp, born of peculiar characteristics which have their roots in the unenviable traits of intense jealousy. And, we may add, covetousness. The real joy of living, the larger satisfactions of life, lie in some reasonable degree of achievement. And the joy is in the doing. A world of perfect sameness in every form could end only in utter banality and boredom. It would overwhelm us, devour us, completely destroy us, and end in madness. The world in which we live, the world of reality, offers a high degree of opportunity and much satisfaction to well adjusted and understanding people. We can partake only of slender portions of this feast. Equal division of material wealth could add but little to the enjoyment of the vast majority of people in the more highly developed industrial countries, particularly in the United States.

3. *Economic inequality and achievement*

Some of the founders of the new republic in America, especially men like Thomas Jefferson, were deeply imbued with the doctrines then prevailing, emanating from Rousseau, of natural rights and human equality: the basis of a marvelous document, the Declaration of Independence. What Jefferson and others had in mind was equality before the law, equality of civil rights. No evidence that the founding fathers believed in economic equality. George Washington was the wealthiest man of his generation in the United States. Robert Morris and John Hancock were both wealthy during the colonial and revolutionary periods. Thomas Jefferson inherited a large fortune, although he died impoverished. It would not have occurred to these men that their views on political equality could be construed as an argument for economic equality.

Close to a century ago this country was swept by a great wave of Utopian Socialism. Many curious experiments were tried. The teachings of Fourier, St. Simon, Robert Owen and many others, were eagerly studied. Brook Farm, Icaria, New Harmony, the North American Phalanx, and other communistic settlements were founded with enthusiasms. Some, particularly those associated with religious sects, prospered for a time. But all ultimately failed. America was never regarded so much as the land of economic equality as it was prized as the land of economic opportunity. While the communistic settlements were carrying on in a precarious way, young men like John Jacob Astor and Stephen Girard were acquiring great fortunes, starting at the foot of the ladder.

The wealthiest of Americans were nearly always children of relatively poor parents. Astor, Girard, were followed by Vanderbilt, Carnegie, Rockefeller, and Ford. Each of these in his generation the wealthiest American. The lack of early wealth did not prevent these men from achieving tremendous economic success. Rather their early upbringing probably contributed much to it; for early want does much to inculcate habits of thrift, patience, and endurance, and develops the urge to succeed, all of which are essential qualities. On the other hand, it has always been a matter of comment that the children of the rich do not, as a rule, amount to much. There are exceptions, of course. W. H. Vanderbilt, Mellon, among others, succeeded in increasing the fortunes left them by their fathers. But as a rule, the children of the rich are content to live on their inheritance; and often early wealth leads to spendthrift habits. More marked in the second generation. So much that we early had the tradition of 'three generations from shirt sleeves to shirt sleeves.' Stretched out a bit nowadays, but still true to a considerable extent.

Probably it is for the same reasons this country has achieved the economic progress that has made it noteworthy among nations. The early settlers came largely to seek fortunes in the New World. They were, in general, an eager and ambitious group, intent on settling the wilderness and acquiring homes and land. The soil was not particularly fertile; they underwent much hardship and privation. The rich lands of the interior remained almost unknown up to the time of the Revolution. The conditions under which these early Americans lived developed character and the urge to succeed; the weak and the shiftless were lost. And the energy and enthusiasm with which these pioneers cleared the land was in later generations applied to the development of American industry. Our reputation for enterprise is largely the product of our early history, when this quality was bred into the national character.

Always a danger that when nations grow rich and powerful that they will become more concerned with the supposed injustice of economic inequality than with the more urgent problem of maintaining progress. It is then that humanitarian and equalitarian legislation undermine the will to achieve. It is then that security becomes more attractive than success. And the financial burden that such legislation imposes on business enterprise, particularly new enterprise, diminishes the opportunity for profit and the willingness to risk capital for expansion and growth. The fibre of the nation is weakened, and its economic life begins to decay. Probably we have not yet reached this stage in the United States; but it is possible that continued pressure for economic equality will some time have this effect.

Not without interest that of all the thousands of volumes on economics and the evils of the economic system, two probably have outsold all others combined: *Progress and Poverty* and *Das Kapital*. More than two million copies of Henry George's masterpiece have been distributed to date; probably even more copies of the monumental work of Karl Marx. At last accounts *Progress and Poverty* had been translated into nineteen languages, and *Das Kapital* probably has an even more amazing record. These two volumes are of profound significance, for they appeal to the deepest of human feelings: the envy of land and of money.

4. *Equalitarianism and capital supply*

Even if an attempt to distribute the national income evenly were not to undermine the enterprise of business men, and thus bring a halt to economic progress, it would of necessity prevent further growth in the capital supply and thus deprive industry of this essential factor to further progress.

The huge income of the people of the United States in 1928 and 1929 was the result of the steady accumulation of capital for more than a century. This capital made it possible for our industries to utilize new inventions and discoveries, new processes and methods. Without this investment all this marvelous advance would have been inconceivable.[10] Without it we could not have attained the high standard of living that is the wonder of all nations. And yet this formula for progress was simple to the last degree.

From the national income each year we invested in reproductive capital something like 5 per cent, and put it into the hands of our most capable business men. We let this small body of hard working men use this capital exactly as they saw fit. Some of the capital was wasted; but the greater part of it was used to increase the production and the income per person at the rate of about 2 per cent per year. Think of what this has meant: doubling the income per capita every thirty-five years, an eightfold increase in a century. Eight times as much comforts and luxuries for everybody.

Now suppose that in the past, instead of diverting the 5 or 6 per cent of the income that went into reproductive capital, we had distributed it equally. Precisely the same to the indolent, the incapable, and the thriftless, as to the finest workers and the keenest thinkers. Suppose this were done, and all the profits of industry and trade had been confiscated and distributed to those who receive wages and small salaries. The difference in income per worker on the average would have been on the order of 8 or 10 per cent. But there would have been no savings, no increase in the capital supply, no gain in the national product, and no long term increase in the wages of the worker. Even if wages and employment remained at their previous level, which is not at all certain, at the end of four or five years the economic position of the worker would have been inferior to that which he was certain to attain under the process of unequal incomes, capital savings, and economic progress. And after the first five years he would go on paying to all eternity for his small and temporary gain at the rate of 2 per cent per annum in the unrealized increase in his income. That is precisely what equalitarianism would have meant if it had been tried.

Many while admitting that this may have been true in the past will deny that it is true in the present or for the future. They will urge that a slower rate of progress is more desirable, that it will prevent or minimize depressions, that our total product is already sufficiently large, and that a more nearly equal distribution of this product is of more importance than an increase in this product. Dangerous delusions. True that our *per capita* output is the highest in the world, as is also our per capita income. But if the largest output were regarded as an adequate total volume of production, we might have stopped our advance half a century ago, for at that time

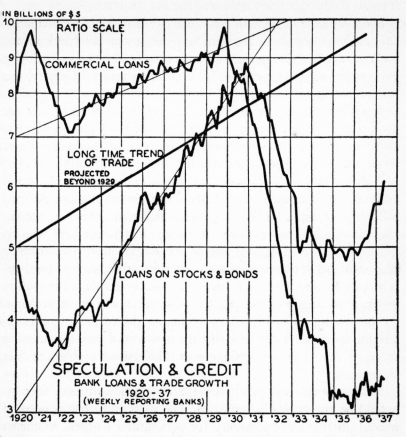

IN BILLIONS OF $ S

RATIO SCALE

COMMERCIAL LOANS

LONG TIME TREND
OF TRADE
PROJECTED
BEYOND 1929

LOANS ON STOCKS & BONDS

SPECULATION & CREDIT
BANK LOANS & TRADE GROWTH
1920-37
(WEEKLY REPORTING BANKS)

XXXIV. WHAT DETERMINES THE VARIATIONS IN BANK CREDIT?

If, as shown, the volume of bank credit is so important to everyone, what determines its variations? Possibly nine out of ten persons would answer, "Business borrowing." No longer true. Above, the uppermost line shows the amount of 'business borrowing,' that is, 'commercial loans,' as far as the data are available; the lower line, the total loans on stocks and bonds—the volume of speculation. From 1922–29, the borrowings of business corresponded closely to the actual measured rate of industrial growth; while the speculative loans rose prodigiously, from less than four to nearly nine billions. The total of speculative loans in all banks was above fourteen billions, bringing a gigantic rise in share prices. When the inevitable crash came, more than three-fourths of this speculative credit was wiped out, with a corresponding effect on all loans and with a terrific contraction of loans to industry.

we had already attained the largest per capita production and income. There is only one test of the adequacy of the present volume of production and that is with reference to the possibilities of the future. So long as we can continue to increase our industrial output, we cannot take the view that we have now product enough. Such a complacent view must destroy all hope for a future of plenty, real plenty for all.

Actually how important is a more equal distribution of income? Not more than 30 per cent of the families of the United States had an income in 1936 much below the average for the country, and some of these families consisted of the unemployed, and the old and infirm, incapable of work. Included in this 30 per cent are also single individuals whose income is adequate to maintain them in decency and comfort, but who are nevertheless reported as families because they live alone. The employed persons in this 30 per cent who receive incomes considerably below the average have a moderately high standard in comparison with other countries, such as England. Thus, in North Carolina, the average weekly earnings for factory workers, including whites and Negroes, men and women, are equal to the average weekly earnings of highly skilled male workers in English factories. The fact is that the problem of very low incomes is largely one of agricultural incomes. The rest is a problem of deep depression.

With progress and prosperity the inadequacy of some incomes would be automatically remedied. The work available in industry would provide an opportunity for agricultural workers to change their occupation. The diminution in unemployment would restore many to the group with adequate incomes. And the progress in production would raise the per capita output and the per capita income so that in a few years the whole level of well-being would be far above what it is today. There can be no satisfactory solution to the problem of inadequate income that does not recognize this fundamental truth: higher incomes can come only with greater production and greater production requires an addition to the capital supply.

It is because the movement for sharing the wealth and redistributing the income of the country endangers progress that it is so important to understand its implications. The capital supply upon which the wealth and well-being of the people of the United States depends was accumulated out of profits by the owners and managers of business enterprises. Every diminution in their income must diminish the capital supply of the future. And it is these incomes—those of the owners and managers of business enterprises—that will be most sharply reduced if the various proposals for sharing the wealth are put into effect. The immediate loss will fall on this comparatively small group of capable and successful men. But the ultimate loss, and this is the tragedy, will fall on the very group that the equalitarian schemes are designed to benefit—the working class.

AGRICULTURAL AID AND PUBLIC WELFARE

The prosperity of commerce is now perceived and acknowledged by all enlightened statesmen to be the most useful as well as the most productive source of national wealth, and has accordingly become a primary object of their political cares. The often-agitated question between agriculture and commerce has, from indubitable experience, received a decision which has silenced the rivalship that once subsisted between them, and has proved, to the satisfaction of their friends, that their interests are intimately blended and interwoven.

—ALEXANDER HAMILTON; 1790

In supporting the present Corn-law, you support a law which inflicts scarcity on the people. You do that, or you do nothing. You cannot operate in any way by this law, but by inflicting scarcity on the people. Entertain that proposition. In fact, you cannot escape it. And if it is true, how many of you will dare to vote for the continuance of the present law?

The present condition of the farmers and labourers of this country is the severest condemnation of the Corn-laws that can possibly be uttered.

—RICHARD COBDEN: *Speech in the House of Commons;* 1843

Chapter XVIII

AGRICULTURAL AID AND PUBLIC WELFARE

1. *Early aid to agriculture*

SAVE among those frankly committed to communism, the equalitarian program does not take the form of proposing equal incomes by direct legislation. Rather, it appears in the guise of attempting to raise the lower incomes, wherever they are found, and for whatever reason they exist. Thus, if agriculture is depressed, legislation must provide higher prices and so higher incomes for farmers; if wages are low, legislation must establish 'minimum wages'; if labor is unemployed, unemployment benefits and 'relief' must be granted. Inevitably the cost of all this must fall upon the other income groups, who are subjected to heavy taxation, or what in the end means exactly the same, to monstrous government borrowing. This latter often only disguised 'inflation.' Sometimes there is an avowed purpose of diminishing the 'disparity' in incomes. Never frankly labelled what it is, the expropriation of the successful few for the benefit of the unsuccessful many. Always given an attractive name, such as 'social security' or 'economic planning.'

Nothing novel in these endless proposals save in the specific form they take. Agricultural aid, for example, is as old almost as the country itself: begun with the colonial settlements. And the first proposal for a bank was as an "aid to agriculture," in the Massachusetts Bay Colony. Later, with the opening of the Middle West, some of the most fertile land in the world was sold to settlers at a dollar or two an acre. The vast areas of the West provided 'free land' until almost recent times.[1]

Ever since, endless aid, 'remedies,' benefits, and devices. There is state supported education for prospective farmers, aided by federal grants. Housewives have demonstrations in homemaking paid for by public money. The farmers may call on the federal and state departments for technical advice, and county agents demonstrate the proper way to plant, cultivate, and harvest crops. The states have been building fine roads, and the federal government has contributed to them, for the purpose of helping the farmer in the marketing of his crops. By various means the agricultural areas have been given the comforts and luxuries that have hitherto been associated with urban life. Beyond all this, direct financial aid in the form of cheap and easy credit, benefit payments for compliance with various schemes designed to 'aid agriculture,' as high, government controlled prices for their crops. Yet with all this the agricultural problem seems still unsolved, the pressure for further aid greater than ever.

Especial efforts to provide farmers with cheap credit. As noted, in 1720, and continuing for more than twenty years, proposals were made in New England to establish a land bank empowered to issue notes on the security of real estate. Some of the proposals provided that the borrowers of such notes could extinguish the obligation by payment in agricultural commodities. "The more the farmer takes out of the public bank and pays in hemp, et cetera," said one writer, "the richer the province will be." [2] The law was not enacted, but demand for a land bank was periodically renewed, despite the fact that under the Bubble Act, such banks could not be established legally. Never a letup from that day to this in the effort to get more 'aid for agriculture.'

Fully two hundred and twenty-five years ago the colony of North Carolina provided that all debts "due or which hereafter may become due on acct. of the Publick or to any Inhabitant or foreignor trading amongst us or in our private dealings amongst ourselves or otherwise howsoever the Debt being contracted or due in Money not expressing Sterling such person or persons to whom such money shall be due shall take & receive" in payment of the debt a variety of commodities at stated prices. The only provision in the act for the protection of the creditor was the requirement that the commodities "be good in their kind & Merchantable & approved by Two substantial Freeholders Indifferently chosen." [3]

In recent years the whole world has been contending with artificially controlled prices for all kinds of agricultural products. Not only have the United States undertaken to maintain high prices for their leading crops, but in many European countries the price of wheat and other grains is maintained well above what it would be under competitive conditions. Restrictions on agricultural production and the fixing of agricultural prices are an old American story. In colonial days, the planting of tobacco was once rigidly controlled o maintain high prices in the face of increasing output. The colony of North Carolina fixed the prices of some fifteen commodities for the purpose of tax and debt payment.

While all these measures were tried, the struggling colonies were spreading over a continent, to become the greatest agricultural nation the world has ever seen, with the finest farms, the largest incomes, the heaviest capital investment, the largest possessions of labor-saving machinery, and the highest product per farm worker; owning six or seven million motor cars, and several billions of dollars' worth of farm machinery, possibly more than are owned by all the farmers in the rest of the world.

Only a slender part of the story. This miracle of agricultural development has been achieved with a steadily smaller and smaller portion of the population. Virtually all the colonists lived on farms. The villages and towns were small, partly because the means of transportation could not sustain any considerable concentration of population.[4]

Even the nominal farm population is now less than a quarter of the total, and a considerable part of these are not farmers at all, and do no farming.[5] They are carpenters, bricklayers, plumbers, electricians, and people of other occupations, living on small holdings. The product of the amazing expansion in the use of motor cars. Everywhere in the United States artisans of every type have gone out into the adjacent country and bought homes and a little land. Thanks to the automobile they go miles and miles to their work, think nothing of distances of twenty and thirty miles. Many of them have gardens; few think of 'farming.' Yet if they own more than three acres they are listed as farmers.

Further, agriculture, like other industries, has been divided into endless specialties, from beekeeping and duck raising to every variety of fruit culture, truck farming, dairying, poultry and eggs, and all the rest. All told, perhaps a quarter of the population on the land now engaged in other than ordinary farming, that is, the tillage of the soil, in raising corn, cotton, wheat, and the like. Probably not more than 12 per cent, 15 per cent at the outside, of the people of the United States are now engaged in raising crops, in what we commonly think of as agriculture.

This wondrous development of agriculture from colonial times to the present was largely the result of forces with which the farmers themselves had little to do. All the long line of inventions, from the days of James Watt to the present, the steam engine, the steamship, the steam railway; all the vast development of modern metallurgy and machinery; the dynamo and the myriad applications of electricity; all the especial devices that have created present day agriculture, the steel plow, the cultivators, the reapers, the harvesters, the threshers, the tractors, the combines, the motor trucks: to all these the farmer has contributed hardly a single device. The steel plow was invented by an Illinois blacksmith, the cotton gin by a Yankee school teacher, the harvester by a Virginia blacksmith, and so for the rest. It is not the farmer, it has rarely been the farmer, who invents, devises, improves. All these things have been done for him by that slender band of inventors and discoverers who are literally the creators of modern civilization. Why the occupation of farming should have been so astonishingly sterile in means and methods by which the farmers' labor has been made so much more fruitful and productive is an interesting problem in itself.

This picture of agricultural progress is hardly one to inspire sympathy for the 'hard lot' of the farmer. It is not a picture of a poverty stricken industry. Yet every generation has seen urgent often peremptory proposals for government aid. The butcher, the baker, the candlestick maker, the blacksmith, the tinsmith, the plumber, the electrician, the carpenter, the chemist, the dressmaker the tailor, the boot maker—all these and workers in a thousand other occupations must accept their lot, take what fate awards them from the table of life. But agriculture has always been the ward of government, the spoiled child of our economic order.

2. *Agriculture and prosperity*

I have already noted that agriculture cannot be the source of great national wealth, nor provide large savings for the reproductive capital essential to economic progress.[6] The nominal remuneration for agricultural work is probably not much above half the average of wages in manufacturing.[7] But this is far from saying that agriculture is underpaid, or that agriculture is impoverished. It is still true that the income of American farmers is far above those of any other country. And there is no evidence that the relative income from farming has declined to any notable extent even in recent years Agriculture has always brought lower returns than industrial or factory work. It is inevitable that industries growing in importance

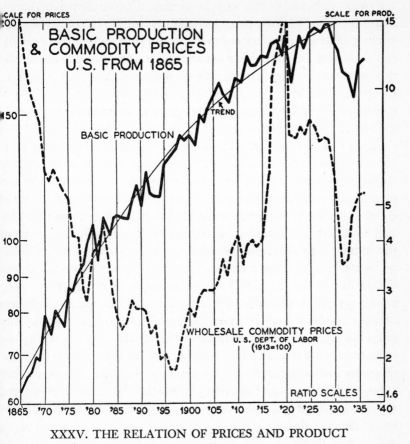

**BASIC PRODUCTION
& COMMODITY PRICES
U.S. FROM 1865**

TREND

BASIC PRODUCTION

WHOLESALE COMMODITY PRICES
U. S. DEPT. OF LABOR
(1913=100)

RATIO SCALES

1865 '70 '75 '80 '85 '90 '95 1900 '05 '10 '15 '20 '25 '30 '35 '40

XXXV. THE RELATION OF PRICES AND PRODUCT

Most intelligent people would say that prices are chiefly determined by 'supply and demand' and 'cost of production.' Only partially so. This is true relative to the minor changes in price, but not regarding the wide changes over the years. There is another, often more powerful factor. The chart above shows the increase in basic production in the United States since the Civil War, and the variations from the long term line of growth. With this is shown the average of commodity prices at wholesale in the same period. A glance at the chart shows that the widest variations in prices have had little to do with the quantity of product and even with the variations from year to year. Some other force or power determines these long term fluctuations, which cause so much havoc in business and so deeply disturb people's minds. It is very important that the instructed public should understand this question a great deal better than they do. The charts here shown may help.

in a progressive society should pay more than an industry that i
relatively declining. This is part of the mechanism for diverting
labor from agriculture to other fields of employment. Since the
settling of the American colonies the more enterprising, capable
and ambitious of those born on farms have been migrating to the
urban centers, to play leading parts in the development of American
industry. In a very real sense there has been a natural selection of the
economically efficient, away from agriculture toward manufacturing, finance, and trade.

And yet more. The emphasis placed on the necessity for 'farm
aid' by the political friends of agriculture has obscured the fact that
we have in farming much the same differences in achievement and
in incomes, as in other industries. As recounted, the Department of
Agriculture at Washington undertook a Census of Farm Income
and tabulated the returns according to income classes.[8] Just as
the Income Tax Bureau does for the returns from the four million
persons who report their incomes for tax purposes. Does this distribution of farm incomes differ from the general distribution of incomes for all, from clerks and shopkeepers up to the Rockefellers
and the Fords? For all practical purposes not at all, as may be seen
from the chart of *Types of Income Distribution*.

Exactly what does this imply? That the average of farm incomes
or of the higher incomes in farming, are the same as in many other
types of industry? On the contrary, notably less. For example, the
highest farm income may be $100,000 a year, in some instances
more. But in other industries there will be incomes of a million or
five million dollars a year.

Inevitable, because the total product of the farms is but now the
smaller part in value, of the total product of industry. We are here
considering simply the distribution of incomes within the farm
group.

The obvious inference is that in agriculture as in industry, the
distribution of income is largely on the basis of ability and energy
just as in other walks of life. There are as many Fords, Carnegies, and
Vanderbilts, in a relative sense, on the farms as in other industries.
The lower average income in agriculture is not due simply to depression, but is related to the same forces that determine the production and income in enterprises of all kinds. It is chiefly because other
industries are able to make larger use of machinery and power that
the average of incomes is greater.

3. *What is wrong with agriculture?*

The difficulty, it is often said, is that it does not yield an adequate return for the labor and capital expended. Undoubtedly that is true in part. But this does not mean that with energy, business ability, and good judgment, farming cannot be made to pay a satisfactory return. Here are two examples.

A little more than a quarter of a century ago a young man in Missouri had ambition to be a doctor; but he stuttered so badly he felt this might be a serious impediment. As a boy he had been deeply interested in raising chickens, and so he obtained a job with a large poultry farm, became superintendent, and soon saved a thousand dollars. With this beginning he rented a poultry farm that for two predecessors had been a failure; at $500 a year. Not five years later he began to be famous. Today perhaps the most widely known poultry man in America, he ships his products all over the earth. At fancy prices. And he is located not in a populous section or close to a great city, but near a little town in far away Oregon. The gross business of this one farm, now 186 acres, runs steadily $50,000 or more a year.

Why such spectacular success? This man produces the finest white leghorn chickens with the most remarkable egg-laying record in the country. And usually he has carried off world prizes wherever he has exhibited. In one year he raised over sixteen hundred pullets, with an average laying record of three hundred eggs a year. Fancy eggs, of unusual size. At fifty cents a dozen, this would yield a gross revenue of $20,000 a year. But he does not sell at fifty cents a dozen; he gets as high as five and ten dollars a dozen, for breeding purposes. And his chickens sell as high as five and ten dollars apiece, and even, occasionally, as much as one hundred dollars. That is why this single farm can have an annual income of $50,000 a year or more.

This is the remarkable record of J. A. Hanson, an honorary 'Doctor,' of Corvallis, Oregon. An example of what enterprise and ability can do. Mr. Hanson's work is a triumph of scientific agriculture, for he has not only produced strains with extraordinary egg-laying records, but hens that are long-lived and free from disease: the fruit of his knowledge of modern methods of sanitation, and of Mendelian breeding. College professors come to his farm to study his methods, and to learn his 'secrets,' of which he has none. But there will be this objection: "What Mr. Hanson has done is not agriculture. This is a special industry, chicken raising. There is no trouble with chicken raising when it is done intelligently. The difficulty we are dealing with is the yield of the fields, that of securing an adequate return from growing crops." So let us take another instance.

Across the continent, on a farm five or six miles from a modest town in lower New Jersey, there was about twenty-five years ago a truck farmer who never seemed to make much of a success. On the proceeds of a good year, he sent his boy to the agricultural college for a short period. The boy came back with ideas, went to work and in the first year the miracle happened for which every farmer lives and dreams: when the yield is magnificent and prices are high. In that year they made $24,000; more money than the father had seen in a lifetime; he wanted to bury it in the ground. The boy had a different idea; he would bury the money, but not in the same way. He would put the money into the purchase of manure and fertilizers. The father was opposed, so the boy bought him out with his share of the profits and carried on by himself.

Just before we entered the World War, this truck farm was capitalized for two million dollars, a good part of this capital raised in Wall Street, and paying 6 per cent on the investment. So prosperous was this farm that two railroads built spurs to get its business. The produce was sold largely by telephone, shipped in carload lots to the larger cities. Almost always among the earliest producers and getting the highest prices. When I saw this farm it had grown to over a thousand acres, and the capital invested, 'buried,' something like four hundred dollars an acre. And hundreds of tons more manure were spread over these fields every year. The man who achieved this success, beginning with meager capital and little experience, was Charles F. Seabrook. Interesting that this magnificent enterprise was forced into bankruptcy by the violent rise in wages during and just after the World War; later reorganized.

Here are two instances of successful farming. Throughout the country there are thousands of similar achievements in agriculture, some well known. If it were not so, whence the twenty-five thousand farms in the United States with an average income of more than $20,000 per year? Many of these farms produce agricultural specialties—poultry, vegetables, fruits, dairy products, and the like. The bulk of the farmers are engaged in field crops and show no such returns for their efforts. And this is one of the reasons. They have followed the time-worn pattern of agriculture, growing much the

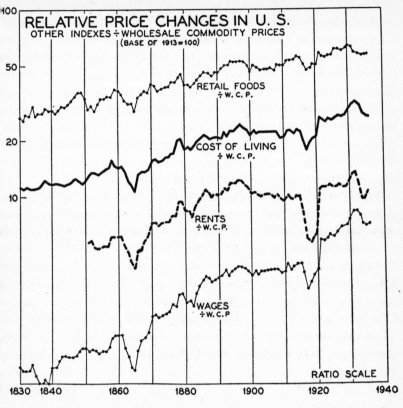

RELATIVE PRICE CHANGES IN U. S.
OTHER INDEXES ÷ WHOLESALE COMMODITY PRICES
(BASE OF 1913=100)

RETAIL FOODS
÷ W. C. P.

COST OF LIVING
÷ W. C. P.

RENTS
÷ W. C. P.

WAGES
÷ W. C. P

RATIO SCALE

XXXVI. RELATIVE PRICE CHANGES VS. ACTUAL

All prices, we know, are related to some one particular thing, which is called the 'medium of exchange'; in the United States the dollar. But they are also closely related to each other, as a glance at the above chart will show. Here the 'actual' price indexes of different groups have been divided by the average for all groups, so as to have a picture of these *relative* price changes. It will be seen, for example, that over a century retail prices of food and the 'cost of living' have risen steadily, relative to the great mass of other products and materials. So, also, have wages, relative to the general average of prices. This means that, proportionally, the prices of many important commodities must have steadily fallen, and that in terms of wages all have fallen.

same crops, year after year: cotton, wheat, corn, tobacco, and the rest.

The result as noted: In a total of six million farms, about one-ninth —660,000 farms—produce about one-half the produce sold from all farms. The other half is produced by some *five and a half million* farms. It is not rash to assume that the agricultural 'problem' is largely confined to the lower group of this five and a half million. They cannot produce enough for a high income because too many are on farms that are economically too small. The solution seems to be: fewer farms and fewer farmers.

Closely associated with this is the steady drain of business ability from the farms. This in a way is helpful, because it relieves the pressure of numbers. But subtracts brains and energy.

These troubles I have enumerated are most evident in the South, where agricultural income is at its lowest. There we find the most dependence on two field crops, cotton and tobacco, each grown the same way for a century or more. The farms are small, the tenants numerous. Extremely little machinery is used, and even farm animals are not plentiful. Fantastic to expect a type of work carried on in such fashion, similar to the primitive agriculture of many backward countries, could yield a level of income comparable with that of American industry, the most modern, the most mechanized, the most enterprising to be found anywhere at any time!

HUMANITARIAN LABOR LEGISLATION

The property which every man has in his own labour as it is the original founda
tion of all other property, so it is the most sacred and inviolable. The patrimony
of a poor man lies in the strength and dexterity of his hands; and to hinder him
from employing the strength and dexterity in what manner he thinks proper with
out injury to his neighbor, is a plain violation of this most sacred property. It is a
manifest encroachment upon the just liberty both of the workman and those who
employ him. . . . The affected anxiety of the law-giver . . . is evidently as im
pertinent as it is oppressive.

—ADAM SMITH: *The Wealth of Nations*

Strong as the passion of meddling is in all political communities, it appear
nowhere so strong as in organizations of workingmen; mischievous as have been
the restrictions upon trade and industry, imposed in the past by governments, i
would be difficult to match some of the latest trades-union edicts out of the statute
of Edward III and Richard II.

—FRANCIS A. WALKER: *The Wages Question*

The struggle of endurance involved in a strike is, really, what it has ofter
been compared to—a war; and, like all war, it lessens wealth. And the organization
for it must, like the organization for war, be tyrannical. As even the man who
would fight for freedom, must, when he enters an army, give up his personal
freedom and become a mere part in a great machine, so must it be with workmen
who organize for a strike. These combinations are, therefore, necessarily destructive of the very things which workmen seek to gain through them—wealth and
freedom.

—HENRY GEORGE: *Progress and Poverty*

Chapter XIX

HUMANITARIAN LABOR LEGISLATION

1. *Labor's wrongs and labor's remedies*

In all the 'wrongs' to which labor is submitted, first place must be reserved for the unending complaint that labor does not get 'a fair share' of the product, that wages are not equal to the value of labor's work. I have often pondered just where lies the origin of this belief. The answer, perhaps, was given in an interesting letter from a working man, in a Boston newspaper. Commenting upon the fact that the gross income of all the manufacturing companies in Massachusetts had been around two billion dollars that year, while the amount paid out in wages was less than a quarter of this sum. To this worker's mind it meant that the employees were deprived of something like three-fourths of the 'value' that they 'created.' Plenty of evidence that this is a prevalent mode of thought; and that it is the basis for the widespread view, encouraged by labor leaders, that labor is not fairly remunerated.

Rarely do such critics go through the accounts of manufacturing corporations. And as rarely do they take cognizance of the fact that raw materials, maintenance, and replacements are the larger items in the total expenditure; the payments for wages, as noted in the letter, are usually only a small part, one half to one fifth. But profits only about one fourth of this; and dividends so small as to be almost negligible.[1] On the average, the percentage of manufacturing income paid out in wages has remained a nearly fixed proportion of total income, as far back as any compilations of data extend. In the United States back to 1849.[2] And the same is true of the proportion for materials and supplies, which has tended to remain at a fixed figure of about 60 per cent. Taxes, depreciation, and other overhead, and interest and dividends, take another 20 per cent. So it is evident that with these costs remaining the same, an increase in the share of wages would either extinguish all the profit, slender as this may be, or else mean an increase in prices passed on to the consumer. Which of course includes the wage-earners.

It has been set forth that high wages are solely the result of high output per worker, which in turn is due almost wholly to the increase in the machinery, capital, and equipment per worker employed. Many intelligent labor leaders understand all this. I have good authority that the foremost of these leaders, and one of the most aggressive, would subscribe to the statement that "the sole way in which wages can generally be materially increased is by a corresponding increase in the product per worker." But such economic understanding is rare among the body of workers; and their leaders seem none too eager to enlighten them.

If inadequate wages come first in the list of alleged wrongs of labor, 'excessive hours' would be a close second. In recent times agitation for shorter hours of work has rather been given precedence. No doubt this is due in part to the belief that with shorter hours it would be possible to spread the available employment among a larger number, and thus relieve, or at least disguise, unemployment. But among some labor leaders, those who regard wage rates as related to the 'supply of and demand' for labor, a decrease in the hours of work is believed to diminish the supply, and thus tend toward an increase in wages. They still think in terms of the old labor jingle of the 1870's:

> "Whether you work by the piece or work by the day,
> Decreasing the hours increases the pay."

This insistence for shorter hours is usually accompanied by the demand that weekly wages must not be decreased. Apparently, in complete disregard of the fact that a reduction in the hours of work must in general lead to a proportionate decrease in production, because the larger part of the 'work' nowadays (often four-fifths or more) is done by machines. And with lessened output, wage rates must fall or unemployment be increased. But even if wages remain the same, so that there is no need to decrease the volume of employment, it is difficult to see what labor can gain from a sharp reduction in the hours of work. What intelligent labor has always wanted and wants above all else is a higher real income. In the past, as the output per worker has increased, labor has taken advantage of these gains to improve its economic position in both ways: in the form of higher wages and of shorter hours. The demand for a 30-hour-week seems little short of a mania.

The third of the alleged wrongs is that labor is subjected to 'tyrannical domination' by the employers, without an opportunity to share in the management. Familiar are such terms as "wage-slavery" and the "tyranny of the wage system." What is wholly overlooked is the complexity of modern methods of production: the large and expensive machinery, the integration of processes, the minute specialization of tasks, all of which necessitate a high degree of administrative direction. Under such conditions industrial discipline is a necessity; otherwise the whole process of production would break down.[3] Even in communistic Russia, the power of workers to dictate the terms of employment is now extremely limited; in fact, some observers find this power rather less than in the average capitalistic society; and distinctly less than what it is at the present time in the United States. Under any circumstances, highly mechanized production cannot be conducted like a town meeting.

In seeking a remedy for these 'wrongs,' labor has chiefly placed its dependence on unionization and on legislation, seeking higher wages and shorter hours. It has sought to determine the conditions of employment through forced collective bargaining, and through the power of the state, by way of labor laws. But the workers of this country have shown in the past little desire for joining unions. The United States were, until recently, the least unionized of the larger industrial countries. For this reason there has been an effort among leaders to gain through legislation what they could not simply by the formation of unions, and to compel, by law, collective bargaining.[4]

So important are these later developments that it is well to consider how far they can contribute to labor's welfare, and what effect they must have on economic progress. The test of the desirability of these measures must be in the effect they will ultimately have on the general well-being. If such legislation can bring about a higher standard of living, it would seem that this should be in evidence in countries where it has been carried furthest; and the reverse seems to be the fact. It seems certain that the coercion of management, either by government or by unions, must in the end impede the processes that make for economic growth: The cost of mistaken and pernicious legislation may be incalculable.

2. *Economic progress by decree*

For near to two centuries, as available data show, the industrial worker in the United States has made steady and noteworthy progress. Even far back, as Adam Smith took note, wages were higher than in any other country. And in 1929, for example, the real wages of an American worker in Philadelphia were, on an average, 25 per cent above those of a Canadian worker in Ottawa, 86 per cent above those of an English worker in London, 180 per cent above those of a German worker in Berlin, 240 per cent above those of a French worker in Paris.[5] Incomparably the highest real wages ever known. And these wages were rising steadily. Even after the war-time increase, in the decade of the 1920's real wages rose more than 20 per cent.

The hours of work per week for the typical industries have been much the same for the United States as for England. Slightly less in the United States than in the continental countries, slightly more than in Australia and New Zealand. Hours of work have been diminishing steadily in all countries. In the United States, the reduction was on the order of 25 per cent in the half century preceding the great depression. Professor Arthur Bowley's note on the reduction in British industries gives a fair indication of changes going on contemporaneously in the United States:

"*Textiles.* In 1847 the 10-hour day Act was passed. In 1874 weekly hours were reduced from 60 to 56½, equivalent to the introduction of a Saturday half-holiday. In 1902 the last hour of Saturday's work was cut off ('so that men could attend football matches'), and hours were 55½. The final reduction took place in 1919 to 48.

"*Engineering.* In 1871 the 9-hour day, or rather the 54-hour week, generally replaced a former 60 hours' week, and there was little change for more than forty years, for the hours in most districts were 53 or 54 in 1914, and were reduced to 47 in 1919. In 1935 about 4 per cent of the operatives in general engineering worked less than 47 hours in a normal week.

"*Coal-mining.* In 1890 a shift of 9 or 9½ hours was usual. In 1909 there was a general reduction of 1 hour per shift. In 1919 another hour was taken off, but after the 1926 general stoppage hours were again increased and an 8-hour shift is now general." [6]

After all our historical experience, and slowly gained understanding of the relation of increased capital to increased output and increased wages, it is proposed that we abandon this one certain

RELATIVE COMMODITY GROUP PRICES
ANNUAL GROUP AVERAGE ÷ B.L.S. INDEX

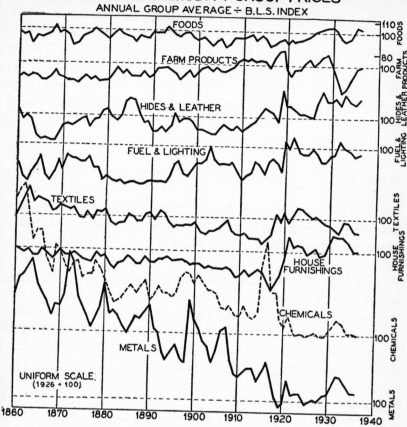

XXXVII. RELATIVE COMMODITY GROUP PRICES

Here are shown the annual price of food products and others, divided by the general commodity price level index. It will be seen that the price of food has changed relatively very little. Enormous change in actual price, as in and after wars and in times of business depression. The same is pretty much true of farm products. But other groups have changed very radically, especially things like minerals and metals and chemicals. All these have been greatly cheapened in price through the years. Interesting that it is just these latter products about which there is often so much complaint and talk of 'monopoly' prices, because so many of them are produced by very large companies.

method and seek economic betterment by decree. The first step is usually by establishing a legal minimum.[7] It is true that most working men will not be affected directly by this minimum wage. But working men as a whole have just as distinct interest in this method of increasing wages as the rest of the consuming public. When higher wages result from increased output everyone is the gainer. But when wages are raised by fiat, and particularly those of one group, there must somewhere be a diminution in the real income of all other groups. A minimum wage in excess of the current rate must result in unemployment for those workers whose product is not equal in value to the new legal minimum.[8] At a time when unemployment is already extensive, additional unemployment through such a wage policy can only increase the difficulty of recovery. Finally, a minimum wage may hinder the establishment of new industries in the agricultural areas, particularly like the South, in which industrial employment is so essential for relieving the pressure of superfluous farms and farmers.

Still less may be said for attempts to maintain high wage rates in fields in which extensive unemployment already prevails. Yet this is precisely the purpose of laws that require the payment of prevailing wages on work performed under government contracts. In substance, this means that contractors doing government work must pay the nominal union rates of wages, which are often higher than the actual wages being paid in that field. The cost of course is borne by the taxpayers, but the effect goes much beyond this burden on public funds.

The same as to others. A well-administered unemployment insurance law would not be objectionable. The fact is, however, that universal experience with such legislation has been unfavorable, for the attempt to prevent the evils that arise out of unemployment insurance is too easily denounced as an "insult to the working classes." These evils are that unemployment insurance seems to encourage unemployment, and adds to the difficulty of revising wage rates during deep depression. Unemployment insurance is certain to lead to the attitude of waiting for a good job to turn up. English experience has shown conclusively that demands of trade unions for higher wages are more insistent when they can be sure that the unemployment the uneconomical wage rates may cause will thus be relieved by the payment of benefits from the unemployment insurance fund.

The old age benefits provision of the Social Security Act is not open to the objections of the type offered against unemployment insurance. The political pressure for old age retirement benefits is always tremendous. The Townsend movement for fantastic pensions to old people has gained many adherents; and it may be that unless a moderate plan is enacted, the danger of extreme legislation could not be avoided. But the *specific* provisions of the section of the Social Security Act relating to the old age retirement benefits are open to many objections. It is doubtful whether it is wise to accumulate a huge reserve fund, in which the accrued obligations under the act are balanced by equal reserves. Not only are there many practical difficulties in investing such a fund; but there is the additional difficulty that such a fund may encourage excessive government expenditure.[9] For the federal government need not seek loans on the market, and the ease of selling government securities at low rates to a trust fund administered by the government would almost inevitably lead to an attitude of indifference in government finances.

There is a widespread impression that unemployment insurance and old age retirement benefits are somehow a net addition to the income of labor. A reflection of the belief that labor's share of the national income can be increased by legislation. The endless illusion. Labor must pay for these benefits. The employer can give his workers only a fixed share of what is added to the value of the product. If in addition the employer must provide unemployment insurance, and contribute to a retirement fund, the wages he can afford to pay must be less by the amount of the premiums to these funds. Although the resistance to wage reductions may postpone for a time the direct shifting of these costs to labor, ultimately they will be shifted.

3.   Collective bargaining and coercion of industry

In the prosperous year 1929, the number of trade union members in the United States and Canada was less than 3,500,000; and the membership had been declining steadily since 1920. The high wages generally paid to American workers, and the faith of labor in the continued improvement of its economic position were not conducive to an organized labor movement. Depression increased the agitation for labor organization. But though some gains were made in a few industries, the total number of trade union members fell even in the years from 1929 to 1932. Since then a heavy rise. But this seems not the result of a strong desire for unionization among workers; it is rather the result of legislation intended to bring about compulsory unionization of labor in American industry. It seems certain that labor cannot hope for any large material benefits from such compulsion. The most noteworthy economic advances, alike in wages and good living, were made while the workers of this country were largely unorganized. The experience of England and Germany with unionization has not been impressive. The halt in industrial growth in these two countries seemed synchronous with the rise of their powerful trade unions. If American unions succeed in thus dominating industry, we may, I think, reasonably expect a similar decline in enterprise, with a halt in progress toward ever higher standards of living.

Few reasonable people would question the advantage of associations of labor, especially as fraternal and insurance benefit organizations. Labor unions could be extremely useful as educational institutions, in the study of economic and social questions. The Monthly Bulletin of the American Federation of Labor has presented intelligent discussions of the economic problems of this country, particularly those in which labor is most interested. Along these lines, labor unions could do valuable work for their members, keeping them informed on the social situation, advising them on matters of policy. But to be highly effective, this would mean recognition of economic realities; and the foremost of these are that wages cannot rise without a corresponding increase in product, and that wages must be revised during deep depressions, if we are blind enough to allow such depressions. Needless otherwise.

Finally, enlightened labor unions could be useful to their members and to their industries in maintaining the labor standards of the more efficient firms. To such unions, voluntarily formed by workers, no capable employer would object. The opposition to trade unions is toward those led by unscrupulous leaders determined to dominate at any cost, and ready to sacrifice the general welfare of labor by forcing wage rates upon industry regardless of their effect.

4. The limits of labor legislation

It seems more than futile to look to legislation for labor's 'salvation.' Wages can never long be maintained by law. The mechanism

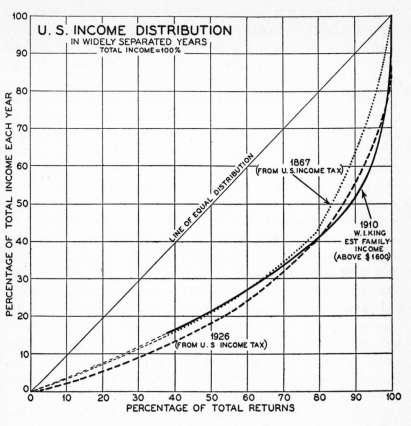

U. S. INCOME DISTRIBUTION
IN WIDELY SEPARATED YEARS
TOTAL INCOME=100%

(Chart axes: PERCENTAGE OF TOTAL INCOME EACH YEAR (vertical, 0–100); PERCENTAGE OF TOTAL RETURNS (horizontal, 0–100). Labels on chart: LINE OF EQUAL DISTRIBUTION; 1867 (FROM U.S. INCOME TAX); 1910 W.I. KING EST FAMILY INCOME (ABOVE $1600); 1926 (FROM U.S INCOME TAX).)

XXXVIII. ON THE DISTRIBUTION OF INCOME IN A NATION

Great numbers of people believe that rich men acquire their wealth by chicane or luck. It is hard to believe that there is an even gradation of ability to make money (and to keep it), and that in its higher forms this is not just as great a talent as a genius for music, or painting, or oratory. Long suspected that there might be some 'law' in the distribution of income, but not until the nations began to adopt the income tax was it possible to prove this. The remarkable outcome is that the distribution of income seems to be very much the same whether a country is rich or poor, old or new, and that it does not change. The chart above gives a guide or map of this income distribution in the United States for three different years since our Civil War. The total sum of all income is taken here as 100; and the distribution is by percentages of this total. Thus, in 1867 the distribution was not very much different than, for example, in 1926, or in 1920. Professor W. I. King has estimated the family income, which supplies much the same picture.

that determines the remuneration of labor cannot be modified by decree. It is certain the real wages of labor can rise only in one way. Attempts to force wages beyond the level determined by economic factors must mean inescapably a rise in prices, thus offsetting the higher wages, or in an increase in unemployment, thus diminishing the total remuneration.

Equally evident that the reduction in hours of work by legislation cannot decrease unemployment. At best, it merely spreads the same amount of unemployment among more workers. At worst, if the shortened hours are not accompanied by a reduction in wages, the total of unemployment must in the end be increased. Almost everyone would favor the progressive shortening of the standard work week, provided it is gradual and output increases. This has been the solid basis in the past for the steady decrease in the hours of work in all American industries. It is unwise to hasten the process by government fiat.

If legislation cannot improve the economic status of labor, what can legislation properly do? Has it any useful function? Undoubtedly. One proper field is the protection of the health and the safety of labor, under the police powers of the states. In this category are included laws relating to sanitation in factories, provisions for adequate fire protection, employment of women and children, safeguards in working with dangerous materials and dangerous machinery. This is an application of the same power that the state ordinarily uses where the public health and safety are involved.[11]

It is possible, too, that the state might contribute much to the maintenance of industrial peace. But there, again, the political pressure of labor may be so great that it would be wiser to avoid state regulation, unless a judicial rather than an administrative body could be entrusted with this duty. The safest rule would be to minimize the functions of government respecting labor, as in other economic matters.

PAUPERS, BREAD, AND CIRCUSES

The man who first invented the art of supporting beggars made many wretched.
—MENANDER; *circa* 330 B.C.

In proportion as the condition of any pauper class is elevated above the condition of independent labourers, the condition of the independent class is depressed, their industry is impaired, their employment becomes unsteady, and its remuneration in wages is diminished.

. . .

If the vital evil of the system, relief to the able-bodied on terms more eligible than regular industry, be allowed to continue, we are convinced that pauperism with its train of evils must steadily advance.
—*Report of the Commissioners of Inquiry on the Poor Laws;* 1834

From the hopes which they hold out of relief from the miseries and iniquities of a state of much inequality of wealth, schemes for a larger application of the same idea (socialism) have reappeared and become popular at all periods of active speculation on the first principles of society. *In an age like the present,* when a general reconsideration of all first principles is felt to be inevitable, and when more than at any former period of history the suffering portions of the community have a voice in the discussion, it was impossible but that ideas of this nature should spread far and wide. The late revolutions in Europe have thrown up a great amount of speculation of this character, and an unusual share of attention has consequently been drawn to the various forms which these ideas have assumed: nor is this attention likely to diminish, but on the contrary, to increase more and more.
—JOHN STUART MILL: *Principles of Political Economy;* 1848

CHAPTER XX

PAUPERS, BREAD, AND CIRCUSES

1. *The Poor Laws*

ALWAYS in times of high prosperity, endless proposals of the 'humanitarian' type—the generous hand-out of other people's money. Then when depression comes, a clamor. At first, it is asked for the deserving poor. But soon broader claims. The aid that is first granted for those in real distress soon becomes a kind of general right for all the unemployed. And especially in our democracies, where governments are dependent on the votes of the masses, it is certain that free-handed measures for relieving distress will be passed. As time goes on, competition for the votes of the recipients of relief lead to larger grants, and these in turn to larger demands. The history of public relief always and everywhere.

In ancient Athens and Rome, public granaries were used to distribute bread to the poor. Not long before bread was supplemented with circuses. Difficult to deny some comforts to those whose necessities are provided by government.[1] In Rome it was a custom for public men to feast the populace; according to Plutarch 22,000 tables for the feast that Caesar gave to the people on the occasion of his triumph. At these entertainments, gifts of money were made to all, to those of rank as well as plebeians.

The bounty of the public purse, first opened to the poor, is soon extended to those in little need. In Athens, too, if we may judge from a statement in Aristotle, the funds of the government were occasionally distributed to the poor by politicians in office, seeking to strengthen their position. In his *Politics*, Aristotle says: "Where there are revenues, the demagogues should not be allowed after their manner to distribute the surplus; the poor are always receiving and always wanting more and more, for such help is like water poured into a leaky cask." Through all the ages.

Prior to the reign of Queen Elizabeth, relief for the poor in England was provided by the monasteries and the guilds.[2] But the confiscation of the possessions of the monastic orders and of the guild deprived the poor of their customary source of aid. The growing problem of poverty and vagrancy led to the enactment of several measures in the reign of Elizabeth for the purpose of providing public funds. The first act directing the levy of a compulsory poor rate, 1572, provided for the appointment of collectors who "shall by their good discretions tax and assess all and every of the inhabitants, dwelling in all and every city, borough, town, village, hamlet and place known within the said limits and divisions, to such weekly charge as they and every of them shall weekly contribute toward the relief of the said poor people."

The Act of 1601 established relief on the basis under which it was administered for more than two centuries. It recognized the obligation of the state to maintain the poor; it provided for the levying of a tax to be collected by overseers; and required that work should be given to the able-bodied needy, and "relief of the lame, impotent, old, blind and such other among them being poor and not able to work, and also for the putting out of such children to be apprentices." [3]

All sorts of difficulties encountered in the administration of the law. Many of the remedies seemed to intensify the evil. Because many paupers flocked to the metropolitan parishes, where relief was perhaps more generous than in rural areas, the Act of Settlement of 1662 denied relief to those who had not established a settlement in a parish. The act undoubtedly had the beneficial effect of keeping beggars from migrating; but it also had the effect of preventing many industrious unemployed from seeking work in other parishes. Against this evil Adam Smith and many others protested. To this pernicious law he attributed many of the local differences in wages. "There is scarce a poor man in England of forty years of age," wrote Smith, "who has not in some part of his life felt himself most cruelly oppressed by this ill-contrived law of settlements." [4] But difficulties are an inevitable by-product of every kind of relief.

The administration of the poor laws in England were at the worst in the last quarter of the eighteenth century and in the first of the nineteenth century. The burden of maintaining the indigent in some parishes was so great, that owners found it better to surrender their property; the poor rates exceeded the rents. The character of the poor was undermined, many preferring relief to work. The authority to establish workhouses, granted for a time, was sharply limited by an act of 1796, which permitted justices to authorize relief in their own homes "to industrious poor persons." Even in the work-houses, no discipline was maintained. Clapham states that "at Chatham the house was in a dreadful state. No work was done; the residents went freely in and out, fed on the finest wheaten bread. Supplied with good ale brewed on the premises, they stood out for porter and gin—and got them." [5]

The custom of supplementing wages by grants from the poor funds encouraged early marriage and large families, with all of its implications for low living standards, always on the border of destitution. Some unscrupulous employers, taking advantage of these supplements, maintained wages below the level they could have afforded to pay. And the hindrance of migrating to other parishes for work made it possible to maintain relatively low wages in restricted areas.

Thus, the poor laws while costing the community much, did nothing to solve the problem. The grants did not prevent many of them from suffering. The Rev. Dr. Malthus was an especial critic of the poor laws; but there is no reason for doubting his summary of their long effect: "I feel persuaded that if the Poor Laws had never existed in this country, though there might have been a few more instances of severe distress, the aggregate mass of happiness among the common people would have been much greater than it is at present." [6]

The first successful attempt towards a remedy was undertaken by the Commission of Inquiry of 1832, among whose able members was Nassau Senior. The result was the Act of 1834, which established these fundamental principles: that paupers must be maintained in a condition less desirable than the humblest worker who lived on his earnings; and that those requiring relief must perform work in a workhouse. This act remained the foundation of the English Poor Laws until the present century. The higher level of incomes since the Industrial Revolution, and the provisions for social insurance, obviated the need for poor relief on the scale of earlier centuries. It is still true, however, that those who are not eligible for these social insurance benefits, or who have exhausted their rights under social insurance, may have recourse to the relief of the poor laws.

In the United States, no federal relief was ever required or granted until the present depression. In the colonial period, relief was largely on the same basis as in contemporary England. But poverty was

much rarer in America than in England. During the nineteenth
century, institutional care in poor farms and poor houses was the
common recourse. In a few states and cities, notably in New York,
New Jersey, and Connecticut, organized departments of public
charity or social welfare administered institutional aid to the needy;
in recent times this has largely been replaced by non-institutional
assistance. Even in those states in which public funds were used,
much of the best work was done by voluntary philanthropic agencies. In the deep depression, the expenditures of the federal government have far exceeded the combined expenditures of all voluntary,
state, and municipal funds for this purpose.

2. *Public expenditure and recovery*

In this country, we have had no experience comparable to that of
England's three and a half centuries. But in the six years in which
federal funds were made available, we seem to have made most of
the mistakes that England made through all the long history of its
poor laws. And this was supplemented by expenditure of billions of
dollars on public works by the federal and local governments, with
the aid of subsidies from Washington. There was a widespread
view that such expenditure would 'contribute to recovery.' In the
attempt to achieve this, we spent far more for relief in six years
than all the sums expended for such purposes in more than one hundred and forty years of this government's existence.

The theory that public expenditure in depression can aid recovery
is not new. The minority report of the Royal Commission on the
Poor Laws, in England, 1909, devoted a section to the suggestion
of Dr. A. L. Bowley that employment could be regularized by de-
creasing public expenditure in good times and increasing it in bad.[7]
This proposal must not be confused with the more recent view
that public expenditure must have a 'multiplicative effect' on employment in bad times, in the manner in which J. M. Keynes has so
elaborately expounded.

The 'multiplicative effect' of public expenditure in depression is
presumed to be achieved by a series of subsequent spendings that
must follow the initial expenditure. Thus, if in bad times the government spends a billion dollars on public works and on relief, the
funds come into the hands of the people, who in turn spend them on
consumption; the increased employment in producing consumption

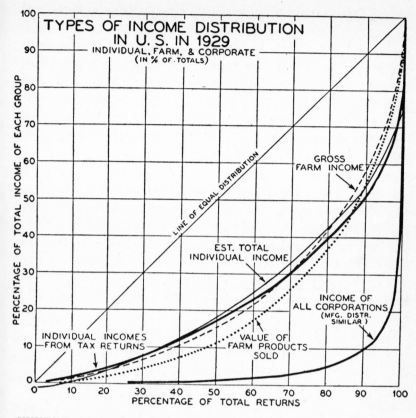

XXXIX. FARM INCOME AND NATIONAL INCOME DISTRIBUTION

A real surprise for the writer in his investigations was the discovery that when farm income is plotted up by income classes, in the same way as the returns from the national income tax, the resulting lines of distribution are nearly identical. Astonishing to find that if we take the value of all farm products *sold*, and distribute this according to the size of the income, the 'inequalities' between classes, so deeply complained of in the high incomes of the rich, appear to be greater on the farm than for the population as a whole. A revelation! Just the same distribution of business ability and genius for management on the farm as in the giant industries. Corporate income, on the other hand, shows enormously greater concentration, as is so clearly set forth in the chart. Alike in manufacturing as in most other corporate activity; one-tenth of the number reporting (about 500,000) have ninety per cent of the total corporate income.

goods increases income, and so successively until various leaks such as "saving" finally bring the series of effects to an end. The result, according to Keynes, depends on the magnitude of the public expenditure and the "multiplier," which may be roughly defined as the inverse of the proportion of the funds that enters into these 'leaks.' Thus, if of additional public expenditure one-fourth on the average is "saved," the multiplier will be four; and the total effect is to increase income four times the amount of the additional public expenditure.[8]

A second method by which the multiplicative effect is to be achieved may be stated in more familiar terms. When public expenditure is increased in depression, the funds for this purpose are almost invariably borrowed. If the bonds are sold to the banks, as most likely they will be, the quantity of credit money is increased. This money presumably will enter into circulation, and its velocity will increase the total of business transactions that arise from the 'injection,' and the income from these transactions becomes a multiple of the original expenditure. In brief, government expenditure increases the quantity of money, and the velocity of money multiplies the effect.[9]

Both views of this multiplicative effect assume that there are no offsetting factors that diminish or obliterate the supposed increase in income. Now it is clear that public expenditure has not had the beneficial effect its advocates expected; and the reasons must be that there are important factors not accounted for. If, for example, an increase in large-scale public expenditure leads to a general fear that taxes will be increased heavily in consequence, and that the costs of production will rise more rapidly than the prices of goods sold, the increase in public disbursements may be offset by an equal or even larger decrease in the expenditures of business. And if there is validity in the concept of a 'multiplier,' the offset must also have a multiplicative effect.

If the offsetting factors lead to a decrease in the quantity of credit money, and in its velocity; if government borrowing takes the place of business borrowing, there is no net increase.[10] When public expenditure leads business men to limit their borrowing because they do not wish to undertake new production, the increase through government loans is partly offset. From impaired confidence there may be a sharp reduction in velocity, so that the increase in the quantity is nullified by the decrease in the velocity. And this seems just what has happened in the United States from large government expenditure. There may have been some positive influence from this enormous outlay, but there certainly has been no multiplicative effect. Throughout the period of halting trade since 1932, there has been a heavy decline in velocity.

Further: as already noted, a heavy increase in public expenditure must sooner or later increase tax rates and thus raise the costs of production, so that business men find that the opportunity for profit is diminished. The haphazard manner in which these vast outlays have been undertaken, the frequently useless purposes for which they are made, undermine the confidence of the public in a policy of prodigality. One reason why recovery, such as it was, collapsed so completely in 1937, with even a moderate reduction in government spending. No supporting foundation can be built up for the increase in business by a policy of excessive public expenditure, for no one will risk the expansion of private enterprise under these uncertain conditions. Only such expansion can provide the basis for a continued and full recovery.

An inevitable effect of a policy of 'generous' relief and huge public expenditure is to diminish the competition for jobs. So long as the unemployed can count on relief or on work on public projects, at prevailing wages, there can be no reduction in wage rates. When government intervenes, offering to maintain those unable to find work at excessive wages, or to provide work on public projects at such wages, competition for the available jobs in private industry is diminished; and the necessary adjustments that must precede recovery cannot take place.

So we find that as the expenditures of government increased, despite the millions of unemployed, wage *rates* for factory work rose from an average of 45 cents per hour in 1933, to over 70 cents per hour in 1937, exceeding even the wage rates of 1929.[11] That this has impeded recovery is impossible to doubt; and the policy of the government has contributed to this unprecedented rise in wage rates at a time of severe unemployment.

Some able men have believed that, properly controlled, government expenditure can be a helpful factor in inducing recovery from a period of depression. A notable instance is that of the late James Harvey Rogers, who proposed that instead of attempting to balance the federal budget every year, it might be made to balance over a reasonable period of years; never more than ten. Within this decen-

nial period, the government might be permitted to run a deficit
during depression, but required to show an equal surplus during
prosperity. He would have each community prepare a program of
necessary construction to which the federal government would
pledge in advance a 50 per cent subsidy if the projects are undertaken whenever widespread depression appears.[12]

Such a program is not conducive to the control of public expenditure. A subsidy of 50 per cent would lead many communities to
extend their projects far beyond the economically desirable. The
temptation too evident. Such projects would needs be worth to the
community only half of the total cost. All this expenditure would
eventually have to be paid out of tax receipts, and the prospect of
heavier taxation would discourage the inducement to expand private
enterprise.

I question the feasibility of varying public expenditure in the
manner that Professor Rogers prescribed. Once pump priming is
undertaken there is always serious resistance to its diminution. It
cannot bring about a self sustaining recovery; and if it is halted, after
once being used, it would be followed by another depression. Each
diminution in expenditure, and depression, will lead to a renewal of
expenditure perhaps on a larger scale. If the federal budget is not
balanced within a much shorter accounting period than a decade, it
is likely it will not be balanced at all. The monetary experiences of
Germany, Austria, France, and Italy, following the World War,
provide us with abundant evidence of the destructive consequences
of long continued deficits.

3.   *Money madness and business confidence*

To England's great Prime Minister, Mr. Gladstone, long Chan-
cellor of the Exchequer, is attributed the remark: "The study of
monetary problems seems as surely to lead to insanity as a grand
passion." Exemplified, and in some part verified, in almost every
generation in the United States. From the early days, when the
Massachusetts Bay Colony began to issue paper IOUs, to the present
time, scarcely a generation without some use of 'fiat money.' And
always with similar results. As in the French Revolution, the colonial
paper money depreciated so rapidly that new issues replaced old,
only to depreciate in turn. Finally, Parliament forbade the further
issue of legal tender notes. During our Revolution, the Continental

Congress and the states issued money in such abundance it was soon worthless. In the Civil War, both the Federal and Confederate governments financed themselves through the easy means of printing money. The result: the Confederate currency became practically valueless, even before the surrender; and the greenbacks depreciated to one-third of their nominal value.

During the World War we devised a method of doing the same thing, issuing money, but more suitable to our business habits. Instead of printing huge quantities of paper money, the government borrowed on its bonds. Many of these bonds were sold to banks, who paid for them by creating deposits for the government; and others were used by private persons as security for loans from the banks for the purpose of buying the bonds. We had a 'credit inflation.' Different in form, but the same outcome. Result: prices increased nearly 150 % in about four years. Again, during the last few years we have been using the same device. The government has sold billions of dollars of bonds to finance its huge program of expenditure. The banks have bought these bonds and created deposits for the government. As yet we have no great rise in prices; none of the usual effects of inflation. Because the velocity of these deposits has declined sharply. But the danger always remains; and it has had its usual pernicious effect in undermining business confidence.

One symptom of this money madness is the frequently expressed view that we need a 'good inflation' to end the depression which we have suffered for a decade.[13] But inflation can never cure anything. The effect of a large increase in the quantity of money—whether greenbacks or deposits—is to give a temporary feeling of elation, much the same as that of several drinks of good whiskey. The parallel is close. Physiologists have found, notably in the case of drunken drivers of motor cars, that too much drink causes an impairment of the judgment of distances and of dangers. Hence the frequency of wrecks and crashes.

Identically the same, apparently, in the case of inflation: an impairment of the judgement, alike of bankers and business men. I can well remember discussing these questions with the late President Havenstein, of the German Reichsbank, in 1921, and asking him why they went on printing this huge quantity of paper money in such reckless fashion. His naive, but I believe perfectly sincere, reply was: "Why, my dear sir, business must go on; business must have money; prices are rising very fast, and business must have more money with which to carry on trade!" An excellent illustration of the ignorance of many financiers of the fundamental relation between the quantity of money and prices.

The notion that inflation means good business is widespread, though not among the wise.[14] It is true that a period of rising prices may temporarily result in an extension of business activity. But it is fictitious and unproductive activity. Speculation becomes a necessary part of business; more, supposedly, is to be gained by predicting the rate of change in prices than by close attention to efficient production. In a very real sense everybody is more occupied in an attempt to intercept nominal profits than to earn the real profits from production. But above all, the most harm done by inflation is that of halting economic progress. There can be no inducement to save when savings are wiped out by rising prices, from the issue of new money by the government. Little inducement to expand production when speculation is more profitable. And the distorted price structure that inflation creates makes it quite impossible to direct production properly into those channels that would best serve both producers and consumers.

The vast inflations of the postwar years in Germany and Austria; to a lesser extent in France and Italy; and to some extent in England and the United States, have made business men conscious of their dangers.[15] They know that despite the rise in prices, despite huge nominal profits, business did not prosper. The money illusion is a powerful force; but the experience of this generation is still near enough so that business is profoundly cautious. It is probably for this reason that we have so far avoided the usual consequences of the huge credit creation in recent years. This caution manifests itself in a reduced velocity of money and of trade.

This fear of inflation and the loss of business confidence is one of the poignant evils resulting from the policy of large expenditure for relief. The funds for this purpose were largely borrowed. The public debt is now at the highest level in our history. In a few years we have expended more for relief than the peak debt of the federal government for all purposes throughout our history, including six wars. There is a prevalent fear that maintaining interest payments on this huge debt may become so difficult that some administration may resort to the printing press in order to reduce the burden of the charges. And so long as all this is a factor that prospective investors must contend with, there is not likely to be a resumption of investment in new corporate securities. The foundations of true recovery.

The great contribution that government can make is to aid in the restoration of business confidence. Just as Alexander Hamilton did much to revive the credit of the young Republic, by putting public finance on a sound and honest basis, so today the surest way to renewed confidence is to allay fear. Economical expenditure will minimize the burden of taxation, reduce the prospective costs of doing business. A balanced budget, at an economical level, will do more to bring an expansion of employment and production than all extravagant public expenditure, with its supposed multiplicative effect on the national income.

4. *Subsidizing pauperism*

In a major depression some aid must be given to unemployed labor. No reasonable person would refuse those who suffer economic misfortune the necessaries of life. But we cannot be indifferent to the dangers inherent in relief on a scandalous scale. The foremost is that relief will come to be regarded as a normal form of income by large numbers of people. When such an attitude becomes prevalent, we have simply subsidized pauperism, with its baneful effects on the social and political life of the nation.

A difficult task; for when people on relief have the right to vote, a policy of frugality and firmness is not attractive to those in office. Far easier to retain political good will by resolving all doubts in favor of relief. Only the most high-minded holders of office can resist the temptation to expand the dole before election. When political clubs become auxiliary bureaus passing on cases, and when politicians make the decisions as to eligibility, there is every reason for fear.

It is important to minimize costs as an inducement to recovery. Equally to administer relief in a manner that will not destroy the self reliance of labor. Always and everywhere prodigality in relief has brought the same evils. In Rome, the handouts of grain and money attracted the riffraff of Europe. And the presence of these mobs intensified the pressure for the dole that destroyed the Roman character. In England, the poor laws brought the paupers of the realm in flocks to the larger cities. And as Adam Smith related, it was "often more difficult for a poor man to pass the artificial boundary of a parish than an arm of the sea or a ridge of high mountains."

Recently in this country we have witnessed a marked migration of the unemployed to California, so that this state has had to take measures to bar the influx. Note that the most fantastic schemes for retiring large numbers of people on generous pensions to be paid by inflationary issues of money have had their origin and maximum strength in California.

Only one way to prevent widespread pauperism: not to subsidize it. The status of the independent laborer working in private enterprise must be more attractive than those on make-work projects; far more attractive than to the recipients of home relief. For the pressure for work is a powerful factor in directing labor into the new fields of employment. And the pressure for work alone will bring about the competitive rates of wages necessary to provide full employment at all times.

Not to be overlooked that the deepest interests of labor are opposed to prodigal relief. Always the costs of relief are a part of the ultimate expenses of production. They must be paid for by the consumers, in higher prices, which reduce real wages. The advance of wages can only continue as economic progress is maintained. Every subsidized pauper is a brake on the economic system; every payment for relief is a drain on the national payroll.

The celebrated report of Mr. Nassau Senior on the Poor Laws held:

that property was being destroyed by the relentless advance of pauperism, that employers were defrauding the public by throwing their wages-bill on the parish, that labourers were being deprived of every motive for doing honest work, that the domestic life of the poor was being ruined by the parish endowment of bastardy and the neglect of all family affection, that the attraction of the so-called benefits of this spurious philanthropic legislation was confining the labourer to his parish, bereft alike of energy and hope. When we consider how entirely the economic progress of the working class has depended on the facility with which labour has been able to distribute itself and find its profit in new and ever-changing conditions of industry, it will be obvious how injurious this perverse legislative endowment of immobility has been.[16]

In the administration of relief in this country, can we avoid these same destructive effects?

THE BLIGHT OF DESTRUCTIVE TAXATION

The subjects of every state ought to contribute towards the support of govern ment, as nearly as possible, in proportion to their respective abilities; that is, i proportion to the revenue which they respectively enjoy under the protection o the state.

. . .

The tax which each individual is bound to pay ought to be certain, and no arbitrary. The time of payment, the manner of payment, the quantity to be paid ought all to be clear and plain to the contributor, and to every other person.

. . .

Every tax ought to be levied at the time, or in the manner, in which it is mos likely to be convenient for the contributor to pay it.

. . .

Every tax ought to be so contrived as both to take out and to keep out of the pockets of the people as little as possible, over and above what it brings into the public treasury of the state. A tax may either take out or keep out of the pocket of the people a great deal more than it brings into the public treasury.

—ADAM SMITH: *The Wealth of Nations*

It has been urged as an objection to exempting savings from taxation, that the law ought not to disturb, by artificial interference, the natural competition be tween the motives for saving and those for spending. But we have seen that the law disturbs this natural competition when it taxes savings, not when it spare them; for as the savings pay at any rate the full tax as soon as they are invested their exemption from payment in the earlier stage is necessary to prevent them from paying twice, while money spent in unproductive consumption pays only once. It has been further objected, that since the rich have the greatest means of saving, any privilege given to savings is an advantage bestowed on the rich at the expense of the poor. I answer, that it is bestowed on them only in proportion as they divert their income from the supply of their own wants to a productive in vestment, through which, instead of being consumed by themselves, it is distributed in wages among the poor.

—JOHN STUART MILL: *Principles of Political Economy*

Not only the wealth but the independence and security of a country appear to be materially connected with the prosperity of manufactures. If, then, it satisfac torily appears, that it is the interest of the United States, generally, to encourage manufactures, it merits particular attention, that there are circumstances which render the present a critical moment for entering, with zeal, upon the important business.

—ALEXANDER HAMILTON: *Report on Manufactures; 1791*

CHAPTER XXI

THE BLIGHT OF DESTRUCTIVE TAXATION

1. *On the incidence of taxation*

N a speech on taxing the Colonies, made before the House of Commons in 1766, the famous Lord Mansfield stated, what has come to be termed the 'equal-diffusion theory' of taxation, in this striking language: "I hold it to be true that a tax laid in any place is like a pebble falling into and making a circle in a lake, till one circle produces and gives motion to another and the whole circumference is agitated from the center." This was ten years before the American Revolution. And such ideas had been prevalent for a long time before Lord Mansfield stated them. The same views on the even diffusion of taxes were set forth in detail by an earlier Italian writer of his period, Pietro Verri of Milan; and they have been repeated in varied form by distinguished writers in every generation since.[1] With what result? The old, infantile belief still prevails that somehow the rich can be made to bear the burden of taxation.

In England, among the earliest taxes to arouse active discussion of incidence—the question of who pays the tax—were the excise taxes of 1641. It is the type we now term 'internal revenue.' Now in almost universal use among the nations, they long continued a favorite target of attack. Denounced by no end of writers, alike in Britain and America.[2] The late E. R. A. Seligman, distinguished tax authority, author of a celebrated work on the question, said of contemporary writings: "It is clear that the discussion of the excise tax called forth almost every conceivable theory as to its incidence. Some thought that the tax was not shifted at all, some maintained that it was shifted to the land only, some believed that it was shifted to the consumer, and some contended that it was again shifted by these to the employers of labor. These views were advanced with all degrees of confidence—but, with few exceptions, with little grasp of fundamental economic principles." [3]

Prevalent views almost as diverse today as in the seventeenth and

337

eighteenth centuries. But it seems that a wider understanding must result from the increasing consideration given to the problem. Almost endless material even in the daily papers. Let us take an example. Here is the heading of an item in a morning journal:

"Telephone taxes equal $12 on each telephone; the New York Company pays over $29,000,000 in taxes."

The gross revenues of the New York Telephone Company, in 1937, were $206,000,000, and of this, 29 millions went in taxes.[4] Who paid this tax: the company, or the customers? Here is a case in which the answer is unequivocal. As is well known, telephone rates are largely fixed by commissions, which endeavor to limit the earnings of the companies to what is regarded as a 'fair' return. In the case of the New York Company, the taxes amounted to nearly as much as the entire net earnings. Were the taxes abolished, would the net be doubled? The answer is certain: not for long! All over the United States, commissions would require a corresponding reduction of telephone rates. In other words, the taxes were paid, almost directly, by every user of the company's lines.

But were these the final payers? In a great number of instances, at least, they assuredly were not. The larger part of these telephones were used by other corporations and business enterprises, rather than by private individuals. Their telephone bills were a part of their running expenses, and, like wages and other costs, were simply added to the price of the goods or services sold. In brief, we may trace the tax near to its final disposition. But even here the ripples described by Lord Mansfield go on and on. And telephone taxes are partially borne by every consumer of every product in the production of which telephone service is used.

The railways, the electric power companies, and all other 'utilities,' are in exactly the same position as the telephone companies. Their rates are largely fixed nowadays by governmental commissions, state or national, and these rates are regulated with a view to providing the companies with an 'adequate return' on their invested capital, and no more. If the billions of dollars that all companies pay in national, state, and municipal taxes were cut off, the companies would have a simply enormous increase in their net profits; perhaps, as in the case of the New York Telephone Company, their net profits would be nearly doubled. But again, only for the moment. Railway

nd utility rates would almost immediately be reduced to corre-
pond with the reduction in the taxes they pay.

Almost identically the same with nearly every business enterprise in the country. Every successful business aims, of course, at a
maximum of profits. But practically all, even among what are termed
monopolies,' realize that the lower the price, the wider the sales,
nd hence the larger the aggregate gain. It is this principle, this *force*,
hat in the long run brings the earnings on capital in nearly every
kind of industry to a common level. For a brief time new enterprises,
new methods, new inventions may enjoy a high level of profits. But
only for a time. As the new inventions, new methods, come into
wider use, profits will again fall to the common level, and this level
is always near the minimum at which business risks may be undertaken.

Now, every expense or outlay involved in every enterprise, of
whatever description, must be added to the costs of production.
Otherwise profits would fall below the minimum at which business
will undertake risks. Nor can business enterprises successfully raise
their prices much beyond these costs. Competition, a hard and fast
regulator of prices, prescribes their prices just as government commissions fix utility rates. Therefore, we may say that the prices of
all goods and of all products are in the same position as the rates on
railways and for other utility services: that is, they are, in the long-
run just sufficient to yield a fair return on the investment. The only
difference between competitive prices and utility rates is that the
former are regulated automatically by competition, while the latter
are regulated by some slow-moving commission. That is why the
railways and utilities suffer so much more from a violent change in
the general level of prices, and therefore in their costs. Especially in
periods of monetary inflation.[5]

No one would contend that in paying for a pair of shoes, say from
Brockton, Massachusetts to Shenandoah, Iowa the purchaser did
not 'pay the freight,' any less than the wages of the working men,
the cost of materials, and the profit of the shoe manufacturer. These
are no more a part of the cost of production than the taxes paid by
the shoe manufacturer. Why and how there could be so little understanding, such a vast divergence of views, is difficult to fathom.
Writers are wont to say that these subjects are 'highly abstruse.' But
everyone familiar with the income and expense accounts of a busi-

ness knows that taxes are part of the costs of production in the sam
sense as wages or materials. And the consumer must pay the taxe
precisely as he pays all the other expenses of production, in the pric
of the goods he buys.

But it will be said: all this is true enough of ordinary taxes; but
it true of the income tax? Does the consumer pay that tax, or doe
it rest on the recipient of the income? Here, again, consider wha
actually happens in the case of a utility. The taxes must be include
in the expenses, and the rates fixed by a commission must be sufficier
to meet all expenses and provide a 'fair return.' The Supreme Cour
has ruled on several occasions that *all* taxes must be included. "Ther
is no difference in this respect between state and federal taxes, o
between income taxes and others." [6] And utility commissions nov
do include income taxes among the expenses determining the leve
of rates.

What of the income taxes of industrial corporations? Are they
too, shifted to consumers? Inevitably these corporate income taxe
are included in the prices of the goods sold. The interest and divi
dends that corporations pay to their bondholders and stockholder
are from the net earnings. Very close to the minimum they requir
in order to stay in business. More than that, on an average, they ar
not likely to earn; for competition will force profits down to thi
level. Less than that, on an average, they cannot earn, for then the
could not obtain the necessary capital for the undertaking. At time
corporate income taxes may be shifted to wages, to labor. For if
business finds that its net earnings available for interest, dividend
and taxes are insufficient to meet these charges, it must diminish it
demand for labor; and if business enterprises generally are in thi
position, the level of wages must fall. If resistance to lower wages i
too strong, the incidence of the tax will ultimately be upon labo
through a diminution in employment.

Very much the same as to the tax on the larger individual in
comes. If a heavy income tax takes a large part of the income o
receivers of interest and dividends, the average rate of interest an
dividends paid by business enterprises must be higher. Otherwis
business cannot attract the necessary capital for expansion. A heavy
income tax will lead investors to the purchase of tax-exempt govern
ment securities; or in extreme cases they may prefer to hold fund
idle rather than to risk them in profitless enterprise. Far more harm
ful is the possibility that if such taxes cannot be shifted to consumers

the form of higher prices, or to labor in the form of lower wages,
they will be borne ultimately by the whole nation. Vividly manifested now in the world's greatest commercial empire.

2. *Progressive taxation and industrial stagnation*

The last forty years or more have seen a huge increase of governmental expenditure in most countries, and therewith a search for
new methods of heavier taxation. Almost universally this has taken
the form of progressive income taxes, Great Britain being a conspicuous leader. But Great Britain has not been conspicuous in this
period in gain of national wealth. Very little, if any, increase in its
real income per capita; and since the income of the workers is a
nearly fixed share of the total, little increase in the average of real
wages. In this same period the United States, at least until 1930,
were going forward at very near the same steady rate, per capita, as
in preceding generations; and with this a steady advance in real
wages and enjoyments.

Why the difference between the United States and Great Britain?
The reason, I think, is clear. In the United States, until 1930, there
was a nearly constant addition to the capital invested in industry, for
at least a hundred and forty years. This has permitted the prompt
introduction of new machinery, new inventions, discoveries, processes, which have steadily augmented the volume of output. While
the rate of expansion in the United States continued, in England it
began to decline, particularly in the last thirty years. Why the
difference? The usual answer is that nations, having grown rich and
powerful, are much like individuals; they lose their vigor and their
enterprise. Perhaps some element of truth. But I believe there are
more positive factors, and one of them is the drive towards heavy
taxation of income.

No one knows just why enterprisers are driven to work so hard,
to accumulate vast fortunes, from which they seem to derive so little
enjoyment in their old age. Probably it is the sheer zest in achievement, and not merely love of gain. But profits are an essential part
of achievement. Without profits they cannot expand their enterprises, adopt new inventions, which are the source of their success.
Evident that one way to dampen this ardor of achievement, and so
to check this gain in well-being, is to confiscate the higher profits.
When there is no favorable prospect, many of the most competent

see no motive for staying in business at all. Which is what has happened recently in the United States.

Nor is it difficult to see why such heavy taxation must bring industrial stagnation.[7] We have seen that in the long run net profits in industry are on the average not much more than 4 or 5 per cent. A few of the most successful may acquire large fortunes in a lifetime. But the Fords, the Rockefellers, and the Vanderbilts are the exception. As is well known, about one-third of enterprises make no profits at all.[8] In computing profits as a whole, we must, of course, take both the small and large earnings, and deduct all losses. The average is far, far below that of the very energetic few. It is not hard to understand why the gains of industry from year to year, taking the broad average, form so small a part either of the capital invested or the value of the product.

From this there arises a curious paradox; first made known, as far as I am aware, by the late Allyn Young.[9] This is that the successful business man works practically for nothing. If on the average, his gain amounts to little more than the going rate of interest, he might just as well put out his fortune at interest and spend his time playing ping-pong. Stronger influences keep him at work. There is the hope of becoming one of the very fortunate few to accumulate a tremendous fortune. But beyond this is the feeling of power, of achievement, in establishing, managing, and expanding a profitable enterprise.

Easy to see that if the fundamental force, the opportunity of profit, the lust for gain, is destroyed, it is much like taking away the main spring of a watch. It simply will not work. Suppose that upon the profits of the more successful a burdensome tax is imposed. Suppose, as many urge, that 20, 30, 40 per cent or more of his gains are taken. He works hard, runs great risks; and the ultimate margin is usually small and easily wiped out. He feels too heavily handicapped. No doubt, also, a deep resentment at what he considers rank injustice. Is it wise, thus, to put a brake upon energy, penalize the highest and finest economic talent? Do we really wish to *promote* industrial stagnation?

The total net earnings of industry in this country even in the 1920's was not much more than six or seven billions annually, plus or minus a little depending on the allowance for depreciation. Subtract two or three billions of this in taxes, as has been done, and it is severely felt, not only by business but by the entire nation. Not

DISTRIBUTION OF REPORTED INCOME IN U. S.

BY INCOME CLASSES IN 1926
(INCOME CLASSES IN $ 1,000)

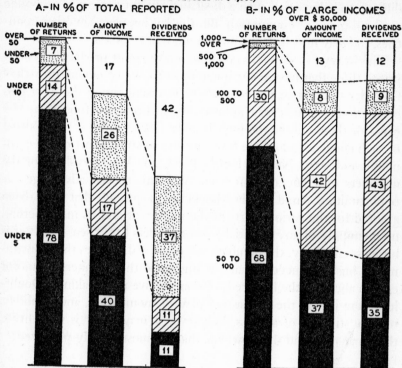

XL. HOW THE REPORTED INCOME IN U.S. IS DIVIDED

The Income Tax Bureau reports the size of incomes among the four or five millions who pay income tax. In the chart above these relations are depicted by income classes. Of the total number of returns in a representative year like 1926, 78 per cent had incomes under $5,000 and received 40 per cent of the total income reported (which is about one-third of the total estimated income of the country). With this is shown the distribution of dividends received, indicating the proportion of stocks and bonds held by the different groups. Thus the 78 per cent (the incomes under $5,000) received 11 per cent of the total dividends reported. In the second half of the chart these percentages are shown for incomes over $50,000. Almost a repetition of the showing as to the total number. Thus, for example, 68 per cent of those with incomes from $50,000 to $100,000 received 37 per cent of the total amount received by this class, and 35 per cent respectively of the income from dividends reported. Roughly, this distribution is found in every country: the division of income from the income tax paying population is much the same.

merely that these taxes are diverted from more important uses. I
is the damper that this raid upon the rich puts upon all industry, and
more fundamentally, upon the spirit of enterprise. Many find i
difficult to believe that such a diversion can put the entire economi
mechanism out of commission. But this has happened in other coun
tries, and may now be happening in the United States.

This heavy taxation falls chiefly upon the most progressive enter
prises, those that have contributed most to our economic growth.¹
Consider the cost to the community in discouraging the most effi
cient producers in every industry, from breakfast food to moto
cars, for these will be the most heavily taxed. Why, if not becaus
of such efficiency, do three firms occupy so large a part of the auto
mobile industry? Neither Henry Ford, nor Mr. Chrysler, nor the
managers of General Motors enjoyed any special advantages o
opportunities. Amid all the thousands of patents that have been
granted for the various parts of the motor car and its manufacture
no monopoly of any essential part or process has arisen. Surely it i
business efficiency, the combination of special abilities that contrib
ute to business success, that has put these three makers of moto
cars so ahead of the hundreds of competitive undertakings. Doubt
less there is here the everlasting play of momentum, and doubtles
too the stimulus of success. Whatever it may be, it is such firms
their managers and their owners, that are most heavily penalized.

3. *Taxation and the capital supply*

In the United States taxation of incomes is comparatively new
Tried for a brief period after the Civil War. Held unconstitutiona
and abandoned over sixty years ago. Then a constitutional amend-
ment and a new income tax. In the beginning mild enough. Bu
seized upon in later years by malevolent minds to become an instrument of oppression and economic terrorism. In the end, perhaps the
most disastrous mistake in the history of our fiscal legislation. Bringing untold ill. Discouraging to enterprise, and thus diminishing the
increase of wages and employment.¹¹ A matter now of great concern.

In an essay upon the sources of our progress and industrial growth
I ventured to offer this postulate:

"Since the highest rate of savings is obviously from the largest fortunes
and progressively increasing with the size, it follows that until we can

devise a more efficient system, the higher the concentration of wealth, that is, income, in the hands of the few, the greater the capital supply, and, therefore, the greater the gain in national well-being." [12]

The purpose of progressive income taxation is to strike hardest at these large incomes, the chief source of new capital supply. The State now expropriates a considerable portion of the income of the rich, the heavy saving class. With what result? The danger of extinguishing the larger part of the capital supply. This seems what has happened in England in recent years. Not merely an impression. It is the conclusion of a competent student of the distribution of income in Great Britain, Colin Clark.[13] And the outcome has been just that which might be predicted, a steady retardation of growth in British industry.

Will the same thing happen in America? If the burdens of taxation continue to rise, if government expenditure continues to take an increasing share of the national income, inevitably it will have exactly the same result, the end of our industrial progress.

Such, as I conceive it, is the invariable and inevitable effect of burdensome taxation, particularly on incomes. The wide approval of progressive taxes upon incomes derives from a profound misunderstanding of the social rôle of wealth. If, as I have endeavored to show, the total personal expenditures of the richer classes constitute but a small part of the total for the nation, the evil that may flow therefrom, under our system of private enterprise, is relatively slight; and the gain to the whole population from its restriction is almost inappreciable.

More recently the view has been urged that we have already reached such a high state of economic development that it would be better to make progress more slowly, to give less thought to the future, and to provide for the more urgent needs for current consumption. Taxation, it is said, can be used for this purpose, to take part of the income of the rich, that would otherwise be saved, and to give it to the poor. Now the extra provision for current consumption, that can be made by diverting a large part of the moderate sum devoted to increasing the country's reproductive capital, cannot be large. If half of the savings that now go into such reproductive capital were distributed among wage earners, including low salaried workers, the increase in their earnings, on the average, would be slight—not more than 5 or 6 per cent. With inevitably a fall in per capita output. Within a few years, the total income available for consumption would be far less than if the accumulation of capital had been allowed to proceed at its normal rate. And every succeeding generation would continue to pay in diminished well-being.

4. *The first principle of taxation*

If the theory of economic progress as here set forth is valid, the principle that should govern the imposition of taxes is obvious. Its primary aim should be the highest positive promotion of capital saving and the conservation of that capital. In no sense a novelty, for this principle is implied by many able writers.

From this point of view the income tax, alike in principle and effect, is perhaps the most harmful that could be devised. The same may be said of other taxes that bear heavily on those who provide most of the savings for productive capital. Among the most objectionable are the capital gains tax, taxes upon corporate savings and corporate surplus, and similar charges on other types of capital savings. Inheritance taxes, or 'death duties,' as they are called in England, plainly destroy one of the strongest motives to accumulation. The same as to the capital gains tax. The purchase of capital goods, or of its titles thereto, must naturally be discouraged if in addition to the tax on the income from such wealth and property, there is a further tax on the increase in the value of the investment.

The tax on the undistributed profits of corporations, that is, on additions to corporate surplus, is in many respects even more pernicious. Most well conducted corporations retain part of their profits to be reinvested in their business. A heavy tax on these undistributed profits compels corporations to diminish, if not to forego, this excellent type of capital saving. While part of the profits so distributed might be saved, most of it would be spent.[14] The financial stability of corporations would be impaired by the amounts they ordinarily add to surplus. Further, an adequate surplus is essential to meet the losses incurred during depression, to continue the payment of interest, and to meet other charges when earnings are insufficient. Onerously to tax the accumulation of surpluses, therefore, is to promote the conditions that deepen depression and intensify the suffering they cause.

Now as to the larger side. If the ideal is the largest possible addition to capital, it follows that the weight of taxes should be removed from savings and placed upon spending. In no way a hardship. The normal fiscal requirements of an economical government could place no serious burden upon the great mass of consumers. The larger part of the tax would fall upon the most conspicuous spenders.

Many able economists have urged an income tax exempting savings. John Stuart Mill went so far as to say that "no income tax is really just from which savings are not exempted; and no income tax ought to be voted without that provision." [15] Why then any income taxes at all? There are endless objections to any kind of income tax. Administratively the most expensive tax device known. It is often evaded entirely; it fosters corruption; its methods are inquisitorial, and frequently outrageous, as in the Mellon case. Much taxable income is under-reported, particularly in the under brackets where supervision is so difficult and expensive. If the same revenue can be obtained far more economically in other ways, such ways would seem vastly preferable.

There is a simple and inexpensive method of taxing all incomes and exempting savings, and that is by a graded tax on all consumers goods, levied at the sources of production; [16] such a tax would seriously affect only those who are heavy spenders; and only to the extent of their spendings. In point of costs, it would be the cheapest tax system conceivable, the simplest and the most beneficent and far-reaching in its effects. It would promote thrift, stimulate saving, and provide the maximum share of the national income for enterprise and expansion. In ten years it could repair the almost irreparable losses and damages of the last ten; and send a nation bounding with prosperity.

As it is, the mass of the people, deluded with the feeling that they, at least, do not pay the taxes, that income and profit taxes fall largely upon the rich, have little care for, no effective interest in these expenditures. So far from this, huge masses clamor for ever greater extravagance. Townsendism, Huey Long's 'share the wealth,' 'ham and eggs,' and all the like.

If, then, depressions did not call forth every imaginable scheme for assessing the rich to provide huge sums for relief and prodigal waste, there would be less reason for fearing the extremes of taxation that destroy the confidence of investors. The severity of depression is intensified by this fear of expropriation. The moment this danger is removed, enterprise is encouraged and industry will resume its normal rate of growth.

Perhaps most salutary of all, such a tax would put a heavy brake upon reckless governmental expenditure. If all consumers could know, beyond peradventure, that every dollar added to the tax would add directly to their daily spendings, they would then be alive, as never before, to the evils of governmental extravagance.

ECONOMIC PLANNING
AND GOVERNMENTAL MUDDLING

Amid a multitude of projects no plan is devised.
                                    —PUBLIUS SYRUS; *circa* 42 B.C.

We are happy in a form of government which cannot envy the laws of our neighbors—for it hath served as a model to others, but is original at Athens. And this our form, as committed not to the few, but to the whole body of the people, is called a democracy. How different soever in a private capacity, we all enjoy the same general equality our laws are fitted to preserve; and superior honors just as we excel.
                —PERICLES: Oration on *The Causes of Athenian Greatness;* 431 B.C.

The employment of public laborers in a democracy is always a thorny problem. They strive to become a favored class, with extra pay and extra privileges. As has already been said, other laborers commonly support them in such endeavors, from a confused notion that the process will raise wages and privileges generally. Elected officials, on the other hand, are apt to accede to their demands; for this compact body of voters needs to be conciliated. At its worst, the employment of large bodies of laborers means a political machine and political corruption. Even at its best, it is likely to bring place-making and easy stints; hence, inefficiency and expense.
                            —F. W. TAUSSIG: *Principles of Economics*

CHAPTER XXII

ECONOMIC PLANNING
AND GOVERNMENTAL MUDDLING

1. *What is planning?*

IN every depression, from the beginning of time, fads and fancies
fill the sky. Every imaginable panacea for economic ills. Usually
nothing new but the name. Thus: the marvelous 'social credit' movement in England, 'technocracy' in the United States, and 'economic
planning' everywhere. No one would regard this rage for planning
as a passing fancy; we shall hear much of it for generations to come.[1]
It had its recent origin in the various schemes utilized in Russia to
achieve a program of industrialization. The 'five-year plans' seem
to have caught the imagination of peoples everywhere. And now
we have 'economic plans' in Germany, Italy.[2] Interesting that it is
chiefly in these countries of totalitarianism. Democratic countries
have as yet formulated no elaborate blueprints for economic development, though we hear much of the need for such planning in the
United States and in England.

One concept of planning, therefore, is that it involves the determination of the kinds and quantities of production under the direct
control of the states—that is, socialism in some form. The extreme
instance, in this sense, is in Russia. The German four-year plan, because its scope is not so wide as that of the Russian, may be regarded
as some intermediate type, short of socialism. But Germany's plan,
though directed more with a view to military than to industrial development, covers so large a part of the productive field, with such
detailed control by government, that its methods are not fundamentally different. Economic planning in this sense is simply the
replacement of private enterprise by the state.

A narrower concept of economic planning involves government
undertakings to achieve long-run economic ends that are ordinarily
outside the scope of private enterprise. This type includes such
policies as city and regional planning. Precisely what governments

351

have done more or less from time immemorial. It was said of the Emperor Augustus that 'he found a Rome of brick and left it a Rome of marble.' Some exaggeration, but perhaps not an incredible accomplishment. But far the greatest achievement in this field was the incomparable beauty brought to Athens by Pericles, Pheidias, Iktinus, and their associates. The splendor of this achievement and its unparalleled results have haunted the imagination of men ever since. Desirable as planning of this quality may be in its field, two reservations may be noted. First, such planning in the hands of inferior ability may force upon future generations an ugly and impossible city or region. Secondly, extravagant planning may prevent all economic progress by increasing government expenditure and reducing the capital supply. But with adequate safeguards, a long run plan for urban and regional development may facilitate the adaptation of community life to new prospective forces. Wide streets, great avenues, large parks: these of necessity must be planned before the growth of a city or region increases enormously the expense of providing these for future generations.

Much the same as to such government undertakings as the Panama Canal, or Boulder Dam. Each of unquestionable value. The huge cost of building the Panama Canal, the risks necessarily associated with such a project, the combination of economic and strategic motives, all contributed to making it an appropriate undertaking for the government. Much the same may be said of Boulder Dam. But shall we go on, endlessly, evolve ever larger projects, of less obvious utility? Shall we go out into the deserts and rear vast structures like the dams at Grand Coulee, or even Muscle Shoals, which may yield no adequate returns for a generation or more? When their utility and advantage may in the meantime be superseded by invention? Are we to plunge into gigantic and often fanciful expenditures merely for the sake of spending public money? Build up enterprises that may be obsolete even in the near future? Within limits, governmental planning has its utility. Perhaps to be said of reforestation, the conservation of soil, and some natural resources.[3] With due restraints, there can be no reasonable objection to careful planning in such fields. They lie outside the scope of private enterprise. But where such undertakings are detrimental to the development of industry, and involve competition with private enterprise, they seem clearly undesirable.

Still more as to planning that embraces governmental regulation of business, the control of prices, wages, and the distribution of income. This type includes the regulation of railroad and utility rates, the maintenance of agricultural prices, the fixing of wages and hours of work, and other forms of industrial control; taxation and public expenditure for the avowed purpose of 'redistributing the wealth.' Planning in this sense means rather the restriction of individual initiative and private enterprise. Full of dangers, for it affects the internal conduct of business, with a consequent decline in efficiency and a retardation.[4] The one type of such regulation that seems desirable is the control of credit, to minimize or avoid depression. And here, it may be emphasized, the control is general, not directly affecting management or enterprise.[5]

Why the need for planning that requires government control of business? The reasons advanced by the advocates of interference are many. Among them are the supposed failure of the competitive system itself to bring about full employment, the supposed failure to 'produce to capacity' even in good times, and the supposed, unjust disparity of income. These questions have in part already been discussed. It seems to me fantastic to say that we have not made progress rapidly enough, even before the last decade, and then to offer as a remedy the very type of action that must inevitably retard progress. We can advance as rapidly as the capital supply permits.[6] The supposed failure to produce in good times is largely imaginary. There is always idle equipment, and idle workers, even in prosperity. But this idle equipment is obsolete and retained for stand-by, emergency use; and some idle equipment is inevitable where seasonal peaks require intensive production for relatively short periods. Beyond that, equipment cannot be used without labor; and the labor supply during prosperity is used to the fullest extent compatible with the moving of labor from job to job and from industry to industry.

The great failure properly charged to our economic system is the failure to avoid depression. And this can be remedied by a relatively simple type of credit control. Further, the general methods of exercising this have in fact been in use for some time. There is nothing to be gained by making such control a part of a more complex scheme of pervasive regulation, as those in favor of 'economic planning' imagine.

2. *The regulation of business*

Consider the effects of government regulation of railroad rates and utility rates; and compare these industries with those that have not been restricted by government regulation.

Just over a hundred years ago this country was in the throes of a feverish speculation, one of the first of our great 'booms.' Chiefly in land, but also in banks and insurance companies, and especially in railroads. The beginnings of a great era of railroad building, and the settlement and development of a continent. At first a dubious beginning. But as has happened so often, almost immediately technology brought progress. The wooden rails with strips of iron quickly gave way to iron rails, then to steel rails; wooden bridges were replaced by iron bridges. And locomotives were built with more tractive power and speed. A vigorous, acquisitive people constructed railroads everywhere—to Lake Erie, to the Mississippi, and over the Rocky Mountains to the Pacific. And as these railroads spread, cities and towns sprang up, the rich prairies of the Middle West were opened to the advancing settlers.[7]

So swiftly did this railroad building proceed that within half a century all the states in the Union, and the territories, were bound together by this iron band. Soon luxury unknown to travel: sleeping cars and dining cars. One could go to sleep at Albany and awake nearing Chicago. Transcontinental travel was far easier than a stage coach trip from New York to Philadelphia had been. And all this innovation lead swiftly to a vast expansion of trade and commerce, a fabulous increase in national wealth. Wheat from the Mississippi Valley sold freely in Liverpool and Hamburg. And later, fruit from California and Florida placed upon the tables of the working men for the price of potatoes. Never in all human existence such a great and bounteous distribution of the good things and the luxuries of this earth.

And the reward to the builders, the enterprisers? After the first flush of enthusiasm, a recriminatory clamor, hostile legislation. Fierce assaults upon 'monopoly,' 'the Robber Barons,' and the 'Railway Kings.' And yet, almost from the beginning the rates for railway transportation fell steadily, from five cents a ton-mile downward to less than a single cent. To carry a pair of shoes from Brockton, Massachusetts, to a remote village on the prairies of Iowa, cost only twenty-two cents. And while rates declined, service improved. And while the speed of transport increased, the clamor grew. The 'regulation of monopolies' became a dominant political issue, recurrently breaking out in every depression from the 70's to 1939. And in 1887, the regulation of railroads was begun by the Interstate Commerce Commission.[8]

All told, the railways of the United States have absorbed at the least twenty to thirty billions of capital; a considerable part through the insurance companies from the savings of the people. It is only a guess, but it is quite possible that the actual total investment through a hundred years may have been nearer to forty billions. Perhaps the larger part of it lost. In spite of the wealth they created, and the wealth they brought to relatively few investors, the railways of this, as of other countries, have never been highly profitable, always run upon a very narrow margin, and recurrently in financial difficulties. To which in the United States the burdens of regulation have added hugely, and the bill, as always paid by the unsuspecting people. The Interstate Commerce Commission and the swarm of state railway commissions that sprang up in its wake have already cost millions, to provide jobs for office holding amateurs, hundreds of millions more, annually, in the retardation and restriction of transportation.

Political pressure for low rates led to forced reductions that made it impossible for the railroads to earn an adequate return, to pay the capital charges, and to provide the best service. How much difference in earnings would have been required to provide the needful capital? Roughly speaking, perhaps like the difference between 4 per cent per annum and 6 per cent. A difference of only 2 per cent at the outside. This small difference of 2 per cent in earnings for only a part of the capital, would have necessitated a very slight rise in rates, or a very moderate lowering of wages and other expenses. Yet, for the purpose of forcing rates to a low level that would soon have been achieved through improvements, the financial stability of the railroads was endangered.

For years it had been charged that the railroads were 'extravagantly run,' and that with 'better management' it would have been possible for them to "save a million dollars a day." The late Justice Brandeis, then interested in these problems, was the reputed author of this phrase. A 'million dollars a day' sounded like a large sum. But it would have amounted to only 365 millions a year; and the gross expenditures of the railroads were then some five billions. So that, even if true, this would have meant a saving of only 7 per cent.

But this amount added to the net revenues of the railroads, would have meant to many the difference between prosperity and near bankruptcy, and enormously raised their credit. One might think that out of all the railway companies then operating, some, at least, would have seized such an opportunity, if it really existed; and there is reason to believe that some tried. But how and where could this saving have been made? Only, in the main, by an economy of labor—by reducing wages or lowering the number of employees. But to this there was resistance, not only from labor, but from the commissions as well.

Despite the dire consequences of railroad regulation, almost every state in the union now attempts to regulate the rates of public utilities, which have now come to mean chiefly the producers of electric power. The development of this industry is almost without a parallel. In less than half a century, it has emerged from hardly more than a scientific toy. Today forty billions or more of capital are invested in the generation and distribution of electric power. Even under the 'dead hand' of regulation and the difficulties of the wartime inflation, when rates were held down while fuel and labor costs rose, the industry made remarkable headway. Today, the production of electricity is at the highest level, and the price at which it is sold at the lowest in history. The need for additional productive capacity is still great. But this outstanding achievement of our generation has, for the time being, been brought to a standstill.[9]

In the light of all this experience with the railroads and public utilities, difficult to see how further governmental control can mean anything less than strangulation, the arrest of progress. The problems of industrial production, prices, and expenses, far exceed in complexity the regulation of railroad and utility rates. Is it wise to entrust the very fundamentals of economic output and well-being to governmental bureaus? Are we to have political bodies, the typical office holding types, determine wage rates? The unavoidable result must be unprofitable production and the discouragement of investment.

3. *Planning and personnel*

Yet other considerations. The purpose behind 'economic' planning, even with many high-minded believers, is plain enough. To them it is a means of raising the economic status of the underprivileged, the supposedly 'underpaid one-third,' who suffer from

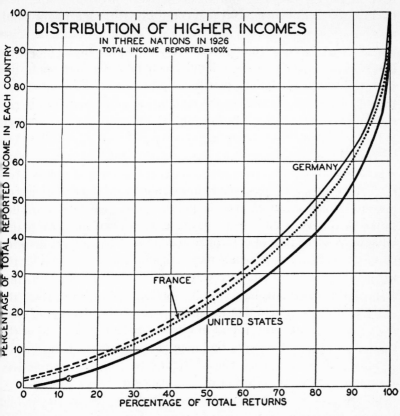

DISTRIBUTION OF HIGHER INCOMES
IN THREE NATIONS IN 1926
TOTAL INCOME REPORTED=100%

Y-axis: PERCENTAGE OF TOTAL REPORTED INCOME IN EACH COUNTRY (0, 10, 20, 30, 40, 50, 60, 70, 80, 90, 100)

X-axis: PERCENTAGE OF TOTAL RETURNS (0, 10, 20, 30, 40, 50, 60, 70, 80, 90, 100)

GERMANY

FRANCE

UNITED STATES

XLI. INCOME DISTRIBUTION IN GERMANY AND FRANCE AND THE UNITED STATES

Here is a story similar to that of the preceding chart: that the distribution of income is strangely alike in all countries and times wherefrom adequate data are available, and does not seem to change as far back as these data extend. France, Germany, and the United States differ enormously in their national incomes. For example, in 1929 this country probably had near to ten times the total income of France, and four or five times that of Germany. But, as will be seen, the modal distribution differs little. In the view of the writer the discovery of this law governing distribution was one of the great contributions yet made to economics and to rational social thinking. If everyone were to know about it, and understand it clearly, there would probably be much less agitation and social unrest. We can not alter human ability any more than we can change the distribution of the stars.

the 'injustices' and inequalities of our competitive system. And what they propose is usually not much more than to redistribute income on a more 'equable' basis. Never successfully achieved anywhere on earth.

Again, successful planning necessarily requires highly competent planners; and these are often difficult to obtain. And the choice must be by the individuals temporarily in power. The business of the government itself is done by the civil service, by the lawyers who are the executives and legislators, and by the army. Presumably the personnel for planning would be chosen from much the same sources. More profitable 'patronage.'

True we have the civil service laws. And examinations for this service are the ideal type in government, and result in a more efficient personnel than selection by the politicians with a view to party interests. But very difficult to devise examinations in industry for choosing leaders, men of enterprise and vision. The civil service may consist of diligent and honest men, but not always of driving and thriving types. Only one sure way of finding these; that is among those who are successful already. It is precisely this natural selection in our economic system that has made possible the high standard of management commonly found in our successful business organizations. Mere planning cannot find men of this type. Nor can we depend upon elected officials for this high type. Judging from almost universal experience, election of the planners would mean principally lawyers. But the legal mind, as a rule, is not suited for this purpose. Accustomed to think in terms of precedent, rather than what could be done. We have had lawyers directing some American enterprises, and the results not always encouraging. The steel industry in America was built up by a group of exceptionally capable, aggressive, perhaps unscrupulous men, typical of those later called Captains of Industry.[10] They brought our steel companies to world leadership, due largely to the demand for steel in the great era of railway building in the 1870's and '80's. By the time of the huge steel merger, America was far in the lead in the production of steel. Then came lawyer control. Enterprise seemed to flag, the industry content with the accustomed ways of doing things. Other nations, Germany in particular, taking the lead in new kinds of steel. Then an awakening in the United States, and in the last ten or fifteen years an astonishing change. America is again in the lead, and turning out metallurgical marvels.

If such things can happen in private enterprise, certain to be worse under state regulation. The decline of the American railways has been discussed. To whom the blame? To the legal profession? That would be absurd. The failure of control is inherent in the system of choosing by popular vote. The legislators, and the railway commissioners who have combined, blindly, in bringing their plight, were largely lawyers, who were not chosen by the legal profession but by the electorate. The choice of the electorate seems largely limited to lawyers, because the law is the chief avenue to political leadership. Not an encouraging thought in 'government planning.'

A planned economy, if it were to reach the stage of a working reality, would inevitably involve a regimented or armyfied sort of society, where the activities of the many would be directed by the few.[11] An armyfied economic system is not conducive to progress. It is true that some of the most notable government achievements, such as the Panama Canal, have been under the direction of the army. But the completion of a gigantic engineering task is no guaranty that the complex problems of an ever-changing economic outlook can be safely entrusted to a group drilled to attach a sacred significance to orders of superiors, accustomed to promotion by seniority, and largely satisfied with the traditional method of getting things done.

Certainly the wartime results of planning by military boards hardly justify the high expectation of those who see the millennium in an armyfied society. Control of industry by the military authorities was as unsatisfactory in the countries with army staffs of high prestige, as in the more democratic countries, suddenly called upon to mobilize their resources for war.

4. *The futilities of planning*

The concept of a planned economy, with its endless boards, and an army of subordinates, seems to involve difficulties still more serious. The core of these is the present curious inability of the human mind, or of human eyes, to look very far through a stone wall. The stone wall in this instance is the future; and the inability of even the most competent minds to see far ahead. This inability is often characteristic of some of the very highest types.

Some day I should like to compile an extended list of what I should term the 'Aberrations of Great Minds.' The list would be long. We may recall that an astronomer, one of the finest minds of the preceding generation, attempted to prove on mathematical grounds that an aeroplane was a manifest impossibility. It could not fly. This was Simon Newcomb, and his demonstration was for his intimate friend Professor Langley, who actually made the first heavier-than-air machine that flew. Again: One of the most comprehensive minds of the nineteenth century was Herbert Spencer, who nevertheless wrote strongly, even fretfully, on the absurdity of trying to make the electric induction motor invented by Faraday into a workable machine. Possibly half a hundred billions of capital now is invested in various countries in this device. Galileo could not believe that there was anything in Kepler's idea that the tides were influenced by the moon. The philosopher Descartes, an accomplished anatomist, reached the conclusion that the seat of the soul was the pineal gland, in the floor of the brain. And so we might go on indefinitely.

Think of the cost, the loss, to society if a planning board, embracing even such men as Herbert Spencer, had rejected a plan to develop the dynamo. Yet the induction motor was a slow growth, from very small beginnings. Well over a century ago, the scientific world was agog with the discoveries of Galvani and Volta. It was found that electricity could be produced from simple chemical reactions, and therewith an electric current, a flow, instead of the sparks from the friction machines with which Franklin and his contemporaries had delighted their time. An outgrowth of the means of generating this strange 'fluid,' as Franklin thought of it, was the electro magnet. A current passed through a wire brought near a magnetic needle would deflect the needle enigmatically. Then there must be some relationship between the peculiar properties of the lodestone, known to the ancients, and electricity. But what?

At Count Benjamin Rumford's Royal Institution in London, a young genius was at work on the problem. Faraday had constructed a powerful magnet, and taking a coil of wire, tried dipping it into the 'magnetic field.' He hoped for some reaction; for months he found one—only a tiny, scarcely noticeable flicker of his galvanometer. Finally it came to him that this was just the effect he was looking for. But it was only momentary; it came only when a coil cut across the lines of magnetic force.

What prophetic mind among all the brilliant and highly gifted workers in that field, could ever have dreamt what would grow from this discovery? Scores of investigators undertook to develop it, for they foresaw that here was a means of manufacturing electricity from mechanical power in unlimited quantities by means of steam engine or waterfall. But who among them could have foreseen that within a hundred years they would be building dynamos, as they came to be known, of a hundred thousand horsepower, supplying whole continents with light and energy and heat? Faraday thought about it. Tens of thousands of pounds were spent on myriad devices. But for thirty years it remained commercially useless. Finally attained simultaneously by several workers in different countries. Within half a century the whole western world was aglow with the electric light, and beginning to drive its machinery with this new power.

Here is a discovery and invention that has already gone a long way towards revolutionizing all industry. Vast chemical developments now depend upon it. Who could have foreseen or planned it?

The lesson of this and similar instances: the vanity and the folly of regimented planning. What mind, even of the highest, could ever have dreamed of these developments, much less guided or directed them? The history of science and technology is replete with the unbelievable prejudices, oppositions, and mistakes of the keenest of creative minds. Not alone the stupidity and myopia of legislatures, or boards, or commissions that prevents the planning of such developments; it lies in the natural limitations of the human mind. We can scarcely entrust the final judgement of the practicality of innovations to any limited group, regardless of its technical competence. The incalculable cost of a single error would be far too excessive to justify the risk. Moreover, the group-mind is inherently conservative, resenting and opposing *change*. Any planning board established by government would inevitably reflect this same antagonism. But the strong hope of profit, gain, riches, makes private enterprise alert for just such opportunities.

For the rest, it may be noted that in this as in other countries, the finest laboratories and technical shops where important new processes and inventions are being developed are not under governmental protection, subsidy, or guidance. Private enterprise has undertaken the risks, and achieved the results: it has been the potent force for creative evolution in the industrial world.[12] The unbelievable advances of the last half century seem to offer almost boundless possibilities. None of this brilliant achievement has been planned; little of it could have been foreseen. It was all so new, in a way unique, it is doubtful whether the most fertile and far-seeing intellects could have made any decisive contribution by means of long-range planning. Any plan must soon be outmoded in a rapidly advancing world; and the temptation to conform to it is so strong that innovations might be stifled long before their import was realized.

5. *Automatic planning and automatic regulation*

All these proposals for planning and government regulation hold implicitly or explicitly that the system of free enterprise is unplanned and unregulated. Pure strabismus. The whole economic mechanism provides for an automatic regulation, and for incessant innovation. The price mechanism, for example, results in the production of just those goods that society wants—those that consumers wish to pay for. The profit mechanism results in the management of all this production by the business men most capable of producing efficiently. Can we speak of an economic system such as this as unregulated because it is not subject to the blundering control of commissions and boards?

Ninety years ago, the French economist Bastiat wrote of this automatic planning for the needs of society. "On entering Paris which I had come to visit, I said to myself—Here are a million of human beings who would all die in a short time if provisions of every kind ceased to flow towards this great metropolis. Imagination is baffled when it tries to appreciate the vast multiplicity of commodities which must enter tomorrow through the barriers in order to preserve the inhabitants from falling a prey to the convulsions of famine, rebellion, and pillage. And yet all sleep at this moment, and their peaceful slumbers are not disturbed for a single instant by the prospect of such a frightful catastrophe. On the other hand, eighty departments have been laboring today, without concert, without any mutual understanding, for the provisioning of Paris." [13] This unconscious co-operation that moved Bastiat to admiration is today on a world-wide scale.

All about us are evident the effects of this automatic industrial planning. The invention and adoption of the dial telephone is an instance; is said to have been undertaken because of the prospect of a future inadequate supply of telephone operators. Here was long range planning by an American industry famous for its efficiency and technical progress. Our iron and steel industry will have spent nearly a billion dollars for new equipment and construction in the five years from 1935 to 1939. Throughout the great depression the iron and steel companies have maintained their research laboratories, seeking new uses for iron and steel and their alloys, developing new products to meet the needs of every industry. Out of these laboratories have come nearly fifty types of stainless steel and iron, each of different chemical composition. Not even long depression and stagnation could diminish the ardor of American industry in seeking new and more efficient methods; and some two thousand laboratories are maintained at a cost of over 200 million dollars a year. To be doubted if those who dream of a scheme of comprehensive planning by government bureaus and boards are aware of the prodigious activity and the real achievements of these private undertakings, each planning for our economic good.

The system they would abandon to seek salvation in countless bureaucracies has been of slow growth, the product of an infinite series of trials and errors, of variation and selection. Its apparently aimless organization has resulted in a marvelous increase of wealth and well-being in the last three hundred years. No one planned it, no one regulated it. Thanks to the advance of science and technology, aided by business initiative, we are already the beneficiaries of its colossal achievement. The microbe on the fly wheel is beginning to gain some understanding of the mechanism that automatically regulates and plans this superb progress.[14] Nor can it be halted if we follow the pattern we have. The past is but an earnest of the promise of the future. We cannot achieve this promise by putting industry under the dead hand of government regulation.

THE NEUROTIC MIND OF NEOLITHIC MAN

In 1914, I was as sorry for the young Germans who lay slain and mutilated on no man's land as for the British lads who lay beside them; so I got no emotional satisfaction out of the war. It was to me a sheer waste of life. I am not forgetting the gratification that war gives to the instinct of pugnacity and admiration of courage, as these are so strong in women. In the old days, when people lived in forests like gorillas or in caves like bears, a woman's life and that of her children depended on the courage and killing capacity of her mate. To this day in Abyssinia, a woman will not marry a man until he proves that he has at least four homicides to his credit.

—BERNARD SHAW

In order to understand the light which the discovery of the vast age of mankind casts on our present position, our relation to the past, our hopes for the future . . . let us imagine the whole history of mankind were crowded into twelve hours and we are living at noon of the long human day. . . . For over eleven and one-half hours there is nothing to record. We know of no persons or events; we only infer that man was on earth, for we find his stone tools, bits of his pottery, and some of his pictures of mammoth and bison. At twenty minutes before twelve the earliest vestiges of Egyptian and Babylonian civilization begin to appear. The Greek literature and philosophy to which we owe so much are not seven minutes old. At one minute before twelve Lord Bacon wrote his "Advancement of Learning," and now one-half a minute has elapsed since man first began to use the steam engine to do his work for him.

—JAMES HARVEY ROBINSON: *The New History*

CHAPTER XXIII

THE NEUROTIC MIND OF NEOLITHIC MAN

1. *Recurring periods of social unrest*

ONE phase, almost elementary, of the continued depression in this and other countries seems lost to view, so long a lapse since its last precursor. That is the quasi regularity of the return of these periods, a pattern molded by a definite series of events.[1] So striking as to suggest that these periods might be induced or produced at will, at any time, simply by setting up the proper mechanism. This mechanism is well disclosed in a review and comparison with preceding troubled eras. One of these was the period of fifty or sixty years ago, with its Molly Maguires in Pennsylvania, the Ku Klux Klan in the South, the Greenback and the Free Silver movement throughout the West, Henry Georgism in New York and elsewhere, and Pefferism with its Senator Peffers and "Sockless Jerry" Simpsons in Kansas. Lasting, all told, through a good quarter of a century.

In the period under view, the great boom that followed the Civil War came in the late 1860's. The smash of '73 ushered in what was then regarded as one of the most serious and prolonged depressions the country had experienced. And the deeper the depression, the more vociferous the agitation by borrowers and by labor and agriculture. All this solely the consequence of the most obvious factors.[2] Why such catastrophes should come to be labeled 'business' cycles is difficult to understand, since these depressions and social unrest are so largely the result of sheer economic ignorance.

Just as in the last twenty years. Practically every phase of this Civil War boom—credit inflation, wild speculation and collapse, followed by widespread unemployment, an epidemic of strikes, and threats of labor uprisings. Repeated, one might say, almost step by step in the same order, and only with different names. Watching the sit down strikes and the mushroom spread of the C.I.O., we seemed in our apprehension to forget that all this was a repetition, letter by letter, of the rise of the Knights of Labor and the days of Powderly and Martin Irons; the vogue of the Greenback Party, the narrow defeat of Henry George for mayor of New York, and finally the free silver fiasco of Bryan in 1896, when he nearly swept the country with his 'Cross of Gold.' Mark Sullivan should have begun his *History of Our Times* a little earlier so that our commentators and moralists might have refreshed their minds, and perhaps added to their knowledge.

So far as this country is concerned, the aftermath of our participation in the World War seemed to be almost a duplicate, a rubber stamp stencil of that of the Civil War. Which suggests that the causes determining the course of events in the two periods were identical, and one may suspect, given human nature as it is and Secretaries of the Treasury as they are, inescapable. Like causes producing like effects.

As if to demonstrate that this order of events was not an effect of war 'psychology' or war 'psychosis,' as commentators love to phrase it. It is instructive to find that the same repetition, the same concatenation of events seemed present in the United States in a turbulent period long before the Civil War. With the banking boom, the canal and railway building boom, the unprecedented land speculation, that preceded the Panic of '37. A long depression, continued to 1844, characterized years after by William Graham Sumner as the severest depression this country ever saw.[3] Followed by the same political unrest. 'Third parties' seemed to first appear in American politics about this time, the Liberty or Abolition party, then the 'Free Soil' party, the American (Know Nothing) party, Greenback parties, Populist parties, Farmer parties, Labor parties, Progressive parties, Union parties, innumerable Socialist parties. They come and go.[4]

2.   *State capitalism and state serfdom*

Proposals for 'reform' grow like mushrooms amid the gloom. In good times most of the 'lunatic fringe' pass out of sight. But socialism especially seems to have a strong attraction for many minds as an ideal form of economic organization. Socialist parties in one form or another, have found root in almost all countries, recurrently, for the last hundred years. So strong is the attraction of the name that in continental Europe almost every political party now finds it indispensable to call itself *socialist*. With wide variants: Socialist parties that appeal in the name of Marx, Lenin, and their successors; but lso in Germany a 'National Socialist Labor Party' (the Nazis) that had as a central doctrine the destruction of Marxian Socialism. n Austria before union with Germany a 'Christian Socialist' party, really opposed to socialism, and in fact very conservative; in France a 'Radical' Socialist party, not very radical and largely representing he lower middle class.

But in England, and especially in the United States, socialism has never made headway. The name itself seems a political liability. The Labor Party in England professes belief in socialism; but in practice more concerned with favorable legislation for labor. In the United States the largest presidential vote for a socialist candidate was in 1920 when Debs polled 900,000 votes out of a total of nearly 27,-000,000. In 1936 Norman Thomas received only 187,000 votes out of a total of 46,000,000.

The intellectual interest in socialism is not to be measured by its vote. Especially in the last century or more, and with the rise of the factory system and the aggregation of industry into large units, endless clamor over the idea of 'wage slavery,' and the right to the whole produce of labor.[5] And therewith the idea that state socialism or communism represented a path to 'freedom, and the larger life': the emancipation of the workers; reiterated, repeated, in thousands of pamphlets, books, and articles. All calling for the 'rights' of the working man. As if, for example, factory employees and the like alone were the 'workers,' somehow in a different status from the farmer, the independent blacksmith, and the carpenter.

Indubitably a widespread belief, even among the more educated classes, that there must be something 'inherently wrong' with the organization of society, and that almost any change would be for the better.[6] They decry the 'inequalities of wealth' and opportunity, rarely the inequalities of talent, capacity, and special abilities. They call for remuneration to 'labor' on the basis of 'needs,' never considering the rest of the population at work. Thus, only 9 million employed in manufacturing, as against a total of 49 millions gainfully employed. A theme for 'advanced thought.'

The literature of this 'liberal' movement, as it is usually termed, is immense. It had begun to gather momentum in the generation before Karl Marx, and in him nineteenth century socialism, of which he was the direct and quite unoriginal product and prophet, found its greatest spokesman. The vogue of this literary and emotional output, often unbelievably dull, is astounding. Far more widely

read than all other economic literature in the world combined. A
real wonder that it should have had such slight effect. It bursts forth
anew with every depression, and prospers even with prosperity.

Is it ominous? Far back in the middle of the 19th century Herbert
Spencer wrote a memorable tract entitled *Man vs. the State*, of
which a notable chapter dealt with "The Coming Slavery." It was
Spencer's idea that the rise of the working class power would inevitably mean their political ascendancy, through sheer numbers,
that therefore some kind of socialistic state was coming. These essays were written just after the wave of 'Fourierism' had swept over
Western Europe and the United States, and the International Working Men's Association had come into being. Even cool, dispassionate
thinkers of the breadth and weight of John Stuart Mill were deeply
influenced by the prevailing tide. In the face of the fact that his
celebrated essay on "liberty" was properly characterized as "one
long indictment of Socialism." A statement in his "Autobiography"
shows that he never resolved this contradiction.[7]

It has been possible for our time to see a little more of the reality
of things, and perhaps to profit by the impressive experiment in
Russia. Especially to realize what Spencer pointed out many years
ago. First, that state socialism is merely a change over to state capitalism, that it does not abolish 'capitalistic production,' or obviate its
necessity; nor emancipate labor from wage slavery; that it means
but a change over to state slavery.[8]

On its industrial side, Russian Communism has differed in no
material way, and has been closely paralleled by the ultra-capitalistic
procedures, in recent years, of Japan. Both countries have sought
to install a kind of ready-made system of industrial production
through the purchase of foreign machinery and the wholesale adoption of western methods and the latest fruits of capitalistic industry.
It will be interesting to follow the industrial progress of these two
countries and to observe which attains the higher degree of success.

Measured by the increase of production, the gain in Russia has
been more rapid than in Japan, until the last few years. But this has
been due largely to the fact that Russia started from an extremely
low level, reached in the demoralization of Russian industry after
the World War and the civil strife that followed. Whether the
'workers' of Russia are any happier or more contented than those
of Japan appears open to question. Nor would the answer be decisive as to the advantages of the two systems, since racial character-

stics might readily enter. But there seems no reason to doubt that
the Japanese worker, like those of the other capitalistic nations, has
had much more freedom.[9]

Be that as it may, it seems clear that we are faced with the same
choice of alternatives present in most human affairs. It is quite probable that we cannot have any wide measure of that general equality
which to many people seems so desirable and just, without a severe
loss of efficiency and individual freedom. Leadership, organization,
and high production seem to imply, and necessitate, a corresponding
degree of direction, discipline, and reward. All this is obvious. The
only serious question is what form of organization affords the highest
efficiency, culture, and comfort, with the largest measure of individual freedom. It is here that the immense superiority of free enterprise is most evident.

But the more passionate advocates of revolutionary change do
not regard this as the chief issue. With them it is the 'tyranny of
capitalism' that deeply stirs their emotions. Forgetful that the unescapable alternative must be the tyranny of the state, which, as
Karl Marx so bluntly put it, means the 'dictatorship of the proletariat.' This the essence of the agitation. Not a struggle for freedom,
for larger individual liberty, for less regimentation. It is the struggle
for power, a part of the everlasting craving of some people to dominate, to dictate, to rule. The itch to run things, to be 'boss,' to issue
autocratic commands. This urge for domination the basic factor.

But it is not only here that socialism must restrict severely the
freedom of the individual. In a society of free enterprise business
men make the 'goods' that consumers want. Essentially, therefore,
consumers direct production. Many foolish types of consumption:
the tremendous expenditure on cosmetics, cigarettes, chewing gum,
candies, soft drinks, and hard liquors. But these represent the consumers' choice. In a regimented economy production is determined
by boards and commissions acting in the name of the state. For all
practical purposes a system of rationing.

3. *Productive efficiency and the state*

Disregarding the supposedly ethical and moral bases for socialism,
summarized in the famous aphorism "Property is theft," the desirability of a socialistic system of production must be tested on economic grounds. Napoleon III is credited with the statement that "all

means of ruling are good, legitimate, and sufficient, provided only that material prosperity is ensured." [10] This doctrine is a dangerou half-truth; but it is worth asking whether socialism, or dictatorship can provide the same degree of prosperity and maintain the same rate of economic progress that private enterprise has so long pro vided.

As an excellent and familiar example of state enterprise, let us take the workings of our Post Office Department. It was begun even before our independent government was established. Benjamin Franklin was the last postmaster general appointed by Great Britain His appointment was cancelled when the colonies declared their independence, but he was immediately reappointed by the Conti- nental Congress. The Constitution gave Congress the power "to establish post offices and post roads," and this has remained an abso- lute monopoly. No competitors allowed; so the government could charge whatever was deemed necessary.

As a matter of fact, the Post Office Department has almost from the beginning been run at a loss, often considerable, and accumulat- ing in the course of nearly a century and a half to a very large sum Who paid this loss? If it had been a private enterprise it would have had to be made up by the owners of the business, the share holders and bond holders; else the enterprise would have gone bankrupt But the government, as a rule, does not go bankrupt. It can increase taxes and let the people pay. Now note first, that this deficit has, on the one hand, been chronic; second, that probably at any time the government could have farmed out its post office department to private enterprise, and at the same rates and probably paying the same salaries, it could have been run at a profit.

Now suppose the government were to take over larger and more important enterprises. Could we expect results even as good as those achieved in the postal system? In the European countries, the tele- phone system is commonly operated as part of the postal system. Yet nowhere in Europe, even in those countries noted for the effi- ciency of the government bureaus, is telephone service as eco- nomical or as good as in the United States. The experience of our government in operating the railways system during the World War is another case. We know the result, but we were told that this was simply a war measure, the railroads were badly demoralized and unable to handle the necessary traffic, and so it was inevitable that the government would have to meet tremendous losses. Which it did. The experiment was so disastrous that the railroads were turned back to the people who had spent their lives in trying to learn the transportation business.[11]

This instance of government operation of a highly organized business that was privately owned and operated before and after the war seems to illustrate vividly the problem of government versus private enterprise; and to reveal precisely what the dreams of collectivism or socialism would really amount to. Almost no one now believes that governmental operation of the railways is likely to be *more* efficient, cost less than private operation. If, then, there could be no material gain, with a large prospect of material loss, how many of the ardent advocates of state enterprise would be eager to have the government buy the railroads at the price of the actual investment? It has been suggested that the government wait until the railroads have been driven into bankruptcy and then buy them up at foreclosure prices. A beautiful thought.

There is, in almost all fields of government enterprise, an inherent and almost automatic weakness. If the field of government enterprise is steadily widened, and correspondingly the number of government jobs, there will be an increased demand that these be brought under the civil service. Some kind of protection at least against the extreme use of this larger employment for party patronage.

But like all good things, even this may have its element of evil. The reason: It is impossible to devise any kind of examination that will differentiate sharply between competent applicants for a job. The proof: that for all the tens of thousands of applicants who are closely scrutinized, year in and year out, by the personnel and employment divisions of our large enterprises, no practical tests have ever been devised. Scores of systems or methods. Proof that no one of these is of decisive value is that none is in even very general use. Personnel managers tend to develop their own technique, in which intuition, impression, or the unconscious plays a considerable rôle. But decisions based on intuition or personal impression are difficult to justify, for they seem to have an arbitrary element in them.

Now in civil service examinations for government jobs, these methods or techniques are almost impossible to apply. They are designed to rule out, as far as possible, the elements of personal choice, and, above all, influence, so that all may have an equal chance. The moment that subjective impressions enter, the primal purpose of the service examination goes out the window. No objective examination can select those applicants who show energy, enthusiasm, and foresight, among the principal requirements for business management.

Yet another, pointed out by Calvin B. Hoover, who has had more opportunity to study regimentation in Russia and Germany than perhaps any other American: that in government organizations, there is only one easy means by which bureau chiefs can get advancement and increases of salary. That is by enlarging the number of men under their direction. A very interesting observation. There is no one at the top, or higher up, whose prime job is to keep down *costs*, and ensure profits. In private enterprise that is the function of the executives. They sit in judgement and compel every division chief to show why the personnel or the forces under them must be increased. Practically the sole method by which enterprise can make profits and survive.

Now if the profit margin is so narrow, what hope can there be for governmental enterprise, with no rigid control of expenses, *no one whose job depends upon minimizing costs?* How can any bureaucracy be as efficient as private enterprise? Civil service examinations and the method of salary ratings provide no safeguard. On the contrary: If the easiest way a bureau chief has of enhancing his own salary is by increasing the number of men under him, no one to stem this powerful motive to increase costs, how can we avoid just what we have had through almost every administration, that is, a steady augmentation in the number of government employees?

True the government may levy taxes, either on individuals or on what remnant of private enterprise remains, and in that way create funds to meet operating deficits. But this merely reduces the capital supply.

4. *Dictatorship and autarchy*

It is not impossible that the historians of a century or two hence may record the happenings of the last twenty or thirty years as the strangest episode of the last two millenniums. Let us suppose that thirty years ago some seer had made the following prophecy:

"A few years will see the outbreak of the first true World War, which will end in a complete political and military stalemate, with wide economic demoralization, leading to the largest changes in governmental, social, and economic organization that Europe has seen since the beginning of the Industrial Revolution.

"The most notable of these will be the rise of dictatorships, not of 'the proletariat,' but of curious types. In Russia there will be one hundred and seventy million people under the iron rule of an obscure adventurer from the distant Russian state of Georgia. In Germany, rich, proud, cultured Germany, the intellectual leader of Europe in the century gone by, the land of Goethe, Kant, Humboldt, Beethoven, and Wagner, will be under the heel of an ignorant and fanatical sign painter. And in Italy the government will be seized by a black shirted mob under the leadership of a once socialistic firebrand. The three having, all told, domination over near to three hundred million peoples. And in the Far East, an island country of sixty million will attempt to subjugate the three hundred and fifty million people of China.

"As the result of all these strange developments, the dominant preoccupation of all the peoples throughout the world will be the prospect of yet another World War, which may go a long way towards destroying civilization itself."

If such a prophecy had been made, who could have believed it? Yet, for the past few years the world has been subject to the menace of arrogant, bellicose dictators, proclaiming that a new form of government has arisen for a new age. And some boldly state that it will last for thousands of years, while democracy and freedom will die. History is against them. No autocracy or tyranny, no dictatorship has ever survived for long. The nearest approach perhaps was the long span of a thousand years in Egypt before Alexander's conquest and the ensuing rule of the Ptolemies. But even that saw repeated changes in dynasty and the incoming of conquering hosts. For the rest, it would appear that the earlier government of Egypt was a kind of huge, well organized bureaucracy, that grew out of the peculiar physical character of the country, and the need for control of the Nile flood.

Dynasties have sometimes maintained their power for centuries, as the Manchus in China. But this seems the exception, even though we go far back into remotest history. The prolonged rule of the Manchus was due to the character of the country, so largely local and agricultural, and the lack of transportation facilities. It is often said that the rapid industrial integration of modern nations, especially the gigantic extension of railways and of the electric power systems, lends itself to a new type of centralized control impossible in former days. But this seems rather doubtful. It is possible that a country like Russia, long under a centralized power and widely divided in its interests, may be more easily controlled with modern means of communication and transportation. But the fact is that a commercial or an industrial people, economically advanced, is not likely to find such dictatorial centralized control to their liking. Economic progress is a mighty stimulus to political freedom.

The whole idea of dictatorship, with its peculiar philosophy, seems rather a survival from the past than an outgrowth of modern institutions. Ancient Rome perhaps came the nearest to such a despotism and to world rule. And one of its emperors, Diocletian, did attempt a scheme of economic regimentation, with price fixing and all the rest, perhaps more ambitious than had ever been tried on such a scale. It did not last long and was a foregone failure, from the mere lack of adequate machinery to enforce it. A monstrous army of supervising officials would have been required to make it effective, and we have some evidence that this was tried. But such a government would fall of its own weight and clumsiness. The Empire rapidly disintegrated and fell easy prey to the marauding hordes of the North. Among the ancients one of the most successful attempts at the domination of a free people came when Peisistratus seized the power in Athens and became its first Tyrant. Regarded by many as the most enlightened of Greek statesmen, his government hardly survived his death, and, moreover, was overthrown at least once, if not twice, by uprisings from within.

The economic philosophy of modern dictatorships, other than the regimentation of industry for the military glory of the country, is embodied in the policy of autarchy, economic self-sufficiency.[12] Not without interest that an ambitious attempt towards an autarchic state should have come in our own time in Italy. Understandable that a country backward industrially, with a crowding population and a low standard of living, should seek some means of advancing itself economically. But an attempt to make Italy self-sufficient is chimerical, unless the Fascist rulers are prepared to see the level of well-being in that country decline. Similarly in Germany; the policy of autarchy, understandable as a military measure, must bring poverty to a country that admittedly must "export or die."

Not surprising that such a policy should arise from a dictatorial government. Powerful appeals to the pride of Nationalism are a

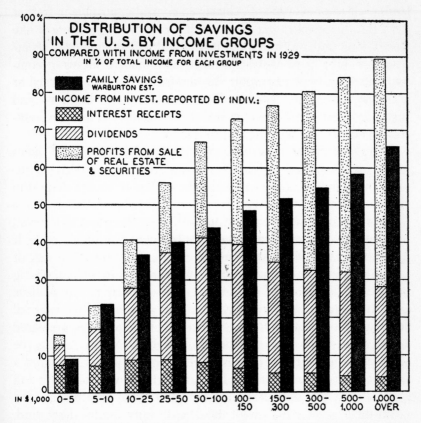

XLII. WHENCE THE GREAT SAVINGS FOR CAPITAL INVESTMENT?

A very old story: The larger the income received in dollars, the larger the percentage of this income *saved*. An almost obvious fact; but its significance not widely understood. In this chart we have taken Clark Warburton's estimates of the percentage of Family Income saved, by groups of incomes from less than $5,000 up to over $1,000,000. It will be seen that the percentage saved rises steadily with the income received. With this is shown the total reported income receipts from dividends, interest, and profits from the sale of real estate and securities, the so-called 'capital gains.' The percentage of income from these sources likewise steadily rises with the total income, so that in the highest brackets it amounts to nearly 90 per cent. This must mean that persons with the larger incomes steadily re-invest the larger part of this income. Vast numbers of persons believe that the rich spend their incomes in luxurious living. As a matter of fact our richest men, like Mr. Rockefeller and Mr. Ford, possibly have the smallest personal expenditures in proportion to their income in the whole world. Practically all of their income goes into further capital investment for the expansion of industry, and therefore for the enrichment of the whole country. Something to ponder over.

most effective means of reaching the crowd mind. And this carries with it the fetish of self-containment. The whole policy leads to actions that seem little short of suicidal. What, for example, if the people of the State of Pennsylvania and the State of Iowa should set up reciprocal embargoes against corn on the one hand, and coal on the other. Pennsylvania can raise some corn at a relatively high cost, Iowa produces considerable coal of low quality. But if such states set embargoes on each other's products, we would infer that they were suffering from the delusion that it would be to their profit to make commodities more difficult to get. Yet this is what is happening in many countries in Europe, largely under dictatorships or the imposing name of autarchy.

How long such a policy can survive, even in regimented countries, idle to predict. The ultimate success of autarchy is at best doubtful. The whole drift of modern times, and especially through the last hundred years and more of the colossal development, seems to belie the possibility of success in a policy of self-sufficiency. For more than one hundred and fifty years world trade has been steadily growing, at a rate even more rapid than the volume of total production. Seriously interrupted by the war, this growing interdependence of peoples is now greater than ever. No industrial power, nowadays, requiring various raw materials from many regions of the earth, can approach national self-sufficiency except at an enormous cost.

But the economic policies of the dictatorships does not stop here. For the purpose of increasing the military power of the state, all industry is regimented, all truly economic aims subordinated.[13] Production is directed by the state for military purposes. Preference in the allocation of capital, raw materials, and labor, is given to firms working on army orders. The rates of wages of labor are held down, profits are restricted, and their use is controlled. Nor does labor, whether in agriculture or in industry, have the right to choose its employment. In a real sense, labor and industry are enslaved in the dictatorships as in the communist state.

A large proportion of the national income is diverted to state purposes. Under such circumstances, it is impossible to provide capital for private enterprises, except those that serve military needs. Even without this provision of capital, the share of the productive output of the country available for general consumption has fallen sharply. As a consequence, the hours of labor have been increased; but even with longer hours and greater production, real wage rates have fallen. And this, to my mind, is one of the ineluctable effects of autocracy. The heavy taxation and borrowing, to say nothing of outright inflation, deprive labor of the consumption goods necessary to maintain high living standards, and they deprive management of the capital goods needful to maintain economic progress.

The key to the prevailing trend towards dictatorships lies, if I mistake not, in the steadily growing ascendancy of the crowd, directly a product of what the French writer Gustave LeBon has aptly termed "crowd psychology." As LeBon takes note, this is essentially a kind of grown-up child psychology, craving a highly paternal type of government. The mass of the people, apparently, do not value independence, liberty of thought, freedom of action, opportunity for individual enterprise. They submit rather to the rule of the omnipotent father, and seem content if only they are assured their daily bread. Otherwise it is difficult to understand how a country with great universities, a splendid literature and art, a proud record of scientific and industrial achievement, could endure the tyranny of a regimentation maintained by coercion, imprisonment, and assassination. It can only be that a large part of the population is still, as Dr. Hooton insists, essentially neolithic in character and in intelligence.

The interest of all this for countries like the United States and Great Britain, where the tradition of economic and political freedom is old, is in regard to their own peoples. Will these also succumb to the propaganda and leadership of kindred fanatics, men of a distinctly neurotic mentality, and often with obsession of a 'mission.' Is there danger that the traditional economic and political systems of these countries will be replaced by dictatorships molded after the Continental fashion? Not an idle question.

For one, I can not believe that in the English speaking world the spirit of independence, the precious gift of freedom, is to be lost through the diablerie of paranoidal maniacs, lusting for self-aggrandizement, and dependent upon the supine submission of a people. But it would be dangerous to overlook the effects that economic desperation may produce, what long depression with wide unemployment may do. It would be a weird outcome if the truly marvelous burst of industrial progress within the last century and a half should eventuate in such a monumental fiasco.

Perhaps the jealousies and antagonisms between nations may forestall such an outcome. For the rest we may depend upon the steady advance in the material well-being of the English speaking peoples and their kindred, the vigorous races of Scandinavia, the growth of general intelligence that must slowly come, to guard us from delusion. In all history no salvation in dictatorship, whether of fascism or communism. The love of freedom, in thought and in action, is not dead or dying. Rather that it will spread among all the peoples as they grow in wisdom and mutual helpfulness; and that from this may arise a genuine international spirit.

PROSPECTS OF ECONOMIC SANITY IN AN
IRRATIONAL WORLD

Surlie common sense would that one region should healpe another when it lacketh. And therefore God hath ordained that no countrie should have all commodities, but that what one lacketh, another bringeth forth . . . to the intent that one maie know they have nede of another healpe and thereby Love and societie to grow amongst them all the more.

—JOHN HALES: *A Discourse of the Commonweal;* 1549

The progress of economic science in the future will depend to a large extent upon the investigation of empirical laws, derived from statistics, which will then be compared with known theoretical laws, or will lead to the discovery of new laws.

—VILFREDO PARETO: *Giornale degli Economisti;* 1895

All this means in the long run *that mankind is solving its economic problem.* I would predict that the standard of life in progressive countries one hundred years hence will be between four and eight times as high as it is to-day. There would be nothing surprising in this even in the light of our present knowledge. It would not be foolish to contemplate the possibility of a far greater progress still.

· · ·

The *pace* at which we can reach our destination of economic bliss will be governed by four things—our power to control population, our determination to avoid wars and civil dissensions, our willingness to entrust to science the direction of those matters which are properly the concern of science, and the rate of accumulation as fixed by the margin between our production and our consumption.

—JOHN MAYNARD KEYNES: "Economic Possibilities for Our Grandchildren," *Essays in Persuasion*

CHAPTER XXIV

PROSPECTS OF ECONOMIC SANITY IN AN
IRRATIONAL WORLD

*The Foundations for a Science of Economics, and
the Present Day Status of This Adventure*

IN view of the extraordinary economic upheaval in the twenty
years that have followed the close of the World War, and in view
of the succession of truly insane economic policies which have characterized at one time or another most of the leading nations in this
period, it may not be amiss to inquire what prospect there is of the
return to sanity in the generation to come.

First we have to note that something of the same kind of upheaval
came with the Napoleonic Wars. In nothing like a similar degree;
and with nothing like the variety of untoward social consequences,
his more equable state of society was due in part to a singular
circumstance. In France, at least, there was little of the customary
monetary inflation characteristic of almost all wars. Napoleon was
one of the rare instances of a statesman who had some flair for economics. He went to war on a cash basis, and stayed there. Perhaps
a derivation from his experience as a young man. He was just out of
military school when the vast inflation of the French Revolution,
the era of the assignacs and mandats, nearly brought ruin to his
adopted country. In later years when Napoleon's rule was in
desperate straits, his financial advisor proposed to print "just a
little" paper money. Napoleon's reply was: "Over my dead body."

Nor did England have a heavy inflation, although what it did have
brought on the usual post-war boom and collapse, in 1819, with its
resultant severe set-back to English industry. But for the rest, the
monetary disturbance was relatively small, and therein, to my mind,
lies the entire difference between the experiences of these twenty
years and those of a hundred years before. For there seems nothing
which so profoundly affects the affairs, the minds, and the morals of
men, as a severe disturbance in prices and in values.

Now the foundations of an economic science were not originated by Adam Smith or Ricardo, nor even by John Stuart Mill, or the other leading economists of that time; for the foundations for all sciences are measurements, computations, correlations, and experimentation where feasible. Economic experiment is largely unattainable, although it would seem that an unconscious or involuntary experimentation had been sufficiently wide and varied as to provide wholly adequate material for a true science. But careful measurements have usually been lacking. Experimentation, it should be observed, is not an absolute essential even for the more exact sciences. This is clear from the example of astronomy, one of the earliest sciences to reach high development. True it might be said that the heavens and the earth are a continuous 'experimental laboratory; but it is none the less an observational science affording the most accurate knowledge, and this because of the variety of exact observation and exact measurement. It has been the latter which has been chiefly lacking in the field of economics. The observational field was wide and varied enough to have furnished a true science long ago.

But the beginnings of economic measurement antedate John Stuart Mill. Among the earliest were the compilers and index makers of the type of Poulett Scrope, although there had been some experiments in this direction sufficient to arouse the wrath and objurgations of that prince of deductive theorizing, David Ricardo. And even back in his day there were at least some proposals towards the maintenance of a 'stable price level.' The pathless ground for the next hundred years, still continuing, with no sign of an end straight into present time.

A curious, and one might think a truly anomalous situation. Anomalous because the facts are fairly simple and the evidence to date quite clear. A definite and unequivocal beginning in England at the time of our Civil War. In 1863 a young student exiled to Australia boldly printed an essay attempting to measure "the changing value of gold." In the minds of the highly respectable, though rather stodgy bankers and money changers of his day, an impious proceeding. And this was precisely by means of these index numbers which David Ricardo had ridiculed as intrinsically absurd. And today they flower as the green bay tree. But no one then realized that here might be the key to the wide ups and downs of prices which the investigations of Jevons had so impressively disclosed. And no one maintained then that in a more distant future they might supply the

ieans for the control of credit,—even then rising to formidable proportions—and therewith obviate the more violent changes in the
eneral level of prices, and thus avoid the ensuing havoc and dis-
urbance.

It was an American and not primarily an economist who first
nvisaged the problem in a precise and indeed mathematical form.
This was Simon Newcomb. Even then perhaps our most eminent
stronomer, and mathematician, and philosopher, with a deep inter-
st in economics. An interest which had been aroused in his early
nanhood by our experience in the Civil War. As a young man under
hirty, he had written a very outstanding little book in criticism of
he financial methods employed to finance that war. Newcomb
nade bold to suggest that the result of these mistaken methods was
o more than double the cost of the war to the nation, and more than
hat, to bring about a violent rise in prices, with the subsequent
lestruction and disaster. A remarkable production, and especially
rom a young and unknown man. It gained slight attention. Newcomb had to pay for the making of the plates and the entire sales
ardly reimbursed his outlay.

But with lectureships first in Johns Hopkins and later at Harvard,
iis interest in economics steadily widened, and in 1884 he produced
a volume which was a favorite companion of the writer's early years,
ind perhaps for this reason gave the impression I still retain: that
t was on the whole the clearest, sanest, and most original volume on
economics yet produced in America. Even to the present day.

It was in this volume that Newcomb first formulated the now
widely known and much embattled equation of exchange. True, his
chief function was simply to put in mathematical form the teachings
of the older economists, notably those of Mill. But in reality its
iervice was far greater. Set forth in algebraic terms, it revealed how
his formula might be submitted to statistical investigation. Its ingredients are simply the volume of currency, and of bank credit,
circulating as a medium of exchange; and the rate at which this exchange fund, as it might be termed, was turned over; that is, the
total volume of business exchanges divided by the amount of
"money" employed. All this as compared with the total value of
things purchased, or the quantity of goods and services multiplied
by the average price.

Again to little effect. True that some of the more active minded
economists of his day caught up his ideas and propagated them.

Notably among these a future president of Yale, Arthur Twining Hadley; one of the ablest economic expositors of his time. But there were not many, and it was twenty years after the publication of Newcomb's volume that his ideas and formula were put to a statistical test. The first of these was by a graduate student at Cornell, later to gain wide recognition as an international authority on monetary systems, Edwin W. Kemmerer. In a thin little volume, written for a doctor's thesis, he endeavored to give numerical measure to the four factors of Newcomb's formula: M (for money), V (for velocity, or rate of turn over), equals T (the total of goods and services), and the average price. In algebraic form $MV = PT$.

This was followed several years later by Irving Fisher's well known volume, "The Purchasing Power of Money," setting forth the same formula, with a new statistical presentation, and indeed dedicated to Newcomb. This was in 1912. The difficulty of both these attempts at mathematical verification was that the material for a rigorous demonstration was still deficient; it was only after the incoming of the Federal Reserve System and the new material relative to the volume of trade, the velocity or rate of turn over of bank deposits, and much else collected and compiled by the new organization, that a closer and more convincing approach was possible.

But there was still one factor which eluded accurate measurement: the variations in the broad averages of prices, begun more than a century ago. Curiously enough this was the first of the numerical computations of an economic nature to be undertaken. Simple enough even from the beginning to compile an adequate index of commodity prices at wholesale. However, it was not then clear that a properly constructed or 'weighted' average would inevitably be largely dominated in its movements by ten or a dozen of the most highly speculative and most widely moving components; and, therefore, that such an index can not be accepted as a representative of the average of the price of everything bought and sold, at retail as well as wholesale; which alone would satisfy the Newcomb Equation of Exchange. Both Kemmerer and Fisher had endeavored to compile such an inclusive index; but adequate material was not then available. I presented in 1923 such a widely inclusive index as the Equation required, along with a variety of other measures of production and exchange, looking towards a statistical measure of the total trade of the nation. With these, new measures of the velocity or rate of turn over of bank deposits, which the new material supplied by the Federal Reserve System had made available.

When these new measures were completed and graphed, they promptly disclosed a very striking result. This was that through a half century or more the growth of this Total Trade, in spite of booms and depressions, was, if taken by four or five year periods, fairly even. But the growth of the volume of Money, that is chiefly Bank Deposits, was quite uneven and manifestly not directly related to the growth of Trade. An easy computation disclosed an astonishing fact: that when this volume of active Money, the Bank Deposits, was divided by the long term indices of this Volume of Trade, the resulting line was a close approach to a new and very inclusive index of general price level. A result that seemed to belie the Newcomb formula, because it took no account of the velocity or rate of turnover of the money factor. A new and inclusive measure of the volume of trade, by months plotted as variations from the long term rate of growth, gave a close reproduction of the month by month variations in the velocity of bank deposits. In other words, as a clear thinking mind might expect, the variations in deposits velocity were a close measure of business activity. Therefore that this deposit velocity was not an important factor in the determination of the price level, according to the Newcomb formula. Clear enough, after discovery of evidence, but so far as I am aware, never previously enunciated.

If true, this, then, would simply mean this, and this alone: that the variation in the volume of active money, from the normal long term growth of trade, determines the general price level. The ancient doctrine known as the Quantity Theory of Money and Prices in its most rigid form. A result, it seems fair to say, probably not accepted by the majority of present day economic teachers and theorists. It is because of this latter fact, and what I conceive to be its bearing upon the future influence of economics, that I have sketched the history of this idea in some detail. Let us examine the data. These findings are of a purely statistical character; they involve no rectification or any kind of juggling with the component indices. Each of these separate indices stands on its own feet, to be examined and justified by the basic material from which they sprang. It is not an anticipated result. So far as I have been able to learn, a pure discovery. Not a product of any preconceived notions. It has seemed to find little unqualified acceptance. Certainly it has not been employed as the chief guide to our vital financial policy, the Control of Credit, which is, of course, the high variable, and the sole controllable variable, in this Equation. Consequent cost to the country since the formula was widely presented, in economic journals and otherwise, a staggering sum. Had the long depression which followed been averted, probably not less than one hundred to one hundred and fifty billions of dollars.

A fantastic thought? I do not find it so, and I have in earlier pages set forth the reasons for this belief in some detail; still more in various papers and speeches. If even approximately true, a result highly significant for our economic future. Consider the facts:

Here is a statistical finding, based upon elements and materials, each one of which is open to independent investigation and verification. In several instances such independent examinations have been made. If the basic facts are true, it would seem that the inevitable conclusion therefrom would merit at least discussion, if not a practical experiment, to demonstrate its validity. Such an experimental verification has never been made. It is said that in most recent years the close relationships here indicated have ceased to hold. Therefore, that the conclusions reached are not rigorously true. But this relationship did hold for half a century, and the deviation therefrom now seems due to the practical suspension of the financial system which had made this country rich and powerful. Only the future, and a return to the historical financial tradition of our country, can reveal whether this view is sound. I have reviewed this incident in our economic history in more detail because it seems highly significant and prophetic for the future. It is now three quarters of a century since the early work of Jevons, more than a half century since the convincing presentation of Newcomb, more than a generation since the first attempt at statistical proof; and there seems no evidence that this doctrine, that this mode of thought has in any way penetrated the minds of those who have charge of our financial affairs. To the situation which developed in 1928, and culminated so disastrously in 1929, few or none paid any serious attention or regarded the situation as fraught with great danger. One remarkable exception, one of the few known to the writer: Ogden L. Mills, then Under Secretary of the Treasury who in a discussion with the writer in the early part of 1928 said without hesitation: "Why, of course we are riding for a crash, but nothing can be done about it. If we attempted to apply a check

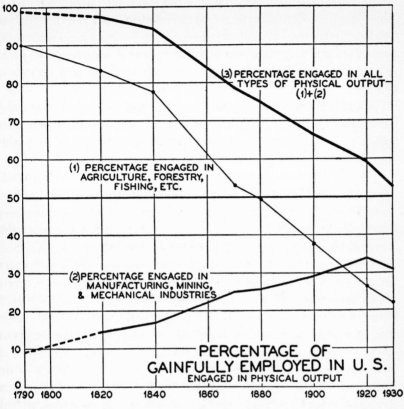

100

90

80 — (3) PERCENTAGE ENGAGED IN ALL TYPES OF PHYSICAL OUTPUT (1)+(2)

70

60 (1) PERCENTAGE ENGAGED IN AGRICULTURE, FORESTRY, FISHING, ETC.

50

40

30 (2) PERCENTAGE ENGAGED IN MANUFACTURING, MINING, & MECHANICAL INDUSTRIES

20

10 PERCENTAGE OF GAINFULLY EMPLOYED IN U.S. ENGAGED IN PHYSICAL OUTPUT

0

1790 1800 1820 1840 1860 1880 1900 1920 1930

XLIII. THE EXTRAORDINARY CHANGE IN OCCUPATIONS

In George Washington's day, it was estimated that nearly all of the population was engaged in what may be termed 'physical output,' such as farm products, black-smithing, and weaving. Now, remarkable to state, hardly more than half. The chart above shows how steadily this percentage has declined in 150 years. This is chiefly due to the long decrease for those engaged in farming and the like—about 90 per cent in Washington's time, now not much more than 20 per cent. A sharp rise in manufacturing and mining. But the most notable increase has been in trade and transportation of every sort, and the vast system of business exchange which has come with modern means of production and railways, the rise of the great cities, and the wide diversification in occupation, creating hundreds of new trades, crafts, and services unknown 100 years ago. Cosmetics and beauty parlors, moving pictures, and no end of others—almost all the hard physical labor now done by machinery. A very much changed world.

Congress would be on our back in a moment." And the Federal Reserve Board in whose deliberation Mr. Mills participated, sat supinely by and tapped the naughty banker and speculator on the wrist.

They were not alone. Some of our most confident prognosticators and financial prophets rode into the maelstrom of '29 without batting an eye. One of them had a calculation in multiple correlation, using 19 variables, who saw not a cloud in the sky. An extraordinary world. But the direful fact is that right through these ten years of depression and opportunity for study even the more instructed in these matters seem to have learned nothing; they are in no greater agreement now than ten or twenty or thirty years ago. Not a basis for undue optimism. Consider the prospect: In the last seven years I have given considerable attention to the statistical analysis of the national elections, which seem to run a much more regular and predictable course than the rather mythical 'business cycle.' If the elections of 1940 should mean a heavy reversal of the last few years and a change in the political administration, this would almost certainly result in a great boom in business and industry. All the pent up Utica of the last ten years will be let loose, and with this the powerful stimulus of the astonishing advance in technology and the general improvement in industrial methods. This backed by a stupendous volume of idle funds in the banks craving for employment in renewed industrial expansion. And undoubtedly there would be a huge wave of almost uncontrollable speculation. Uncontrolled because there will be few who wish, and assuredly no politician or governmental authority, to apply the brakes for adequate control. A case of 1928–29 over again? There are reasonable grounds for such a fear.

This renewed industrial activity will be in effect and appearance the resumption of our normal long-time rate of industrial growth. And the general belief will be that we are simply 'making up' for lost time.

There is little on the purely industrial side to suggest that such a rapid recovery, to perhaps the projected long line of normal growth, would be in any way unhealthy or unwise. On the contrary, in many ways highly salutary. For the tremendous unemployment of the last six or eight years, a highly dangerous and explosive element, would evaporate like snow in the sunshine. The ensuing increase in wages would clearly reveal that only the incompetent and the unskilled, the ever present army of the incapables, need be out of work. And therewith would go like the fuzz of an old dandelion a great part of all the fantastic suppositions that our industrial growth is at an end, that we have reached the stage of 'stationary society' and, most of all, that there is 'something wrong with our economic system.'

But this revival of industry, with the application of all the magnificent results of present day Tectonics, would naturally mean a renewal of a high rate of profits, and this in turn would inevitably bring a terrific speculation. All to be followed by heavy borrowings at the banks for purely speculative purposes, thus unduly expanding the volume of bank credit and therewith public purchasing power, giving rise, as always, to an inflated price level and a highly dangerous situation. Have we anywhere an authority, either among our bankers or our governmental agencies, with the courage and understanding and assured position to provide reasonable control? How many even among our economic statesmen will there be to proclaim that credit expansion is at a higher rate than the physical growth of production and trade; and that this rate of growth can be and has been carefully and accurately measured; and that the excess of credit over this rate of growth spells sheer inflation, and inflation sheerly spells renewed disaster? I fear, not many.

But contemplate the fateful consequences which would ensue if we are to have another great boom, another revival of insane speculation, another outburst of unquenchable optimism with complete disregard for results of the last century and of the baleful Blight of the last eight or ten years? What will be the inescapable result? We shall inevitably have another major crash, as utterly needless as in 1929, followed by another terrific decline in values; with increasing bank failures and bankruptcies of every kind, (all as needless, as that of '29 to '35), followed again by enormous unemployment and genuine suffering, (again wholly needless, and ever will be). All this naturally followed by the expulsion of the party in power, by the renewal of the 'New Deal' or something far worse; again an utter disillusionment and loss of our faith in free institutions and sane economics (because of the lack of sane economics!) with every wild and crazy proposal or 'theory' that the human mind can contrive; a new burst of 'social experimentation,' all the fads and follies and futilities and bungling absurdities of the last decennium. The weary grinding of the remorseless Wheel of Fate.

Are we never to have control, never to have understanding and foresight, to prevent all these things? And where are these to come from if not from the solid foundations of careful, scientific, methods of approach, careful measurements and correlations, instead of unprovable theories and idle conjectures? When is a true Science of Economics to get underway? This, I believe, is the real problem, and that on the answer the future of this great country, and perhaps of present day civilization itself, almost wholely depends.

THE UNLIMITED POTENTIALS OF TECTONICS

As for the new Inventions, for the saving of mens workes in an overpeopled Common-wealth, it is disputable whether they be for the generall good or not; yet in regard that the chiefe policie consisteth in finding out wayes, how the same quantitie of land may maintaine more people than it did before, which cannot be done any way, but by industrie of the people; therefore I conceive, that in the new Inventions, it is for the generall good to save mens workes by Engines; for if one workeman can doe as much with his Engine, as ten men can doe without it, there is nine mens maintenance saved to the Common-wealth; whereby plenty is increased to every one: I must needs confesse, that if the common practice in Husbandry now used, was to set their Corne the common way, that then the Engine new invented for that purpose, might doe more hurt than good; for that so many would then want employment; as we see in London; there was an Invention to grinde the Needles many at once, whereby halfe the Needle-makers had gone a begging, if the new device had not bin restrained; but in this case it is farre otherwayes, for here is imployment for many more people than before; though there be many mens workes saved, which would be lost working the rude way: also here is a great improvement in the quantitie of land; for by this meanes the new people set on worke doe get maintenance for many more than themselves, by their industry upon the same quantitie of land which would maintain but a few before. And it is to be conceived, that when these Inventions and Improvements shall be thoroughly put in practice, then the Common-wealth will not be overpeopled; but rather there will want people to accomplish the worke, whereby it will appeare that the saving of mens workes will then be a profitable Invention.

—GABRIEL PLATTES: (*circa* 1650) Quoted by Lord Stamp,
The Calculus of Plenty; 1937

Chapter XXV

THE UNLIMITED POTENTIALS OF TECTONICS

THERE is one great danger: the fear, the apathy, the give-up spirit that comes in all periods of depression, the product, perhaps sheerly, of economic and historic ignorance, and the inevitable myopia, lack of wide perspective that invariably moves with it. So easy to lose the sense of time, to see only the immediate difficulties, which often loom so portentously. Always a waning faith in progress, in invention, in energy and initiative. Always the same supine superstition that somehow the great advance of mankind has come to a tragic end.

It seems for nothing that all these ideas and beliefs have been regularly recurrent in practically every generation so far back as we have any record: that we have not the energy of former times; that we can not keep up the previous pace of advancement; that new industries are coming in to ruin old industries and create unemployment.

Hardly anyone is now ignorant of the fact that a generation after the weavers and spinners of England smashed up the new spinning jennies and looms, there were ten times as many employed in these industries as before the new inventions had come in. And identically the same with the reapers and mowers and harvesting machines in farming. Always partly and for the moment true. Today the average man on a well equipped farm can produce, at the least, five times as much food, or total product as a hundred years ago. The result: that where the farms employed 80 per cent of the population a hundred years ago, today it is really less than 20 per cent. And in consequence food costs, in terms of average hours of labor, about one-fourth what it would have been early in the last century. And what variety. What nation ever had such an extraordinary diversity of foods, of grains, and vegetables and fruits, and meats? And yet with all this general diffusion of comfort and luxury, we pine and despair.

The same throughout all human activity—the railroad ruined the canals, because canal transport was too costly, and yet there are three canals, at Suez, Panama, and the Sault Ste. Marie which today carry scores of times the tonnage of all the canals in the world when the railroads came in. Because in certain positions they are highly economic and advantageous.

The same with electricity and gas. Freely predicted, as many living can remember, that when electricity came into general use, the gas industry was doomed! Forty or fifty years later and the production and use of gas has pretty steadily increased, up to the Blight.

The same with radios and the cables. With youthful enthusiasm I can remember that I was one of those who thought that the cables might now fold up as they would no longer be needed. After thirty years, several times as much is in use as when the radio was perfected. And the same with the autos and airplanes and the railroads; the same with the telephones and telegraphs; the same with moving pictures and the theaters. If the railroads had not been shackled by unwise interference, their growth would have continued just as has the use of coal and the telegraph, and even the canals.

When the long distance transmission of electricity began to loom, it was a wide belief that we should derive all our electric power from water power; even in such a prescient mind as Steinmetz. Yet steadily for thirty years now, the production from steam power has gained on water power as a source; the latter is now the minor element. To many minds almost incredible that this could be. Again a product of unbelief in the powers of Tectonics; even in our generation the development of steam power either from coal or from oil has been stupendously advanced. And there seems hardly any limit to this steady improvement, because as the steam pressures and the consequent efficiency have been steadily raised, wondrous new alloys have been making stronger and stronger steel jackets and pistons and valves. In the production of water power no such improvement possible. And yet we are squandering hundreds of millions upon visionary projects of great power production from water.

Some years ago a large company refused to contract for the power of Muscle Shoals at what was thought to be a bargain price, because it calculated that by the proper location of plants, steam

AN EXAMPLE OF CAPITALISTIC INDUSTRY
DISTRIBUTION OF FORD COMPANY INCOME THROUGH 33 YEARS
(PARTLY ESTIMATED)

TOTAL INCOME
12,500 MILL. OF $'S

NET PROFITS
844 MILL. OF $'S(=7%)

TOTAL INCOME 12,500 MILL. OF $'S
NET PROFITS 844 MILL. OF $'S
TAXES 600 MILL. OF $'S
COST OF MATERIALS & OVERHEAD
WAGES IN SUPPLYING INDUSTRIES EST.
WAGES EST. 3,400 MILL. OF $'S

NET PROFITS 844 MILL. OF $'S
DIVIDENDS 125 MILL. OF $'S
NET CASH & RECEIVABLES 300 MILL. OF $'S
INVESTED IN PLANT & EQUIPMENT EST. 420 MILL. OF $'S

XLIV. HOW ONE COMPANY BECAME A "BILLIONAIRE"

The Ford Company was started with $29,000 gross capital, barely half of it cash. In the thirty odd years of its existence, it has had a gross income of more than thirteen billions of dollars. All its present capital, upwards of seven or eight hundred million dollars, has come from its profits. Out of twelve and a half billions of dollars total income, dividends amounted to $125 million—1 per cent of the total income. So, if the buyers of Ford cars had been allowed all the realized profit paid out, the cars would have cost them 1 per cent less than they actually paid. This is undoubtedly one of the most spectacular instances of how largely capital is derived directly from the business, and, of course, directly from profits. In other words, no profits, no capital, no growth, and ultimately failure. Were the public, who paid thirteen billions for Ford cars, or the workmen, who received more than half this amount in wages, losers by the bargain?

power would be cheaper as well as more flexible and more reliable. But there is no curbing the Visionaries.

Another wonderful rejuvenation of an industry: in the last ten years of stagnation we have been hearing much about the difficulties of the coal industry, and dismal prophecies as to its future. That its growth had ceased. And now come new methods of mining and cleaning the coal so that where adequate capital can be employed, there will be cheaper and more efficient methods. This is only the beginning. The rest is a vista of a dumbfounding revolution: that coal may in large part be no longer used for fuel! At least save where it is exceptionally advantageous, and perhaps then principally in the form of coke or briquettes. Its all important value will be the vast variety of chemicals which will come from coal tar. Already, a perfect troop of new medicines, new dyes, and new plastics, and a wide variety of other products. So that the prediction has already been made that with this astounding advance of industrial chemistry, a day is near when coal will be too valuable to burn as of yore.

This industrial wizardry may likewise invade the food producing industry, and so, to the minds of many, threatens to ruin the farms! As if invention and capitalistic enterprise had not been "ruining" the farms steadily for over a hundred years. So that today the capital invested in American farms is probably ten or twenty, if not fifty, times what it was when the larger part of the population gained therefrom an extremely modest and ofttimes precarious living. And this will go on mightily. Perhaps to double the food supply from half the workers now engaged. As noted, 11 per cent of the farms are now producing one-half of the total farm products marketed. For they can produce better and cheaper food. And this, needless to say, is possible only through the larger investment of capital.

In the same way cotton may in the near future be no longer used as cotton, save under special conditions, and in the higher grades. Already experiments are well advanced toward the planting and cultivating and harvesting of cotton just as if it were wheat, sowing the plants closely together so as to conserve the moisture and save the cost of cultivation; then to harvest with a mowing machine, or perhaps with a harvester-combine. Then to put the entire plant with the cotton boles into the digester, and rapidly ransform it into high grade cellulose. Estimated to be a cheaper product, of a higher quality, than that being made from any other kind of pulp. Possibly a new future and a new hope for the dying agriculture of the southern states.

And all this but the merest beginning; the science of the quickened pace, of the new knowledge, and the new power that is marching throughout the world. There is an exhibit of a new glass thread almost as strong as steel and flexible, impervious to water, and *mirabile dictu*, it is now being woven into glass cloth for a wide variety of uses. Glass dresses have been made for some years. They may soon drive out silk and rayon as these have driven out cotton.

And so we might go on and on. The finest steel plant today in existence is now in the heart of India, where once the art of steel making flourished in its highest degree. Portents of the change that will come when the Other Half, the teeming millions of an undeveloped hemisphere awake! Not merely to the making of steel; for even its kingdom is now threatened by new metals and new alloys that will be lighter, stronger, cheaper, more ductile. New processes in the production of aluminium and of magnesium and several other metals give great promise of what already has begun to be talked of as the new Metallurgy.

And all this is but a part of the Tectonic advance that will involve every kind of product and every form of production. Already the physicist is beginning to play with the elements as if these were merely chemical compounds, which he will take apart and recombine at his will. Just as the chemist is now taking coal tar and a variety of other substances and converting these into myriad forms and varieties of unbelievable complexity. Something like ninety of the so-called 'elements' have undergone transmutation, one into another, realizing the dream of the alchemist. It is true that these transmutations are as yet only in spectroscopic quantities, infinitesimally small.

But even as I write the daily papers give an account of a wonderful new 'atomic gun' that has been invented at Cornell University that may far outstrip the amazing achievements of the hundred ton cyclotron. A simple glass tube on the order of an X-ray tube, six feet long, but capable of much greater extension. Able to handle heavy atoms as well as the lightest elements like hydrogen and helium.

Opening wider and wider vistas, day by day. Where will it all end? So far as the human mind can perceive there is no end in sight, conceivably no end possible, for such vistas of time as we can now envisage. For what science and tectonics are doing is steadily to increase and utilize our knowledge of *relations*. Permitting, stimulating, an almost infinite variety of new compounds and syntheses, that is to say, new *uses;* and to all this there seems no present limit. Even two generations ago it was the stupendous vision of Helmholtz that, providing this earth becomes involved in no cosmic catastrophe, everything in the universe that is in relation to any other thing, will one day be known. Perhaps the most daring flight of the human mind, and yet grounded upon solid knowledge and likelihood.

But all this is only the physical side of the almost unbelievable transformation and transmutation of a life already under way. No less revolutionary, in all probability, are the portents for social and psychic change. Perhaps *breeding* a New World!

SUMMARY

For those who have not followed in detail the thesis presented in the preceding pages, a brief review of the doctrine, in summary form, is given in the eight short chapters which follow.

I

THE TRANSFORMATION OF THE WORLD

Through Invention and Machinery

1. The Background: Five thousand years or more of a nearly stationary civilization; then a momentous advance. Apparently little industrial change over a long period. (From 4,000 or 5,000 B. C.?) The amazingly slow development of tools and invention, co-operative industry, the accumulation of wealth and the beginnings of modern industrial economy.

2. The Source of the Transformation: The singular linkage of isolated events; the well known consequences of the introduction of the compass, gunpowder, printing, and from the fall of Constantinople the damming up of the trade routes by land and by the Red Sea; the impulsion to navigation and discovery, leading to the voyages of Vasco da Gama, Columbus, the Cabots, the search for new lands; the conquest of Mexico and Peru. The Old World had been pretty well mined out. The enormous stimulation to exploration from the discovery of vast stores of silver in America and its effect upon prices and trade, leading to:

3. The *Price Revolution* of the 16th and 17th centuries, a long steady rise, through a century and a half, without a parallel in at least 2,000 years, leading directly to:

4. *The Industrial Revolution* of the 18th and 19th centuries, and the coming of the Power Age. The long continued rise of prices gave an enormous impulse to commercial enterprise, since profits and gains were almost assured. The enterpriser could not lose. This was the true beginnings of modern capitalism, which lead to:

5. *The Coming of the Power Age* and the enormous expansion of product in manufacture, first in England, then in the United States, Germany and other countries. The exhaustion of the oak forests in England led to the development of coal mining, long neglected, and this in turn to pumping machinery, leading to the invention and perfecting of the steam engine, and this to the vast

increase in coal mining itself and in iron mining, copper mining and the like.

6. The consequent rise of commerce and of trade, the wide dissemination of the new profits, and the unprecedented accumulation of capital. The rise of modern banking and insurance, and a "credit economy" with a marked increase in the efficiency of capital, and a corresponding stimulus to invention and the utilization of new processes and devices, and the foundation of modern technology. The development of the steam engine followed by the steamship and the railroad, ushering in an era of high profits and quickened enterprise.

7. The development of electricity, and especially the discovery of electro-magnetism by Faraday, perhaps the greatest single invention of modern times, leading to the manufacture, literally, of vast quantities of electric power. Followed by the invention of the telegraph, the telephone, the electric motor, and the easy dissemination of power. Then the invention of oil and gas engines, especially the Diesel type, and the automobile, and a great cheapening of transportation. The rise of the chemical industry and metallurgy, farm machinery and the like, leading to a revolution in the means of communication and transport, furthering the increase of trade and the exchange of goods, and methods and information, an immense increase in the mining and use of metals, a powerful stimulus to agriculture, resulting in a steady lowering of production costs, the concomitant increase of wages, shortened hours of labor and the general lightening of human toil.

8. The corresponding advance in all the sciences, the discoveries in geology, physiology, and medicine, leading to vital improvements in hygiene and the prevention of plagues and similar disorders. The accumulation of wealth supplied funds for this rapid advance in scientific methods and knowledge, perhaps greater in sheer quantity within a century or so than in the long creeping advance of human knowledge in the preceding 5,000 years. The invention of dynamite, the power drill and new methods of refining gave a similar impulse to mining and exploration. The discovery of oil, rubber gave to the world new products and stimulated the search for others. Yet another effect was the enormous expansion of education and technical training, the achievements of applied science opening new pathways to wealth, the accumulation of capital, and abundant funds for research.

II

THE ENORMOUS GAIN WITH THE COMING
OF THE POWER AGE

1. Historical research, especially of the last 30 years, has revealed that the average of human product in the most civilized
countries apparently varied very little over a wide expanse of
time. Probably little increase from the domestication of the ox and
horse (5th millennium or earlier). Navigation had become much
more widely developed; and likewise the trade routes by land, but
the ships of Vasco and Columbus were no larger than those of
the ancient Phoenicians or Greeks, over 2,000 years before. Alexander or Caesar could travel no faster than Hammurabi or Sargon,
except as the Romans built roads. And Napoleon hardly faster than
Caesar.

2. The development of iron mining and especially the discovery
of the process for coking coal, led to a great development of the
coal mining industry in England, which directly preceded and
stimulated the development of the steam engine. At first a dire
failure. Watt worked eight years on his first engine; not a success.
Inventions in the textile industry and the power loom brought
further demand for cheap power and opened the market for the
steam engine. The rise of British industry from the middle of the
17th century and its spread to adjacent nations and America; an
epic of human history!

Why did not all this happen in France or Germany or Spain?
Spain was always rich in minerals; and these were mined before the
Roman occupation, when Tartessos was a rich pre-historic state.
France, Germany and Belgium have large stores of coal. It is now
clear that a degree of civilization throughout most of Europe goes
back 6,000 or 8,000 years. The peculiar conjuncture of natural resources, wealth, sea-trade, the spirit of enterprise and adventure,
and the inventive genius of its people, that gave England the long
lead it held till the opening of the 20th century.

3. The swift expansion of industry and transportation from
1750, unparalleled before or since. Leading to the vast extension of
commerce, labor saving machinery, and the increase of human comforts. The rise of a strong indigenous English population in

America, a powerful stimulus to this increase. Immigration up to a little before our Civil War was scant, possibly not over 250,000 up to the American Revolution. An almost purely Anglo-Saxon population, that grew with astonishing rapidity; the basis of Malthus' calculations and gloomy predictions. The latter confounded by the inventions and discoveries of his own time.

4. Regular repetition of predictions that this intense industrial advance could not possibly continue. Witness Carroll Wright's famous pronouncement in 1884. The rate of increase of the population has declined steadily since our Civil War, and the surge of immigration from the Old World brought thirty millions in fifty years. But the growth of product *per capita* in America, so far as the broadest and most careful measures will disclose, has not materially varied in any decennium from the founding of the Republic up to 1930.

Why did this vast extension of human enterprise and human product have its chief genesis among a single people on either side of the Atlantic, and not all over the world? At the beginning of the Industrial Revolution, about 1750, England had a population of only six or eight millions. Today English is spoken by perhaps a quarter of a billion people, and this population has probably more than two-thirds of the wealth and income, the industrial product, the banking capital, the railways and steamships of the entire world. And though the world population has tripled within these three centuries, the huge proportion of this enormous number is still, save for the invasions of foreign machinery, goods and enjoyments, almost as backward as in the days of Marco Polo and Jenghis Khan. An amazing contrast.

5. Long time measures and comparisons of this mighty growth by nations and by industries are now available. They disclose a remarkable evenness of growth and the development of distinct long time *Trends;* therewith the possibility of a long time planning.

6. These new measures of long time growth shed much light upon the question of business "cycles," so much discussed in recent years; they seem to negative the idea of world cycles in production or trade. The variations from the long time rate of growth, even among the most sensitive types of indices, as those measuring basic production, reveal but little deviation from the trend. The larger part of the oscillations or cycles seems due to the variations in world crops and, therefore, to meteorological conditions rather

than to variations in mining and manufacture. Yet it has been from these that the idea of business cycles has been chiefly derived. Broader and more inclusive indices of industrial growth in the United States and other countries seem to bear the same testimony. There are often heavy declines in the making of what are called capital or durable goods; but these are so irregular they can scarcely be called "cycles." The importance of these, at least up to 1930, seems to have been highly exaggerated. What we have to discover is the primal cause of these variations and that of such an unexampled collapse as followed 1929.

III

THE PRICE PROBLEM AND THE PRICE REVOLUTION

What Determines Prices and Why No Solution of This Age Old Problem Until Now?

1. WE HAVE growing evidence, from the discoveries in archaeology, that the general level or wide average of prices, like the average human product, did not greatly change over a long period, possibly three or four thousand years. There were, of course, wide oscillations as, for example, when Alexander's huge plunder of the treasures of Persia were brought back and distributed to his soldiers. But little evidence of any continued long time or secular trend.

This view is supported by the slight change in the cost of production of the chief commodities. In terms of human labor, the production of wheat, barley and the like, did not vary much and the production of minerals and metals was so small that it counted for little. There was practically no coal, very little iron mining, some copper and silver and gold. But we know that from the earliest days when gold and silver began to be used as the medium of exchange, the ratio of one to the other, save for short periods, varied from between 10 and 12 to 1. From the earliest records up to the discovery of the American treasure. Thereafter a long, and mighty rise, due to the huge increase of the silver product and later of gold.

2. With stable ratios of gold and silver and slender variations in the cost of production, obvious that there was slight basis for wide fluctuations in the general level of prices (or wages). The plunder of war, under the Caesars in Rome, brought rather wide variations. And so also the sack of the pagan temples by Constantine, whose Christian zeal seems to have been stimulated by this highly profitable enterprise. But prices in Europe through the Dark Ages, and even later, seemed to have been generally low, rising sharply with epidemics of plagues, like the Black Death of the 14th century.

But the discoveries of vast stores of gold and silver from conquests of Cortez and the Pizarros, and the rapid spread of mining in the Americas, brought to Europe a huge supply of precious metals. Therewith the greatest sustained rise in prices of which we have any record; and this record extends dimly at least over something like four thousand years. Adam Smith sets the discovery of America and the sea routes to India as probably the most noteworthy events in human history; the rage for seeking the American treasure brought a burst of exploration which might otherwise have proceeded slowly through centuries. Within fifty or one hundred years after the Pizarros' discoveries, and of Potosi, the larger part of the gold and silver bearing areas of the two continents had been overrun by prospectors.

3. But this tremendous rise in prices came to an end at the close of the 17th century. Since then the broader measures of prices, in England and the United States, reveal no clear secular trend. The averages in the 18th and 19th century did not differ greatly from that of the last fifty years. There were rather wide oscillations, as in ancient times: as in the Napoleonic Wars and the World War, and in our Civil War. But these, it seems clear, did not result from any imaginary scarcity of goods, but almost solely from the huge issues of paper money which are almost invariably resorted to. We have then a long background for the discussion of the question: What determines prices?

4. Ingenious attempts have been made from the days of Jevons and Newmarch to Castle to give a rigorous statistical answer. But it is only within the last fifteen years that adequate materials have been available for the solution: broad measures of commerce and trade as a whole, the volume of the circulating medium, now chiefly bank credit, the rate of turnover or velocity of this credit, and finally an adequate measure of the General Price Level, as con-

trasted with special indexes like those of commodity prices at wholesale.

5. Supporting these conclusions, these broad measures of production and prices reveal that there is little relation between the long term trends of production, or their variations, and the prices of commodities. All prices tend, more or less, to rise or fall together, while production grows steadily and with relatively small deviations. Changes in prices, therefore, cannot be closely related to commodities themselves. They are due, it is now clear, rather to variations in the money supply, a fact of profound importance in, economic and monetary theory. The thesis is supported by a wide series of graphs depicting these long time relationships.

IV

THE RELATION OF MONEY, CREDIT AND PRICES
and
The Unsolved Problem of Monetary and Economic Stability

1. THE vast extension of trade which followed the discovery of the Americas and of a sea route to India, brought with it the expansion of the system of banking and credit that had existed in a crude way for two thousand years or more. Therewith a fluidity, and likewise a new kind of instability, in the mercantile world, that has slowly come to play an important rôle in human affairs. Money must always have been a major factor in our later cultural stage. But in no such degree as in the last two centuries.

The Bank of England was founded in 1694. Within the next two hundred years a spread of banking without parallel. The famous scheme of John Law, known as the "Mississippi Bubble" in 1720 and the "South Sea Bubble" which followed quickly after, were the beginning of a long series of speculative orgies that have introduced a distinctly new influence in social polity. In the 19th century the wide adoption of the gold standard as a system of international exchange brought with it a larger degree of stability, which came to an end with the outbreak of the World War. Therewith a new problem: The control of credit.

2. It had been recognized from the days of Ricardo and Mill that the expansion and contraction of the volume of the money

supply might be a disturbing factor, but the full recognition of this did not come until after the World War and the period of monetary chaos which ensued. Therewith a deeper interest in the relations of money and credit to trade, and the so-called trade "cycle."

Fifty years ago Simon Newcomb, a distinguished American astronomer and economist, endeavored to formulate these relations in a simple algebraic equation. Slowly perfected by Kemmerer and Fisher, its validity could not be established until wider and more accurate measures of the growth of industry and trade, the velocity or rate of turnover of the credit volume, and finally, a broader and more representative index of the General Price Level, were available.

These measures have been provided within the last fifteen years. We are now able to determine, statistically and mathematically, the exact significance of these several factors. It was found that in normal times the velocity, or rate of turnover, corresponded closely with the variations in trade activity, so that these two factors cancelled out, leaving only a constant, representing the long time rate of trade growth. Thus the Newcomb formula becomes a simple ratio of the volume of credit money to this long time rate of growth; and this ratio is very closely the General Price Level. Our familiar commodity price indexes tend to vary, at times, too widely to be acceptable as a broad measure of prices. So we have now the solid foundations for a system of credit control based on purely statistical methods.

This conception is new, and has not yet had any considerable recognition. It promises, however, to become the foundation of a rational and quantitative Monetary Theory. This rests upon the obvious fact that while the volume of trade or the rate of growth cannot, in a system of free exchange and in a world-wide commercial economy, be controlled, the volume of credit can. We have then a variable factor which, under a more enlightened banking management, may solve one of the paramount questions of our time: The maintenance of at least a reasonable degree of monetary and economic stability.

The social consequences that would flow from the general adoption of such a rational system rest upon the fact that nothing seems more deeply troubling to the human mind and, it may be added, to public and governmental morals, than a violent fall in the price level, and in values of all kinds. Such a fall seems deeply to affect general sanity, a fact which has been vividly in evidence, especially in England and the United States, since the close of the Napoleonic Wars and the long continued fall in prices which ensued. An especially violent fall has been invariably followed by a deep feeling of unrest and dissatisfaction with the existing human order, leading to widespread attacks upon the economic system and every variety of fantastic proposals for a new social order, such as those of Saint Simon and Fourier, and similar Utopian experiments; and in our time highly instructive attempts to realize these wild dreams upon a national scale, as in Russia: the dictatorship of the Proletariat, with the expropriation of the capitalist class. Similar outgrowths are the Fascist and Nazi movements in Italy, Germany and elsewhere.

It has been difficult to reveal the impracticable nature of these proposals until this recent development of statistical measures, which show how small a share of the total product is consumed by the 'capitalist class' and how little difference a redistribution of property and income towards a more complete equality would affect the masses. Now evident that the personal expenditures of the rich amount to very little, and if their "wealth" and incomes were evenly distributed this would materially affect only the large body of incapables, derelicts, and mentally deficient, survivals of the neolithic population out of which modern civilization has arisen. It probably would not materially alter the status of by far the larger part of those gainfully employed; possibly 80% or more; while such a 'redistribution' would threaten seriously the supply of new capital.

It is now certain from these investigations that if the industrial progress of this period is to continue, the capital supply must somehow be maintained and that the alternative is either State Capitalism, as in Russia, or what may be termed Commercial Capitalism, such as now obtains over the larger part of the world. In other words, we have now a precise formulation of the conditions of economic growth. In brief, the mechanism for a progressive amelioration of the human lot.

The utilization of this new knowledge seems to the writer the great problem and the portentous task of the immediate future. A period of economic chaos such as has more or less characterized the twenty years since the close of the World War, might readily destroy our modern civilization, and lead to such a disheartening

decline as followed the breakup of the Roman Empire and the
Roman domination. Now still more threatening since these lines
were first written.

V

HIGH WAGES, HIGH PROFITS, AND THE CAPITAL SUPPLY

ALMOST universal knowledge, now, that in the United States we
have the widest dissemination of general comfort and well-being
of any nation. The average of wages, real wages, as measured in
purchasing power, was in 1930, as computed by the International
Labor Office, at least one half again as much as the next leading
nation, Great Britain, near to twice the average real wage of Germany, and between two and three times that of Italy.

Actual wages in this country are at least ten times the average
wage in the factories of India, and perhaps also of China. They
seem at least five or six times those of Japan. Whence these high
wages? What created all this wealth and comfort?

We now have solid statistical evidence that the extraordinary
growth of the United States in manufacturing, mining and transportation has been closely parallel to the increase of the capital
invested. In turn, this capital investment seems in the last hundred
years or more to have grown almost parallel to the amount of
horsepower employed in our industries. This quantity of horsepower in turn seems to measure closely the average amount of machinery employed in industry as a whole.

All this means that the amount of machinery or horsepower employed in industry, *per worker*, has risen almost exactly with the
amount of capital invested per worker; and in turn, the wages of
the workers appear to have risen at a corresponding rate.

In other words, we now have a definite picture of the process or
mechanism by which our high wages have been created. They are
due solely to the increased product per worker, which in turn in
the last one hundred years has steadily risen in almost exact proportion to the amount of machinery employed, and to the amount
of capital invested in industry.

This increase is not due to any fabled gain in the "efficiency" of
the workers. There is little evidence that skilled workers are today

any more skillful than they were a hundred years ago. The increase in product seems due solely to invention, discovery, the creation of new processes, and the realization of them through largely automatic machinery. This in turn has required a vast expenditure of capital. The capital supply then is an ineluctable factor in high wages and a higher standard of living.

Whence now comes this capital employed in industry and especially in manufacturing of all kinds, wherein has been our greatest industrial gain? The rather surprising answer is that it has come, in by far the larger part, from the industries themselves, and even each industry to a large degree generating its own capital. The supposed rôle of "the savings of the nation," or of "the people," seems to play a quite subordinate part. And this is especially true of new industries, a crucial point. For it is almost solely through new industries that the increase in real wages comes. In the older industries, long established and often showing little more than a population rate of growth, there is little incentive or capacity to raise the general wage level, because their profits are relatively low and tend to be stationary.

Now it is almost wholly through the profits of industry that the new capital, and especially the new capital for new industries, is derived, either through dividends or from the attendant capital gains. In turn, it is the new industries which expand most rapidly, and make, therefore, the larger profits providing the larger supply of capital funds, for expansion and improvements, and for technical research. (The commercial corporations of the United States are today expending more than three quarters of a million dollars per day in scientific investigations.) It is these new industries which create new demands for labor and from their high profits are able to bid for the most capable working men. The chief source of the rise in real wages in the United States. This increase is automatic, and for all practical purposes the influence of legislation, or of labor unions, or the altruistic sentiments of employers, has been zero.

It is difficult for the vast majority of people (and especially reformers) to believe that wages are not fixed by employers, or by combinations of them, or by "custom," or that they cannot be materially raised by "collective bargaining," or labor unions. Hard for them to realize that they are a fixed part of the money-value of the product, varying somewhat from industry to industry, but on the average not changing significantly in the United States through at least the last 80 years.

These findings have an important bearing on the question as to whether Socialism, or what is termed a 'more equitable distribution of wealth,' would have any material effect upon the average income of the average worker. In point of fact it would appear that we actually have in this country, to a high degree, a kind of "co-operative commonwealth" in which the share of total product or income is far more equitably distributed than is generally imagined. Or that an entirely equal distribution among all the workers would not increase their incomes, in all probability, by much more than 5%. Possibly less, since it seems the universal experience that when the stimulus of individual enterprise and initiative, with "the profit motive," is taken away, the result is a decline in the total product.

VI

IT IS CAPITAL THAT CREATES CAPITAL
And the Wealth of Nations

OF THE existing Wealth and active Capital of the world, and especially that of the Western or 'economic world,' more than 95 per cent probably has been created in the 150 years that have passed since the Industrial Revolution. And this is the proof: If at that time all the real capital, exclusive of the nominal value of land, amounted to only one billion dollars, and had increased at the net rate of 4 per cent per annum (in modern times this would now amount to around 1,000 billions), it would vastly exceed the present actual invested capital.

Capital can gain this net of 4 per cent only if the product of a country increases at 4 per cent or more; 'or more' because of the constant losses of the invested capital in obsolescence.

The evidence seems clear that the *per capita* product of the leading industrial countries increased very little over an enormous period, perhaps a thousand or even two thousand years, and up to about the 17th century. Therefore the *per capita* real wealth of the world likewise could not have increased, in this same period, because real wealth implies the production of 'goods and enjoyments,' not mere money.

If, now, the actual product has increased only about as fast as the net gain in capital invested, it follows that on balance there has then been no addition to this capital from the outside, from 'Labor'; that is, the amount subtracted from the total product for the payment of interest on capital (around 4 per cent) is about the minimum amount that will induce the average man to save and invest. This has been especially true at least in the last century, the most important period.

The net increase in the product per worker or per capita (nearly the same) has averaged in the last one hundred years between 2 and 2¼ per cent per annum. The average increase in real wages through this same period has been about 1½ per cent per annum.

As in the long run the entire net proceeds of industry (except the parts that go to taxes) go to labor and to capital, it follows that the entire 'expropriation' of Labor by the Capitalistic System has been on the order of less than 1 per cent per annum.

This 1 per cent, added to the realizable minimum interest rate, is what has created the hundred billions and more of industrial capital now employed in industry in the United States.

The population has increased from about 3 million at the time of the Revolution to around 130 millions, or more than 40 times. Yet the product has increased probably 100 or 200 times.

If the annual product of industry or real net 'income' in the United States in prosperous times, as in 1928–29, was 90 billions, it would now be about half as much again if it had increased at the average rate of the preceding century. This is what ten years of complete arrest of growth has meant to the people of the country.

Of this colossal increase, 90 per cent or more would have gone directly to the improvement in the 'standard of living' and the enjoyment of the people. If, instead, 100 per cent had gone to the people, that would have augmented the average income by not more than 10 per cent, probably less, because possibly half this remaining 10 per cent would have been wasted or lost. There would have been no increase in the *per capita* product nor in the average real wage. Thus, the whole population would have been no better off than when this country began as a nation.

Only in the last generation has there been any material savings of the great body of the people; and these savings have gone largely to investments in homes and in life insurance and the like, and have represented but a very small part of the net investment in productive industry. If the total savings had been larger than the estimated 4 or 5 per cent, the increase in the total product and wealth of the country also would have been larger.

The evidence seems to be that most persons save very little and almost the entire gain in productive capital and in total product has come from 4 or 5 per cent of the population, the original owners of capital who have larger incomes than the average wage. In other words, capital creates itself: it is not the product of Labor. It is the *earnings of capital* which have supplied practically all the increase, and therefore all of the improvement, in the income and well being of the country.

VII

THE PARETO CURVE AND ITS SIGNIFICANCE FOR OUR TIME

IN THE world in which we live we discover everywhere the most extraordinary variety, and likewise disparity. From the billions of suns that blaze in the sky to the ultra-microscopic particles that float in the air. So in the world of life; from the giant sequoias and the monstrous whales, to microbes and the ultraviruses that bring us plagues and epidemics. So also in human affairs: some few are very successful, highly talented, endowed with capacities and abilities far beyond the mass of their fellows. The rule throughout all nature: inequality.

Does this almost infinite variety and disparity present merely a random or haphazard distribution or is it, everywhere, dominated by a remarkable law? This is a statistical problem, difficult at present to answer because, curiously enough, we have not measures of distribution amid a wide variety of different kinds of populations. In reality, hardly more than one wide field is open for investigation.

This is the distribution of income, and to a certain extent of wealth, in highly developed commercial states like our own, or in the leading nations of Europe; largely derived from income-tax data. Long ago it was suspicioned that this distribution did follow a definite law, but the first to give the problem a careful, laborious investigation was Vilfredo Pareto, born in Paris of an Italian father, an emigré, and a French mother; educated as an engineer, who became director of state railways in Italy; later Professor of Economics in Lausanne.

What, very simply, Pareto found was that from the highest to the lowest brackets of income there was a steady progression in numbers, and that if the numbers in these different brackets were plotted they followed a remarkable and almost uniform curve. Plotted on double-log paper and the data cumulated, this closely approached a straight line. First presented about 1896, and thereafter subjected to a recurrent gunfire of criticism and objection. Largely these objections arise from meticulous observations, that under a microscope, at least, there are some variations detectable in the slope of the line. Considering the nature of the data and especially the obvious inadequacy of the reported incomes in the lower brackets, this is hardly surprising.

But there is a wider interest in these findings, and that is whether the Pareto Curve is not a general expression for almost every kind of highly specialized ability, from that of the billiard player or baseball pitcher to the spectacular performance of the chess player, or the lightning calculator in mathematics. Evident that there are not in this world many Newtons or Shakespeares or Faradays, any more than there is a large population of Dizzy Deans or Willie Hoppes. Any more than there are thousands of John D. Rockefellers or Henry Fords, or the Croesuses of old. Everywhere a vast variety of talent, and disparity in ability. Such at least was the conception to which the writer had given a good deal of attention for a number of years, without being able to gather adequate factual data in support of the idea. Interesting to find last year that Professor Harold T. Davis had hit upon the same concept and made the same effort towards statistical proof of its validity. Not a wide variety of available data. Enough, however, it has seemed to me, to indicate that the thesis is valid, and further that the Pareto Curve is destined to take its place as one of the great generalizations of human knowledge.

I believe we may go much further and say that it has a profound significance in the field of economics and still more broadly what we may call the political economy. Manifest that we can not by legislation or any fanciful law create a Newton, a Shakespeare, or an Edison. No more than we can legislate the number or variety of very excellent poets or mathematicians, or inventors, who follow, in considerable numbers, in their wake. One thing in this difficult field seems clear; we cannot plan for or regiment, or in any artificial way create genius. And all of high value and interest, and understanding, and color, in this rather perplexing and sometimes difficult world, has been derived from the especially talented few.

Not so clear that the wealth, capital, and broad diffusion of comforts in the more highly developed civilizations like those of the United States and Europe, are the product of an extraordinarily small number of men: the inventors, the discoverers, the contrivers and innovators, and the singularly gifted, with the very rare talent for organization, and likewise the accumulation of wealth. These are the true creators and, I believe, will prove the true saviours of our modern world.

I have endeavored to show how small is this accumulation, how very slight the difference in income if it was all equally distributed, and yet how momentous would be the effect if this capital accumulation, likewise the talent, the energy and foresight of the men who have created it, were destroyed. All history is filled with the tragic results from the extinction of this capital supply.

Equally fateful, it would seem, upon every variety of activity and aspiration, whose fruits derive from this fine flower which we call civilization. Throughout all history this fierce urge to destroy, to level up, to abase the talented, the capable and the rich: one of the strongest drives within those vast lower levels of our neolithic population. Over and over again, throughout the ten, twenty or thirty thousand years in which high levels have been attained, the ruthless destruction of civilization by these barbarian hordes. Let us beware that in the guise of a seductive altruism it may not happen again.

VIII

TECTONICS WILL SAVE THE WORLD

(But Not the Techno-crats!)

1. ONE of the revelations of archaeology has been the evidence of the sometimes dumbfounding technical skill and attainments of the ancients. Witness the majestic pyramids in Egypt, which long remained a mystery as to how they were built. So also with hundreds of similar achievements throughout the early history of civilization.

The boats of the Phoenicians often exceeded in size any vessels constructed for two thousand years after. The Egyptians had large irrigation works; the Babylonians as well. A distinguished engineer remarks that many of the most epochal inventions had been made before the rise of Greece and Rome. The ancients indeed had almost everything but *power*, in the broader sense, that is not merely traction power, but the strength of materials to use such powers to the utmost. The ancients had some steel and iron; but the pyramids were erected a thousand years or more before iron came into general use. Yet for uncounted centuries, the rate of progress was amazingly slow. Then a sudden change: In a double sense, discovery of a New World.

2. "Necessity Is the Mother of Invention," throughout all history. Growing commerce of the inland seas brought the demand for larger ships, and the need for strength brought a demand for iron. So in turn the use of iron created the market for coal and coke, which led to the steam engine, to railroads, and to steamships. These in turn stimulating the development of modern metallurgy, steel making, the use of alloys and the like.

3. But all this was not *planned*, because the greatest discoveries have often been accidents, or fortuitous: a kind of product of their time. Columbus merely blundered into his finding of a new world. It took about 2,000 years, or more, to develop the steam engine; no one had any clear idea as to how it could be done; nor could anyone foresee that it would transform the world. Very much the same with the electric dynamo, the automobile, the radio, and hundreds of other inventions. These were all the products of discoveries that were often accidental, as that of petroleum, which, in a little more than a generation, had led to the gas, and then to the gasoline motor. All unforeseen. No human being can look far ahead; hence the futility of more than a minimum of planning. Also that of most predictions.

Likewise the unending reiteration of the idea that human progress cannot continue indefinitely at the marvelous pace of the last one hundred and fifty years. Every decennium since Watt's invention of a working steam engine has belied this prediction. In 1884 Carroll Wright, an economist of high attainments, took this discouraged view:

"It is true that new processes of manufacture will undoubtedly continue, and this will act as an ameliorating influence, but it will not leave room for a marked extension, such as has been witnessed during the last 50 years. . . . There may be room for further intensive, but not extensive, development of industry, in the present era of civilization." The half century that has elapsed since this prediction has never been surpassed in the variety and importance of its achievements.

No reason to suppose that there is any near limit to this astonishing advance. Often one invention breeds another. Almost every notable discovery is fertile, that is, finds applications in unexpected ways. Thus, for example, when fifty years ago Hertz discovered electric waves, probably neither his brain nor any other could have dreamt of the present day universal organization of radio systems, with their entertainment programs or communication with airplanes.

4. But there is in this field something *vitally new*. The *machinery* of invention and discovery has entered upon a new stage. Instead of scattered workers in improvised shops, researches now are being carried on in magnificent laboratories, costing often millions of dollars, with thousands of research workers, the most highly trained and educated class in the world. These laboratories are the pure product of capitalistic enterprise, *in search of profit*. They have received a powerful impulse from corporation tax laws, designed expressively to limit profits, and thus check the growth of industrial enterprise and the advance in wages. Hard for even the most rabid trust-baiter to forbid companies or individuals to engage in highly fruitful and marvelously beneficent scientific research.

5. So, in all probability, the triumphant march of Technology will go on, unchecked, and therewith the increase of wealth and wages, comforts and enjoyments; and human toil will be steadily lightened. The average hours of work in the factories are now only one-half what they were as a rule two thousand or two hundred years ago. We can scarcely imagine what it will all be like in even another hundred years. We can set no limits upon human ingenuity and inventiveness. In 300 years, greater progress than in 3,000 years before. In these three centuries, our senses, our powers, and to some extent even our intelligence, have been notably extended. Gathering momentum as it advances, Technology will take over all industry; and its methods will remake our lives.

6. And all this increase of plenty will be followed by social se-

curity and general happiness. We shall not need old age pensions
or security laws, because the advance in Technology will not be
confined to machinery and to processes; we shall have an equal
advance in the technique (very simple and, as we now know, easily
attained) of economic and monetary stability, so that we shall have
no more business depressions, nor crazy speculation, nor wide unemployment and decline in the production of wealth. And these
will be eradicated, not by childish and futile attempts at government fiat, but by the unbelievably simple methods of *credit control.*
That is, we shall learn to understand and run the economic mechanism as smoothly as we do now that of a powerful electro-generat-
ing plant, or a Leviathan of the sea; and economics and economists,
perhaps, will rise to larger knowledge and a new dignity and sphere
of usefulness.

———

> Rouse, O people! Wake to wonder,
> You who mourn the age as dead,
> Cold, mechanical and godless—
> 'Tis a flaming age instead.
> Speak no more of this our epoch
> As a monster's iron plan;
> 'Tis the age of God's creators—
> Dawn of His creator, man!
>   ANGELA MORGAN

NOTES AND COMMENTS

NOTES AND COMMENTS

CHAPTER I

1. Mechanism is essentially a concept designed to show that all phenomena are the result of relatively simple laws of matter and motion, a philosophy whose spirit is reflected in the statement of Descartes, "Give me matter and I will construct the world." The quest for mechanism is man's oldest philosophical problem, and out of this search came the atomic theory of Thales and Democritus. As I stated in *The World Machine*, "it is fairly certain that Descartes was the first concretely to picture this world as a mechanism, the first to explain its phenomena upon a mechanical basis, the first to analyze the universe into terms of matter and motion. This he did, not as pure astronomer, not simply as regards the sun and planets, but through the tides and winds, through physiology and all the phenomena of life, down to the last flutter of an eyelid." It only remains to add to the mechanism of the universe and of life, the mechanism of society. For an analysis of the concept of mechanism, see P. A. R. Janet, *Final Causes;* James Ward, *Naturalism and Agnosticism.*

2. Aristarchus of Samos, sometimes called "the mathematician," was a Greek astronomer, *c.* 310–230 B. C., who anticipated by nearly 1,800 years the heliocentric hypothesis of Copernicus, and brought upon himself the accusation of impiety for "putting in motion the Hearth of the Universe." Copernicus admits his indebtedness to Aristarchus' work, *On the Sizes and Distances of the Sun and Moon.* Although this work does not contain the heliocentric hypothesis, the certainty of Aristarchus' priority is established by Archimedes' rebuttal in the *Sand-reckoner.* See, T. L. Heath, *Aristarchus of Samos, the Ancient Copernicus;* and Carl Snyder, *The World Machine,* chap. VII.

3. One fascinating business cycle theory attempts to connect the phenomenon of prosperity and depression with the appearance of spots on the sun. The English astronomer Herschel first speculated on the significance of sun spots in mundane affairs. W. S. Jevons, and the many who have followed him, connected solar phenomena with business conditions through the influence of sun spots on weather, agricultural production and prices, and general business activity. An account of the significance of sun spots is given by Professor H. T. Stetson in his book, *Sunspots and Their Effects.* For discussions of the relation of sun spots to business cycles, see W. S. Jevons, *Investigations in Currency and Finance;* H. S. Jevons, "The Sun's Heat and Trade Activity," *Contemporary Review,* Aug., 1909; J. H. Kirk, *Agriculture and the Trade Cycle;* C. Garcia-Mata and F. I. Shaffner, "Solar and Economic Relations," *Quarterly Journal of Economics,* Nov., 1934.

4. The deductive school is a partly mechanistic one, making use of the concept of equilibrium, particularly in price analysis. The more recent and popular institutionalist school of economics denies completely the validity of equilibrium analysis and the entire mechanistic concept.

6. Simon Newcomb, *Principles of Political Economy,* Part IV, "The Societary Circulation;" especially chap. VII, "Effect of a Diminution in the Flow of the Currency."

7. I have discussed the relationship of the volume of bank credit to the general level of prices in the following papers: "The Problem of Monetary and Economic Stability," *Quarterly Journal of Economics,* March, 1935; "New Measures of the Relations of Credit and Trade," *Proceedings of the Academy of Political and Social Science,* Jan., 1930; "Industrial Growth and Monetary Theory," *Economic*

Forum, Summer, 1933; "The Problem of Prosperity," *Journal of the American Statistical Association,* March, 1929.

8. For an account of the bank holiday of March, 1933, see H. P. Willis and J. M. Chapman, *The Banking Situation, American Post-War Problems and Developments;* J. F. T. O'Connor, *Banking Crisis and Recovery under the Roosevelt Administration;* "73d Congress Faces the Banking Problem," *Congressional Digest,* April, 1933.

9. In this use of the scientific method in the study of business cycles, Professor Wesley C. Mitchell has been a notable pioneer. His use of statistical methods in analyzing time series of cyclical fluctuations has added much to our knowledge of business cycles.

10. *Cf.* my article "On the Statistical Relation of Trade, Credit, and Prices," *Revue de l'Institut International de Statistique,* vol. II, no. 3, 1934.

11. For an analysis of rates of growth in the United States see my papers, "The Index of the Volume of Trade: Second Revision," *Journal of the American Statistical Association,* June, 1928; and "The Capital Supply and National Well Being," *American Economic Review,* June, 1936.

12. On this question, see S. J. Chapman, *Outlines of Political Economy,* chap. I. The distinction between economics as a science and as an art, somewhat related to the question of what ought to be, is considered by F. A. Walker, *Political Economy,* pp. 19-23.

13. Despite the great advance in statistical economics, there is still reason to believe that much of our economic thinking consists of theorizing in a vacuum. There have been notable exceptions. Professor Mitchell in this country and Dr. A. L. Bowley in England insist on the need to verify theory with statistics. For the progress and possibilities of a quantitative science of economics, see G. Cassel, *On Quantitative Thinking in Economics,* and my paper on "Measurement Versus Theory in Economics" in the *Essays Contributed in Honour of Gustav Cassel.*

Chapter II

1. These differences are in many instances so fundamental that economists are frequently classified into schools of economic thought, based on their method of analysis, their point of emphasis, or their traditional origin: Thus we have the English classical school, deriving from Smith, Ricardo, and Mill, and the neo-classical, sometimes called the Cambridge, following Marshall and Pigou; the new Cambridge, following Keynes, and claiming kinship with Malthus; the Austrian, giving emphasis to marginal utility and following Menger, Wieser, and Böhm-Bawerk; the new Austrian, using Böhm-Bawerk's interest theory in analyzing business cycles; the German historical, following Roscher and Schmoller; and more recently the statistical and mathematical schools. The institutionalist school, quite prominent in the United States, gives emphasis to social and legal institutions as factors affecting economic life.

2. At best there is the attitude prevalent among economists that economics is both a deductive and inductive science. Many of the older economists, including Mill and Jevons, were logicians. But Jevons' use of deduction did not keep him from developing statistical analysis and utilizing it in economics far beyond his contemporaries and predecessors. See, for example, his *Investigations in Currency and Finance.*

3. Prior to 1919 the data for most cycles, although fairly complete for some types of production and for many price and banking series, are not very full. Nevertheless, the most important series are sufficiently complete and reliable for an analysis of the causes of booms and depressions.

4. On the devaluations in England, consult R. G. Hawtrey, *Currency and Credit,* third edition, chap. XVI; and the *Dictionary of Political Economy,* I, p. 500.

Amongst continental countries, France is the classic example of repeated currency devaluation. The original French mark of eight ounces of silver was coined into 58 sous in the days of St. Louis. The Hundred Years' War, and numerous regal difficulties, led to a rapid increase in the number of sous coined from the mark of silver. By 1360 the mark was coined into 100 sous, and by 1454 into 175. The sou finally became so small that a new coin of account, the livre of 20 sous, was instituted. By the time of the Revolution, the standard coin was ⅟₁₈ of its weight under St. Louis. During the Revolution the name of the *livre* was changed to the *franc*. Since the World War, the franc has been very considerably devalued. For a history of the debasement of French money, see Albert Despaux, *Les Dévaluations Monétaires dans l'Histoire*, Part III.

5. Alexander Del Mar, of the late nineteenth century, wrote an entertaining volume on the historical effects of changes in the quantity of money. His theory of history is expounded in *Money and Civilization*.

6. Hinton Rowan Helper (1839-1909) was a North Carolinian of the poor, non-slave-holding class. Helper's anti-slavery argument was purely economic, for he was a rabid Negrophobe and spent the latter part of his life advocating African colonization of the Negroes. "Indeed," he wrote, "the *unprofitableness* of slavery is a monstrous evil, when considered in all its bearings; it makes us poor; poverty makes us ignorant; ignorance makes us wretched; wretchedness makes us wicked; and wickedness leads to the devil." For a short account of his life see H. T. Lefler, *Hinton Rowan Helper, Advocate of a "White America."*

7. Reviewing American tariffs before the Civil War, Professor Taussig concludes: "In the main, the changes in duties have had much less effect on the protected industries than is generally supposed. Their growth has been steady and continuous, and seems to have been little stimulated by the high duties of 1842, and little checked by the more moderate duties of 1846 and 1857." *The Tariff History of the United States*, p. 152.

8. Index numbers were probably invented by the Italian mathematician, G. R. Carli, who was investigating the effects of the discovery of America on prices. His work was published in 1764. An important contribution was made by the Englishman, Sir George Schuckburg-Evelyn, in 1798, in the course of a study of the effects of the paper pound on prices. Jevons, Soetbeer, and Edgeworth also made significant contributions to the theory and construction of index numbers. A short account of the history of index numbers can be found in W. C. Mitchell, *Index Numbers of Wholesale Prices*, Bulletin 173, United States Bureau of Labor Statistics, and the revision in Bulletin 284. On the construction of index numbers, see Irving Fisher, *The Making of Index Numbers;* W. I. King, *Index Numbers Elucidated;* and C. M. Walsh, *The Measurement of General Exchange Value.*

9. On the theoretical impossibility of measuring the general level of prices, Ricardo wrote: "It has indeed been said that we might judge of the value of money by its relation, not to one, but to the mass of commodities. When we consider that commodities are continually varying in value, as compared with each other; and that when such variation takes place, it is impossible to ascertain which commodity has increased, which diminished in value, it must be allowed that such a test would be of no use whatever. Some commodities are rising in value, from the effects of taxation, from the scarcity of the raw material of which they are made, or from any other cause which increases the difficulty of production. Others again are falling, from improvements in machinery, from the better division of labour, and the improved skill of workmen; from the greater abundance of the raw material, and generally from greater facility of production. To determine the value of a currency by the test proposed, it would be necessary to compare it successively with the thousands of commodities which are circulating in the community, allowing to each all the effects which may have been produced upon its value by the above causes. To do this is evidently impossible." David Ricardo, *Proposals for an Economical and Secure Currency.*

10. On international price measurements, see A. L. Bowley, *International Comparison of Price Changes*, London and Cambridge Economic Service (London, 1926); A. L. Bowley and K. C. Smith, *Comparative Price Index-numbers for Eleven Principal Countries*, London and Cambridge Economic Service (London, 1927), W. C. Mitchell (assisted by M. S. Goldsmith and F. K. Middough), *International Price Comparisons*, Department of Commerce, in co-operation with the War Industries Board, Washington, 1919.

11. The equation of exchange, now generally familiar in the form $PT = MV$, was stated in 1885 by Simon Newcomb in the form $VR = KP$; where V is equal to the number of dollars in circulation; R is "the average number of times . . . a dollar changes hands during the year;" K is the volume of wealth and services changing hands, and P the average price for a unit of them. Simon Newcomb, *Principles of Political Economy*, Part IV, chap. II. For earlier formulations of the equation of exchange somewhat similar to those of Newcomb, Kemmerer, and Fisher, see A. W. Marget, *The Theory of Prices*, pp. 9–12.

12. On the measurement of velocity, see my articles, "Turnover of Deposits: A Measure of Business Activity," *American Bankers' Association Journal*, Feb., 1924; and "New Measures in the Equation of Exchange," *American Economic Review*, Dec., 1924. See also, Irving Fisher, *A Practical Method of Estimating the Velocity of Circulation of Money*, (London, 1909).

13. For the present status of my index of trade, see "The Index of the Volume of Trade: Third Revision," *Journal of the American Statistical Association*, Dec., 1931. *Cf.*, E. E. Day and W. Thomas, *The Growth of Manufactures, 1899 to 1923*, U. S. Government Printing Office, 1928; and W. M. Persons, *Indexes of General Business Conditions*, Harvard University Committee on Economic Research, 1919.

14. See my papers, "New Measures in the Equation of Exchange," *American Economic Review*, Dec., 1924; "Deposits Activity as a Measure of Business Activity," *Review of Economic Statistics*, Oct., 1924; "Turnover of Deposits: A Measure of Business Activity," *American Bankers' Association Journal*, Feb., 1924. See also *Business Cycles and Business Measurements*, chap. VII. The root of the argument is that cyclical variations in trade and in the velocity of money tend to be equal, so that in the equation $PT = MV$, V/T is a constant. If this is true, the general price level and the quantity of money vary in direct proportion, and the equation can be written $P = MK$, where K is a constant.

15. Carl Snyder, "Industrial Growth and Monetary Theory," *Economic Forum*, Summer, 1933.

16. E. W. Kemmerer, *Money and Credit Instruments in Their Relation to General Prices*.

17. Irving Fisher, *The Purchasing Power of Money*; and *A Practical Method of Estimating the Velocity of Circulation of Money*.

18. This is the purpose of my index of the General Price Level. The price groups and weights in this index number are as follows:

Price group	Weight	Price group	Weight
Industrial prices, wholesale	10	Realty values, urban and farm	10
Farm prices at the farm	10	Securities, stocks, and bonds	10
Retail food, 51 cities	10	Equipment and machinery	10
Rents, 32 cities	5	Hardware	3
Clothing, fuel, *etc.*, retail	10	Automobile	2
Freight and transportation costs	5	**Wages**	15

The index is described in the *Review of Economic Statistics*, Feb., 1928; and is published in the *Monthly Review of Credit and Business Conditions*, Federal Reserve Bank of New York.

19. Gustav Cassel tested the relationship of note issues to prices in Sweden by comparing the note circulation from 1915 to 1920 with an arithmetic average of

wholesale prices and retail food prices for the same years. Expressing the note circulation as a percentage of the price index, he obtained figures ranging from 113 to 88. The results are fair, but clearly not so good as those in which deposits as well as notes are compared with a general price level. Gustav Cassel, *Money and Foreign Exchange after 1914*, pp. 57–60.

20. "Economic theory surely cannot remain in its present backward position if it wants to be recognized as a discipline on an equal footing with other branches of modern science, in which clear quantitative thinking is a self-evident prerequisite for the student." Gustav Cassel, *On Quantitative Thinking in Economics*, p. 4.

21. Tench Coxe (1775–1824) was the best informed man of his time on the state of commerce and industry in the United States. He advocated protective tariffs and the development of a merchant marine. He was assistant secretary of the treasury from 1789 to 1792 and commissioner of the revenue from 1792 to 1798. He compiled the digest of the first census of manufacturers in 1810. See Harold Hutcheson, *Tench Coxe: A Study in American Economic Development*.

Chapter III

1. For a study of industrial growth in the United States, see chap. II of my *Business Cycles and Business Measurements*, where a comparison is made with the earlier indexes of Day, Stewart, and King. All these indexes agree that production has grown at a remarkably regular rate. Further proof of the regularity of growth is provided by W. M. Persons, *Forecasting Business Cycles*. I have discussed this question in several papers: "Measures of Industrial Growth and Their Significance," *Beiträge zur Konjunkturlehre*, edited by E. F. Wagemann, Hamburg, 1936; "New Measures of Trade and of Economic Growth," *Revue de l'Institut International de Statistique*, vol. I, no. 4, 1933; "The Index of the Volume of Trade," *Journal of the American Statistical Association*, Dec., 1923; and subsequent revisions in that Journal, Sept., 1925; June, 1928; and Dec., 1931.

2. See my paper "Capital Supply and National Well-being," *American Economic Review*, June, 1936. Professor Hansen objects to the statement that there is a unique relationship between the flow of savings and the rise of real income. Referring to Colin Clark, he points out that technological and managerial innovations are factors to be considered, and because these innovations can be either capital-using or capital-saving, he maintains that it is quite possible to have an increase in real income concomitant with a decline in the volume of savings. A. H. Hansen. *Full Recovery or Stagnation*, p. 310.

3. United States Treasury Department, *Statistics of Income for 1931*, pp. 10, 13, 18.

4. For information on the industrialization of Russia and the working of its economic system, see C. B. Hoover, *The Economic Life of Soviet Russia*, and I. F. Hubbard, *Soviet Trade and Distribution*.

5. This equation is known as Pareto's Law. It can be expressed in the form $A = Nx^a$, or $N = Ax^{-a}$. To eliminate the exponents it can be expressed as $log\ N = log\ A - a\ log\ x$. In these equations, x is an amount of income; N is the number of persons receiving that amount or more; A is a constant varying with the total number of incomes considered; and a is a constant which contains the essence of the law, for in all countries and at all times a is almost exactly 1.5. Graphically, the law tells us that on double logarithmic paper, with one axis for sizes of incomes and the other for the numbers of persons receiving the assigned incomes or more, the points when connected will form a straight line negatively inclined at an angle very close to 53°. It is this angle of inclination which represents the constant a, 1.5 being the tangent of 53°.

6. Rufus Tucker has shown this conclusively. Using the recent income tax data and that of the Civil War, he has demonstrated that the angle of inclination of the Pareto curve is the same now as in the post-Civil War period, and concludes that

the degree of inequality in the distribution of income has not changed. R. Tucker, "Distribution of Income," *Quarterly Journal of Economics*, Aug., 1938. For other discussions of Pareto's law, see N. O. Johnson, "The Pareto Law," *Review of Economic Statistics*, Feb., 1937; W. L. Crum, "Individual Shares in the National Income," *Review of Economic Statistics*, Nov., 1935.

7. The law is stated by Vilfredo Pareto, *Cours d'Economie Politique*, vol. II, Book 3, chap. I. The significance of Pareto's law is considered in chaps. XIV–XVI, below.

8. See chaps. XI–XIII, below.

9. I have expounded this view at some length in my paper "On the Structure and Inertia of Prices," *American Economic Review*, June, 1934.

10. A good account of land speculation in this country in the last century and its influence on business cycles is given in W. B. Smith and A. H. Cole, *Fluctuations in American Business, 1790–1860*, chaps. X and XVIII.

11. For a discussion of this question, see my address "The Concept of Momentum and Inertia in Economics," delivered at the meeting of the American Association for the Advancement of Science, Dec. 27, 1932, and published in *Stabilization of Employment* (Principia Press, Bloomington, Ind.).

12. I have been shown a statement in the Talmudic tract *Pirke Aboth* (The Sayings of the Fathers) which shows clearly the prevalence of installment selling in ancient Palestine. "Rabbi Akiba was wont to say: Everything is given on pledge, and a net is spread for all the living; the shop is open, and the dealer gives credit, and the ledger lies open, and the hand writes, and whosoever wishes to borrow may come and borrow; but the collectors go round continually every day, and exact payment from man whether he wills or not; and they have whereon they can rely in their demand." *Pirke Aboth*, III, 20.

13. The greater part of cyclical fluctuation in production is in the remote stages of the process, that is, in the production of capital goods rather than consumers'. I have elsewhere pointed out that "the amplitude of fluctuation of trade series increases generally according to their distance from the ultimate consumer." See, "The Index of the Volume of Trade: Third Revision," *Journal of the American Statistical Association*, Dec., 1931. Cf. Gustav Cassel, *The Theory of Social Economy*, revised edition, p. 550.

14. For instance, the widely known index of business published in *The Guaranty Survey* fell from 115 in 1929 to 55 in 1932, a decline of 52 per cent. Other well known indexes of production fell by as much or more. In comparison my index of production and trade fell from 112 to 67, a decline of 40 per cent. I have always pointed out that the movements of my index represent an outside limit of variability. There is no way of measuring directly the precise decline in economic activity between 1929 and 1932. An indirect estimate may be made by taking the Department of Commerce statistics for income produced for these years and correcting them for the change in the general price level. This calculation indicates that from 1929 to 1932 the decline in economic activity was only 33.8 per cent.

15. On cyclical price movements see F. C. Mills, *The Behavior of Prices;* on price movements in war and post-war periods see E. M. Bernstein, *Money and the Economic System*, p. 176; W. C. Mitchell, *History of Prices during the War*.

16. In *The Wealth of Nations*, Smith makes a single reference to the steam engine: "In the first fire-engines, a boy was constantly employed to open and shut alternately the communication between the boiler and the cylinder, according as the piston either ascended or decended. One of these boys, who loved to play with his companions, observed that, by tying a string from the handle of the valve which opened this communication, to another part of the machine, the valve would open and shut without his assistance, and leave him at liberty to divert himself with his playfellows." Cannan edition, 1904, vol. I, p. 11.

17. The classic illustration of the economist's mechanism of equilibrium is Marshall's illustration of three balls in a basin. There are three factors in the determination of value: supply price, demand price, and amount produced. No one determines the other, but like balls in a basin, the position of each in equilibrium is affected by the others. Alfred Marshall, *Principles of Economics*, p. 818.

CHAPTER IV

1. H. T. Buckle's *History of Civilization in England* was one of the first great historical works to give emphasis to soil and climate as a factor in history. More recently the "climatic hypothesis of civilization" has been emphasized in the works of Ellsworth Huntington. See particularly his *Civilization and Climate*, and *Economic and Social Geography*.

2. An interesting account of the evolution and life of early man is given in H. F. Osborn's *Men of the Old Stone Age*. See also, J. Geikie, *The Antiquity of Man in Europe*. On the discovery of fire, see W. Hough, *The Story of Fire*.

3. See my article, "The Concept of Momentum and Inertia in Economics," an address at a meeting of the American Association for the Advancement of Science, Dec. 27, 1932, and published in *Stabilization of Employment*.

4. A. E. Douglass, *Climatic Cycles and Tree Growth;* E. Antevs, *Rainfall and Tree Growth*.

5. See, J. F. Palmer, "Pestilences: Their Influence on the Destiny of Nations, as Shown in the History of the Plague," *Transactions of the Royal Historical Society*, London, 1883; and H. Zinsser, *Rats, Lice, and History*.

6. L. Biart, *The Aztecs;* P. A. Means, *Ancient Civilization of the Andes* (Incas); T. W. F. Gann, *The Maya Indians of Southern Yucatan and Northern British Honduras*.

7. They did have the dog travois, but obviously this was of limited usefulness. After the introduction of the horse, they had pack animals and the horse travois. The travois was a type of dog or horse-drawn sled, with a net or platform for carrying loads.

8. Chaps. XVII, XXIII, and XXV.

9. E. A. Hooton, *Up from the Ape; Apes, Men, and Morons;* and *The Twilight of Man*.

10. W. Ridgeway, *The Origin of Metallic Currency and Weight Standards*, chap. IV, describes the "primaeval trade routes." From the most remote times intercourse existed between Western Europe and the Far East.

11. Consult J. H. Breasted, *Ancient Times, A History of the Ancient World*, pp. 265–269.

12. Plato, *The Timaeus*. The quotation above is a free translation. R. G. Bury gives the passage: "O Solon, Solon, you Greeks are always children: there is not such a thing as an old Greek. . . . You are young in soul, everyone of you. For therein you possess not a single belief that is ancient and derived from old tradition." R. G. Bury, *Plato's Works*, vol. VII, p. 33.

13. The owls or "maidens" were first struck in the middle of the sixth century B. C. They are the earliest known coins which bear a type on both sides, and their form set the style for many years to come: the use of a deity on the obverse side and the attribute of the deity on the reverse. The coin was the greatest commercial coin of the period. See P. Gardner, *History of Ancient Coinage*.

14. S. Higginbottom, "The Cattle Drain in India," *Asia*, Aug., 1938, p. 473.

15. That England is not rich in natural resources is clearly shown in a recent book by H. Kranold, *The International Distribution of Raw Materials*. The author attempts to construct an index of resources, based on each country's proportion of

the world production and export of basic raw materials corrected for differences in population. The result gives Great Britain, including the crown colonies but not the dominions, an index of 1.5, compared with an index of 4.4 for the United States, and 8.3 for Canada.

16. Consult, T. Frank, *An Economic History of Rome*, and *An Economic Survey of Ancient Rome;* W. S. Davis, *The Influence of Wealth in Imperial Rome;* G. M. Calhoun, *The Ancient Greeks and the Evolution of Standards in Business,* and *The Business Life of Ancient Athens;* G. Glotz, *Ancient Rome at Work,* and *Le Travail dans la Grèce Ancienne;* and Jules Toutain, *The economic Life of the Ancient World.*

17. Fritz Heichelheim, *Wirtschaftliche Schwankungen der Zeit von Alexander bis Augustus;* E. J. Hamilton, *American Treasure and the Price Revolution in Spain, 1501–1650,* and *Money, Prices, and Wages in Valencia, Aragon, and Navarre, 1351–1500;* J. E. T. Rogers, *Six Centuries of Work and Wages,* chap. XIV; Alexander Del Mar, *A History of the Precious Metals from the Earliest Times to the Present,* and *A History of Money in Ancient Countries from the Earliest Times to the Present.*

Chapter V

1. The mediocrity of the average man is described by Buckle in these words: "An immense majority of men must always remain in a middle state, neither very foolish nor very able, neither very virtuous nor very vicious, but slumbering on in a peaceful and decent mediocrity, adopting without much difficulty the current opinions of the day, making no inquiry, exciting no scandal, causing no wonder, just holding themselves on a level with their generation, and noiselessly conforming to the standard of morals and of knowledge common to the age and country in which they live." H. T. Buckle, *History of Civilization in England,* vol. I, pp. 128–29.

2. Buckle said, "There is, unquestionably, nothing to be found in the world which has undergone so little change as those great dogmas of which moral systems are composed," while "in reference to the conduct of our intellect, the moderns have not only made the most important additions to every department of knowledge that the ancients ever attempted to study, but besides this, they have upset and revolutionized the old methods of inquiry." Hence, Buckle held, progress must be manifested in the changing factor, intellect, and not in the constant factor, morals. H. T. Buckle, *History of Civilization in England,* vol. I, pp. 129–30. See also, J. B. Bury, *The Idea of Progress.*

3. Clarence Day in *This Simian World* discusses in humorous and penetrating fashion what would have been the nature of the world if an animal not of the simian family had evolved into a civilized creature. He describes the sort of world that the industrious bees and ants might have built, magnificent in its physical structures but given over wholly to soul-withering work. Similarly, the cats, pigs, goats, elephants, and eagles come in for appraisal, each being found to have some characteristics more desirable than man, but greater drawbacks too.

4. Becquerel, for instance, is said to have stumbled upon the discovery of radio-activity when he found that uranium salts, with which he had been working, were affecting photographic plates protected in an opaque case. A pure accident. For a wealth of similar instances, see D. B. Hammond, *Stories of Scientific Discovery,* and many recent popular works on the history of science.

6. "The cortex of a man is twice as massive as that of an ape of equal body weight. Anatomically, the cerebral cortex is by far the most distinctive human characteristic. . . . Man is a mammal and his brain in all respects but one is essentially similar to that of an ape. But the association centers of his cortex are magnified and in internal texture complicated in measure commensurate with enlarged and glorified mental powers." C. J. Herrick, *Brains of Rats and Men,* pp. 68, 70.

7. Carl Van Doren, *Benjamin Franklin*, pp. 104–5, 117.

8. J. W. Draper, *A History of the Intellectual Development of Europe*.

9. For a more sympathetic view of Columbus, see the article by Professor S. E. Morison in the *New York Times Magazine*, Oct. 9, 1938.

10. J. J. Fahie, *Galileo, His Life and Work*.

11. Professor Ogburn's list of inventions and discoveries made almost simultaneously by two or more investigators covers thirteen pages. Among them are the following: In astronomy, Adams and Leverrier both discovered the planet Neptune in 1845; in mathematics, logarithms were discovered by Bürgi in 1620, by Napier-Briggs in 1614, the calculus was discovered by Newton in 1671, by Leibnitz in 1676; in chemistry, oxygen was discovered by Scheele in 1774, by Priestley in the same year; in the field of electricity, the telegraph was invented by Henry in 1831, by Morse, by Cooke-Wheatstone, and by Steinheil in 1837; the telephone was invented in 1876 by both Bell and Gray. W. F. Ogburn, *Social Change, with Respect to Cultural and Original Nature*, pp. 90–102.

12. Henry Clews, *Fifty Years in Wall Street*, chaps. XIII, XV, and XXXIV; and A. D. H. Smith, *Commodore Vanderbilt, an Epic of American Achievement*.

13. Consult Richard Ehrenberg, *Das Zeitalter der Fugger*, part of which has been translated as *Capital and Finance in the Age of the Renaissance*.

14. Adam Smith, *The Wealth of Nations*, Book I, chap. I. See also, chap. III, note 16, ibid.

15. In *Inventors and Money-Makers*, Professor Taussig makes much of the point that inventors are seldom money-makers, that they need a business partner to keep them working profitably and to dispose of their products advantageously. Regarding Watt and Boulton and Professor Taussig's view of their business relations, see *Inventors and Money-Makers*, pp. 34–35.

16. W. Ridgeway, *Origin of Currency and Weight Standards*, chap. IV on ancient trade routes; M. P. Charlesworth, *Trade Routes and Commerce of the Roman Empire*; and A. H. Lybyer, "The Ottoman Turks and the Routes of Oriental Trade," *English Historical Review*, vol. XXX, 1915, pp. 577–88.

17. E. J. Hamilton, *American Treasure and the Price Revolution in Spain, 1501–1650; Money, Prices, and Wages in Valencia, Aragon, and Navarre, 1351–1500*. See also the following papers by Professor Hamilton: "American Treasure and Andalusian Prices, 1503–1660," *Journal of Economic and Business History*, Nov., 1928; "American Treasure and the Rise of Capitalism, 1500–1700," *Economica*, Nov., 1929; "Imports of American Gold and Silver into Spain, 1503–1660," *Quarterly Journal of Economics*, May, 1929; "Wages and Subsistence on Spanish Treasure Ships, 1503–1660," *Journal of Political Economy*, Aug., 1929.

18. A short history of gold production is available in K. Helfferich, *Money*, chap. III (Infield translation). Tooke and Newmarch, *The History of Prices*, Part VII, gives a discussion of mining operations in California and Australia. The best account of gold mining in South Africa is found in W. J. Busschau, *The Theory of the Gold Supply, with Special Reference to the Problems of the Witwatersrand*. See also, J. Kitchen, "Gold Production," in *The International Gold Problem: Collected Papers*; L. D. Edie, *Gold Production and Prices before and after the World War*; and C. O. Hardy, *Is There Enough Gold?* J. C. Stamp, *Papers on Gold and the Price Level*.

19. The King's minister was Malestroit, and his pamphlet was entitled *Paradoxes Concerning the Dearness of All Things*. Jean Bodin's *Response to the Paradoxes of M. de Malestroit* was published in 1568. It is reprinted in Professor A. E. Monroe's *Early Economic Thought*.

CHAPTER VI

1. This is not precisely an economic interpretation of history, although it includes much of that philosophy. See E. R. A. Seligman, *The Economic Interpreta-*

tion of History. Contrast the view presented here with such statements as that of E. A. Freeman, the English historian, that "history is past politics, and politics is present history;" and of P. V. N. Myers, the American historian, who regarded history as past ethics.

2. "Insecurity of person and property," wrote John Stuart Mill in explaining the important and justifiable work of the government, "means uncertainty whether they who sow shall reap, whether they who produce shall consume, and they who spare today shall enjoy tomorrow. It means not only that labour and frugality are not the road of acquisition, but that violence is." J. S. Mill, *Principles of Political Economy*, p. 881, Ashley edition. *Cf.* what Adam Smith said on the necessity of protecting property, *The Wealth of Nations*, Book V, chap. I, part II. The classical economists while recognizing the necessity of protecting life and property, emphasized at the same time the danger of paternalism.

3. The gifts of the Rockefellers to education and to science are too numerous to record in detail. The most notable of these gifts are the Rockefeller Foundation, the General Education Board, and the University of Chicago. Andrew Carnegie endowed the Carnegie Foundation, the Carnegie Institute, and innumerable libraries. The Vanderbilts endowed Vanderbilt University, and have made contributions to Harvard, Yale, and Columbia. The Armour Institute of Northwestern University is the gift of the Armours.

4. Thomas Jefferson and his age were the heirs to the philosophy of the Physiocrats, a French school of economists. This group, led by Quesnay and Turgot, flourished in the second half of the eighteenth century. While their elaborate attempt to demonstrate that agriculture was the source of wealth may be regarded as a complete failure, their basic economic philosophy has remained a permanent contribution to economic thought. The physiocrats were naturalists, or mechanists. The world to them was an orderly place, governed by immutable, natural law; the art of the legislator was to interpret this law, but not necessarily to implement natural law with what Quesnay called "positive law." The physiocrats regarded the realm of government regulation as restricted in extreme degree, and the best rule of thumb for the government is the physiocratic principle "laissez-faire, laissez passer."

5. Oswald Spengler's *Decline of the West* is probably the best known and the most scholarly of these pessimistic works of recent times. But Spengler is not alone, for the view that Western civilization is decadent has been widely held, and has been particularly common in Germany. The view that society is an organism rather than a mechanism, that it grows, matures, and decays, is found in Hegel, Nietzsche, and Schopenhauer.

6. Iron ore cannot be smelted with coal, since the sulphur released in combustion deteriorates the iron, making it brittle and completely unmalleable. This characteristic necessitated using charcoal, a practice which deforested much of England, and stopped the growth of the English iron manufacturing industry by 1600. Significant that at this date Russia was producing more iron ore than England. The use of coal suggested itself early, and many attempts were made to perfect a coal-using process. In 1619, one Dud Dudley is said to have produced "good merchantable iron" from coal, but being a Royalist he lost his patents and his fortune with the beheading of Charles I and failed to regain them from Charles II. The final discovery was made by Abraham Darby, a Quaker, a manufacturer of cast iron pots. His process was the "coking" or cindering of coal to remove the sulphur. Darby's son, also named Abraham Darby, took over the Coalbrookdale works in 1730 and made many significant improvements. Consult T. S. Ashton, *Iron and Steel in the Industrial Revolution*, and P. Mantoux, *The Industrial Revolution in the Eighteenth Century*.

7. Professor Usher states that the original Newcomen engine consumed 20 pounds of coal per hour per horsepower. With Smeaton's improvements the Newcomen engine consumed 15.87 pounds. Watt's engine in 1780 burned from 6.3 to 8.4.

Compare these figures with the coal consumption of engines in use in 1929. At that time a good reciprocating engine consumed 1.9 pounds of coal per hour per horsepower, and a steam turbine about .96 pounds. Thus a 1929 turbine was more than twenty times as efficient as a Newcomen engine and nearly ten times as efficient as Watt's. It should be noted, of course, that further improvements have been made in the last ten years. A. P. Usher, *A History of Mechanical Inventions*, pp. 362–363.

8. An interesting and authoritative account of the development of oil, electric, and gasoline engines is found in a volume by two members of the faculty of Massachusetts Institute of Technology, E. Hodgins, and F. A. Magoun, *Behemoth, the Story of Power*.

9. The fifteenth census, 1930, reports nearly fifty million persons gainfully employed, with ten millions listed as in agriculture. With this one-fifth, there was a mounting surplus of agricultural production. It should be added that many farmers are not employed full time, but partly supplement their work with industrial jobs during the winter.

10. The fundamental concept of Malthusianism is found in the Old Testament: "When goods are increased, they are increased that eat them." *Ecclesiastes*, 5, 11. A half century before Malthus, Benjamin Franklin gave this statement of the principles of population: "There is, in short, no bound to the prolific nature of plants or animals but what is made by their crowding and interfering with each other's means of subsistence. . . . Thus there are supposed to be now upwards of one million English souls in North America (though 'tis thought scarce 80,000 have been brought over sea), and yet perhaps there is no one fewer in Britain, but rather many more, on account of the employment the colonies afforded to manufactures at home. This million, doubling suppose but once in twenty-five years, will in another century be more than the people of England, and the greatest number of Englishmen will be on this side the water." *Observations Concerning the Increase of Mankind, Peopling of Countries, etc.* Adam Smith, in discussing the high rate of wages in the American colonies, also pointed out the rapidity with which the people multiply: "they double in twenty or twenty-five years." *The Wealth of Nations*, Book I, chap. VIII.

11. For an account of the life and work of Malthus, see J. M. Keynes, *Essays in Biography*, Part II, chap. I; and James Bonar, *Malthus and His Work*.

12. The rapid rise in population during the late eighteenth and early nineteenth century, and the decline in the rate of growth since 1860, have vitiated many forecasts of future population. Gregory King in his *Natural and Political Observations and Conclusions upon the State and Condition of England*, predicted in 1696: "In all probability the next doubling of the people in England will be in about six hundred years to come, or by the year of our Lord 2300, at which time it will have eleven millions of people. . . . The next doubling after that will not be, in all probability, in less than twelve or thirteen hundred years, or by the year of our Lord 3500 or 3600. At which time the Kingdom will have 22 millions of souls . . . in case the world should last so long." King was the optimist of his time, for contemporary pamphleteers stated that the population was declining and predicted a further fall. Actually, the population of England increased eight-fold in the less than 250 years since King made his prediction. Americans, however, seeing the rapid growth of population, have been inclined to overestimate the future population of the United States. In 1815 Elkanah Watson estimated the decennial population that would be found in this country from 1820 to 1900. Through 1860 his error was less than 1 per cent, but it became progressively greater and by 1900 the error was 30 per cent. DeBow, superintendent of the seventh census, followed Watson's predictions closely and overestimated the 1900 population of the United States to the same extent.

13. See my paper, "On the Structure and Inertia of Prices," *American Economic Review*, June, 1934.

14. E. A. Hooton, *Apes, Men, and Morons;* J. Ortega y Gasset, *The Revolt of the Masses;* W. Rathenau, *The New Society.*

15. The story of John Winthrop and other early American chemical manufacturers is told in W. Haynes, *Men, Money, and Molecules,* chap. IV.

16. Tyndall wrote: "Nourished by knowledge patiently won; bounded and conditioned by co-operant Reason; imagination becomes the prime mover of the physical discoverer." J. Tyndall, *Fragments of Science,* chap. IV. Tyndall realized that without imagination science would deteriorate to mere description.

Chapter VII

1. Alexandria was founded in 332 B.C. by Alexander the Great, and under his successors it became the most important commercial city of the world, as well as the center of culture and scholarship. The Ptolemies were city-builders of imagination, and ambitious patrons of the arts. They built a museum, a "home of the muses," to which the best of the Athenian scholars were attracted. The Alexandrian scholars were chiefly grammarians, writing textual criticisms of the Greek poets. They were also mathematicians and anatomists; and some scholars hold that chemistry had its origin in the work of the Alexandrian Anaximenes. By 30 B.C. the school had degenerated into a group of mystical theological speculators. Consult, Sandys, *History of Scholarship,* vol. I.

2. The subtle distinctions involved in the definition of capital are elaborately considered by E. von Böhm-Bawerk, *Capital and Interest,* and Irving Fisher, *The Theory of Interest.*

3. See, W. R. Nelson, "Boulder Canyon Project," *Annual Report of the Board of Regents of the Smithsonian Institution,* 1935. For a description of the Colorado River aqueduct project, see A. R. Boone, "Billion Gallons a Day," *Scientific American,* Jan., 1939.

4. One point on which I agree with the new Keynsian economics is this necessity of growth—new investment—to keep the economic system fully employed and progressing. But I regard the provision of an adequate capital supply through savings as a necessary condition for growth and progress.

5. Carl Snyder, "The Capital Supply and National Well Being," *American Economic Review,* June, 1936. This is shown by the fact that wages have tended to be a fairly constant proportion of the national income. Income distributed to the owners of business enterprises seems also to bear a constant relationship to the national income. This is true in periods of prosperity and depression. Cf. E. M. Bernstein, "Wage-Rates, Investment, and Employment," *Journal of Political Economy,* April, 1939, p. 223.

6. In 1805 the cost of land carriage was about fifty cents per ton mile. At this period corn sold for about thirty-five cents a bushel, and could not, therefore, be transported as far as twenty-five miles. Similarly, the radius of wheat transportation was between fifty and seventy-five miles. I. Lippincott, "Pioneer Industry in the West," *Journal of Political Economy,* April, 1920.

7. The physiocrats held precisely the opposite view: that agriculture alone could produce what they called a *produit net,* and that agriculture is more favorable to the accumulation of wealth than any other form of economic activity. Adam Smith was under the influence of this school when he wrote: "It is thus that through the great part of Europe the commerce and manufactures of cities, instead of being the effect, have been the cause and occasion of the improvement and cultivation of the country. This order, however, being contrary to the natural course of things, is necessarily both slow and uncertain. Compare the slow progress of those European countries of which the wealth depends very much upon their commerce and manufactures, with the rapid advances of our North American colonies, of which the wealth is founded altogether in agriculture." *Wealth of Nations,* Book III, chap. IV.

Malthus, on the other hand, recognized clearly the relationship between commerce and manufactures and the wealth of a nation. In his *Principles*, he said: ". . . in all rich manufacturing and commercial countries, the value of manufactured and commercial products bears a very high proportion to the raw products; whereas, in comparatively poor countries, without much internal trade and foreign commerce, the value of their raw produce constitutes almost the whole of their wealth." T. R. Malthus, *Principles of Political Economy*, p. 171.

8. The census of 1930 shows that the total value of machinery and farm implements on the more than six million farms was only $2,700,000,000, about $450 per farm, and about $375 per farm worker for the more than seven million full-time farm workers.

9. In 1930 the average compensation per active employee for all manufacturing industries was $1,454, while the average compensation of farmers and farm laborers was only $759. Department of Commerce, *National Income in the United States, 1929–35*, pp. 68, 71, 115.

10. The Luddites, as the machine wreckers were known, took their name from "King Ludd," the pseudonym of their leader. Gathering at night in bands, the Luddites stormed factories, wrecking machinery. Real difficulties began in 1812, and in a mass trial in 1813 many were condemned to death or emigration, among them probably "King Ludd." Ernst Toller wrote a powerful drama on the subject, *The Machine Wreckers*.

11. The fear that perfection of mechanical means of production will result in unemployment goes back to the time in which man still worked with simple tools, using his own energy as a source of power. In the time of Queen Elizabeth a statute was enacted prohibiting the use of gig mills in finishing cloth, for fear that it would replace the hand cloth-finishers. And Elizabeth also refused a patent to William Lee, an Oxford fellow, for his knitting machine, on the ground that it would diminish the opportunity for employment. In the time of James I, the use of a machine for making needles was prohibited at the request of the men engaged in making needles by hand. And Charles I issued a proclamation against the use of brass buckles because "those who cast the brasse buckles can make more in one day than ten of those that make iron buckles can do." W. Cunningham, *Growth of English Commerce and Industry*, vol. II, p. 76.

12. *Cf.* P. H. Douglas, "Technological Unemployment," *American Federationist*, Aug., 1930.

13. "One may say that there is always—lying in stock as it were—any amount of technical possibilities in the way of substituting the use of capital for other factors of production. Every fall in the rate of interest will result in the setting free of a part of these possibilities and the conversion of them into actualities; and thereby a further fall will be prevented. If in this process the stock occasionally shrinks, it is abundantly compensated for by the continual addition of new possibilities, consequent upon technical progress." G. Cassel, *The Nature and Necessity of Interest*, p. 123. See also Chapter XXV of this volume.

14. *Cf.* D. H. Robertson, *Banking Policy and the Price Level*, pp. 11, 21; and J. A. Schumpeter, *The Theory of Economic Development*.

Chapter VIII

1. Sismondi, Rodbertus, and Marx are the most important in this group. Their views are considered in section 4 of this chapter.

2. Benjamin Franklin, *Hints to Those that Would Be Rich*.

3. Franklin was an untiring advocate of thrift. "The way to wealth, if you desire it," he wrote, "is as plain as the way to market. It depends chiefly on two words, industry and frugality." *Advice to a Young Tradesman*, 1748. See the resemblance of this advice to Smith's statement in *The Wealth of Nations* regarding parsimony and industry in the accumulation of capital.

4. Adam Smith, *The Wealth of Nations*, Book II, chap. III.

5. See my papers, "The Capital Supply and National Well Being," *American Economic Review*, June, 1936; "Measures of Industrial Growth and Their Significance," *Beiträge zur Konjunkturlehre*, edited by E. F. Wagemann; and "New Measures of Trade and of Economic Growth," *Revue de l'Institut International de Statistique*, vol. I, No. 4, 1933.

6. W. I. King has made estimates of net savings in the United States from 1909 to 1918. See his paper "The Net Volume of Savings in the United States," *Journal of the American Statistical Association*, Dec., 1922. Other estimates made by Professor King are available in *The Wealth and Income of the People of the United States*, p. 132, and his estimates of corporate savings are to be found in *The National Income and Its Purchasing Power*, p. 280. Clark Warburton estimates the sum of gross savings available for the purchase of capital items in 1929 at 18.7 billion dollars. I am inclined to believe that the estimate is too high. *Cf.* National Bureau of Economic Research, *Studies in Income and Wealth*, vol. I, p. 109. See also, Clark Warburton, "The Trend of Savings, 1900–1929," *Journal of Political Economy*, Feb., 1935. As to the destination of our national savings, see the admirable work of the Bureau of Economic Research, University of Notre Dame, *A Study of the Physical Assets, Sometimes Called Wealth, of the United States*, 1922–1923.

7. "About 2.3 per cent of all families—those with incomes in excess of $10,000—contributed two-thirds of the entire savings of all families. At the bottom of the scale 59 per cent of the families contributed only about 1.6 per cent of the total savings. Approximately 60,000 families at the top of the income scale, with incomes of more than $50,000 per year, saved almost as much as the 25 million families (91 per cent of the total) having incomes from zero to $5,000." M. Leven, H. G. Moulton, and Clark Warburton, *America's Capacity to Consume*, p. 94.

8. Although many corporations do induce their employees to buy stock, offering very attractive terms for the purchase, the fact is that by and large American workers do not own stock in the corporations that employ them. This is in sharp contrast to the view of Professor T. N. Carver as stated in *The Present Economic Revolution in the United States*.

9. U. S. Treasury Department, *Statistics of Income for 1929*.

10. National Association of Underwriters, *The March Through Life*. Federal Trade Commission, *National Wealth and Income*, p. 58.

11. Sismondi wrote: "By an inherent contradiction in modern economic conditions, while their great wealth push the wealthy to build vast factories, their riches also exclude the products of these very great factories from the consumption of the rich. Those who receive the selling price of the merchandise, those who benefit from fabrication, are not the same as those who consume them. The production thus goes on accumulating while consumption is restrained." Sismondi, *Nouveaux Principes d'Economie Politique*, vol. I, p. 361 (cited by H. L. McCracken, *Value Theory and Business Cycles*, 2nd edition, p. 26). Marx wrote: "The last cause of all real crises always remains the poverty and restricted consumption of the masses as compared to the tendency of capitalist production to develop the productive forces in such a way, that only the absolute power of consumption of the entire society would be their limit." K. Marx, *Capital*, vol. III (Kerr edition), p. 568.

12. K. Rodbertus, *Overproduction and Crises*, pp. 51, 53.

13. The new group under Keynes carries this dogma much further, for they hold that an attempt to save more of the national income will induce business men to restrict investment, because with less consumption business will be unprofitable and business men will refuse to invest. A corollary to this proposition is that if people spend more investment will be increased. However, even this proposition is not held to be universally true. Joan Robinson, a disciple of Keynes, writes: "If we were to imagine a Nineteenth Century that conducted itself according to the precepts of Mr. Keynes, so that thriftiness was actively discouraged, while full employment was always maintained, and contrast it with the Nineteenth Century

which received the blessing of the classical economists, there can be little doubt that, although the level of employment would have been higher, the accumulation of capital would have been very much less in Mr. Keynes' Nineteenth Century than in the Nineteenth Century which actually came to pass." *Essays in the Theory of Employment*, p. 59.

14. The earlier economists understood this quite well as may be seen from their distinction between "productive and unproductive consumption," a concept found in the writings of many classical economists. Cf. Adam Smith, *The Wealth of Nations*, Book II, chap. III; T. R. Malthus, *Principles of Political Economy*, pp. 29 ff; Nassau Senior, *Industrial Efficiency and Social Economy*, vol. I, pp. 135–42; J. R. MacCulloch, *Principles of Political Economy*, p. 411; Tooke and Newmarch, *History of Prices*, vol. I, chap. III. The fallacy that saving reduces demand is most effectively refuted by J. S. Mill, who states that a demand for commodities of a particular type affects the direction in which labor is employed, but does not increase the volume of employment. J. S. Mill, *Principles of Political Economy*, pp. 79, 87 (Ashley edition).

15. Alfred Marshall, *Principles of Economics*, pp. 222–23.

CHAPTER IX

1. "Possessing utility, commodities derive their exchangeable value from two sources, from their scarcity, and from the quantity of labour required to obtain them." David Ricardo, *Principles of Political Economy and Taxation*, chap. I. Similarly, Marx, who borrowed heavily from Ricardo, wrote: ". . . that which determines the magnitude of the value of any article is the amount of labour socially necessary . . . for its production." Karl Marx, *Capital* (Kerr edition). Ricardo, of course, hedged considerably on the labor theory of value, limiting its universality to "the early stages of society," and then stating that value depends "almost exclusively" on embodied labor. Ricardo realized that the use of capital and the necessity of profits prevented labor from being the source or measure of value. Ricardo did say that "in every state of society, the tools, implements, buildings, and machinery employed in different trades may be of various degrees of durability. . . . This difference . . . introduces another cause, besides the greater or less quantity of labour necessary to produce commodities, for the variations in their relative values."

2. Although not in direct proportion to the size of the business. Cf. Alfred Marshall, *Principles of Economics*, pp. 613–14.

3. An interesting statistical analysis based upon the figures of the Securities and Exchange Commission demonstrates a high degree of correlation between the per cent profit of business and the salary of the highest paid executive. See B. T. Beckwith, "The Relation of Top Salaries and the Profits of Manufacturing Companies," *Southern Economic Journal*, October, 1939, and J. C. Baker, "Executive Compensation Payments by Large and Small Industrial Companies," *Quarterly Journal of Economics*, May, 1939.

4. "Profits," said Walker, "are the creation of the business men that receive them. This surplus, in the case of any employer, represents that which he is able to produce over and above what an employer of the lowest industrial grade can produce with equal amounts of labor and capital. In other words, this surplus is of his own creation, produced wholly by that business ability which raises him above and distinguishes him from, the employers of what may be called the no-profits class." F. A. Walker, "The Source of Business Profits," *Quarterly Journal of Economics*, April, 1887.

5. Max Eastman, "The End of Socialism in Russia," *Harper's Magazine*, Feb., 1937.

6. Even the wage incentive, which unions have often opposed in this country, has been introduced in Russia. This ancient device to stimulate efficient workers

has been introduced in Russia under the name of Stakhanovism. There is an All-Union Stakhanovist Conference, which probably discusses much the same questions as the Taylor Society in this country. The conference first met from November 17 to 23, 1935.

7. The doctrine of surplus value, derived from Rodbertus, is older than Marx. But even before Rodbertus, Sismondi had used the term *vaux mieux* in much the same sense as Marx later used 'surplus value.' In England there was a large group of literary liberals—Ravenstone, Gray, William Thompson, Hodgskin, Robert Owen, and others—who believed that any income going to persons other than laborers was an unjust deduction from wages. On the continent, Saint-Simon and Proudhon held that property was the right to enjoy the fruits of labor without working. These men differ from Sismondi, Rodbertus, and Marx in that the latter relate the doctrine of surplus value to a theory of economic value. In recent times, ingenious applications of similar concepts have been developed by Franz Oppenheimer and John A. Hobson.

8. "Ten Years of Steel," Extension of the Remarks of Myron C. Taylor at the Annual Meeting of Stockholders of the United States Steel Corporation, April 4, 1938, p. 48.

9. English history abounds with laws such as that of the 25th, Henry VIII: "Forasmuch as divers and sundry of the king's subjects of this realm, to whom God of his goodness hath disposed great plenty and abundance of moveable substance, now of late within few years have daily studied, practised and invented ways and means how they might accumulate and gather together into few hands as well, great multitude of farms, as great plenty of cattle, and in especial sheep . . . but have also raised and enhanced the prices of all manner of corn, cattle, wool, pigs, geese, hens, chickens, eggs and such other almost double above the prices which hath been accustomed . . . it may therefore please the King's Highness of his most gracious and godly disposition, and the Lords Spiritual and Temporal of their goodness and charity, with the assent of the Commons in this present parliament assembled, to ordain and enact . . . that no person or persons from the feast of St. Michael the Archangel which shall be in the year of our Lord God 1535 shall keep, occupy or have in his possession in his own proper lands . . . above the number of 2,000 sheep." For many such laws see A. E. Bland, P. A. Brown, and R. H. Tawney, *English Economic History: Select Documents*.

10. Adam Smith pointed out that in Holland, the wealthiest country of his day, profits and interest were low. "The province of Holland, on the other hand, in proportion to the extent of its territory and the number of its people, is a richer country than England. The government there borrows at two per cent., and private people of good credit at three." *The Wealth of Nations*, Book I, chap. III.

11. John Stuart Mill accounted for the accumulation of capital at low rates of interest in England in this manner: "There are many circumstances, which, in England, give a peculiar force to the accumulating propensity. The long exemption of the country from the ravages of war, and the far earlier period than elsewhere at which property was secure from military violence or arbitrary spoliation. . . Much also depended on the better political institutions of this country, which by the scope they have allowed to individual freedom of action, have encouraged personal activity and self-reliance, while by the liberty they confer of association and combination, they facilitate industrial enterprise on a large-scale." *Principles of Political Economy*, pp. 173-75 (Ashley edition).

12. Walker believed firmly that it was better to give business men somewhat excessive profits rather than to risk giving them insufficient ones. While agreeing that high profits might lead to reckless investment, he added: "But it clearly does follow from the fact that the sole initiative in industry resides in the employing class, that it is exceedingly important that profits should be kept up to the point to encourage the largest production which can be maintained without repletion." F. A. Walker, *Money and Its Relation to Trade and Industry*, p. 91.

13. See chap. VII, sect. 5.

14. The steadiness of the rate of interest has been noted by many economists. Professor Taussig states: "The steadiness of the rate of interest during the vast changes since the industrial revolution of the eighteenth century is a remarkable phenomenon. . . . The trend of this rate . . . in view of the extraordinary increase alike in the demand for capital and in the supply of capital, has been remarkably even." *Principles of Economics,* vol. II, pp. 30–31 (3rd edition). Professor Cannan in a lecture given to the staff of the Bank of England made a similar observation. "When you think of these great contending forces, increase of capital struggling against increase of population, and the invention of elaborate machinery struggling against the invention of simplificatory devices, and remember that the first of these two struggles may be going one way while the second is going the other way, you will not find it extraordinary that the rate of interest is as stable as it is, whether you think of thousands of years or of the few years which you have known." Edwin Cannan, *An Economist's Protest,* p. 292. For the behavior of the interest rate in the United States, see F. R. Macaulay, *Some Theoretical Problems Suggested by the Movements of Interest Rates, Bond Yields and Stock Prices in the United States since 1856.*

15. "The margin of profit in ordinary business is so small that a reduction in profits . . . cannot fail to tell heavily upon the vitality of the commercial and industrial system." F. A. Walker, "The Relation of Changes in the Volume of Currency to Prosperity," American Economic Association, *Economic Studies,* 1896.

CHAPTER X

1. For a discussion of wage theories, see J. R. Hicks, *The Theory of Wages;* P. H. Douglas, *The Theory of Wages;* M. Dobb, *Wages;* and H. A. Millis and R. E. Montgomery, *Labor's Progress and Some Basic Labor Problems,* chap. IV.

2. That wages are nothing more nor less than the product of labor was the famous wage theory of Francis A. Walker, so simple and obvious that once it was expounded it became, as Taussig points out, the almost universal theory taught in class rooms and text books. Laborers are hired, Walker argued, because business men know they are productive, and their productivity will determine how much business men can afford to pay. F. A. Walker, *The Wages Question,* chaps. VIII and IX. Unfortunately, Walker denied that the product per worker is determined by the capital used in industry. On this question there were no statistical data available; and although Cairnes in his restatement of the wages fund stressed the relationship between product and capital, Walker was not convinced. See F. W. Taussig, *Wages and Capital;* Alfred Marshall, *Principles of Economics,* Appendix J; J. E. Cairnes, *Some Leading Principles of Political Economy,* Part II, chap. I.

3. Although the process by which excessively high wages will diminish employment is in dispute among economists, there is general agreement that this result will follow. Given the quantity and velocity of money, there can be only one rate of wages that will permit full employment of labor. This is the view implicit in Newcomb's concept of the societary circulation. See S. Newcomb, *Principles of Economics,* Book IV. From the productivity side, a high rate of wages induces business men to diminish the employment of labor up to the point at which high wages are equalled by high product per worker. This is the theory of J. B. Clark, *The Distribution of Wealth,* and E. von Böhm-Bawerk, *The Positive Theory of Capital.* Finally, emphasis has recently been given on the effect of a high level of wages on the need for money to finance the wages bill, and the consequent rise in interest rates and diminution in investment and employment. This view offered by J. M. Keynes in *The General Theory of Employment, Interest, and Money,* bears a faint resemblance to Newcomb's view.

5. Adam Smith, *The Wealth of Nations,* Book I, chap. VIII.

6. The extent of manufactures in Colonial America has been a moot question. The colonists, as Franklin said, "puffed" accounts, while the governors in their

reports to the home country deprecated colonial achievement lest they lose their places for having permitted competitors of English manufacturers to arise in the colonies. Victor S. Clark quotes with approval from a letter of Comptroller Weare to the president of the Board of Trade: "Upon actual knowledge, therefore, of these northern colonies, one is surprised to find that, notwithstanding the indifference of their wool and the extravagant price of labor, the planters throughout all New England, New York, the Jersies, Pennsylvania, Maryland (for south of that province no knowledge is here pretended) almost entirely clothed themselves in their own woolens, and that generally the people are sliding into manufactures proper to the mother country." V. S. Clark, *History of Manufactures in the United States,* vol. I, p. 213.

7. Adam Smith noted: "But though North America is not yet so rich as England, it is much more thriving, and advancing with much greater rapidity to the further acquisition of riches. . . . Notwithstanding the great increase [in population] occasioned by such early marriages, there is a continual complaint of the scarcity of hands in North America. The demand for labourers, the funds destined for maintaining them, increase, it seems, still faster than they can find labourers to employ." *The Wealth of Nations,* Book I, chap. VIII.

8. On this point see my papers, "The Capital Supply and National Well Being," *American Economic Review,* June, 1936; "Measures of Industrial Growth and Their Significance," *Beiträge zur Konjunkturlehre,* edited by E. F. Wagemann.

9. The old axiom that if the worker will not seek his interest, his interest will seek him, had in it much truth. It is certainly nearer the truth than the view that wages are the result of the relative economic strength of labor and business.

10. This is the official position of the socialist economists. Marx himself very clearly stated this view: "The last cause of all real crises always remains the poverty and restricted consumption of the masses as compared to the tendency of capitalist production to develop the productive forces in such a way, that only the absolute power of consumption of the entire society would be their limit." Karl Marx, *Capital,* vol. III, Part V, chap. XXX.

11. Differences in wages are of two types: compensating and non-compensating. On "inequalities arising from the nature of the employments," see Adam Smith, *The Wealth of Nations,* Book I, chap. X, Part I. J. S. Mill has an excellent discussion of "the differences of wages in different employments," in his *Principles of Political Economy,* Book II, chap. XIV. For an analysis of non-compensating differences in wages in our economic system, see F. W. Taussig, *Principles of Economics,* 3rd edition, vol. II, pp. 141–44. Smith said of the differences in wages that have persisted: "The proportion between the different rates . . . of wages . . . in the different employments of labour . . . , seems not to be much affected, as has already been observed, by the riches or poverty, the advancing, stationary, or declining state of the society. Such revolutions in the public welfare, though they affect the general rates . . . of wages . . . , must in the end affect them equally in all different employments." *The Wealth of Nations,* Book I, chap. X, Part II.

12. For example, unions propagate the "lump of labor" fallacy, the notion that the amount of work to be done is a fixed amount, for which a "lump" of so many man-hours is required. It follows from this that the cure for many of labor's troubles is shorter hours. Hence, Samuel Gompers declared in 1887: "So long as there is one man who seeks employment and cannot find it the hours of labor are too long." It is this same error that lies behind the practice of stretching the work and similar tactics; and it has led to labor opposition to innovations and scientific management.

13. No one knows the economic cost of strikes, but a rough measure of the direct loss in income can be attempted. According to the *Monthly Labor Review,* more than 28 million man-days of employment were lost by strikers. During the same year, the average wage of industrial workers, as reported by the Department of Labor, was about $.65 per hour. On this basis approximately $150,000,000 was lost

in wages. But this sum is not the total direct cost of the strikes. When laborers strike, machines are idle, and the value that these machines might have added to the product is likewise lost. Allowing one-half the wage loss for other income than wages, the direct loss in incomes due to strikes was approximately $225,000,000 in 1937. But there were indirect losses, too, losses suffered by the producers of raw materials, and losses suffered by the users of the goods produced by the strikers. Beyond these losses, some allowance must be made for the destruction and the costs of protection of property during strikes.

14. Ferdinand Lassalle (1825–64) applied the term to a subsistence rate of wages. The iron law of wages, *ehernes Lohn Gesetz*, was stated by Lassalle as follows: "Under the domination of supply and demand the average wages of labor remain always reduced to the bare subsistence which, according to the standard of living of a nation, is necessary for maintenance and reproduction." The name was originated by Lassalle, but the law itself is to be found in Turgot, Ricardo, and others.

CHAPTER XI

1. For a history of depressions in the United States, see Carroll D. Wright, *Industrial Depressions*, First Annual Report of the Commissioner of Labor; O. M. W. Sprague, *History of Crises under the National Banking System;* W. Thorp and W. C. Mitchell, *Business Annals;* W. B. Smith and A. H. Cole, *Fluctuations in American Business, 1790–1860;* O. C. Lightner, *The History of Business Depressions;* C. A. Wardwell, *An Investigation of Economic Data for Major Cycles.* For histories of some of the more severe crises and depressions, see R. C. McGrane, *The Panic of 1837; Some Financial Problems of the Jackson Era;* J. McCulloch, "Crisis in the American Trade," *Edinburgh Review,* July, 1837; Ira Ryner, *On the Crises of 1837, 1847, 1857, in England, France, and the United States: An Analysis and Comparison;* E. R. McCartney, *Crisis of 1873;* D. A. Wells, "The Great Depression of Trade," *Contemporary Review,* Aug. and Sept., 1887; W. J. Lauck, *The Causes of the Panic of 1893;* A. H. Hanson, *Cycles of Prosperity and Depression in the United States, Great Britain, and Germany; a Study of Monthly Data, 1902–1908;* W. C. Schluter, *The Pre-war Business Cycle, 1907–1914;* C. C. Jackson, *Six Industrial Crises.* For the great depression, see chapter XII, note 5.

2. At a "Conference on Cycles" in 1922, Dr. F. E. Clements offered the following definition as to the use of the term cycle: "It seems desirable to use *cycle* as the inclusive term for all recurrences that lend themselves to measurement, and period or periodicity for those with a definite time interval, recognizing, however, that there is no fixed line between the two." Cited by W. C. Mitchell, *Business Cycles: The Problem and Its Setting,* p. 377.

3. Professor Mitchell's works on business cycles include: *Business Cycles* (1913); *Business Cycles: The Problem and Its Setting* (1927); *Gold, Prices, and Wages under the Greenback Standard* (1908); *History of Prices during the War* (1919); *A History of the Greenbacks with Special Reference to the Economic Consequences of Their Issue* (1903); and *History of the Legal Tender Acts* (1903). Professor Mitchell's students and associates have made important contributions to business cycle research, particularly F. C. Mills, A. F. Burns, and S. Kuznets. For further reference on the study of cycles, see the masterly work of Joseph A. Schumpeter, *Business Cycles.*

4. See chapter XII, sections 2–4, below.

5. In an article, "Shall We Modify Our View of the Business Cycle?," *Administration,* May, 1923, the idea was expressed that the usual business cycle represented a fluctuation of production of 5 per cent above and below the line of trend, rather than the much larger percentages frequently stated. Very evident that "the amplitude of fluctuation of trade series increases generally according to their distance from the ultimate consumers"; therefore that "the fluctuations of trade are not nearly so large as was formerly supposed, when the only data available were production of a few basic commodities." See my paper, "The Index of the Volume of

Trade: Third Revision," *Journal of the American Statistical Association*, Dec., 1931.

6. In my index of the volume of trade, production is given a weight of 25, primary distribution 22, retail trade 24, and finance 8. The index also gives weight to a general series and bank debits outside New York. For a complete description of this index composed of 89 separate series, all adjusted for seasonal variation, for trend, and where necessary, for price changes, see Carl Snyder, *Business Cycles and Business Measurements*, chap. V, and my paper "A New Index of the Volume of Trade," *Journal of the American Statistical Association*, Dec., 1923, and subsequent revisions published in the same journal, September, 1925, June, 1928, and December, 1931.

7. My index of production and trade shows a decline of 40 per cent from 1929 to 1932. For the same period, the index of the Board of Governors of the Federal Reserve System declined 46 per cent, and the index of Standard Statistics declined 49. I believe that all indexes exaggerated the real amplitude of the depression. Professor Mitchell presents a number of interesting comparisons of the index of production and trade with the American Telephone and Telegraph Company's business index, Frickey's clearings index, and Persons' trade index. The comparison shows clearly that my index is subject to less fluctuation in prosperity and depression than the others. See, W. C. Mitchell, *Business Cycles: The Problem and Its Setting*, pp. 346–348.

8. Carl Snyder, *American Railways As Investments*, The Moody Corporation, 1907.

9. See Marcus Nadler and J. I. Bogen, *The Banking Crisis*.

10. Great Britain left the gold standard September 21, 1931. All the Empire except Canada and South Africa followed immediately. The Scandinavian countries suspended on September 21, and Finland on October 12. Japan and many other countries followed Great Britain's lead before the end of the year. By December, 1932, 44 countries, according to a report of the Department of Commerce, had abandoned gold. The United States did not leave the gold standard until April 20, 1933.

11. Carroll D. Wright, *Industrial Depressions*, First Annual Report of the Commissioner of Labor, pp. 61–63.

12. It has been shown with considerable probability that the prosperity phase of a business cycle is comparatively long when the secular trend of prices is upward, and conversely, that the depression phase is comparatively long when the secular trend of prices is downward. On this question, see W. L. Thorp, *Business Annals*, pp. 62–67, and W. C. Mitchell, *Business Cycles: The Problem and Its Setting*, pp. 410–11.

13. On the effect of money wages on employment, consult E. Cannan, "The Demand for Labour," *Economic Journal*, September, 1932; A. C. Pigou, "Real and Money Wage Rates in Relation to Unemployment," *Economic Journal*, September, 1937; and E. M. Bernstein, "Wage-Rates, Investment, and Employment," *Journal of Political Economy*, April, 1939.

14. The Harvard Graduate School of Business Administration has published an excellent study of *The Behavior of Consumption in Business Depression*, by Arthur R. Tebbutt (vol. XX, No. 6, August, 1933).

Chapter XII

1. William of Occam (1280–1349) was a medieval scholar, a member of the Franciscan order, and a precursor of the protestant revolt. An advocate of poverty, individual faith, and the independence of national states, he was accused of heresy and held prisoner for a short time at Avignon. For the details of his interesting life see, *Dictionary of National Biography*, XIV, pp. 802–7; *Encyclopedia of the Social Sciences*, XI, pp. 435–6; *Dictionary of Philosophy and Psychology*, II, p. 199; and

A. J. Little, *Grey Friars in Oxford*. A statement of his famous principle may be found in the *Dictionary of Philosophy and Psychology*, II, p. 264.

2. The literature of the "under and over" theories is voluminous. Over-production is the layman's explanation of depression. A statement of this theory may be found in T. R. Malthus, *Principles of Political Economy* (1820); J. C. L. S. de Sismondi, *Etudes sur l'Economie Politique* (1836). The distinction between over-production and over-saving is not made by Rodbertus, Marx, and many of the modern socialists. For over-saving theories in which emphasis is given to saving, see J. A. Hobson, *Economics of Unemployment;* J. M. Keynes, *A Treatise on Money,* and *The General Theory of Employment, Interest, and Money.* Under-consumption theories are in many respects similar to over-production and over-saving theories. Among these may be mentioned, W. T. Foster and W. Catchings, *Profits,* and *The Dilemma of Thrift;* C. H. Douglas, *Economic Democracy,* and *Social Credit;* and S. Gesell, *The Natural Economic Order.*

3. A list of the major crises, including some not regarded as of major significance by other writers, can be found in W. C. Mitchell, *Business Cycles: The Problem and Its Setting,* p. 387.

4. These characteristics have also been discussed above, chap. I, sect. 2; chap. III, sect. 2; chap. VIII, sect. 4.

5. R. G. Hawtrey gives strong emphasis to the monetary aspects of business cycles, and regards business cycles as purely a monetary phenomenon. He holds that "whatever other characteristics the trade cycle may have, it is, above all, a periodical fluctuation in productive activity and in the price level." And he adds that "the essential characteristic of the trade cycle is that maximum productive activity synchronizes with the maximum price level, and minimum productive activity with the minimum price level." R. G. Hawtrey, "The Monetary Theory of the Trade Cycle and Its Statistical Test," *Quarterly Journal of Economics,* May, 1927, pp. 472, 473. See also his *Currency and Credit,* and *The Economic Problem.*

6. For these data on department store inventories, and stocks of manufactured goods and raw materials, see the *Survey of Current Business,* 1932 Supplement, pp. 19, 51.

7. See my measurements of production growth, "The Capital Supply and National Well-Being," *American Economic Review,* June, 1936; "The Problem of Monetary and Economic Stability," *Quarterly Journal of Economics,* February, 1935; "New Measures of Trade and of Economic Growth," *Revue de l'Institut International de Statistique,* vol. I, No. 4, 1933; and "Growth of World Trade vs. Basic Production," *ibid.,* vol. II, No. 1, 1934. Note that Professor F. C. Mills does not share this view. He writes: "Between the depressions which bounded the decade of the 'twenties the rate of increase in the physical volume of production in the United States was clearly in excess of that which prevailed during the period of expansion prior to the World War. . . . (Pre-war and post-war rates of production growth, excluding construction, were, respectively, 3.1 per cent per year, and 3.8 per cent.) It is more conspicuously true if account be taken of the post-war retardation of population growth." F. C. Mills, *Economic Tendencies in the United States,* p. 530.

8. For a discussion of the great depression, see L. Robbins, *The Great Depression;* P. Einzig, *World Finance, 1914–1938,* part III; I. Fisher, *The Stock Market Crash and After;* G. Cassel, *The Crisis in the World's Monetary System;* and my article, "The World Wide Depression," *American Economic Review,* Supplement, 1931.

9. Marcus Nadler and J. I. Bogen, *The Banking Crisis.*

10. For an account of the crisis of 1907, see W. C. Schluter, *The Pre-War Business Cycle, 1907–1914;* A. H. Hanson, *Cycles of Prosperity and Depression in the United States, Great Britain, and Germany.*

11. Benjamin Strong, *Interpretations of Federal Reserve Policy in the Speeches and Writings of Benjamin Strong,* edited by W. Randolph Burgess.

12. On the German crisis, see L. Robbins, *The Great Depression,* chap. VI, and P. Einzig, *World Finance, 1914–1938,* chaps. XXVII and XLI.

13. On British monetary policy and experience since the suspension of the gold standard, see H. F. Fraser, *Great Britain and the Gold Standard;* and N. F. Hall, *The Exchange Equalization Account.* On England's earlier post-war policy, see S. E. Harris, *Monetary Problems of the British Empire.*

14. For a discussion of the depression of 1937 and its origins, see O. M. W. Sprague, "The Recovery Problem in the United States," *American Economic Review,* March, 1938; S. H. Slichter, "Must We Have Another Boom?," *Atlantic Monthly,* May, 1937, S. H. Slichter, "Risks, the Key to Recovery," *Nation,* March 12, 1938.

15. The manner in which public expenditure is supposed to lead to an expansion of income is discussed by J. M. Keynes, *The Means to Prosperity;* J. M. Clark, "Cumulative Effects of Changes in Aggregate Spending as Illustrated by Public Works," *American Economic Review,* March, 1935; A. D. Gayer, *Public Works in Prosperity and Depression,* chap. I.

16. The fall in bond prices in 1937 is strikingly revealed by the behavior of the Dow Jones index of prices of 10 industrial bonds, the index being given in the form of the per cent of par value of 4 per cent bonds. The index declined from 107.50 in January, 1937 to 97.21 in December, 1937.

17. In his *Principles of Political Economy,* Newcomb wrote: "The real trouble in such cases is that wages and prices are higher than they should be to correspond to the monetary flow. Were there any power which could by its own fiat diminish all prices ten per cent, that act would operate exactly like taking the load off a wheel when the driving force became insufficient to turn it. The wheel would immediately commence turning again. In order that such a fiat should be effective it would have to include not only a scaling down of prices and wages, but of debts. The payment of a debt is an integral portion of the monetary flow; but it is a portion which cannot be diminished in response to a general diminution in the flow, except through the disaster of bankruptcy on the part of the debtor. The result is that when the general flow of currency diminishes, the intensity of its effect is exaggerated, not only because there are such large classes of men who cannot command the same prices as before, but because in every mercantile community large payments of debts are always due. This is why a commercial panic is first felt at the monetary centers, where business is conducted and debts incurred on a large scale, and why in case of such a panic the obstruction to current business is proportionally greater than the diminution of the total monetary flow." Simon Newcomb, *Principles of Political Economy,* p. 385.

18. For a presentation of the debt theory of depression, see T. Veblen, *Theory of Business Enterprise,* pp. 177–227; I. Fisher, *Booms and Depressions,* chaps. II–IV, and "The Debt Deflation Theory of Great Depressions," *Econometrica,* October, 1933.

19. See my paper, "The Increase of Long-Term Debt in the United States," *Journal of the American Statistical Association,* June, 1934.

Chapter XIII

1. I claim no novelty for this view. It was the central point of the theory of crises held by Lord Overstone and other supporters of the currency principle.

2. This is the point I have made many times. See, for instance, "The Problem of Monetary and Economic Stability," *Quarterly Journal of Economics,* February, 1935. *Cf.* Lionel Edie's statement on this question: "Central banks should aim at so regulating reserves of the banking system that the outstanding credit built upon those reserves will expand at the same rate as the long-term growth of production.

There is enough credit when the curves of credit growth and production growth parallel each other. More than this is too much; less than this is too little." L. D. Edie, *The Banks and Prosperity*, p. 117.

3. Many writers have stressed the importance of business confidence. Marshall wrote: "But though men have the power to purchase they may not choose to use it. For when confidence has been shaken by failures, capital cannot be got to start new companies or extend old ones. Projects for new railways meet with no favour, ships lie idle, and there are no orders for new ships. . . . The chief cause of the evil is a want of confidence. The greater part of it could be removed almost in an instant if confidence could return. . . . Confidence by growing would cause itself to grow; credit would give increased means of purchase, and thus prices would recover." Alfred Marshall, *Principles of Economics*, pp. 710–11.

4. J. T. Flynn, *God's Gold, the Story of Rockefeller and His Times*, p. 69.

5. D. R. Dewey, *Financial History of the United States*, pp. 89–92.

6. As I have pointed out: "Outside debits are almost perfectly correlated with the total Volume of Trade Index, both as regards time movement and the amplitude of the fluctuations." *Business Cycles and Business Measurements*, p. 132.

7. The annual average rates of discount charged by banks to customers in New York, in eight Northern and Eastern cities, and in 27 Southern and Western cities, are given below. Note that except during the great depression, changes in these rates have never been large. The data are taken from the *Survey of Current Business*, 1938 Supplement, p. 56.

Year	New York City	Northern and Eastern Cities	Southern and Western Cities
1919	5.51 per cent	5.73 per cent	6.00 per cent
1920	6.25	6.74	6.75
1921	6.34	6.76	6.99
1922	5.07	5.48	6.14
1923	5.19	5.50	5.94
1924	4.60	5.11	5.71
1925	4.47	4.98	5.58
1926	4.67	5.06	5.61
1927	4.53	4.88	5.60
1928	5.15	5.34	5.70
1929	5.88	6.04	6.14
1930	4.69	5.07	5.72
1931	4.22	4.61	5.39
1932	4.49	5.05	5.62
1933	4.02	4.83	5.56
1934	3.33	4.29	5.17
1935	2.70	3.86	4.69
1936	2.49	3.52	4.35
1937	2.43	3.36	4.17

8. Consider what Tooke and Newmarch said on this point: "There are, doubtless, persons who, upon imperfect information, and upon insufficient grounds, or with too sanguine a view of contingencies in their favour, speculate improvidently; but their *motive* or *inducement* so to speculate is the opinion which, whether well or ill founded, or whether upon their own view or upon the authority or example of other persons, they entertain of the probability of an advance of price. It is not the mere facility of borrowing, or the difference between being able to discount at 3 or 6 per cent., that supplies the *motive* for purchasing, or even for selling." *A History of Prices and of the State of the Circulation from 1792 to 1856*, vol. III, p. 153. Hawtrey holds that low interest rates and the prospect of a rise in prices occur simultaneously.

9. After the crisis of 1837 a committee of bankers at a New York convention stated: "If the share of the blame which may justly be imputed to the banks be

analyzed, it will be found to consist in their not having, at any early period, duly appreciated the magnitude of the impending danger, and taken, in time, the measures necessary to guard against it; in their want of firmness—when the danger was more apparent than alarming—in yielding to the demand for increased, or continued, bank facilities, instead of resolutely curtailing their loans and lessening their liabilities." Cited by H. E. Miller, *Banking Theories in the United States before 1860,* p. 210.

10. Carl Snyder, "The Problem of Monetary and Economic Stability," *Quarterly Journal of Economics,* February, 1935.

11. D. Ricardo, *Principles of Political Economy,* chap. XXVII.

12. This is Bagehot's principal thesis, which he drives home in every chapter: "The ultimate banking reserve of a country (by whomsoever kept) is not kept out of show, but for certain essential purposes, and one of those purposes is the meeting a demand for cash caused by an alarm within the country. It is not unreasonable that our ultimate treasure in particular cases should be lent; on the contrary, we keep that treasure for the very reason that in particular cases it should be lent." W. Bagehot, *Lombard Street,* p. 53. Again, he wrote: "Very large loans at very high rates are the best remedy for the worst malady of the money market when a foreign drain is added to a domestic drain." *Ibid.,* pp. 56–57.

13. See O. M. W. Sprague, *Crises under the National Banking System.*

14. In a statement for the press, released March 13, 1939, the Board of Governors of the Federal Reserve System said: "Experience has shown, however, that (1) prices cannot be controlled by changes in the amount and cost of money; (2) the Board's control of the amount of money is not complete and cannot be made complete; (3) a steady average of prices does not necessarily result in lasting prosperity; and (4) a steady level of average prices is not nearly as important to the people as a fair relationship between the prices of the commodities which they produce and those which they must buy.

"Steady prices and lasting prosperity cannot be brought about by action of the Federal Reserve System alone, because they are affected by many factors beyond the control of the Federal Reserve System."

15. For the legal powers of the Federal Reserve Banks and the Board of Governors of the Federal Reserve System, see *Federal Reserve Act of 1913 with Amendments and Laws Relating to Banking,* compiled by Elmer A. Lewis (Government Printing Office).

16. Gross earnings of the Federal Reserve Banks declined 25 per cent in 1924 from the level of 1922–1923. This decline in earnings was accompanied by a 100 per cent increase in the earnings of the banks on government securities. Report of the Federal Reserve Board for 1924, pp. 12–13.

17. The author was Benjamin M. Anderson.

18. In testimony before a Congressional Committee, Governor Strong said: "In the latter part of 1921 and early 1922, the member banks had liquidated so large a portion of their discounts at the Reserve Banks that there was some concern felt by some of the Federal Reserve Banks as to their earnings. I would like to explain that with so little experience in banking of this character, it is quite impossible to ask nine active, intelligent, progressive business men, three of them bankers, to serve as directors of a Reserve Bank, and at once, before they learn a little of the philosophy of reserve banking, not to assume that one of their responsibilities is to earn enough money to pay dividends on their stock. . . . So that in that period the Reserve Banks, being autonomous and having the power to invest money, were making considerable investments in the market, buying bills and buying government securities." *Interpretations of Federal Reserve Policy in the Speeches and Writings of Benjamin Strong,* edited by W. R. Burgess.

19. The policy of the Federal Reserve System in 1931 and for a time in 1932 was to restrict credit in order to assure continuance of the gold standard, particularly

after England abandoned gold in September, 1931. The rediscount rate in New York had been 1½ per cent since May, 1931. It was raised to 2½ per cent on October 9, and to 3½ per cent on October 16. *Report of the Federal Reserve Board for 1932*, p. 104.

CHAPTER XIV

1. The size, weight, and density of stars vary enormously. Antares, the largest known star, has a diameter 450 times the size of our sun, that is to say, its diameter is slightly more than twice the size of the earth's orbit. And the smallest known star is van Maanen's, which is just about the size of the earth. Over a million stars of this size would fit inside our sun. Sir James Jean, *The Universe Around Us*, pp. 257–58.

2. A recent writer, Herman Kranold, has constructed an index of the resources of the major countries of the world, which shows markedly the inequality in the distribution of resources. Herman Kranold, *The International Distribution of Raw Materials*.

3. Some form of double entry book keeping was undoubtedly in use in Greek and Roman times. But as John Bauer says, double entry bookkeeping "was extensively developed and applied during the great Italian commercial era of the fourteenth and fifteenth centuries." *Encyclopedia of the Social Sciences*, vol. I, p. 404. E. Peragallo denies that the ancient world used the double entry system. *Origin and Evaluation of Double Entry Bookkeeping*, p. 2.

4. Dr. Thomas DeWitt Talmage, 1832–1902, was a Presbyterian preacher. He attracted the largest congregations in America. Although he married a woman of great fortune, his own business ability was considerable, and he accumulated great wealth. *Dictionary of American Biography*, vol. XVIII, pp. 287–88.

5. Pareto lived from 1848 to 1923. A short biographical sketch and an excellent account of his system is given by Luigi Amoroso, "Vilfredo Pareto," *Econometrica*, February, 1938. F. Borkenau, *Pareto*, chap. I, is also a good source of biographical material.

6. The equation expressing this relationship, the Pareto equation, is

$$N = Ax^{-a}$$

where

x equals an amount of income;
N represents the number of people receiving that income or more;
A is a constant dependent on the size of the community; and
a is a constant which tends always to be about 1.5.

It is this constant a which determines the slope of the straight line in the Pareto curve, 1.5 being the tangent of 56 degrees.

7. The discrepancy at the lower end of the curve, the end representing the larger incomes, is not great, nor is it particularly important, for the share of the national income represented by incomes of a million dollars or more is negligible. At the upper end, the end representing the lower incomes, the curve bends at the mode, but the modal income is comparatively small, so that the straight line gives a true picture of the great range of incomes. This criticism that the Pareto curve is not a completely straight line has been much over-stressed, for as Macgregor points out, even Boyle's law does not hold at the limiting ends. D. H. Macgregor, "Pareto's Law," *Economic Journal*, March, 1936.

8. Empiricism was a strong point in Pareto's attitude toward economics. "The progress of economic science in the future," he said, "will depend to a large extent upon the investigation of empirical laws, derived from statistics, which will then be compared with known theoretical laws, or will lead to the discovery of new laws." *Giornale degli Economisti*, May, 1907, p. 366.

9. Vilfredo Pareto, *Cours d'Economie Politique*, vol. II, Book III, chap. I.

10. A. L. Bowley, *Measurement of Social Phenomena*, chap. V; *The Changes in*

the Distribution of the National Income, 1880–1913; and "The British Super-Tax and the Distribution of Incomes," *Quarterly Journal of Economics,* February, 1914.

11. Lord Stamp gave a remarkable demonstration of the practical utility of the Pareto curve. He plotted the returns of the British super-tax, and noted that the line was not straight. He informed the government that "they had missed over 1,000 payers in the lowest class [of the super-tax], £5,000 to £10,000," and he adds, "they promptly went and found them." *Wealth and Taxable Capacity,* p. 83.

12. Rufus Tucker has studied these data. "When plotted cumulatively on double logarithmic paper," he says, "they make beautifully straight lines, except for slight irregularities in 1867 and a very slight convexity in 1870 and 1871." Rufus Tucker, "Distribution of Income," *Quarterly Journal of Economics,* August, 1938.

13. Frederick R. Macaulay, *Income in the United States: Its Amount and Distribution, 1909–1919,* National Bureau of Economic Research; G. F. Shirras, "The Pareto Law and the Distribution of Income," *Economic Journal,* December, 1935. N. O. Johnson considers these criticisms and offers a very level-headed defense. See his paper, "The Pareto Law," *Review of Economic Statistics,* February, 1937.

14. Carl Snyder, "The Pareto Curve and Its Significance for Our Time," Coles Commission for Research in Economics, *Report of Third Annual Research Conference on Economics and Statistics,* 1937. Bresciani-Turroni writes that "the profound significance of Pareto's law lies in that it states the existence of an 'order' in the distribution of individual incomes. Pareto's discovery is a positive contribution to the theory of the persistence of the social groups, which, in Lexis's conception, affords the basis for the explanation of the statistical regularities in human actions. Thanks to Pareto, another important field of social phenomena—besides those discovered by Graunt, Süssmilch, Quetelet, and Lexis—was shown to be dominated by statistical uniformities." C. Bresciani-Turroni, "Annual Survey of Statistical Data: Pareto's Law and the Index of Inequality of Incomes," *Econometrica,* April, 1939.

15. H. M. Stout, *Public Service in Great Britain,* chap. IV.

16. This is further borne out by the study of the National Resources Committee, *Consumer Incomes in the United States,* 1935–36, p. 97.

17. U. S. Treasury Department, *Statistics of Income,* 1929, p. 23.

Chapter XV

1. The "normal curve," also called the "curve of error," because it was originally developed to describe errors made in measurements, and sometimes called the "Gaussian curve" after one of its discoverers, looks like a bell, or the profile of a World War helmet. Its ordinates represent the expansion of the binomial theorem, which is the distribution of values to be expected when chance is given full play.

2. See Carl Seashore, *Psychology of Music,* and his many other works on this subject.

3. F. W. Taussig, *Principles of Economics,* 3rd edition, vol. II, pp. 170–71.

5. The Federal Trade Commission in an attempt to estimate the national wealth of the United States from estate returns, studied all probated estates in 24 counties of 13 states for the years 1912–1923. They found 43,512 estates, while 259,908 had died in these counties. Thus 216,396, or 84 per cent had left estates too small to be worth probating. Even of the 16 per cent who left estates that were probated, many were extremely small. United States Federal Trade Commission, *National Wealth and Income,* p. 58. Cf. W. L. Crum, *The Distribution of Wealth; a Factual Survey Based upon Federal Estate-Tax Returns.* Graduate School of Business Administration, Harvard University.

6. This statement was made in Proudhon's pamphlet, *Qu'est-ce que la propriété?,* Paris, 1840.

7. It must be persons holding such views that Edgeworth had in mind when h

wrote that "confusion between ends and means is entertained by those well-meaning, generally working, members of the social hive, who seem more concerned about the equilateralness of the honeycomb than the abundance of the honey." F. Y. Edgeworth, *Mathematical Psychics*, p. 129.

8. Cited by Vilfredo Pareto, *Cours d'Economie Politique*, vol. II, book III, chap. I.

9. Pareto remarked, quite justly, that society should be more concerned with the production of wealth than with its distribution. This stricture follows logically from his law. The point, as made by Bresciani-Turroni, is as follows: "A rise in the minimum income, or a diminution of the inequality of incomes, is possible only when the aggregate income increases faster than the population. Conversely, when the income per capita increases, the lowest incomes will also rise, or the distribution will become less uneven, or both these two effects will be produced in combination." C. Bresciani-Turroni, "Annual Survey of Statistical Data: Pareto's Law and the Index of Inequality of Incomes," *Econometrica*, April, 1939.

Chapter XVI

1. R. S. Tucker, "The Distribution of Income among Income Taxpayers in the United States, 1863–1935," *Quarterly Journal of Economics*, August, 1938. On the constancy of the distribution of income in England, see A. L. Bowley, *The Changes in the Distribution of the National Income*, 1880–1913, p. 27; Lord Stamp, *Wealth and Taxable Capacity*, p. 87; D. H. Macgregor, "Pareto's Law," *Economic Journal*, March, 1936. Macgregor took a large number of income estimates for England in different years, estimates in the form of percentage of persons receiving percentage of income. He arranged these estimates from smallest to largest according to the proportion of persons and applied the Pareto formula to this series. At a value of 1.43 for *a* he found good results, indicating that these independent estimates for different years measured the same degree of inequality.

Other studies showing constancy of income distribution should be mentioned. Giffen found that distribution in 1883 was nearly the same as from 1835 to 1840. *Essays in Finance*, vol. II, "Further Notes on the Progress of the Working Classes." Schmoller studies incomes in Basle, Frankfort, and Augsburg in the 15th century, and in Saxony and Oldenburg in recent years. He formulated no general law, but pointed out that the percentage of persons receiving various percentages of income was remarkably constant, and that income distribution in these places and times was the same as in England in 1867. He concluded that personal qualities rather than institutions were the chief factors determining the distribution of income. "Die Einkommensverteilung in alter und neuer Zeit," *Jahrbuch für Gesetzgebung, Verwaltung und Volkswirtschaft*, 1895. Even C. L. E. Engel remarked of the seeming stability in distribution of income. "Die Klassensteuer und klassifizierte Einkommensteuer in preussischen Staate, 1852–1875," *Zeitschrift des konigliche statistischen Bureaus*, 1875.

2. National Resources Committee, *Consumer Incomes in the United States, 1935–36*, p. 6.

4. W. I. King, *The Wealth and Income of the People of the United States*.

5. Allen A. Young collaborated with R. T. Ely in the writing of the famous text, *Outlines of Economics*. The sixth edition of this work, published after Professor Young's death, contains this statement: "From the social point of view, and in the long run, it is probably true that pure profits are negligible or, possibly, even a negative, quantity. In the aggregate, society probably secures the services of entrepreneurs without paying them anything additional to what would be regarded as a fair estimate of the return necessary to compensate all expenses of production, including a competitive valuation of his own productive services. . . . Collectively considered, therefore, pure profits are at once necessary and probably non-existent." R. T. Ely, *Outlines of Economics*, p. 510.

6. N. O. Johnson has studied the Pareto curves of American income tax data. From 1914 to 1933 he finds the slope ranges from 53 to 62 degrees. In 16 of the 20

years the range is only between 54 and 60 degrees. Furthermore, there is no consistent tendency to change in any direction. The tangents of the slopes for the years 1914 to 1933 are:

1914—1.54	1924—1.67
1915—1.40	1925—1.54
1916—1.34	1926—1.55
1917—1.49	1927—1.52
1918—1.65	1928—1.42
1919—1.71	1929—1.42
1920—1.82	1930—1.62
1921—1.90	1931—1.71
1922—1.71	1932—1.76
1923—1.73	1933—1.70

The variations, expressed as tangents of the slopes, appear greater than if they were expressed as angles of the slopes, since tangents vary from zero to infinity for angles that vary from 0 to 90 degrees.

7. A. L. Bowley, *The Changes in the Distribution of the National Income, 1880–1913*, p. 27; Lord Stamp, *Wealth and Taxable Capacity*, p. 87.

8. For a fuller discussion, see chapter XIX, section 2 of this volume.

9. The National Industrial Conference Board's data for average hourly earnings in factory employment from 1920 to 1937 are:

1920—$.606	1929—$.590
1921— .524	1930— .589
1922— .494	1931— .564
1923— .541	1932— .498
1924— .562	1933— .491
1925— .561	1934— .581
1926— .568	1935— .600
1927— .576	1936— .617
1928— .579	1937— .693

Survey of Current Business, 1938 Supplement, p. 47.

10. M. C. Rorty argued that the gross savings must be 10 to 16 per cent of the national income. In the period of which he wrote, income increased at the rate of 3 or 4 per cent per annum, and physical wealth (excluding land) was four times the national income. On this basis Colonel Rorty argued that physical wealth (excluding land) must increase at a rate of 12 to 16 per cent of each year's income. M. C. Rorty, *Some Problems in Current Economics*, pp. 106–7. The reproductive capital of which I speak is not the same as the total physical wealth excluding land. Rorty's estimate can be modified to yield an estimate of savings going into reproductive capital. As I have shown, the reproductive capital grows at a slightly greater rate, dollar for dollar, than does the national income. Thus, to maintain a national income growth of 4 per cent, reproductive capital would have to be increased by slightly more than 4 per cent of the national income.

11. Difficult to agree with Mill's view of progress as "the mere increase of production and accumulation," nor to contemplate with complacency the prospect of a static world to which Mill looked forward. John Stuart Mill, *Principles of Political Economy*, Ashley edition, pp. 746–51.

12. If clear profits are defined as the difference between the money value of goods and services produced and income payments which business men made in having these goods and services produced, then business men suffered a loss in every year from 1930 to 1934. These losses, as estimated by the Department of Commerce, were

1930	$4,903 million
1931	8,052
1932	8,942

1933 $3,094 million
1934 1,429

Survey of Current Business, June, 1937, pp. 11–17.

14. In Pareto's words, "(1) an increase in minimum revenue, (2) a diminution of the inequality of income, can occur, either singly or cumulatively, only if the total of incomes increases more rapidly than the population." Vilfredo Pareto, *Cours d'Economie Politique*, chap. I, book III, vol. II.

CHAPTER XVII

1. Max Eastman, "The End of Socialism in Russia," *Harper's Magazine*, February, 1937.

2. *The New York Times*, February 5, 1939. See Sidney and Beatrice Webb, *Soviet Communism—A New Civilization?*

3. Dryden's translation of Plutarch's life of Solon states: "And the disparity of fortune between the rich and the poor, at that time, also reached its height. . . . All the people were indebted to the rich. . . . Then the wisest of the Athenians, perceiving Solon was of all men the only one not implicated in the troubles, that he had not joined in the exactions of the rich, and was not involved in the necessities of the poor, pressed him to succor the commonwealth and compose the differences. . . . The first thing which he settled was, that what debts remained should be forgiven, and no man, for the future, should engage the body of his debtor for security. Though some, as Androtion, affirm that the debts were not cancelled, but the interest only lessened, which sufficiently pleased the people; so that they named this benefit the Seisachtheia, together with the enlarging their measures, and raising the value of their money [*sic*]; for he made a pound, which before passed for seventy-three drachmas, go for a hundred; so that, though the number of pieces in the payment was equal, the value was less." Cf., C. J. Bullock, "The New Deal in Ancient Greece," *Harvard Business Review*, vol. XIV, Summer, 1936.

4. Dr. Erich Fromm: *Die Entwicklung des Christusdogmas*, 1931.

5. *Matthew* is particularly full of passages warning against the accumulation of wealth. "Lay up for yourselves treasures in heaven," vi:2; "Ye cannot serve God and Mammon," vi:24; "What is a man profited if he shall gain the whole world, and lose his own soul?" xvi:26; "It is easier for a camel to go through the eye of a needle, than for a rich man to enter into the kingdom of God," xix:24.

6. *Matthew*, xxi:12–13: "And Jesus went into the temple of God, and cast out all them that sold and bought in the temple, and overthrew the tables of the money changers, and the seats of them that sold doves. And said unto them, It is written, My house shall be called the house of prayer; but ye have made it a den of thieves."

7. See what Aristotle says in his *Politics*, Book I, chap. IX, where a distinction is made between natural and unnatural economic activity. Husbandry and stock raising were regarded as the most natural form of economic activity. Commerce and trade were regarded as unnatural forms.

8. On this point, Professor Taussig writes: "Those possessed of the qualities of leadership must not only be given a free field; they must also be stimulated to the full exercise of their gifts. Inequality of some sort appears to be indispensable as a stimulus." F. W. Taussig, *Principles of Economics*, 3rd edition, vol. I, p. 102. Cf. J. M. Clark, *Social Control of Business*, 1st edition, p. 139.

9. Faraday held a professorship founded by John Fuller, which paid at first £100, and later £200 a year. But in his early days he did commercial analyses and earned well over £1,000 a year from this source. The demands upon his time were too great, however, and he chose to give up this income in the interest of his scientific work. By 1832 his independent earnings were down to £155, and never again amounted to that much. J. H. Gladstone, *Michael Faraday*, pp. 42–43.

10. Carl Snyder, "The Capital Supply and National Well Being," *American Economic Review*, June, 1936.

Chapter XVIII

1. B. H. Hibbard, *A History of the Public Land Policies;* and R. T. Hill, *The Public Domain and Democracy;* T. C. Donaldson, *The Public Domain: Its History.*

2. "Some Proposals to Benefit the Province," by an anonymous pamphleteer, Boston, 1720; quoted by A. M. Davis, "Currency and Banking in the Province of the Massachusetts-Bay," *Publications of the American Economic Association*, Third Series, vol. II, p. 97.

3. H. T. Lefler, *North Carolina History Told by Contemporaries*, pp. 49–50. The commodities whose debt paying values were fixed by law included:

	£	s.	d.
"Tobacco per Cwt.	0	10	0
Indyan Corn per Bush.		1	8
Wheat " "		3	6
Tallow Tryed, per lb.			5
Leather Tanned & Uncured, per lb.			8
Beaver & other Skins per lb.		2	6
Wild Cat Skins per piece		1	0
Butter per lb.			6
Cheese per lb.			4
Buck & Doe Skins (raw) per lb.			9
do. do. (drest) "		2	6
Feathers per lb.		1	4
Pitch (Full Gauged) per Barl.	1	0	0
Whale Oil " "	1	10	0
Porke " "	2	5	0
Beef " "	1	10	0"

4. In 1805 the cost of land carriage was about 50 cents per ton mile. Since corn was then selling for 35 cents per bushel, it could be transported only 25 miles, even if the whole price of the product were used to pay transportation costs. Similarly, the wheat radius was 75 miles. I. Lippincott, "Pioneer Industry in the West," *Journal of Political Economy*, April, 1920.

5. The nominal farm population includes all persons living on three acres or more.

6. See above, chap. VII, sections 1–3.

7. The ratios of compensation per employee (full time equivalent) in agriculture and in manufacturing, have been as follows in recent years:

Year	Agricultural compensation as per cent of manufacturing compensation
1929	54
1930	51
1931	42
1932	40
1933	39
1934	40
1935	41
1936	41

These ratios are found by dividing the per capita income of employees in the two divisions as reported by the Department of Commerce, *National Income in the United States, 1929–1936*, p. 27.

8. National Resources Committee, *Consumer Incomes in the United States, 1935–1936*, p. 97.

CHAPTER XIX

1. In 1929, for example, admittedly a most prosperous year for manufacturing, the gross income from manufactures was $67,720 million. Profits (dividends and additions to corporate surplus) were $4,454 million, that is, 6.6 per cent of the product. Dividends distributed to the owners of stock in manufacturing corporations were $3,159 million, that is, 4.6 per cent of the product. The data are taken from pp. 24, 31, U. S. Department of Commerce, *National Income, 1929-1936.*

2. This is true not only of the ratio of wages to gross income from manufacturing, but also of the ratio of wages to value added by manufacture. On this point, see P. Douglas, *Real Wages in the United States*, p. 540; M. Leven, and others, *America's Capacity to Consume*, p. 158; W. I. King, *The Wealth and Income of the People of the United States;* Frederick A. Macaulay, *Income in the United States;* E. F. Gay and L. Wolman, in *Recent Social Trends*, vol. I, pp. 228-237; and M. Copeland in *Recent Economic Changes*, vol. II, pp. 757-766.

3. "The wages system as it stands is the outcome of the division of labor; and its present most pressing problems are due to the increasing complexity which characterizes large-scale production. In ever growing measure the modern development of industry has necessitated organization, direction, discipline—single-minded management. . . . The liberty of the individual workman is necessarily restricted. . . . This limitation of freedom is often regarded as a special characteristic of employing capitalism and private property. But it is the inevitable result of highly organized production. . . . What is true in regard to its bearing on the present wages system is that this system has made the necessity plain and unmistakable; for it alone has developed the methods of large-scale production and thus arrived at the advantages as well as the disadvantages of the complex division of labor." F. W. Taussig, *Principles of Economics*, 3rd edition, vol. II, p. 283.

4. The Wagner Labor Relations Act, the National Industrial Recovery Act (section 7a), and other laws have all directly encouraged unionization and collective bargaining. In the railroad and coal industries particularly, legislation has long promoted trade union activities.

5. *International Labor Review*, vol. XIX, p. 572.

6. A. L. Bowley, *Wages and Income in the United Kingdom since 1860*, p. 25. The answer to the share-the-work people was given years ago by John Rae, *Eight Hours for Work*. "The only way to increase the demand for labor all round," he said, "is to increase the production of labor all round, and a general or serious diminution of production always causes a general or serious decrease in the demand for labor." Even the new Cambridge school of economists agrees that reducing hours does not increase employment. Mrs. Robinson, a follower of Keynes, states: "A reduction of hours is not in any sense a remedy for a low level of employment. It merely leads to a redistribution of a smaller total of employment amongst a larger number of individuals." Joan Robinson, *Essays in the Theory of Employment*, p. 69. See also, T. N. Carver, "Theory of the Shortened Work Week," *American Economic Review*, September, 1936.

7. This is the method of the Fair Labor Standards Act of 1938.

8. J. B. Clark, "The Minimum Wage," *Atlantic Monthly*, September, 1913; F. W. Taussig, "Minimum Wages for Women," *Quarterly Journal of Economics*, May, 1916.

9. Professor Hansen emphasizes the very real difficulties in any attempt, such as unemployment insurance, to transfer purchasing power from one period to another. He considers eight possible methods that might be used to build up a reserve in one period to be distributed in another. For most of these methods, he finds that the fund would become a serious competitor of the Federal Reserve System, and make more difficult the problem of intelligent credit control. A. H. Hansen, *Full Recovery or Stagnation?*, chap. VIII.

11. Professor Taussig, after describing the great decline in the hours of work which has occurred in western countries since the industrial revolution, says: "This general reduction in hours, *pari passu* with a general advance in wages, has been due to the gain in productive capacity." *Principles of Economics*, 3rd edition, vol. II, p. 328. The demand for a still shorter working day, he adds, "is entitled to all sympathy and support," provided such reductions proceed slowly in accordance with the increased technical efficiency of industry. *Ibid.*, p. 330.

Chapter XX

1. T. Frank, *Economic History of Rome*, p. 196. For a popular account of Rome's experiences with relief, see H. J. Haskell, *The New Deal in Old Rome*.

2. Thorold Rogers, *Six Centuries of Work and Wages*, chap. XV.

3. A. E. Bland, P. A. Brown, and R. H. Tawney, *English Economic History: Select Documents*, p. 372 (14 Elizabeth, c. 5, 1572), and p. 380 (43 and 44 Elizabeth, c. 2, 1601).

4. Adam Smith, *Wealth of Nations*, Book I, chap. X, part 2.

5. J. H. Clapham, *An Economic History of Modern Britain*, vol. I, p. 358.

6. T. R. Malthus, *Essay on Population*, 7th edition, III, vi, p. 305. For Malthus' view of the effect of the poor laws on prices, see his essay, *An Investigation of the Cause of the High Price of Provisions*, 1800.

7. Even before this suggestion of Bowley, proposals had been made to use public expenditure to relieve unemployment. Malthus suggested in his *Principles* that "the employment of the poor in roads and public works . . . is the means most within our power and most directly calculated to remedy the evils arising from . . . disturbance in the balance of produce and consumption." For a history of these proposals, see A. D. Gayer, *Public Works in Prosperity and Depression*, chap. I.

8. J. M. Keynes, *The Means to Prosperity;* and *The General Theory of Employment, Interest and Money*, chap. X. The concept of the multiplier was developed by R. F. Kahn in his paper, "The Relation of Home Investment to Unemployment," *Economic Journal*, June, 1931.

9. Hawtrey states that the creation of credit is the sole advantage of expenditure on public works during depression. "If the new works are financed by the creation of bank credits, they *will* give additional employment. . . . The public works are only a piece of ritual, convenient to people who want to be able to say that they are doing something. To stimulate an expansion of credit is usually only too easy. To resort for the purpose to the construction of expensive public works is to burn down the house for the sake of the roast pig." R. G. Hawtrey, "Public Expenditure and the Demand for Labour," *Economica*, March, 1925.

10. A view given great emphasis by R. G. Hawtrey, *Trade and Credit*, chap. VI.

11. These hourly wage rates are for all factory workers in 25 industries as computed by the National Industrial Conference Board. These rates for June, 1933, and November, 1937, may be compared with an annual average hourly rate of 59 cents in 1929. *Survey of Current Business, 1936 Supplement*, p. 41; *Survey of Current Business, 1938 Supplement*, p. 47.

12. J. H. Rogers, *Capitalism in Crisis*, pp. 161–163.

13. The word *inflation*, now so familiar to the layman as well as the economist, was coined by Alexander Del Mar, a critic of the Federal government's financial policy during the Civil War. Del Mar in *The Great Paper Bubble; Or the Coming Financial Explosion*, compared Secretary Chase to a man blowing bubbles with a pipe, and prophesied that the "inflated" bubble was about to burst. Earl Hicks, "Alexander Del Mar, Critic of Metallism," *Southern Economic Journal*, October, 1939.

14. There seems always to be a considerable number of advocates of inflation as a remedy for unemployment. One of the most noted was John Law. "A plentiful

supply of money in usage among the people," he said, "would remedy the plight of the idle and find work for those unable to be paid for lack of money." *Oeuvres Complètes*, p. 190. For the effect of John Law's system on the economic life of France, see Earl J. Hamilton, "Prices and Wages in Southern France under John Law's System," *Economic History*, February, 1937; "Prices and Wages at Paris under John Law's System," *Quarterly Journal of Economics*, November, 1936. For some early English proposals for inflation, see Thomas Attwood, *Letter to N. Vansittart on the Creation of Money and Its Action upon National Prosperity* (1817); John Gray, *Gray's Lectures on the Nature and Use of Money* (1848); and Sir Archibald Alison, *Free Trade and a Fettered Currency* (1847).

15. The literature of inflation is plentiful. See particularly: C. Bresciani-Turroni, *The Economics of Inflation*; G. Cassel, *The World's Monetary Problems*; F. D. Graham, *Exchange, Prices and Production in Hyper-inflation: Germany, 1920–1923*; J. H. Rogers, *The Process of Inflation in France, 1914–1927*; S. E. Harris, *Monetary Problems of the British Empire*, Parts I–III.

16. Report of the Commissioners of Inquiry, appointed 1832, drafted by Nassau Senior and Edwin Chadwick. See the *Dictionary of Political Economy*, vol. III, p. 156.

CHAPTER XXI

1. The thesis of the equal diffusion theory of taxation is that the burden of taxation is distributed through the automatic operation of the mechanics of exchange in proportion to the consumption of individuals. When once a tax is levied, the prices of all goods, and the rewards of all factors of production, are adjusted to distribute this burden. "The vein from which the surgeon has taken the blood is not more bloodless after the operation than any of the other veins of the body." N. F. Canard, *Principes d'Economie Politique* (1802), pp. 168–69. Seligman states that the term "equal diffusion" was first used by Andrew Hamilton, a professor at Aberdeen, in a book on taxation published in 1790. The theory, of course, is far older than this use of the term.

2. Here is one American outburst against the excise tax. "Were some future congress to enforce, in all its horrors, a Portuguese, or a British system of Excise, were an hundred thousand mercenaries prepared to support it, the geographical situation of this continent would, in a few years, defeat the plan. The western shore of the Mississippi would afford a capacious asylum, and an impenetrable rampart to millions of fugitives from the Atlantic states. Excise would yelp in solitude; while new nations and empires of freedom would stretch along the banks of the Missouri." This was in 1786. Quoted by E. R. A. Seligman, *The Shifting and Incidence of Taxation*, p. 77.

3. *Ibid.*, pp. 77–78.

4. These figures are for the New York Telephone Company, 1937. The Bell system in 1938 paid $147 million in taxes. This was equal to $550 per employee, $9.50 per telephone, and $7.54 per share of American Telephone and Telegraph stock.

5. Professor Taussig explains that the public utility industries usually sell their services at a rigid "fair" price, which is why a rise in the general price level works hardship on the utility companies. He points out that the slow rise in prices during the early twentieth century put more and more pressure on the utilities, and "the abrupt advance during the war of 1914–18 brought the tendency to a sudden climax. The public furiously and vociferously opposed changes from the accustomed scale of charges. Increases finally had to be accepted; they were as inevitable as those in salaries, in taxes, in rentals of dwellings and shops; but they were sparingly allowed. The problem for the owners and investors was no longer how to conceal and pocket profits, but how to avoid losses; and the problem for the public became for the time being that of assuring the maintenance and extension of essential industries, not that of controlling the profits of monopolies." F. W. Taussig, *Principles of Economics*, 3rd edition, vol. II, p. 118.

6. *Galveston Electric Co. v. Galveston*, P.U.R. 1922 D, 159; also, *Georgia Railway and Power Co. v. Railroad Commission*, P.U.R. 1923 D, 1.

7. Among the causes of the prosperity of England's American colonies, Adam Smith listed moderate taxes. This moderation of taxation also accounted for the accumulation of capital in the colonies. "The labour of the English colonists is not only likely to afford a greater and more valuable produce, but, in consequence of the moderation of their taxes, a greater proportion of this produce belongs to themselves, which they may store up and employ in putting into motion a still greater quantity of labour." *Wealth of Nations*, Book III, chap. VII, part 2.

8. In 1928, out of 443,611 corporations reporting for the corporate income tax, 174,828, that is, 39 per cent, reported a deficit. In 1931, 62 per cent, fully 283,806 out of 459,704, reported a deficit. U. S. Treasury Department, *Statistics of Income*, 1928, pp. 30–31; *Statistics of Income*, 1931, p. 24.

9. Chapter XVI.

10. This, of course, is the primary objection to punitive taxation of undistributed profits. It discriminates against the successful, the progressive, and the growing business enterprises.

11. See chapter XVI, section 3.

12. Carl Snyder, "The Capital Supply and National Well Being," *American Economic Review*, June, 1936.

13. A. C. Pigou and Colin Clark, *The Economic Position of Great Britain, 1936*, demonstrate that the secondary distribution of income through taxation has resulted in the anomalous situation that there is no longer *any* net personal savings in Great Britain. All net savings today are institutional. Total savings in Great Britain have fallen from some 12 or 13 per cent of the national income in pre-war times to 7 per cent by 1929, and to 5 per cent by 1934. Pigou and Clark conclude that saving is now certainly not half as great as in pre-war times.

14. A recent estimate states that of the dividends distributed as a result of the undistributed profits tax, only about one-fourth will be saved and made available for increasing industrial capital. G. Colm and F. Lehmann, *Economic Consequences of Recent American Tax Policy*, p. 37.

15. J. S. Mill, *Principles of Political Economy*, Ashley edition, pp. 814–15. See pp. 812–17 for Mill's full discussion of the point.

16. This proposal has also been made by J. H. R. Cromwell and H. E. Czerwonky, *In Defense of Capitalism*, pp. 145–46.

CHAPTER XXII

1. The literature of economic planning is enormous. Among the more important books are the following: *Collective Economic Planning*, edited by F. A. Hayek; J. M. Clark, and others, *Long Range Planning for the Regularization of Industry*; George Soule, *A Planned Society*; G. D. H. Cole, *Economic Planning*; Lionel Robbins, *Economic Planning and International Order*; Barbara Wooten, *Plan or No Plan*.

2. On Russia's plans, see Calvin B. Hoover, *The Economic Life of Soviet Russia*; and W. H. Chamberlin, *The Soviet Planned Economic Order*. On Germany, see Calvin B. Hoover, *Germany Enters the Third Reich*; and Max Ascoli and Arthur Feiler, *Fascism for Whom?* On Italy, see Fausto Pitigliani, *The Italian Corporative State*; and William G. Welk, *Fascist Economic Policy*.

3. The National Resources Committee has issued some publications on this aspect of Planning: *Drainage Basin Problems and Programs; Water Planning; Planning Our Resources; National Resources Planning Facts;* and many others.

4. According to the Brookings Institution, *The Recovery Problem in the United States*, the N.R.A. sought to bring about recovery by raising business costs, a policy that was bound to fail. L. P. Ayres, *The Economics of Recovery*, states that "the

malady from which N.I.R.A. suffers is a compound fallacy of her economic hypotheses." See also, Leverett S. Lyon, and others, *The National Recovery Administration: An Analysis and Appraisal;* George Terborgh, *Price-Control Devices in N.R.A. Codes;* and Otto Nathan, "The N.I.R.A. and Stabilization," *American Economic Review,* March, 1935.

5. This distinction is of major significance. Credit control properly involves a limitation upon the total volume of credit created. It does not attempt to direct this credit into some channels rather than others. Nor does it attempt to restrict the right of bank managers to pass on the credit standing of applicants for loans and either to give or refuse bank credit. The limitation is purely quantitative and general.

6. See, for example, the recent publications of the Machinery Institute of Chicago, particularly, *Savings and American Progress,* and *Capital Goods and American Progress.*

7. For statistical data on the American railroads and the railroad building era, see L. H. Haney, *A Congressional History of Railways in the United States;* and S. Thompson, *A Short History of American Railways.*

8. Professor I. L. Sharfman has written a definitive study of the Interstate Commerce Commission. *The Interstate Commerce Commission: A Study in Administrative Law and Procedure.*

9. The new capital raised for public utilities through security issues indicates the tremendous growth of these industries from 1920–1930, and the sharp decline under the impact of depression. The data are reported by the *Commercial and Financial Chronicle.*

1920	$ 375 million		1930	$2,335 million
1921	490		1931	955
1922	725		1932	275
1923	890		1933	35
1924	1,325		1934	50
1925	1,480		1935	85
1926	1,600		1936	125
1927	2,065		1937	155
1928	1,810			
1929	1,930			

10. The term "Captains of Industry" seems to have been first used by Francis A. Walker.

11. It is not surprising, therefore, that the planning of Germany and Italy are largely related to a society organized for military rather than economic well being. Individual freedom, whether of workers to leave and take jobs, or of business men to expand and contract production, is severely limited, if not entirely abolished. Such regimentation is not compatible with democracy. On this question, see the address of Winthrop W. Aldrich, "The Incompatibility of Democracy and a 'Planned Economy.'" A statement by Walter Lippmann is distinctly to the point: "Though the planned economy is proposed as a form of social organization which will provide peace and plenty, thus far in all its concrete manifestations it has been associated with scarcity and war. . . . That, I believe, is where all planned economies have originated and must in the very nature of things originate. For it can be demonstrated, I am confident, that there is only one purpose to which a whole society can be directed by a deliberate plan. That purpose is war, and there is no other." Walter Lippmann, *An Inquiry into the Principles of the Good Society,* pp. 89–90.

12. The development of ethyl gasoline is an interesting instance of this sort. Thomas Midgley, Jr., vice president of the Ethyl Gasoline Corporation, in a talk before the American Chemical Society, had this to say of the discovery. "It should be evident to any one who knows all the facts that the discovery of ethyl and the benefactions it has brought were possible only because of the American way of business, only because courageous corporate executives had the foresight to invest

large sums of money and continue backing an idea through periods when less astute minds might have dropped it. They would not have done this had they not believed in the end they would make a profit from it for their stockholders. They would not have been able to do it had they not previously made large sums of money for their corporations from other ventures, which allowed them to finance this one. They would not have been able to do it had there been any law against their taking the chance of losing the money put into it." He added that the corporation "was over $3,000,000 in the red before it [ethyl] began to earn a profit for those who had backed it." *The New York Times*, June 6, 1939.

13. Quoted by H. D. Henderson, *Supply and Demand*, p. 6.

14. Carl Snyder, *The World Machine*.

Chapter XXIII

1. These periods of political unrest recur at approximately the time of the end of the down-swing of the long waves of business activity. See N. D. Kondratiev, "Die Langen Wellen der Konjunktur," *Archiv für Sozialwissenschaft und Sozialpolitik*, vol. LXI, pp. 573–609; "The Long Waves in Economic Life," *Review of Economic Statistics*, November, 1935; A. H. Hansen, *Economic Stabilization in an Unbalanced World*, pp. 93–100; and E. Wagemann, *Economic Rhythm*, chapter V.

2. Cf. what has been said of the pattern of depression in chapter XII, section 1.

3. W. G. Sumner, *History of Banking in the United States;* and *History of American Currency*. See also, R. C. McGrane, *The Panic of 1837: Some Financial Problems of the Jackson Era*.

4. Charles A. Beard, *The American Party Battle;* E. E. Robinson, *The Evolution of American Political Parties;* Stuart A. Rice, *Farmers and Workers in American Politics;* and H. J. Ford, *The Rise and Growth of American Politics*.

5. Anton Menger, the brother of the distinguished Austrian economist Carl Menger, held that legal rights are meaningful only to the propertied class in a capitalistic society. Meaningful rights for laborers, he said, would be (1) the right to work, (2) the right to exist, and (3) the right to the whole produce of labor. Anton Menger, *The Right to the Whole Produce of Labour: The Origin and Development of the Theory*.

6. Philosophers, and novelists, have always found the existing world far from ideal, and have busied themselves with setting up impossible and unworkable worlds of their own, Utopias. Amongst the Utopia builders are found Plato, More, Bacon, Rousseau, and many others. For this general attitude, see Mrs. Frances Russell's book, *Touring Utopia*.

7. Mill's writings on socialism have been collected and published in a volume entitled *Socialism* (New York, 1891). The introduction quotes from Wadsworth Donisthrope's *Individualism, a System of Politics*, the statement that Mill's essay *On Liberty* "is one long indictment of Socialism." In his *Autobiography*, Mill revealed the confusion in his mind on this important subject when he wrote: "The social problem of the future we considered to be how to unite the greatest individual liberty of action with a common ownership in the raw material of the globe and an equal participation of all in the benefits of combined labour." *Autobiography*, chapter VII. This statement seems to aim at a reconciliation of contradictions, socialism and individual liberty, an impossible task.

8. Calvin B. Hoover, *The Economic Life of Soviet Russia;* L. E. Hubbard, *Soviet Trade and Distribution;* W. B. Reddaway, *The Russian Financial System;* and Susan M. Kingsbury and Mildred Fairchild, *Factory, Family, and Woman in the Soviet Union*.

9. The industrial freedom of the Japanese worker has been restricted to a considerable extent during the current war with China. Nevertheless, it is probably greater than that of a worker in Russia.

10. Quoted by Carlton J. H. Hayes, *A Political and Social History of Modern Europe*, vol. II, p. 151.

11. W. M. Splawn, *Government Ownership and Operation of Railroads;* I. L. Sharfman, *The American Railroad Problem;* W. J. Cunningham, *American Railroads: Government Control and Reconstruction Policies;* and F. H. Dixon, *Railroads and Government.*

12. C. S. Pippetts, *Autarchy: National Self-Sufficiency,* is a well documented statement of the world's trend in that direction. See also, Max Ascoli and Arthur Feiler, *Fascism for Whom?;* and Paul Einzig, *The Economic Foundations of Fascism.*

13. In Germany, the present economic system is frankly called a military economy, *Wehrwirtschaft.*

BRIEF BIBLIOGRAPHY

Some of the writer's recent papers dealing with the questions here under view are listed below:

New Measures of Trade and of Economic Growth. Revue de l'Institut International de Statistique, Vol. I, No. 4, 1933.

Growth of World Trade vs. Basic Production. Ibid., Vol. II, No. 1, 1934.

On the Statistical Relation of Trade, Credit and Prices. Ibid., Vol. II, No. 3, 1934.

Concerning Economic Disequilibria and Maladjustments. Proceedings of 22d Congress of l'Institut International de Statistique, London, April 16–21, 1934.

The Debt Theory of Depressions. Ibid., reprinted under the title: The Increase of Long-Term Debt in the United States, in: The Journal of the American Statistical Association, June 1934.

Measurement Versus Theory in Economics. Festschrift für Cassel, 1933.

The Concept of Momentum and Inertia in Economics. Festschrift für Arthur Spiethoff: Der Stand und die nächste Zukunft der Konjunkturforschung, 1933. Ibid. in Stabilization of Employment, ed. Roos, Principia Press, Bloomington, Ind.

On the Structure and Inertia of Prices. American Economic Review, June 1934.

Commodity Prices Versus the General Price Level. Ibid., September 1934.

The Problem of Monetary and Economic Stability. Quarterly Journal of Econ., March 1935.

Industrial Growth and Monetary Theory. Economic Forum, Summer 1933.

Overproduction and Business Cycles. Academy of Political Science, New York; Proceedings, June 1931.

New Measures of the Relations of Credit and Trade. Academy of Political Science, New York; Proceedings, January 1930.

The Problem of Prosperity. Presidential Address, American Statistical Association, Journal of Asso., March 1929.

The Measure of the General Price Level. Harvard Review of Economic Statistics, February 1928.

Deposits Activity as a Measure of Business Activity. Harvard Review of Economic Statistics, October 1924.

Measures of the Growth of British Industry. Economica, November 1934.

Die Bedeutung des Kapitalangebots für den Industrialisierungsprozeß aufgezeigt am Beispiel der Vereinigten Staaten. Weltwirtschaftliches Archiv, hersg. vom Institut für Weltwirtschaft an der Universität Kiel (Dr. Andreas Predöhl), September 1935.

The Problem of Monetary and Economic Stability. Quarterly Journal of Economics, February 1935.

Capital Supply and National Well-being. American Economic Review, June 1936.

Measures of Industrial Growth and Their Significance. Beiträge zur Konjunkturlehre. Festschrift für Wagemann. 1936.

Business Cycles and Business Measurements. The Macmillan Company, 1927. 326pp.

IN APPRECIATION

The writer is deeply indebted to many friends and associates who, in the last twenty years or more, have given so freely of their time and counsel, especially in the earlier years of the work here passed in review. In foremost line to Wesley C. Mitchell, W. I. King, and Frederick Macaulay of the National Bureau of Economic Research; the late Warren M. Persons of Harvard and Henry Schultz of Chicago; stimulating suggestions from Edwin Bidwell Wilson and Joseph Schumpeter; to the remarkable investigations of Orlando F. Weber; to the writer's former associates in the Bank, and especially to Miss Lucile Bagwell, who has carried out the larger part of the statistical investigations which form the basis of the present volume and prepared the materials for several hundred charts, zealous and unwearied; to Harold Roelse and Miss Alice Carlson; to John H. Hendrickson who drew all the charts here presented; to Dr. W. R. Burgess, Bradford Smith, and others; to Dr. E. M. Bernstein of the University of North Carolina who undertook the arduous work of reducing a voluminous manuscript to more practical limits, and has supplied the notes; and to Trufant Foster who has edited the volume and seen it through the press, with much care and many valued suggestions. Finally, to hold in pious memory many interesting and sometimes stormy discussions with the late Benjamin Strong, possibly the ablest financial mind of this country since Alexander Hamilton —whose genius might have saved this nation from a disastrous depression and much else, had he lived.

INDEX

Abilities, complex, and fundamental faculties, **254**

Act of 1601, establishment of relief in England, 324

Act of Settlement, 324

Agriculture, proof of indigenous character in America, 68; concentration of, 129; difficulties inherent in, 130; Department of, studies of farm income distribution, 246; early aid to, 299; wondrous development, 301; Department of, census of farm income, 304; what is wrong with? 305

Agriculture and prosperity, 302

d'Ailly, Cardinal, ideas of opening up New World, 91

Alexander, Mediterranean trading world, 33; and his city, 236

Aluminium industry, whither profits? 158

America, discovery of, 91, 99

American colonies, survey of wages, 165; rapid growth, 166

American Federation of Labor monthly bulletin, discussion of economic problems, 318

American Telephone and Telegraph, largely creation of Theodore Vail, 258

Ants, tropical, armies, 58

Archimedes, profound contriver, 91

Aristarchus, observations of earth, 17

Aristotle, ideas on chemistry and physics, 24; quoted, 323

Arts and sciences, success in, 253

Asia, contribution to science, 85

Astor, John Jacob, fur trade of the Pacific Northwest, 241

Athenian Owls as international currency, 235

'Atomic gun' at Cornell University, 399

Aurigae, Epsilon, density of, 233

Autocracy and history, 374

Automobile in U.S., astonishing growth in production of, see Chart XIX, 169; cost per family, 288

Babylon, ancient, industrial organization, 5; and Persia, contributions to science, 85

Bacon, Sir Francis, quoted, 16

Bagehot, Walter, on lending freely in a crisis, but at a high rate, 222

Bailly, Jean Sylvain, quoted, 84

Bank credit and stock market speculation, 23; causes of expansion and contraction, 52; destruction of, 186-88; dominant factor in expansion, 199; contraction of, since 1907, 202; determiners of, variations in, see Chart XXXIV, 293; expanding volume, 391

Bank deposits, velocity of circulation and price level, 26

Bank failures all needless, 391

Bank of England, effect of interest rates on bank credit, 221; cooperation with Federal Reserve Bank of New York, 227

Bankers of Babylonia, system of drafts, 235

Banking in antiquity, 79

Banks, solvency in 1933, 23

Baseball, hitting and normal probability curve, 254

Bastiat, on automatic planning, 362

Billionaire company. Chart of Ford income and its employment from inception, see Chart XLIV, 397

Birkeland, nature of solar corona, 115

Bismarck, his high attainment, 278

Bloemfontein gold reefs, 99

Bodin, Jean, on rise in prices, 100; quoted, 118

Booms and depressions, invariable linkage, 20; causes, 53

Boulder Dam, see: Capitalism, an analogy to, 120; its real source of power, 122

Boulton, faith in Watt, 96

Bowley, Arthur L., on reduction of hours in British industry, 314

British Civil Service and oral examination, 246

Bubble Act, 300

Buckle, Henry Thomas, on moral improvement, 86

Bureaucracies, salvation in, 363

Business confidence, monetary control, 215; and money madness, 330

2